SPEECH: *A FIRST COURSE*

❧ ❧ SPEECH ❧ ❧

A FIRST COURSE

E. C. BUEHLER
PROFESSOR OF SPEECH AND DRAMA
UNIVERSITY OF KANSAS

WIL A. LINKUGEL
ASSISTANT PROFESSOR OF SPEECH AND DRAMA
UNIVERSITY OF KANSAS

HARPER & ROW, PUBLISHERS
NEW YORK, EVANSTON, AND LONDON

SPEECH: A FIRST COURSE

Library of Congress catalog number: 62–8883

M-N

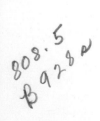

Preface

This book grows out of many years of experience in working closely with beginning speech students. Its tone and content are geared to the inexperienced speech student, who may take only one college speech course. It seeks to give him practical guidance for developing his speaking abilities, yet goes beyond matters of "how to do it." It aims to make the student intelligent about speech by equipping him with critical standards for making his own speeches and for evaluating the speeches of others long after graduation. More important, its aim is not only to develop *the able speaker,* but *the mature, articulate person who is a responsible individual in our society.*

The book is also written for the teacher. Since we believe that the teacher must always be the central force in a speech class, we have earnestly tried to write a book the teacher will find stimulating, helpful and teachable. Projects and exercises to help him elicit thinking and discussion are provided at the ends of chapters, but all classroom practice work in speaking, which we consider the core of the speech course, is presented in Part Three, as described on the next page.

Part One points the way and sets the tone for the course and the book. Its aim is to motivate the student as well as enlighten him, to build constructive attitudes as well as to give a general perspective of the subject. As the sower first prepares the soil before spreading

v

the seed, so the student, by reading Part One, prepares his mind for the learning and practice of speech which lie before him.

In the light of the complex nature of speech, we believe that text materials should be simple, clear, and functional. We therefore present all basic theories and principles relating to the oral communication of the creative piece under six main topic areas—the Six Dimensions of Speech which form Part Two, the heart of the book. Speech communication structured in this manner gives the student a picture which he can easily grasp and readily retain. We believe that this organizational approach is more meaningful to the student than that of a book whose chapters are highly particularized and somewhat unrelated.

Speech communication moves about the axis of people and ideas. Improvement in speaking ability does not come in so many separate parts, but is a process involving the total person and the integration of the Six Dimensions of Speech. The beginning student worried about what to do with his hands has the symptom of a problem which lies deep within himself—a problem of poise and confidence, which he best can meet by a concern for ideas and for the listener. For this reason it seems to us logical to arrange the topic areas as a natural unfolding of the speech act—the order found in Part Two. The first three dimensions in this continuum seem to us the roots from which the phases of speaking manner gain their growth and reach their fulfillment. The teacher, however, who wants to work intensively on delivery early in the semester may of course do so by rearranging the order in which the dimensions are discussed.

Part Three provides a program of assignments for the application of the theories covered in Part Two. These assignments have all been thoroughly tested; many have been used and refined under classroom conditions over a period of thirty years. Similarly, the topics listed under each assignment are the product of actual classroom experience. In the selection of both assignments and topics we have had the following aims:

1. To give the student maximum growth and development in speaking
2. To provide a balanced and diversified program of classroom speaking experiences
3. To challenge each student individually according to his capacity to learn

4. Generally to enrich the minds of class members with knowledge and information of academic worth

Although Part Three is directed generally to the student, many concepts and suggestions are interwoven which concern both student and teacher working as a team. It often seemed to us best to keep both in mind in trying to communicate the full spirit and purpose of an assignment. However, in no sense should this approach interfere with the teacher's initiative in working out his own lesson plans or adapting any of the assignments to suit his purpose. Part Three is a pool of projects and assignments from which the instructor can freely draw, according to his course plan and goals. Obviously not all assignments can be used; perhaps less than half can be effectively worked into any given semester.

No attempt is made to rate assignments; however, we recommend that the first cluster of assignments in Group One come during the opening days of the course, since they are designed to get the term rolling and to create class spirit. They may be effectively used to give the student several brief speaking experiences before he has read much of the text or has studied basic speech theories in depth. Thus practice will help to verify theory, and theory, when applied to the more challenging assignments of the latter part of the course, will become more meaningful. If the committee symposium speeches, based upon the Six Dimensions, are assigned, they should be completed during the first half of the semester. The more challenging speeches in Group Two, which require more research and preparation, should logically come during the latter half or two-thirds of the course.

Theory logically precedes practice; we therefore recommend that the text be thoroughly studied early in the course. Then, as special problems arise, a review of principles or a more intensive study should be made. Such a distribution of study time seems feasible, since the shorter speeches demanding less preparation come in the early stages of the course, the heavy speeches later.

E. C. B.
W. A. L.

January, 1962

Contents

ix

PART ONE

THE KEY TO THE COURSE

Speech is our principal tool of communication. Yet it is more than a merely functional instrument; it is a means by which we develop and sustain our minds and our souls that we may live harmoniously with ourselves and with others. It is uniquely important in a society such as ours, whose lifeblood is the free flow and exchange of ideas. You, as a college student and a future leader, face both the challenge and the opportunity of being an articulate and responsible citizen.

Although this book seeks primarily to bring into sharp focus the skills of speaking before groups, it also encompasses areas involving the education of the total person: the development of his powers of analysis, his awareness of human motives, his sensitivity to spiritual problems, and his capacity to think and act with wisdom. In short, this book is concerned with liberal education.

Part One presents the essential concepts and personal attitudes necessary to the growth and development of the able speaker. It contains insights into the speech course itself and words of guidance to you as a speech student. These pages are designed to give you the proper perspective on the role of speech in a free society, the role of speech in a liberal education, and the role of speech in your life, a perspective which is the key to the course.

THE SPOKEN WORD AND HUMAN DESTINY

Man's greatest achievement is perhaps his ability to talk; yet most of us take this gift for granted. We look upon it much as we do the color of our eyes or the size of our feet, appallingly unaware how vitally speech is tied to the normal processes of living. Yet we think, visit with friends, rear and educate our children, pray, and carry on all kinds of commerce through the medium of speech. Professor Andrew Weaver, one of our leading speech authorities, crystallized the role of speech in human lives with these words:

> Speech forms that inner stream of awareness which we call mind. Speech molds us in its own image. Speech teaches us to know and to sympathize with one another. Speech enables us to think clearly, feel truly, judge justly, and act wisely.
>
> Were speech to fail, our intelligence would lapse to the level of beasts, each individual would dwell apart from his fellows, the structure of society would crumble, the very fabric of life itself would disintegrate, and all the vital processes of civilization would grind to a faltering stop. . . .
>
> Speech is man's greatest achievement and his crowning glory.[1]

One cannot easily grasp the far-reaching influence of speech in human history. The spoken word, man's most effective tool for communication, is deeply rooted in the whole story of the human race. Countless examples show that the texture of our present civilization was determined by the power of speech, generations, even centuries, ago.

During the golden age of Pericles, a tiny segment of the world's population created a civilization which flowered into a glory seldom equaled in human history. Here a handful of people were bent upon the search for the true, the beautiful, and the good. They lived in houses without furnaces; they wore clothes without buttons or zippers; they studied politics without newspapers or radios and discussed philosophy without books. Yet they created a culture so rich and a design for living so plausible that to this day each great university in America would become a hollow shell if from its libraries, its art departments, and its classrooms were stripped the contributions of these Greeks who lived more than three thousand years ago. Although the printed word has preserved something of what they had

[1] Andrew Weaver, "What Is Speech? A Symposium," *Quarterly Journal of Speech,* April, 1955, p. 153.

to offer, the birth and growth of their culture came largely through the medium of speech. The Greeks verbalized their ideas. Conversations, discussions, and assemblies were common practice for disciplining their minds and sharing their knowledge. One of the greatest of all the Greeks—Socrates—relied wholly upon discussion for the development of his ideas.

We cannot escape the example of Jesus, who lived his short life nearly twenty centuries ago. Without formal education, He was, nevertheless, articulate about a way of life. He had something to say and preached the world's most unforgettable sermons—without chancel, pulpit, or notes. By word of mouth He organized a committee mainly of rugged, poor men—fishermen, tradesmen, and craftsmen of Galilee—who nourished the early Christian faith. That faith spread over half the globe by means of preaching and personal testimony. The followers of Jesus went into all lands to *preach* the gospel, not to write it.

Fifty-five men met in an early American assembly and for weeks and months committed their collective mind to a common cause. Here was discussion with a definite purpose. In the spirit of cooperation and compromise these men hammered out, by talk, a design for a national government which became the marvel of the age. When Gladstone, the English statesman, examined the product of this convention, he called it "the most wonderful work ever struck off at a given time by the pen and purpose of man." The prime medium in the formulating of this Constitution was speech.

Many other historical illustrations can be cited. The Crusades were set in motion by a speech made by Pope Urban II in 1095, of which historian William C. Lang writes: "The responsive chord had been struck; the first crusade was soon under way."[2] In our own day Winston Churchill's oratory helped to rally a nation in grave danger of defeat. Franklin Roosevelt's "fireside chats" gave confidence to the United States when it was gripped by a great depression, as well as when it was faced with a second global war. Thus the power of speech has been a vital instrument in shaping the course of history.

Unfortunately, speech is not always a force for human good; it can destroy as well as build. Used by the selfish, ambitious demagogues, it has brought its share of scourges to this world. Adolf

[2] William C. Lang, "Public Address as a Force in History," *Quarterly Journal of Speech*, February, 1951, p. 33.

Hitler proclaimed, "The power which has set in motion the great avalanches in politics and religion has been, from the beginning of time, the magic force of the spoken word—that and that alone." This same man made effective use of speech in launching his avalanche of destruction. Dictators, demagogues, and criminal conspirators have at their command the power of the spoken word. The Communists of today are highly skilled in oral propaganda. The skill of the tongue belongs to saint and devil alike.

Yet speech is still man's greatest achievement. We may well be guided by Aristotle's sage advice: ". . . if it be objected that one who uses such power of speech unjustly might do great harm, *that* is a charge which may be made in common against all good things except virtue, and above all against the things that are most useful, as strength, health, wealth, generalship. A man can confer the greatest of benefits by a right use of these, and inflict the greatest of injuries by using them wrongly."[3] The well-trained citizenry of a democratic society, which depends upon free discussion, must be able to articulate thought effectively. It also must develop critical ability and ethical values in order to detect chicanery in the speech of others. The student of speech therefore studies both speaking and listening.

YOUR SPEECH AND BETTER LIVING

Why Study and Training Are Important

Although most people may agree that it would be well for them to speak effectively, relatively few realize how closely speech is related to their well-being. It is natural that we often do not appreciate the true worth of things closest to us. So it is with speech, which is so interwoven with the rest of life. Its boundless facets cannot easily be separated; we talk because it is our nature to do so. But before we embark upon a long course of study, it will be well to examine more closely some of the larger rewards and benefits which gravitate around speech. Although its values are many and varied, let us consider those which in particular concern man and society.

1. *Speech serves as a highly functional tool for communication.*

[3] *The Rhetoric of Aristotle*, W. Rhys Roberts (trans.), The Modern Library, 1954, p. 23.

It is a utilitarian device which we use daily in our conversations, conferences, and public forums. We use it like the food we eat— for survival. From the idle gossip across the garden fence to the world-shaking debates of the United Nations, we talk to make decisions, share ideas, and get things done. We raise families, educate our children, operate the market place, govern ourselves, and offer our prayers through the spoken word. But the point which matters most is that effective speakers have the advantage over poor ones. Those who talk easily and well make more sales, get more votes, secure better jobs and more promotions, and, in our competitive society, generally outdo those who talk poorly.

2. *Speech is the measure of the man.* People come to know us largely by the way we talk. A stranger steps into our midst, and one word from his lips may tell us whether or not he is a gentleman. A well-known speech expert, Dr. Lee Travis, says, ". . . speech is a reflection of the personality of the speaker. With every utterance, the speaker gives himself away. His speech is a microscope directed toward his own inner self, through which others may get the most intimate glimpses."[4] Whether we like it or not, we cannot escape the fact that we do make impressions, favorable or unfavorable, upon our listeners, both in private conversations and before groups. When we talk, our beliefs, mental attitudes, emotional balance, sense of justice, educational background—the countless attributes that form an impression of our total personality—are reflected in the listener's mind. Whether this speech-created impression is accurate or erroneous is not the issue. The fact to remember is that it is made.

3. *Speech is a primary energizer of ideas.* The story of man offers countless examples of how speech has energized ideas and thus influenced human behavior. It always has been and always will be a prime force for social betterment and human enlightenment; the world's great reform movements have been kindled by public speech. A good idea that is never expressed is of no real value to anyone. It is like a great book locked in the library vault, gathering dust and read by no one. Students in a speech class can learn much from each other's ideas. A speech class should thus provide adventures in learning.

4. *Speech is an agent of personality growth and development.* It poses not only the posture of character and personality, but the

---

[4] Lee Edward Travis, "A Point of View in Speech Correction," *Quarterly Journal of Speech,* February, 1936, p. 57.

way to self-discovery and fulfillment. A person who, for organic or psychological reasons, finds it difficult to be articulate, tends to withdraw further into himself. Irregularities in human behavior can often be traced to the frustrations and feelings of inadequacy which are associated with being inarticulate. A well-organized personality is thus related to the normal functioning of the speech process. A sociologist once said that if every person were completely articulate there would be no need for jails.

Normal oral expression stimulated by a group of appreciative listeners often unlocks talents which lie hidden within us. The sense of personal achievement that can come from talking to a group helps to release the creative powers of the mind and those elements of our nature by which the personality may best develop. An objective study by Glenn E. Moore reveals that speech training produces statistically significant changes in the personality "in the direction of increased emotional stability, increased self-sufficiency, decreased introversion, and an increase in dominance."[5]

5. *Speech is our most reliable medium for feeding our social hungers.* Man is not only a talking animal—he is also a social animal. His sixth sense might be called the sense of belonging. He loves company, he does not want to be alone, he craves recognition and social approval. Solitary confinement is generally looked upon as his cruelest punishment; the hermit is seen as an eccentric of humanity. Man's great bulwark against loneliness, his defense against isolation from others, is speech.

6. *Speech is a means of thinking.* Our mind is always at work. We may even discover in the midst of conversation with another or while listening to a speech that we are carrying on conversational bits with ourselves. This inner dialogue goes on almost constantly during waking hours, consciously and unconsciously. Whether we are engaged in the most leisurely type of day-dreaming or the deepest of thoughts, we fall back on inner speech to symbolize our thoughts with words. And by this inner speech we find within ourselves, as Wendell Johnson aptly put it, our "most enchanted listener."

7. *Speech binds the past with the present.* The idea that speech is boundless in its potential was provocatively posed more than a generation ago in the book *Science and Sanity* by Alfred Korzybski. Its thesis is that whereas plants are space-bound and limited by chem-

---

[5] Glenn E. Moore, "Personality Changes Resulting from Training in Speech Fundamentals," *Speech Monographs*, 2 (1935), 56–59.

istry and time to the cycle of one life, man's spoken word, translated into thought and action, may potentially live for countless centuries. We see, therefore, that speech can reach beyond the barriers of chemistry, space, and time. Every meaningful word and phrase has a chance for immortality. Records of the words of Socrates, Plato, Milton, Jesus, Washington, and Lincoln, as well as thousands of others, testify that words spoken by man may live perpetually.

Speech Values of a More Personal Nature

Aside from the larger blessings to man and society, speech may affect you more directly and personally. Not all of its more personal by-products can be specifically itemized, however, since they represent intangible values. Obviously the main purpose of this course is to help you become a better speaker. Most adults know how to talk and many give speeches without ever receiving any formal training, although to a large number of the latter one must apply Ben Jonson's statement, "To speak, and to speak well, are two things."

Employers place an increasing amount of stress on the employee's ability to communicate effectively. The economist Peter Drucker points out: ". . . colleges teach the one thing that it is perhaps most valuable for the future employee to know. But very few students bother to learn it. This one basic skill is the ability to organize and express ideas in writing and speaking." He adds that the "letter, the report or memorandum, the ten-minute spoken 'presentation' to a committee are basic tools of the employees."[6] Southwestern Bell Telephone requires some of its executives to make two speeches, have four film showings, and interview eight important citizens each month. A well-known speech teacher, Seth A. Fessenden, conducted a study of the relationship of teaching successes to speech competency in over four hundred teachers; it revealed that the teachers rated as "superior" had taken 27 percent more courses in speech in college than those rated "inferior."[7]

The ability to express yourself clearly through speech has unlimited value. It will help you in recitations and discussions in almost all college courses. Should you enter a profession—law, medicine, teaching, and so forth—you will undoubtedly profit from the

6 Peter Drucker, "How to Be an Employee," *Fortune*, May, 1952, p. 126.
7 Seth A. Fessenden, "Speech for the Classroom Teacher," *The Bulletin of the National Association of Secondary School Principals*, January, 1948, p. 202.

ability to speak well. As the President's Commission on Higher Education asserted, "Few of the abilities men possess are of greater human significance than their power to order ideas clearly and to set these before their fellows by tongue or pen."[8] Perhaps Aristotle offers the proper summation: ". . . it is absurd to hold that a man ought to be ashamed of being unable to defend himself with his limbs, but not of being unable to defend himself with speech and reason, when the use of rational speech is more distinctive of a human being than the use of his limbs."[9]

The speech course is designed to give you confidence when addressing a group of listeners and to teach you practical skills in the preparation, organization, and presentation of speeches. You may also expect a degree of voice improvement; Howard Gilkinson, another speech teacher, has demonstrated that recordings of speech students' voices at the end of the semester show a decided improvement over those made at the beginning.[10]

In the process of developing and mastering speaking skills, you should, moreover, realize many "fringe benefits." The course should help you to understand people as it brings you into close touch with the thoughts and feelings of your colleagues. It will help you to think more clearly, logically, and objectively. You will widen your horizon of knowledge and become a better-informed person. You will develop critical standards by which to evaluate speeches, both in and out of the classroom. You will improve your listening habits to better comprehend what you hear. You will be stimulated to develop your powers of imagination and creative thinking. More important still, the course should develop in you the inner poise and self-assurance by which your personality can unfold and develop. A speech class can be the door to self-discovery; better speech can often lead to better living.

THE NATURE OF SPEECH

The term *speech* brings varied concepts to the mind. It has so many meanings that a short, simple definition is difficult. Its separate

---

[8] Gail Kennedy (ed.), "Higher Education for American Democracy," in *Education for Democracy*, Heath, 1952, p. 27.

[9] *The Rhetoric of Aristotle, op. cit.*, p. 23.

[10] Howard Gilkinson, "Indexes of Change in Attitude and Behavior Among Students Enrolled in General Speech Courses," *Speech Monographs*, 8 (1941), 23–33.

aspects can, however, be identified. Gray and Wise list nine specific "bases of speech": social, physical, physiological, phonetic, neurological, psychological, genetic, linguistic, and semantic.[11] To these we might add one more, the philosophical basis. We shall not, however, attempt to explain or discuss all these bases of speech. The beginning student should be mainly concerned with the physiological, psychological, and social bases, with the other aspects left largely to advanced speech courses.

By *the physiological basis of speech* we mean the bodily structures and mechanisms which produce the speech sound through the process of respiration, phonation, resonation, and articulation. The *psychological basis* refers to the stimuli and responses involved in the speech act. When people speak, they do so in terms of their reactions to past experiences. Since they do not perceive and react identically to a stimulus, there is a constant threat of a breakdown in communication between them. To avoid misunderstanding, the speaker should constantly observe the "feedback"—the visible reactions of his listeners—and gauge his speech accordingly. The necessity for this cooperative action provides us with the *social* nature of speech. We speak for the purpose of communicating with our fellow men, often so that we may secure their cooperation toward the fulfillment of a desired end. It is impossible to imagine society without the ability to communicate.

The very nature of speech and the act of speaking are geared toward communication; hence, we may broadly define speech as the process by which ideas and feelings are expressed or transmitted through the integration of words, voice, action, and the personality of the speaker in order to gain a desired response.

Confusion in our thinking often comes from a failure to distinguish adequately between private and public speaking, between the act of talking and that of making a speech. This distinction is not always easy to make. For instance, consider two motorists involved in a minor automobile accident at a crowded city intersection. After the two drivers survey the damage done to their respective cars, a traffic officer appears to question them. Almost instantly a sizeable crowd surrounds the drivers and the policeman, each one straining

[11] Giles W. Gray and Claude M. Wise, *The Bases of Speech*, 3rd ed., Harper, 1959.

to hear every word they speak. Are we witnessing private or public speech? In another instance we attend a party in honor of a celebrated guest. At times during the discussions our honored guest seems to have the floor even though he remains seated and a whole roomful of people is listening to his conversation with the person next to him. Again, is this private or public speech? Or consider what so often happens in a college classroom when during the course of a lively discussion some student takes several minutes to make his point. In his enthusiasm he may rise to his feet in the middle of his remarks or even step to the front of the class before he is finished. Is this private or public speech? Or is it both? Where, in short, does private speech end and public speech begin?

Most people seem to believe that public speaking is an austere, formal, and formidable undertaking. They think of a man engaged in some kind of performance, standing on a platform before a large audience. They look upon the speaker in awe and wonderment, as though there were something of the oracular about the whole occasion. But great, dramatic oratory is rare in modern times and is certainly an unrealistic goal for the average college student.

Some speech texts tell us that public speaking is basically enlarged and elevated conversation with a group of people. However, this overly simple definition does not cover the creative side of public speaking. Making a speech is after all a special undertaking, whereas talking is about as common as eating, and does not in itself comprise making *a speech*. Our problem may be to distinguish not so much between private and public speech as between speech in day-to-day living and *a speech*. We observe the speech of children at play, of football players barking their signals, of neighbors chatting across the garden fence, and of countless other situations of life and living; but these are not the art form of speech.

What do we mean by *a speech?* A speech is not a recitation, a declamation, a report, play acting, or an essay; yet an essay read aloud comes close to being a speech. But does mere vocalization of a written composition make it a speech? If it does, the written themes of an English course could readily be shifted to meet the requirements of a speech class. As an earlier American speech authority wrote, "A speech is something other than a composition done with the mouth. Speeches may be read, spoken from memory, or extemporized; even essays and papers may be read. But, where in the world is there a place for a thing neither speech nor essay, but a composition standing on its hind legs?"[12] When we think of *a speech* we have in mind a creative piece in which ideas are expressed by means of spoken language for a specific purpose by a specific person before a specific audience at a specific time and place.

The basic elements which characterize a speech are: the speaker, audience and occasion, substance, composition (language and form), and delivery.

The Speaker

The speaker is a factor which cannot be divorced from the speech itself. Stories, poems, and other written matter may appear in print anonymously, but how can there be an anonymous speech? In rare instances, such as in the event of sickness or other emergency, one person may be called upon to read a speech prepared by another. A ghost writer may also give a speech its essential substance and shape. The man, however, who does the presentation is the responsible author and communicator. The substitute reader of another's speech and the ghost writer are the exceptions, not the rule, and do not violate the general truth that the speaker is an essential part of the speech.

Audience and Occasion

All speeches must have an audience and an occasion. The audience may vary in size from one person to many millions—as in the cases of radio listeners and television viewers. In a very few instances a prepared speech may never be heard—in fact, never made. For instance, in the United States Congress a speech may be merely inserted in the Congressional Record to be distributed among constituents. An undelivered manuscript, however, cannot properly be called a speech. In still other instances, speeches of unusual social or historical significance and rhetorical worth, may be both delivered before audiences and published in newspapers and even books. Some oral literature may have a wide reading audience and be read for generations. We have, indeed, a rich heritage of speech literature which reaches into the distant past for more than 3000 years.

[12] James Winans, "Aims and Standards in Public Speaking Work," *The English Journal,* 7 (1923), 230–231.

Substance

To say that a speech must have substance or content may be to belabor the obvious. But it is important to note that the sole justification for a speech remains the communication of thought related to a definite purpose. We all deplore the speaker who, saying little, talks loud and long. The full measure of speech content is, however, dependent upon its relationship to the speaker, the speaker's purpose, and the occasion. Merely to say something is not always enough. What is said must, in general, fit the speaker, his listeners, and the situation.

Composition

A speech is an idea expressed through words and form. Its language is essentially that of prose—though there may be poetic phrases and even a poetic style, and figures of speech may abound. There may be many variations of form and pattern in the arrangement of ideas vocalized. Some speeches reflect total lack of organization and no orderly sequence of ideas, whereas others stand as models of architectural design. There is no set form, such as in a sonnet; a speech, like a river, must flow and have direction, moving thought toward a determined end. The real challenge in the composition of a speech lies in the creation of that flow. The basis of much of the craftsmanship which gives speech its ultimate artistic form is thus in the area of language and structure. Although most speeches heard in a college speech class may not reflect a high level of creative art, there are, nevertheless, thousands of speeches, covering centuries of time, which, because of their thought and superior rhetorical procedures, stand as a form of literature. Composition, more than any other single factor, is the measure of the art of a speech.

Oral Presentation

A speech becomes an accomplished fact when it is orally presented to an audience. It then is something actual and real. Delivery may be of four types: memorized presentation, reading from manuscript, extemporaneous, and impromptu. These four types are fully explained in Chapter 12, "The Dynamics of Delivery."

This speech process, which we tend to take for granted, is complex. It is not a single specific act like flicking a fly off the sleeve or yanking a weed out of the garden. In speaking, a person becomes totally energized. We see with our eyes and hear with our ears, but we speak with our whole selves.

Speech is a form of learned behavior in which basic biological organs are used. These organs, however, have other more important functions: the lungs help to supply oxygen to the blood; the lips, tongue, teeth, palate, and mouth are essential for taking food into the body. Thus we can say that speech is an *overlaid,* secondary, or superimposed function.

The purposes, uses, forms, and personal motivations of speech may vary widely from day to day, hour to hour, even minute to minute. When we make small talk in personal or social conversation there may be an air of ease and casualness in our speech. During such conversational bits we are in a sense engaging in a kind of random social movement. It is our way of being comfortable and relaxed in the presence of others. When we talk before groups and become more conscious of the larger demands of our listeners, our fuller nature and personal resources become activated. Thus, when we make a speech, greater demands are made upon us; reserve energies and resources of mind, body, voice, and inner nature are drawn upon. Speaking is not dependent upon one single organ or part of the person, nor is it solely a matter of gesture or word or voice inflection or idea; it is all these and more. It is voice, body, language, thought, attitudes, character, and a thousand other attributes integrated into one single operation. And we use this complex act of speech for myriad purposes: conversation, public speaking, dictation, debating, discussion, reading aloud, acting, story-telling, emceeing, preaching, newscasting, and many more.

In conclusion, the all-important factor in speech is that it is the prime medium by which people communicate with one another. Other forms of communication exist, but speech is the principal means.

Trends in Style and Uses of Speech

Today's style of public address is not the same as that of previous generations. Old-fashioned oratory, characterized by the flowery, ornamental language and flamboyant, high-sounding manner of delivery common in the days of our grandfathers and great-grandfathers, is now as out of date as high-buttoned shoes, celluloid collars, and muttonchop whiskers. (Speech in a free society should minister to the needs of its people and reflect the culture of their time.) This it did in the days of Webster, Ingersoll, and Bryan. Formal platform public speaking, geared as it was to the concept of performance, had its place in earlier American life. At a time when there were no moving pictures, no radio or television to bring entertainment into the home, no automobiles to whisk people away to vacation spots or sports events, the people naturally craved some entertainment. The public speaker felt called upon to give a good show as well as to bring a message. The popular speaker was often an able actor and a masterful storyteller. People would come by horseback, buggy, wagon, and train, some of them traveling one way a full day or more, to hear him. Naturally he would be expected to hold forth long and loud. A lecture lasting two or three full hours was not unusual.

As we compare mid-twentieth century speech and all its ramifications with that of a century ago, we are impressed not only with the number of changes but with the drastic nature and degree of some of them. It may be helpful to call attention to a few which seem most useful in orienting us to the demands of effective oral communication.

1. *Today speechmaking has become everybody's business.* No longer do we consider public speaking something reserved for politicians, preachers, college presidents, or the gifted few. A man or woman from any walk of life may encounter a speaking situation of considerable importance. The merchant, the farmer, the doctor, the housewife, the shop foreman, the salesman, and all the rest of us must from time to time share a responsibility of leadership which requires the spoken word. Thus the "layman," not the "professional," is called upon to do most of the speech-making today. Norman Thomas, who has done about as much public speaking as any living American, writes in a recent book: "In our day, the occasions for Websterian oratory are few and the men capable of it still fewer."[13] He points out that the Astor Hotel in New York averages 4223 events a year at which there are addresses requiring a podium, the Waldorf-Astoria about ten speeches daily—with an over-all attendance of close to 5000.

[13] Norman Thomas, *Mr. Chairman, Ladies and Gentlemen*, Hermitage, 1955, p. 24.

2. *Speeches are much shorter than they used to be.* The increased
tempo of modern living and the wide diffusion of information by
press, radio, and television are influences which encourage brevity
on the platform. Three rules for the speaker are often invoked: "Be
brave, be brief, be seated." Sermons, courtroom speeches, and political speeches are scarcely half as long as they used to be. Even college
debaters and orators have had their time limits cut nearly in half
since Harvard and Yale first met on the forensic platform in 1892.

3. *There have been drastic changes in style and manner of delivery.* For more than half a century following the Civil War the
mark of the elocutionist was evident among platform speakers. It
remained for a time and then began to fade with the new century.
Today the influence of the elocution movement has for all practical
purposes vanished from American public-speaking platforms. This
movement was overly concerned with the technicalities and mechanics of delivery. Ultimately these outward skills of vocal and bodily
expression produced speakers who were lacking in naturalness and
sincerity. Their artificial, stylized, declamatory manner failed to convince and persuade audiences.

Speakers are now more direct, more conversational, and much
more informal in manner. The central goal in their language and
delivery today is effective communication of ideas. No doubt the
"share and tell" emphasis in our public schools has influenced speakers to speak with less flourish. Also, the wide use of public address
systems, radio, and television has all but eliminated the shouting,
podium-pounding speaker.

4. *This is a time for talk other than formal speechmaking.* Our
complex, competitive free society, with its inventions such as the
telephone, radio, television, moving pictures, intercom systems, voice
amplifiers, and recording machines, has vastly multiplied the uses
of oral communication, thus revitalizing in many respects its manner
of speaking. New techniques are constantly devised to improve the
effectiveness of communication by these media. Speech is also used
increasingly in carrying out functions of emceeing and conducting
conferences, interviews, committee meetings, and group discussions
of all sorts. Scores of books have been written to explore methods
and principles for effective group deliberations and oral decision-
making. As the late Dr. Irving Lee, in his book, *How to Talk with*

People, writes, ". . . the phenomena of discussion are being studied now as never before."[14]

Is Speech Merely Oral English?

Students and others sometimes think of speech merely as oral English. Such a concept is in large measure erroneous. Of course, speaking and writing are mutual: thought, language, grammar, syntax, organization and logical sequence of ideas characterize both written and spoken English. But in a larger and more realistic sense there are important differences. Speech and writing courses differ in their over-all goals, orientation, and types of learning experience. Speech is concerned with more than language and literature, which are the bases of an English course.

Speech demands immediate comprehension and response by a group of listeners; the reader's reaction toward the written word may be delayed, set aside, or reviewed at intervals of time. The meaning of the spoken word can be amplified and colored by voice and action. Spoken words thus reflect the speaker's personality more obviously than written words reflect the personality of the writer.

The ideas symbolized by the speaker's language in a speech class may be instantly tested, examined, and evaluated by both students and teacher. This immediacy entails disciplines which are basic to a speech course, yet are fundamentally quite different from those of theme writing in an English course. Further essential differences between oral and written language are discussed in Chapter 11, "Language in the Speech."

Other characteristics distinguish a speech class from an English class, such as the need for understanding the mechanics of vocal production, skill in vocal manipulation, effective use of gesture and bodily expression, audience empathy and audience control. All in all, the goals, methods, and practices of oral and written communications in the college classroom are not the same.

The Role of Speech in Liberal Education

The goal of speech instruction is the creation of the whole man, the growth and development of his many-sided personality—to teach him not merely to talk, but to talk about something of intellectual

[14] Irving J. Lee, *How to Talk with People,* Harper, 1952, p. ix.

worth. Education is concerned with the world of ideas and ideals. Ideas attain worthiness as they are tempered by clear, hard, independent thinking. An effective speech must have the contours of a creative piece; this requires rigorous structure of thought, careful analysis, and assimilation of isolated materials from which ideas are developed. Finally, the process requires a variety of methods for testing the truthfulness of statements. Thus speaker and listener alike must seek and develop standards of judgment for measuring and evaluating content.

Form and substance represent the initial phases of the speech-making process. Beyond this there must be appropriate language style and manner of delivery geared to the sensitivity of the listeners. One central goal in a speech class is to help the student to be more articulate. No man is truly educated if he remains inarticulate, but just to be articulate is not enough; the educated man is richly endowed with knowledge which becomes useful and meaningful through the process of logical and creative thinking. He is sensitive to the feelings and wants of others and is a discriminating judge of values in all his relationships with people. All these are aspects of the discipline we call speech, and they all must be considered as a measure of the educated man.

Educators generally are aware of the dynamic nature of speech training as it is related to our culture, to the conduct of human affairs, to the development of the mind, and to the creation of a mature, socially adjusted, responsible person. Colleges today generally recognize speech as an academic discipline. It is a vital area of academic activity, and its growth during the last few decades has been phenomenal.

The first real sign of speech as a modern academic discipline came in 1915, when the National Association of Academic Teachers of Public Speaking was formed. This association has grown from 165 members then to nearly 8,000 today; counting membership in related organizations of Theater Arts, Speech and Hearing, and Radio Broadcasters of America, the total exceeds 20,000 members, almost all of whom are teachers in academic speech fields. Few colleges offered a speech major in the early 1920s, and advanced speech degrees were almost unknown. In less than four decades after this, over 18,000 advanced degrees in speech were granted. Today about 150 colleges offer a Master's Degree, and 35 a Ph.D. in speech. More than 1,000 departments, divisions, or schools of speech exist today among our colleges, junior colleges, and universities. About 6,000 speech majors are graduated each year, and nearly half of our colleges require at least one speech course for graduation. The catalogs of several large midwestern universities list more than 100 courses in speech and related areas. Whereas the field provided at first only three major areas of speech for study—original speaking, oral reading, and drama—there are now a dozen or more; these include theater, radio and television, speech and hearing, communication studies, speech pedagogy, semantics, phonetics, rhetoric, history and criticism of public addresses, and group discussion.

Beyond these specific areas of study in which speech is represented in one way or another as the key to the communication act are many other academic dimensions in which speech is deeply rooted. Among these are physics, psychology, philosophy, physiology, biology, logic, and the social sciences.

From kindergarten through college, our schools have wisely placed great stress upon the development of phases of communication other than speech, such as reading and writing. They have been slow, however, to emphasize development in speaking and listening, those phases of communication we use most frequently in directing the course of our lives. Yet responsible people in a democracy must know how to handle well all the tools of communication. The truth can never make us free, no matter how well we may know it, unless we are also articulate about it and are able to share it with our fellow man by means of spoken language.

YOUR ROLE IN THIS COURSE

The Uniqueness of a Speech Course

There are pronounced differences between a speech class and other courses in the curriculum. It is important that you fully understand and appreciate these differences and the problems that grow out of them. With this awareness you will be able to make the necessary adjustments to the speech class environment, its learning processes, and the objectives of the course.

1. *The central activity of the speech class deals with elements of public performance.* The very nature of the course involves making

short talks before a group. Although related problems of speech in interpersonal relations and of underlying principles and theories are significant, the actual experience of making talks under audience conditions is the core of the work. What other class in a college of liberal arts is so oriented?

2. *A speech class revolves around human factors.* It is through personal relations that the class moves and has its being. Personality patterns are brought into such close proximity that they inevitably influence one another.

3. *Speech itself is a complex process.* As we have mentioned earlier in this chapter, speech has many facets which invoke many sciences, many arts, and many phases of interpersonal relationships. The problems, therefore, for both teacher and student are perhaps more varied and complex than those of any other course.

4. *Any poor emotional attitudes you may have will create unusual hazards in speech work.* They will have a more significant bearing upon the quality of work done and your relative success than in most other courses. Here dread of facing the class is a more serious deterrent to the learning process than it is in other classes. Such apprehension can not only destroy your own motivation, but it can have a deadening effect upon other students and upon class spirit.

5. *Individuality is a most valuable asset in determining the quality of your work.* You have a unique claim to personal resources upon which you alone can draw in your speech-making. Capitalize upon your individuality and make it count in a distinctive way every time you give a talk. In other courses, textbooks and teachers' methods may deter your individuality, but not in an effective speech course.

6. *The speech class, like most science classes, has its laboratory,* but not one composed of test tubes, microscopes, and physical properties. Its laboratory is composed of living matter—fellow classmates —and thus is never static; it is always in a state of flux and is created anew with each class meeting. In no other course, consequently, is class attendance, good listening behavior, and group spirit so important to the educational objectives as in a speech class. The class is a social entity and a constructive force, ready to share your joys and triumphs as a speaker. It has a mood and a soul of its own which you help to create. The right kind of class spirit provides a mysterious, wonderful motivating force to draw out your hidden

and latent speaking talents. In no course in the curriculum does classroom atmosphere so vitally influence the quality of your work.

7. *There are no absolutes in speech such as one might find in mathematics, accounting, or engineering.* There are no perfect scores in the usual sense, and work can seldom be 100 percent completed, as in the solving of a mathematical equation or a chemical formula.

8. *Self-generated purpose is doubly rewarding to you.* Actions prompted from within are rewarding not only in the immediate classroom undertaking but, because of the lasting mental discipline they encourage, in all speech situations you will face in later life. You will do your best work if you compete *with yourself* instead of *for grades*. Each triumph generates new strength, increased self-reliance, and greater desire for further speaking ventures. Probably nowhere in the college curriculum does success succeed as it does in a speech class.

9. *Effort will be rewarded.* Your speech grades will improve, to some degree, if you make an honest try. For effort is reflected in careful, thorough preparation of speeches, cooperation and courtesy as a listener, and willing participation in class projects and assignments without complaints or excuses.

10. *In a speech class you are not always learning something new or mastering an unfamiliar process.* You are improving upon something you already can do. Speech is a process or function familiar to you from the time of infancy. Speech training thus takes something which already is part of you and helps you to use it more effectively.

These few indications of the uniqueness of a speech class will soon become familiar to you; there are many more. It is important that you give serious consideration to these fundamental elements of your speech class. Adjust yourself to the demands peculiar to this class and you will be richly rewarded.

How to Get the Most Out of This Course

We cannot prescribe a simple formula that will give you those constructive attitudes so essential to your progress in speech. No book can force you to embrace this course with open arms. The right mental attitude is something you must work out for yourself in your own way. The problem is yours and yours alone; solving it will require patience and determination. Yet neither you nor even others can judge your true potential in speech, for ultimate success as a speaker is, at your age, quite unpredictable.

History shows that accomplished orators often come from the ranks of those who show the least promise in their youth. As youths, Demosthenes, Patrick Henry, Benjamin Disraeli, Daniel Webster, Abraham Lincoln, Robert Ingersoll, Wendell Phillips, Winston Churchill, and Franklin Roosevelt offered little hope that some day they might become speakers of renown. Most of these men, in fact, at the age of 18 or 20 years suffered either from a speech impediment, extreme shyness, or unusual awkwardness of manner. Yet they learned to overcome their limitations and handicaps to achieve greatness on the platform.

Many suggestions will be offered to guide you toward fulfillment of the goals of this course. You no doubt will devise numerous study procedures of your own to suit your individual needs. However, we urge that as supplement to your own study plans you consider the following recommendations, devised for your guidance and assistance.

1. *Look upon the course as an opportunity for personal growth and development.* Welcome each speaking experience as a venture in human growth, rather than as an assignment measured in terms of absolute success or failure. Doing it is what counts, and doing it the best you can. The speeches for which you get your highest grades may not always be the ones most valuable to you in terms of your total growth and educational progress. Some speeches on which you make your poorest grades may ultimately be the source of great personal satisfaction. It is the larger educational rewards and enduring personal satisfactions which matter most.

2. *Get off to a good start in the preparation of your speeches.* Begin by jotting down early any ideas which come to you—even while your instructor is making the assignment. Put your mind to work at once. Even though your initial thoughts may be discarded, the chances are your speeches will be better if you do not yield to the temptation to procrastinate.

3. *Take pride in your speaking endeavors.* Does this speech really represent your best efforts? If you are more concerned about making the most of your abilities than about your grade, you will probably make a higher grade than you expected.

4. *Be patient with yourself.* Be your own severest critic, yet do not expect everything to happen at once. The self cannot grow to

full strength overnight. It takes time to build the attitudes and gain the insights which will form the basis of your growth and development as a speaker.

5. *Be a full-fledged member of the class group.* Integrate yourself into the class in such a way that your presence would be missed by your teacher and every student. Think of your speech class as a laboratory made up of living human beings. In a purely mathematical sense, you represent, in a class of twenty students only five percent of the total; but your contribution toward group awareness and class spirit can be something much more than one-twentieth of the whole. Be the most cooperative member of the group in all matters pertaining to assignments and class projects. Speaking is a process in which one gives and others receive, giver and receiver acting upon each other to produce a kind of circular response. This human interaction generates from attentive listening, a spirit of mutual helpfulness, and a sense of sharing each other's problems as well as each other's triumphs. Class spirit is usually at its best when the precept "one for all and all for one" prevails. Therefore, privately cherish the thought that every student who speaks will do a little better because you are present.

6. *Always bring your total self into the speech act.* Beyond the specific skills of speechmaking, you possess a self from which radiates countless clues that are effective in the communication process. We are first aware, for instance, of a tree as a totality, not as a collection of separate leaves, branches, roots, and trunk. A tree stands as an object of symmetry, color, balance, and beauty in which component parts are wonderfully blended and integrated to form the whole. Man also is a totality. He communicates with his total experiences, his total character and personality, his feelings, his thoughts, and his attitudes. In other words, all that he is or hopes to be in body, mind, and soul reach beyond the raw machinery of making a speech. That is why it is important that you bring your total self into the speech act.

7. *Use the "whole" method in the study and application of basic theory.* Before proceeding to build a bridge one must first study all the blueprints in their entirety; theory precedes practice. Speaking similarly cannot be learned piece by piece or step by step in the usual sense. Hence the "whole" method should be applied in the study and reading of Part One and Part Two of this volume. Read

Part Two carefully early in the course, as though it contained one single master plan to guide you for the whole course. Absorb as much as you can from the materials as a whole, combing the pages for ideas, 'suggestions, and clues which will be most helpful and useful for you. Underscore parts which appeal to you. Make marginal comments and keep diary notes for your personal use. Many portions of the book should then be reviewed and reread later, when they are needed for more thorough digesting.

PART TWO

THE DIMENSIONS OF EFFECTIVE SPEECH

Part Two contains the basic theory and principles of speech. We have brought into sharp focus the six major dimensions of the speech communication act. To both the preparation and the criticism of speeches, these dimensions are essential topic areas. Each dimension with its cluster of concepts is oriented to the total speaking process.

Some dimensions naturally precede others in our thinking. First, there must be the person speaking; he initiates and originates the signals; he is the sender, the giver of the message. Second is the receiver, or the audience; there can be no speech if there is no listener or receiver. Third, there must be an idea or message; the sender must have something to send. Speech thus moves about the axis of people and ideas, its greatest function being to facilitate the communication of thought. The three factors—man, audience, and message—are the basic dimensions in which oral communication takes place.

Organization, language, and delivery are all produced by the speaker. These are most rewardingly studied and applied only after adequate insight has been reached into the first three dimensions—"speaker," "audience," and "content." Although the section on delivery, in this book, comes last, that does not mean it is least important. It means the speaker should first be concerned about having something to say to the listener. The man with an idea, eager to share it with others, is on the surest road to speech effectiveness.

The Speaker

❧ 1 ❧
Poise and Confidence

No function in life is more bound up with your total being than that of speech. Listeners, both consciously and unconsciously, form opinions and develop attitudes about you as a person from your ideas, your logical processes, the language you use, even your gestures and vocal inflection. They react to your mood as well as to your message, your appearance and behavior as well as your words and subject. In fact, they have an initial impression about you even before you say a word. Your speech, then, is measured and appraised by listeners through a thousand clues about you as a person.

It is a compelling thought that, with the three billion people on this earth, you are a unique individual. True, all people have two eyes and two ears and walk on two legs; they eat, drink, sleep, laugh, cry, use the same senses, are subject to the same diseases, and communicate with each other by means of speech. Yet beyond what they have in common, every human being carries the stamp of a "self" that is his alone.

There is something in the force of the individual personality which is appealing to most people. Woodrow Wilson once said: "The most exciting thing in the world is the human personality." Will Rogers' words, "I never met a man I didn't like," were engraved on the commemoration stamp in his honor issued in 1948. Speech teachers who have heard thousands of classroom speeches often remark that they never get bored with their students. To them it is exciting to observe the behavior of the human personality as manifested by the speech process.

In the act of communication, your total personality tends to become alive and activated. Speech has been referred to as the oral communication of ideas with the personality of the speaker wrapped around them. The Greeks taught us that we cannot separate the speaker from his platform performance. The great Roman speech teacher, Quintilian, taught that the ideal speaker must be first of all a good man. Your life, your ideals, and the way you view the world are all revealed to others when you speak. All the qualities that make up the human character, no matter how complex they may be, are a source of eloquence which you alone can claim. The full measure of who and what you are becomes an intricate, inescapable part of the total communication act.

For these reasons, two major problems in the dimension of the speaker become important. The first concerns the optimum functioning of your *total self;* this problem brings your personal resources to bear, for better or for worse, upon the speechmaking venture. One great barrier to your optimum functioning as a self before an audience is lack of poise and confidence. The word that strikes at the heart of this problem is *stage fright.* The second problem concerns the speaker's image and is often discussed under the term *ethical proof.* The first of these concepts is discussed in this chapter, the second concept in the next.

WHY UNDERSTANDING AND CONTROL
OF STAGE FRIGHT ARE IMPORTANT

Basic insight into the role and nature of stage fright is essential to your maximum progress and development as a speech student. Before we attempt to define stage fright and discuss its possible remedies and methods of control, let us consider five pertinent questions:

How Does Self-Confidence Influence the Maximum Effectiveness of a Speech?

The beginning speech student tends to place self-confidence far too high on the list of basic factors which contribute to speech effectiveness. He seems to look upon it as a virtue in itself, a kind of magic element which will guarantee his success, as if no speech can succeed so long as stage fright exists. In one survey, beginning college speech students ranked self-confidence at the top of twelve speech factors, whereas national speech experts ranked it at the bottom.[1] Of course, the beginning student is deeply concerned about the tensions, fears, and apprehensions he experiences when making a speech. But his feelings of ego involvement throw the total picture of speech-making out of its true perspective. He is prone to allow this attitude to overshadow other cardinal factors such as content, organization, clear purpose, logical thinking, preparation, and the like. One nationally known speech authority wrote a letter in response to the study just mentioned, in which he made the following worthwhile observation:

As you say, and as your survey indicates, most beginning speakers (in college, or among adults) rank confidence as what they most wish to achieve in a speech class. For myself, I think this is a nonsensical goal! What would your track coach say if a youngster told him he wanted to learn to run the 100-yard dash "comfortably!" I always tell my students I don't care how much they suffer on the platform, as long as they do a truly good job of communicating ideas that are worthwhile for the audience. My own hunch is that their stage fright arises in large part from having to do in public something they don't know how to do well—with the acute realization that their listeners are judging not only what they do but what they are. This would scare anyone. The remedy: learn to speak well! Hence, the best "cure" for stage fright is to master analysis, organization, illustration, modes of proof, etc., etc.[2]

All the self-confidence in the world does not by itself lead to an effective speech. Many speakers who suffer miserably from stage fright nevertheless reach a high level of effectiveness—they succeed in spite of the difficulty. What they say and their sincerity and clarity of purpose in saying it carry them through. Of course, we may also admit that they might have done a still better job had stage fright been overcome or minimized.

Stage fright may indeed give a false or distorted picture of the true personality of the speaker and thus hamper the effectiveness of his efforts. More significantly, stage fright in its acute stages may in

[1] See the Appendix for a report of this study.
[2] Letter from Robert T. Oliver, Pennsylvania State University, February 2, 1959. Reprinted by permission.

varying degrees cause the speaker to forget and thus perhaps omit important points in his speech. It also may impair his delivery, his posture, gestures, and quality of voice, as well as his rate of speaking, vocal pitch, and cadence. Fidgety, meaningless gestures, and a shaky voice are common and unfortunate results of tension.

Some speakers who are normally warm and friendly, take on long severe faces on the platform, with glowering looks and aggressive or belligerent manner. The result is that personal attributes which would be important assets are strangely dissolved by the emotional complexes that exist.

What Role Does Self-Confidence Play in Your Progress and Development in Becoming an Able Speaker?

Progress in minimizing and controlling stage fright is almost mandatory before you can make satisfactory progress in speech-making. It is important that all of your faculties which apply to the speaking process be fully operative; only when the faculties of your mind and your physical self are free from the inhibitions generated by stage fright can you reach your best level of performance. No teacher can offer or should try to offer pertinent criticism of your efforts while you remain in a state of near shock. You are not your real self then: your basic speech processes are not working properly; the voice we hear may not be your natural voice; you may give ideas improper emphasis; even the order of ideas may get mixed up and important points of your speech be entirely omitted. At times, your words and phrases may not fit the meaning you wish to convey, and you may violate even the simplest rules of grammar. Worse yet, you may convey the wrong mental attitudes—you may appear cold and aloof when you want to be friendly, indifferent when you want to be enthusiastic, belligerent when you want to cooperate. Under such circumstances the teacher's critical comments cannot be based upon sound insights into your real speech needs. Therefore, it is crucial that you make as much progress as possible as fast as possible in the management and control of stage fright.

How Prevalent Is Stage Fright?

Stage fright is so widely prevalent that it is experienced by most speakers. Plutarch recorded twenty-three hundred years ago that

Demosthenes, in his first public address, was afflicted by "weakness in his voice, a perplexed and indistinct utterance and a shortness of breath . . . so that in the end, being quite disheartened, he forsook the assembly." Cicero said of himself, "I turn pale at the outset of each speech, and quake in every limb and in all my soul." Even such famous speakers as Daniel Webster, Mark Twain, William Jennings Bryan, Will Rogers, and Winston Churchill complained about stage fright. Numerous studies have indicated that most college students have some difficulty with stage fright. Greenleaf found that of 789 college students only 11 percent experienced no stage fright, all the others being afflicted by varying degrees of the malady.[3] In a recent survey covering 699 University of Kansas beginning speech students, only 3 percent claimed to experience no stage fright whatsoever.

If you are bothered by feelings of self-consciousness and apprehension when making classroom speeches, remember that the classmate next to you may feel more miserable than you. Is stage fright, then, an affliction which you must shun like the plague? Or is it a blessing heaven-sent to help you? These questions will be answered later in this chapter.

Can Stage Fright Be Overcome or Controlled?

In a survey conducted by a committee of the Speech Association of America and reported by its chairman, Professor Donald E. Hargis, 87 percent of the responding teachers reported that students made a more adequate platform adjustment after taking the beginning speech course; 75 percent of them gained in poise and confidence, and 9.8 percent manifested social and emotional growth.[4]

The University of Kansas study just mentioned covered the attitudes of students toward stage fright in a required course in speech. Twenty-seven percent of 699 beginning speech students said that at the beginning of the course they definitely dreaded making speeches before groups, while only 8 percent dreaded it at the time the course was completed; 30 percent said they experienced "much" or "very much" stage fright at the outset of the course, but only 14 percent did so after completing the course. The study indicated a strong

[3] Floyd I. Greenleaf, *An Experimental Study of Social Speech Fright,* M. A. Thesis, State University of Iowa, 1947.

[4] Donald E. Hargis, "The First Course in Speech," *The Speech Teacher,* January, 1956, p. 31.

shift in student attitudes toward the course itself. After completing it, 76 percent said they had less feeling of dread toward it than at the beginning, 1 percent dreaded it more, and 23 percent dreaded it about the same as before.

What Is Your Attitude Toward Your Physical Self as Related to Speech Delivery?

Many beginning students, when they first think of making a speech, form a mental image of themselves standing before an audience. This image frequently grows out of the feelings of self-consciousness which concern them in matters of outward appearances, looks, posture, bodily action, and dress. The beginner perhaps worries to himself, "The audience can't look into my mind, but they can see me." This concern over outward impressions may be troublesome in many situations. Remember when you graduated from high school and walked alone across the wide stage before a packed house to receive your diploma? No doubt what many seniors dread most about their graduation is that walk across the platform. When being interviewed for your first important job, you may have difficulty in showing physical composure, in knowing just what to do at all times with your hands. Similarly, if, when you first consider making a speech, you say, "I don't know what to do with my hands," you are really talking about the symptoms of your self-consciousness. You are announcing the fact that you are more worried about your ego than about what you have to say.

Of course you know that your outward appearance and what you do with your hands are not the primary or basic factors which make a good speech. These are superficial and trivial compared to other things. The problem of your physical self and all matters pertaining to bodily expression in delivery are discussed at length in Chapter 13, "Bodily Communication." If this matter looms in your mind as a major problem, it might be well to turn to these pages for help.

WHAT STAGE FRIGHT IS

Stage fright is a psychological condition caused by worry and feelings of anxiety. The nature and intensity of the emotion experienced may be determined by complexities of personality structure, physiological conditions, patterns of social behavior, and many psychological factors. In spite of certain common denominators among symptoms, causes, remedies, and methods of control, nevertheless stage fright remains a highly individualistic problem. No two cases of stage fright are identical; neither symptoms nor methods of elimination or control are the same. Each case is separate. Therefore, the person with the affliction, if we may call it that, must for the most part be his own doctor.

In a study of social speech fright one researcher presents this definition: "an evaluative disability occurring in social speech situations and characterized by anticipatory negative reactions of fear, avoidance, and various internal and overt manifestations of tension and behavioral manifestations."[5]

Low and Sheets describe stage fright largely on the basis of its symptoms: "The emotional disturbances of mental and physical behavior of the speaker as manifested by poor eye contact, nervous hand movements, restless shifting of feet, awkward posture, quivering of body, timid voice, embarrassment and other physical and vocal cues emphatically perceived."[6]

Another writer observes still other aspects of the fear phenomenon: "Stage fright may be a manifestation of neurotic behavior resulting from the conflict between two instinctive reactions, specifically, the longing for an audience and the fear of appearing before it. These two reactions are equal in strength; stage fright is the result." He further states: "Poise is a state of inner calm, serenity and well-being. It is a balance of tensions, an equilibrium, as a result of both inner health and satisfactory relations with the outside environment. When there is lack of poise the entire speech personality is disturbed and made less efficient in its adjustment. This lack of poise is known as stage fright."[7]

The patterns of physical reaction to fear stimuli in stage fright may resemble those we have when we are shocked by tragic news or by a threat of danger. Nature comes to our rescue in these moments of emotional stress with its complicated system of superchargers. The respiratory and circulatory organs of the body are "souped up" by the secretion of glandular fluids which supply added energy to meet

[5] Greenleaf, *op. cit.*

[6] Gordon M. Low and Boyd V. Sheets, "The Relation of Psychometric Factors to Stage Fright," *Speech Monographs*, 18, no. 4 (1951), 266–271.

[7] Elwood Murray, *The Speech Personality*, Lippincott, 1939, p. 91.

the crisis. Although this is a physiological phenomenon, stage fright is also a social fear in which the ego is deeply involved, a fear which is mainly a form of learned behavior. Yet the spot on the platform behind the lectern is in some ways the safest place in the whole room. What then are you afraid of?

You are afraid of yourself, the kind of impression you will make upon your audience or your teacher or even upon yourself. Your sense of pride in accomplishment is part of the picture. You want approval of others. You fear their ridicule. Thus you worry about your limitations, your inadequacies, and a thousand imperfections—real or imaginary. In countless ways you become aware of possible deficiencies which reflect upon yourself. In other words, you become "self-conscious," and, your interloping self-consciousness shoves aside your real self, with the result that the audience receives a false image of you.

SYMPTOMS OF STAGE FRIGHT

It is through its symptoms that we most easily recognize our stage fright. We have already mentioned some of them. It will be helpful if we now take a closer look at those common behavior patterns which accompany the emotion fear, limiting our attentions to those most prevalent and most obvious.

Withdrawal Behavior

APOLOGETIC ATTITUDES. The frequently heard phrase, "Unaccustomed as I am," and its relatives, are the mark of the apologetic speaker. This type of speaker tells the audience in advance that he is a poor speaker, will probably fail, knows little about the subject, is ill prepared, is inexperienced—and generally belittles himself. He thus not only knocks the props from under whatever he may have to say, but he also often undermines his purpose and the worthiness of his thoughts by indifferent posture, meaningless gestures, hesitant manner, and upward inflections of the voice—all of which connote doubt, uncertainty, and general negative attitudes. Obviously this type of speaker cannot win the respect and admiration of his listeners; his efforts indeed are doomed to failure.

AVOIDANCE OF DIRECT COMMUNICATION WITH AUDIENCE. The speaker showing this symptom usually shuns direct contact with his listeners by looking at the floor, the ceiling, or out of the windows, or by burying himself in his notes or manuscript. His posture is usually slouchy, characterized by nervous shifting from one foot to the other or by retreat behind the lectern. His withdrawal tendency is further manifested by the way he sinks his hands in his pockets or locks them behind his back for a long period of time, fumbles with his notes, mumbles, and speaks in a deadly monotone. Such a speaker seems to be completely oblivious to his audience with no interest or desire to communicate with it.

RUNNING AWAY FROM IT ALL.   In one variation of withdrawal behavior, the would-be speaker never really speaks at all—he simply runs away from the speaking situation. Figuratively speaking, he stays home on the night of the banquet during which he will be called upon to say a few words. One brilliant high school senior, headed for the highest scholastic honors in his class, learned that because of this honor he would be expected to make the valedictory speech on commencement night. He promptly proceeded to flunk a quiz or two to gain second rank in his class in order to avoid being valedictorian.

Physiological Activity and Vocal Expression

Physical responses symptomatic of stage fright are numerous and easily recognized. Emotional pressures tend to seek outlets through muscular activity, both involuntary and voluntary. Behavior which is largely involuntary includes the pounding heart, rapid breathing, perspiration, blushing or blanching, dry mouth, quickened pulse beat, loss of memory, and muscular conflicts which cause trembling of the knees or other parts of the body. Actions which are more or less voluntary include rigid posture, fidgety random movements, shuffling of feet, jingling coins, fumbling notes, rubbing hands, rising pitch of the voice, talking rapidly, cluttering speech with "uhs," slips of the tongue, and grammatical, articulatory, or language irregularities.

CAUSES OF STAGE FRIGHT

Sources of Stage Fright

Many factors, some complex, others more simple, contribute to the over-all experience of stage fright. Yet they all are concerned with man's basic need for personal adequacy. We all want to maintain and enhance our perception of ourselves. Public speaking places our self-concept in jeopardy—it is a threat to our adequacy—and in the minds of all but the fully confident fears arise. Immediate sources of speech fears vary widely from person to person and, for the same person, from speech to speech. Intensity of fear varies also. As we consider the many ramifications of this phenomenon and attempt to analyze its causes, we must first look at the character and personality structure of the speaker himself. The speaker must, at the start, discern those traits which make up his mental, physical, spiritual, and social self. Within the "self" are found the basic elements which may be shaped, adjusted, and used to control the fright response.

FEAR OF PHYSICAL UNATTRACTIVENESS.   Feelings of inferiority are often generated by the thought that one is not physically attractive or is lacking in charm. Have you ever felt you were too tall or too short, too skinny or too fat, not pretty or handsome, or underdeveloped sexually? Have you ever worried about the color or complexion of your skin, the shape of your figure or of your nose? You may, in other words, feel you do not measure up to the standards of the ideal man or woman. Such feelings may build tensions and thus become barriers to self-confidence.

FEAR OF SOCIAL INADEQUACY.   Stage fright is a form of social fear. Its roots may extend back to your earliest childhood, to your home life, your playmates, your neighborhood activities, and your social life in the grades and high school. Did you get along well socially and feel accepted by children of your group and age? Were you and are you now conscious of your social status? Do you ever feel that your family has come from the "wrong side of the tracks," that you cannot afford to dress as well as others, that you belong to a minority group, social or religious? Whether imaginary or real, any ideas you may have that you are socially unpopular stand as barriers in building self-confidence.

FEAR OF CRITICISM.   On the other hand, some people experience stage fright because they have an exaggerated sense of pride, an inflated ego, that makes them far too sensitive to criticism. How about you? Are you afraid of criticism? Do you get angry or hurt even when you know the criticism is justified and you are wrong? Do you carry a chip on your shoulder? If your answer to these questions is yes, you have added difficulties in controlling and overcoming stage fright.

FEAR OF FAILURE. Stage fright may be in part the result of a fear of failure. We are afraid we will forget or embarrass ourselves in some other way. Frequently these feelings are associated with an unfortunate previous experience such as the loss of a job, the loss of a high school election, failure to make a fraternity, being jilted in love, flunking an examination, or, more significantly, an embarrassing childhood experience while participating in some public performance, such as making a speech, giving a recitation at a school program, or bungling a musical recital. Such experiences often leave their wounds upon the unconscious mind, generating a tendency to withdraw and thus avoid humiliation and embarrassment.

FEAR OF THE UNKNOWN. We are afraid of the dark because darkness creates an area of the unknown which gives us a feeling of insecurity. There is always a certain amount of the unknown, the new, the unpredictable in every speaking situation. No two situations or audiences are exactly alike; there are so many human equations involved that some elements of uncertainty are always bound to be present. Speaking experiences are not like walking to school a hundred times on a road where you see the same familiar sights again and again, where the physical environment, after a while, becomes comfortably routine. The road you travel as a speaker is entirely flanked by human beings with changing moods and unpredictable behavior.

Feelings of fear and anxiety may arise with almost any new experience. How composed were you at your first formal party, your first airplane ride, the first time you tried the high diving board or drove the family car? How did you feel at your first interview for a job? Our fear of speaking to an audience may be natural because we have done so little of it. Fortunately, as we become more familiar with the speaking experience, tensions tend to subside.

FEAR OF STAGE FRIGHT. The late President Franklin D. Roosevelt, speaking over the radio to a nation in the depths of the worst economic depression of the century, said, "The only thing we have to fear is fear itself." Thus he struck an effective blow at national anxiety. Many students have an aversion to speechmaking because they are afraid of being afraid. They are afraid of stage fright. The very thought of stage fright, more than the speech or the audience, produces a state of panic. Their actual fear of fear, which often feeds on itself, may be one of the most difficult to control.

CONFLICTING EMOTIONS.   There are times when sweet thoughts of triumph conflict sharply with bitter thoughts of failure. The strong desire to do and the fear of failure work against each other so forcefully that the will to action approaches dead center—as the farmer said of his fractious horse: "He's rarin' to go but can't go for rarin'." When thoughts of personal glory conflict with those of possible failure, a good case of stage fright develops. Similar experiences of mixed emotions may come to the student at examination time, to the football player at the crucial game of the year, to the surgeon before a complicated operation, or to the groom at the altar on his wedding day.

EXCITEMENT FROM ANTICIPATION.   Mere anticipation of a big event often causes bodily reactions such as increased pulse rate, sweating hands, and other symptoms of stage fright. A fully confident football player may experience an increase in adrenalin flow before a big game, even though he is not afraid. An experienced actor who has performed his role many times may undergo considerable excitation before going on stage. This excitement is the result of anticipation. Better still, take an experience from everyday life. Have you ever planned a big trip and felt a physical reaction or stimulation when thinking of it? The public speaker also anticipates his speech. Fully confident and experienced speakers are usually at least a little excited before they speak. Their "keyed up" feeling may be the result of certain fears, but it is more likely to be that of mere anticipation. In fact, it usually helps the speaker "warm up" to the speech. The next time you experience slight excitement before giving a speech, remember that it may be the result of mere anticipation, and that the increased adrenalin flow is nature's way of helping you soar to greater heights than you would otherwise find possible.

Misconceptions and Faulty Attitudes Aggravate Stage Fright

One anomaly of life seems to be that people inexperienced in speech making have so many silly, senseless notions about it. It is indeed rare to find honest, objective, sound thinking about qualifications of speakers and what is required for their success. Some think that good speakers are born—that speaking well is a gift of the few; others feel that the audience is a hostile, unfriendly force, ready to laugh at their failures. These unsound concepts and attitudes have kept and no doubt will continue to keep many a promising person from developing his speaking ability. Such misconceptions about speech may induce as well as aggravate stage fright.

Character Traits Affect the Problem

Although the structure of one's character may not always be the sole cause of stage fright, certain traits of character, nevertheless, tend to create conditions either favorable or unfavorable to its elimination or control. Some character traits provide the instruments by which the speaker can fashion self-reliance and self-assurance. Without their use he may continue to suffer disgrace, humiliation, and failure. The speaker who has developed a full measure of such virtues as *courage, determination, patience, enthusiasm,* and *friendliness* has within his reach the tools for building his self-confidence. The speaker who lacks these qualities of character or has the misfortune to possess largely opposing traits, like timidity, cowardice, laziness, indifference, impatience, and unfriendliness, has only useless tools at his command. There is an old saying, "You can't make a silk purse out of a sow's ear"; we might also say, "You can't make a confident speaker out of a characterless man."

DESIGN FOR ACTION

Having defined and discussed both symptoms and causes of stage fright, we are now ready to set forth a *design for action,* based not on any single remedy or method but on four major approaches to the problem.

Examine Yourself and the Sources of Your Stage Fright

"Know thyself" must be your initial step in the control of stage fright. Begin by putting yourself, so to speak, on the psychiatrist's couch, and probe for the true sources of your tensions and fears when speaking before a group.

What fears, if any, are linked to faulty notions or misconceptions? Can you recall any of these silly notions? Have you also had difficulty with unreasonable fears? Do you imagine something dreadful about making a speech? The audience to be hostile? The occasion as something unpleasant or awful? If you do, you are, like Don Quixote, fighting windmills and giants that do not exist.

Are you by nature timid and reticent? When you are with people, do you find it difficult to join in conversation? When you are in a group, do you prefer to withdraw into your shell? Is it hard for you to "mix" at a party?

Is your aversion to making a speech really due to your lack of speaking experience and preparation, or is it lack of faith in your ideas? Do you have confidence in your own opinions? Or have you had the habit of saying to yourself, "Little me, who cares what I think?" What of your desire to grow in strength as an oral communicator? Would you really like to be an effective speaker, or don't you care? Finally, are your character traits in order? Do you have those qualities which are effective wellsprings of communication?

Before you make satisfactory progress toward building self-assurance, it is important that you be honest with yourself and truly attempt to bring your personal resources fully to bear upon your speaking. Make an inventory, therefore, of your assets and liabilities so that you may determine those sources of strength which will help you most toward speech achievement.

Stage fright is something you must face alone. How you meet this challenge is entirely up to you. We have attempted to give some insights as to the nature of stage fright, its role in the speaking process, its symptoms, causes, and methods of control; but all this is futile unless you, of your own free will and accord, make a serious effort to do something about it.

In this design of self-evaluation a few summary reminders may help:

1. Stage fright is entirely an individualistic matter. No other case is exactly like yours. Make your own diagnosis and prescribe your own methods for conquering fears.

2. Stage fright is natural and probably does more good than harm —when viewed in its entirety. It is harmful only when it is undisciplined. Learn how to control it and to use it constructively, for here lies an added source of physical energy, mental alertness, and dynamic personal power. Without stage fright many public speakers, actors, singers, and athletes would never achieve success.

3. Meeting the challenge of stage fright is not like peeling an apple. An apple once peeled stays peeled; but stage fright, once overcome, may have to be reconquered again and again. Tensions may recur any time in different forms. As you progress from one level of their control to another, you will need continually to redesign your plans for self-mastery. Always remain alert and ready to meet any surprise attack.

4. Compete with yourself first, then compete for grades. In the final analysis, the grades you make or how you compare with your classmates matters less than how well you have done in comparison with yourself. Have you made the most of your resources and abilities? Have you been completely true to the talents available to you? Time will eventually take the measure of your progress toward self-confidence in this course; the true test of your growth will come five, ten, twenty years from now. Then the rewards of self-mastery may prove that your greatest day was when you made your lowest grade in speech, your least rewarding day when you made your highest.

5. Make each speaking venture a new game. Make a fresh start every time you speak—no matter how well you know your audience, how often you have talked on the same subject, or even how often you have made the same speech. Decide that this is a brand new challenge requiring a brand new design and purpose. Never be complacent for this attitude breeds staleness of ideas, language, and delivery.

Develop Useful and Positive Attitudes

You may think that speakers are born, that public speaking is a gift of the few. Nonsense! Speakers are not born any more than teachers, doctors, carpenters, stenographers, or truck drivers are "born." Ability in speaking is developed by industrious application of sound principles which underlie the speaking process. Anyone with normal intelligence, an acceptable voice, a pleasing personality, and a strong desire to succeed can become an able speaker.

Perhaps you may think that all that is required for effective speaking is mastery of a few tricks. This, too, is nonsense. Speaking is not a skill based on a few devices for holding an audience spellbound. There are no clever stunts by which you can really deceive the discriminating listener. The bulk of good speeches given in this country are made by honest, sincere men and women from all walks of life, who speak of worthwhile ideas or inspire others to do good. They do not put on stunts nor rely on tricks.

To think of the audience as a hostile, unfriendly force is also foolish. Rarely will you have an unfriendly audience; at worst you may face a neutral one. Why then fret about an imaginary enemy? The audience is most often on your side and wants you to have your say, even though it may not always agree with what you say.

You may think that to make a good speech you must be witty, clever, or entertaining. Again, nonsense. To be sure, audiences like to be stimulated. But although they may applaud clever remarks and laugh at humorous jokes, their laughter, applause, and even rapt attention are not reliable yardsticks for measuring the effectiveness of a speech. There was little applause when Abraham Lincoln finished his speech at Gettysburg.

You may think that stage fright is something fixed and permanent, like the color of your eyes. More nonsense. Stage fright is *learned behavior,* and you can unlearn it.

You may think you ought to imitate well-known speakers. Nonsense again. It is ridiculous to try to be like someone else when making a speech. The fact is, you cannot imitate another and be true to yourself or honest with your audience. Why try to pretend? Be the author of your own ideas; draw upon your individuality, your personal and mental powers. The worst possible way to develop self-confidence is to think that imitation can help you. Above all else be yourself. You are unique. You carry the sole copyright of your personality. Make full use of it, for it is one of your most cherished possessions.

You may be ready to give up if you cannot become perfect at once. Nonsense! No truly perfect speech has ever been made. Many effective speeches approach perfection, while others are packed with flaws. Speaking is a lifetime challenge. Don't be discouraged just because you can't become a Daniel Webster in one semester.

In concluding this section on useful and positive attitudes, let us make two suggestions:

1. Do not be afraid of minor faults and mistakes. If you notice a slip of tongue, a mispronounced word or grammatical error, just keep on going. Henry Ward Beecher, a great pulpit orator of Civil War days, was said to have been careless about his grammar. On one occasion an old friend, an English professor, chided him for the

grammatical errors in his sermons. Beecher replied, "If the English language gets into my way, it doesn't have a ghost of a show." Please note, though, that good grammar is of great importance to a speaker.

2. Look upon your speech as a valuable experience, rather than something rated in terms of absolute triumph or failure. Consider it as a piece of research or experiment in learning. Try to develop the attitude of the scientist as he carries out his experimental work. A detached attitude will take much of the pressure off your ego and will help you to pay more attention to what works best for you in the oral communication process.

Reduce the Area of the Unknown

Be well prepared and know what you are going to say. This is perhaps the best single piece of advice anyone can give you for controlling stage fright. Beginning speech students at the University of Kansas, asked early in the semester to check items which they believed to be most helpful in their efforts to control stage fright, ranked them in this order:

1. Be prepared. Know what you are going to say.
2. Dare to be yourself. Remember that your individuality is an asset you alone can claim.
3. Know that you are neatly and appropriately dressed.
4. Remember that the audience is on your side and wants you to succeed.
5. Use visual aids and bodily action in speech.

Preparation not only ranked first, but it outranked all other items nearly three to one.

Speak from a position of basic faith. Use a subject about which you can be sincere and enthusiastic. When you say something that springs from your sincere belief and conviction, you will not be afraid. In fact, you may forget about yourself because you are standing for a principle or a cause which is bigger than you. Your self-consciousness tends to be forgotten when a compelling motive sweeps you into vital human communication.

Become more familiar with speaking. Develop opportunities for gaining experience as a speaker before different audiences. We learn to do by doing; so it is with making speeches.

Spot Remedies and Controls

We have talked about much that a speaker can do to minimize and control his fears before speaking. There are also a few things he can do while he is making his speech or just before he takes his place before the audience.

The process of producing and articulating vocal tones involves physical energy and muscular action; vocal expression is therefore a phase of bodily activity. We are concerned primarily with the bearing of bodily action and voice upon the fear complex. Visual and auditory aspects of communication are discussed in detail in the chapters on delivery.

Bodily action is of course an important part of oral communication. We learn to talk with our bodies before we learn to use language as a tool to convey meaning. Infants learn to reach, kick, and throw things to get what they want before they learn to use words. We grow up and continue to talk with our bodies all through our lives. Children, however, demonstrate most convincingly the role of bodily action in communication when their play is uninhibited and free from the scrutinizing eyes of their elders. They shake their heads, wiggle their bodies, gesticulate with arms, legs, fingers, dance and hop about from place to place to emphasize and punctuate their chatter. Watch a youngster aged six to twelve come home with a vivid tale about a fire he has seen, a circus act, a snake in the woods, or an exciting game at school. Here we have dramatic action which seems to vibrate from every muscle and issue from the very pores of the body. What about adults? They, too—especially when excited and uninhibited, but even when engaged in casual social conversation—talk with total bodily action. Yet what happens when they face an audience? They freeze and stand stiff with muscles tense, as if paralyzed—victims of a bad case of stage fright. Fortunately, something can be done about this momentary shock.

Free the body and it will help free the mind. Some psychologists support a theory that muscular activity and emotional experience complement each other. We run because we are afraid, and we are afraid because we run. We fight because we are angry and we are angry because we fight.[8] Actors have thus long been known to put

[8] For an exposition of this concept as it pertains to speech see James A. Winans, *Public Speaking*, rev. ed., Century, 1917, pp. 101–104.

themselves in the mood for their parts by climbing or shaking ladders or engaging in some violent bodily action behind the scenes just before their cue for entrance.

The speaker can get his body under control by two types of activity. The first, which might be called *inwardly motivated* action, is generated and inspired by meanings and emotions which arise from within the speaker: from his attitude toward his subject and his responsiveness to his audience, from his purpose, thinking, feelings, and desires. The second type of activity is consciously imposed by the speaker from without and may be, therefore, more artificial and automatic—like participating in setting-up exercises and climbing ladders. Act excited and you will tend to feel excited; look interested and you will tend to feel interested.

The following suggestions may be helpful in encouraging inwardly motivated activity:

1. Surrender to the meaning and emotion of your speech. Keep your mind on what you say, rather than on how well you are doing.
2. Use the blackboard and other visual aids as much as possible to clarify your meaning. Handling objects tends to reduce tensions, but they must of course be related to your speech.
3. Make what you say sound important through vocal and bodily emphasis.
4. Be sure you can be heard in all parts of the room; think of the people in the back row.
5. Give particular vocal and bodily emphasis to key points.
6. When dealing with events or incidents, use descriptive gestures.
7. Make your story vivid and clear so that your audience can follow you.

More superficially, you can build confidence through outward management of vocal and bodily activity by following these suggestions:

1. Take several long, deep breaths just before you speak.
2. Walk to the platform briskly but with a full stride and firm step.
3. Look straight into the eyes of the audience and maintain eye contact at all times.
4. Stand tall, think tall, and walk tall.
5. Speak up with a full, strong voice.
6. Take a good drink of water just before you speak.
7. Smile occasionally, even if it is difficult for you.
8. Make your remarks directly to individual members of your audience.
9. Keep up a lively vocal tempo which carries your thoughts along.

Other Reinforcements for Building Confidence

1. If you use notes, be sure they are clear so that you can easily follow them.
2. Memorize opening and closing statements, but no more.
3. Glance over the audience several times before you get up to talk, and in this manner collect images of interested, sympathetic faces in advance.
4. Before speaking, review the highlights of your talk and hold a kind of cue rehearsal of your own.
5. Dress for the occasion.

PROJECTS AND EXERCISES
For speaking projects see Part Three.

1. Do you experience stage fright? If so, what are your symptoms? Make an inventory of symptoms which fit your case. Are the symptoms always the same? If not, try to list those you experience repeatedly in one column and those which seem to come and go in another column.
2. Describe in one single statement of less than 100 words the feelings you had at the time of your worst case of stage fright. Do the same for the time you had the most self-confidence.
3. Select three people—for example a student from your speech class, a college professor, and a minister or priest—who you think demonstrate much poise and confidence when speaking before a group. Observe each one closely and thoughtfully as they speak. Then ascribe to them three to six main sources of their self-assurance. After completing your analysis with notations, interview each separately and ask them what they think helps them most to gain poise and confidence. Find out how good an analyst you are.
4. The following is a list of seven constructive ways of building self-confidence. Read them over carefully and rank in order the items most helpful to you. Give (1) to your first choice, (2) to your second choice, and so forth.
   _____ Adequate preparation.
   _____ Use of objects and visual aids.
   _____ Use of more than ordinary amount of bodily action and physical activity.
   _____ Concentration upon what you are saying, rather than upon yourself.
   _____ Dealing with a subject in which you are especially interested.
   _____ Knowledge that other students also experience stage fright.
   _____ Approaching the speech enthusiastically.
5. How serious and determined are you in acquiring ample self-confidence? You can do wonders for yourself in the privacy of your room or while

doing odd jobs. Use the flash topic technique as outlined and described in *Tapping your subconscious mind*, Part Three, page 354. Try the daily exercises by yourself for a minimum period of two weeks. In your practice do at least two or three flash topic exercises two minutes in length each day.

TOPICS FOR DISCUSSION

1. Why do you think college students ranked self-confidence first and speech experts ranked it last in the survey described on page 388?
2. Can you think of aids for conquering stage fright other than those given in the preceding chapter?
3. How are character traits related to the phenomenon of stage fright? Do you think character traits are a strong influence? How do they compare in importance with personality factors?
4. Discuss the definitions of stage fright presented in this chapter. Which do you think is most accurate? Formulate your own definition of stage fright.
5. How does the stage fright experienced by the public speaker compare with that of the aviator, athlete, or actor?
6. Explain what is meant by the statement, "Stage fright is more of a blessing than a curse."
7. Is "buck fever"—a hunter's sudden inability to perform at the sight of game—the same as stage fright?
8. Which of the sources of stage fright listed in this chapter do you think is the greatest? Do you think this varies from one person to the next?

ADDITIONAL READINGS

Baird, A. Craig, and Knower, Franklin H., *General Speech*, 2nd ed., McGraw-Hill, 1957, pp. 113–129, 206–217.

Brigance, William Norwood, *Speech, Its Techniques and Disciplines in a Free Society*, 2nd ed., Appleton-Century Crofts, 1961, pp. 68–74.

Clevenger, Theodore, Jr., "A Synthesis of Experimental Research in Stage Fright," *Quarterly Journal of Speech*, April, 1959, pp.134–145.

Dickens, Milton, *Speech, Dynamic Communication*, Harcourt, Brace, 1954, pp. 39–53, 194–209.

Gilman, Wilbur E., Aly, Bower, and Reid, Loren D., *The Fundamentals of Speaking*, Macmillan, 1951, pp. 137–144.

Murray, Elwood, *The Speech Personality*, Lippincott, 1937.

Oliver, Robert T., and Cortright, Rupert L., *New Training for Effective Speech*, rev. ed., Dryden, 1951, pp. 50–71.

Sarett, Lew, and Foster, William Trufant, *Basic Principles of Speech,* rev. ed., Houghton Mifflin, 1946, pp. 52–92.

Sarett, Lew, Foster, William Trufant, and Sarett, Alma Johnson, *Basic Principles of Speech,* 3rd ed., Houghton Mifflin, 1958, pp. 184–207.

Thonssen, Lester, and Gilkinson, Howard, *Basic Training in Speech,* 2nd ed., Heath, 1953, pp. 36–59.

White, Eugene E., *Practical Speech Fundamentals,* Macmillan, 1960, pp. 29–38.

❧ 2 ❧
The Speaker's Image

The listener, although he may be unaware of it, usually says to himself of the speaker, "Who is this talking? Where is he from? What does he do? What does he know and why is he here?" As if it matters, one might object, who says what. Isn't truth still truth, no matter who utters it? Aren't pearls of wisdom still pearls of wisdom, whether they fall from the lips of a peasant or a Solomon? Perhaps, but it does matter, for the listener judges for himself the quality of the pearls. Truth exists for him only when he recognizes and accepts it as such. He must have faith in the speaker to have faith in what the speaker says. The light of what is said in a speech reaches the listener's mind only as it is filtered through the prism of his total self—his life, deeds, purpose, personality, and character. If the speaker has truth to reveal, he must first be sure that his image will not stand in the way of its revelation.

THE "AUTHENTIC SIGN"

Ralph Waldo Emerson comments freely in his journals upon the importance of the speaker in the oral communication process. At one point he says, "What you are stands over you . . . and thunders so that I cannot hear what you say to the contrary;" and again, "The reason why anyone refuses his assent to your opinion, or his aid to your benevolent design is in you. He refuses to accept you as a bringer of truth, because . . . you have not given him the authentic sign." This is a key to the problem—"you have not given him the *authentic sign*." Emerson here echoes the classical theory that the authenticity of what is said lies within the speaker himself.

Thus authenticity comes less from substance, rhetoric, or style, than from the man who is making the speech. You cannot put it on the way you put on a coat and hat; integrity can never be worked into your speech to meet the expediency of a given moment. It is something bound up with your entire way of life. The elders in the temple sensed this in Jesus when he was but twelve years old; they said he spoke as one having authority. They saw the *authentic sign*.

What Emerson was talking about in the lines just quoted Aristotle outlined in detail. In his *Rhetoric* he presented three modes of persuasive proof: *logos,* the use of logic and evidence; *pathos,* appeals to human emotions and motives; and *ethos,* the persuasive effect of the "personal character of the speaker." He maintained that the speaker carries the most effective means of persuasion available to him—his *ethos.*

The character (*ethos*) of the speaker is a cause of persuasion when the speech is so uttered as to make him worthy of belief; for as a rule we trust men of probity more, and more quickly, about things in general, while on points outside the realm of exact knowledge, where opinion is divided, we trust them absolutely. This trust, however, should be created by the speech itself, and not left to depend upon an antecedent impression that the speaker is this or that kind of man. It is not true, as some writers on the art maintain, that the probity of the speaker contributes nothing to his persuasiveness; on the contrary, we might almost affirm that his character (*ethos*) is the most potent of all the means to persuasion.[1]

From the time of the ancient Greeks to the present day, many attempts have been made to designate and classify the elements of ethos, or "ethical proof," as modern writers call it. Aristotle said ethos consists of good sense, good moral character, and good will. Cicero, the Roman rhetorician, observed that ethos encompasses "a person's dignity . . . his actions and the character of his life." He placed more weight than did Aristotle upon the speaker's ethos be-

[1] *The Rhetoric of Aristotle,* Lane Cooper (trans.), Appleton-Century-Crofts, 1932, pp. 8–9.

fore he speaks, rather than on what he says to build ethos during the speech. Quintilian, one of the most renowned speech teachers of all time, put more stress on the importance of the speaker's character than did any of the ancient rhetoricians. He advocated that a child's character be developed in the early grades as an essential step in his training and preparation for becoming an orator. He said, "The orator must above all things devote his attention to the formation of moral character and must acquire a complete knowledge of all that is just and honorable."

ETHOS IN DAY-TO-DAY LIVING

It will help to deepen our understanding of the role of ethos in a speech by observing how it works in day-to-day living. We have all at times witnessed the impact of a person's character upon the lives of others. Perhaps in your immediate family there is someone— father or mother, brother or sister, uncle or aunt, grandfather or grandmother—who stands out as a person of unique strength and force. Although this person may have eccentricities and faults, yet he is loved, admired, and respected by all. Or perhaps you have a friend, roommate, teacher, minister, or employer who, because of his character, has made a deep and lasting impression upon you. Our lives are governed by more than laws, customs, and habits; they are also governed by the people with whom we live, work, and play. The whole hierarchy of our beliefs is shaped and modified by the character of those with whom we communicate, as well as the institutions by which we are governed. At some time or other, we all become salesmen and ambassadors for human values, and spiritual truths. We succeed or fail because of the aura of ethos which radiates from us.

In the realm of speech communication, private or public, we cannot escape this factor of personal prestige. It embraces a wide and complicated network of elements, such as breadth of knowledge, experience, judgment, emotional maturity, physical attributes, character traits, age, personality patterns, creative thinking, special abilities, special accomplishments, and so forth.

Trust, Like, and Respect

A simple and useful approach to the subject of prestige in general rests in answers to the following questions: (1) Do we *trust* the person? (2) Do we *like* the person? (3) Do we *respect* the person? These three elements are not necessarily independent of each other; they may interact. For instance, observing a student cheating on an examination, no matter how well you may have liked him before, may cause you not only to distrust him but to dislike him also. Furthermore, these three elements cannot be valued equally in the formation of the personal prestige image. Thus when we contemplate a difficult surgical operation for a member of the family, we look for the most competent and skilled surgeon—one whom we can trust; but when we select a new president of the country club we pay more attention to his friendly, likable qualities.

What has been your experience in observing the workings of these three aspects of personal prestige? Haven't you enjoyed more and worked harder in a class in which you had a teacher whom you liked? Didn't you also trust him because of his integrity and devotion to the truth and respect him because of his knowledge of the subject and his ability as a teacher. Consider the case of your parents. Where do they buy most of their furniture, electrical appliances, casualty insurance, gasoline, groceries, and even life insurance? The chances are they do most of their buying from salesmen, clerks, and attendants they like, trust, and respect. Churches are usually fullest where the preacher is best liked. And so the story goes—for barbershops, beauty parlors, and drugstores, and even for lawyers and doctors, where respect for professional competence should, however, weigh more heavily.

And what about political elections? Prestige factors are particularly noticeable where the voters like and trust a candidate; respecting him, or at least doing so for the right reasons, unfortunately seems less prevalent. After the Civil War, Ulysses S. Grant was the great victorious general of the Union forces—a national hero, loved and admired as a fighter for a noble cause. The authority he carried was that of a soldier, not of a political scientist or experienced government administrator or politician. But he was liked and admired, and he got the votes.

When General Dwight D. Eisenhower ran for president the first time, people had the image of an heroic figure, a triumphant general who had fought for a great cause. Moreover, he had a warm, sincere smile; *The New York Times,* even in the midst of the campaign, observed that people might distrust his words but would trust the look in his face. The Washington bureau of *The New York Times* on September 28, 1952, quoted Eisenhower himself on this point: "It is not what you say that matters. Question is, do you leave an impression of sincerity; do they believe you when they leave?" The key slogan in that campaign was "I like Ike," and it swept him into the White House.

In the presidential campaign of 1960, the Democratic candidate, Senator John Kennedy, found that the image of his youthfulness was perhaps the toughest and most troublesome handicap he had to overcome. Here again was a matter of *ethos,* a matter of personal prestige, where the public associated age and experience with wisdom and sound judgment. Senator Kennedy worked hard to project an image of sober maturity in order to offset preformed impressions.

THREE APPROACHES TO SPEAKER ETHOS

As we study and analyze the components of the speaker's total image, we shall direct our attention to (1) the speaker's character, (2) his personality, and (3) his prestige. Although in this triple approach we may in some instances encounter overlapping concepts, there is sufficient merit in the classification to warrant its use.

Character

Character constitutes a whole complex of a man's qualities. It should not be confused with reputation, for reputation is the image others have of you, whereas character exists within you. Character is what you really are and represents that phase of your total self about which others may make ethical evaluations. To have a good character is to know and live by society's highest moral demands—integrity, trustworthiness, sincerity, sense of justice, unselfishness, and courage. Though not all may agree upon the components of character, it is, in the ultimate sense, the foundation stone upon which society must rest. Civilization would be utterly impossible if some standard qualities of character did not prevail.

In the mature person character may have a relatively stable pattern, but even then it should not be viewed as something static or absolutely fixed. It can be altered, modified, and reconstructed. It can grow in stature, shrivel in size, become weaker or stronger in its texture. In speaking, however, it always remains a primary source of reinforcement.

Many salient attributes of character apply to the speaker and his speech in our society. For the sake of brevity, we shall limit our discussion to (1) integrity, (2) sincerity, (3) humility, (4) personal values, and (5) emotional control.

INTEGRITY. Integrity, another word for honesty, lies at the core of a good character. "An honest man is the noblest work of God." "Thou shalt not steal" and "Thou shalt not bear false witness" have always been parts of the code of conduct of civilized people. Perhaps this is belaboring the obvious, but it is the obvious which sometimes goes unappreciated. It is difficult for us to imagine how persuasive power and speech success can rest upon integrity. Abraham Lincoln is a case in point. Much has been written about his honesty. Many stories about "honest Abe" have been told and retold to inspire our youth. More important, could Lincoln have led this nation through its greatest crisis without this virtue we call integrity? Could Lincoln the orator, without it, have been spokesman for the Union? The image of Lincoln and the image of honesty are interwoven. If this were not true, imagine the hollow mockery of the words, "with malice towards none and charity towards all," "a house divided against itself cannot stand," "bind up the nation's wounds," "government of the people, by the people, and for the people . . ." Abraham Lincoln's integrity breathed the breath of truth into every word he spoke.

There is the case of Dwight D. Eisenhower, who twice was elected to the Presidency, each time far outrunning the other candidates. In addition to liking him for his warm smile and friendly looks, people trusted him; they believed in his honesty and integrity. A counter-image of fraud and deceit would have spelled disaster for him at the polls.

Honesty in the speaking process is reflected in many ways other than through the image of the speaker's character. There is a complex of manifestations of integrity, or the lack of it, in the speaker's language, his use of evidence, his ideas, his method of reasoning, his manner of vocal expression, his gestures, and his attitudes toward himself, his subject, and his audience.

SINCERITY.   In the ideal sense sincerity in a speech is the sign of a speaker's conviction, coupled with his real desire to communicate with the audience. That is, the speaker means what he says, says what he means, and has an urgent desire to share his meanings with the listener. There is a genuine ring to what he says and to his manner of speaking. He does not pretend to be something he is not, nor does he espouse ideas about which he cares little or in which he does not believe. Sincerity, then, is an aid to eloquence and, when properly controlled and tempered by sound sense, can be a most useful tool for persuasive speech. On the other hand, insincerity can damage a speaker's ethos beyond repair. There is an old saying, "He who is not skilled in speech but has sincerity will be forgiven, but he who speaks skillfully without sincerity commits a wrong for which there is no forgiveness."

We must take warning, however, for evil men can be as sincere as good men. We cannot equate sincerity only with that which is good, just, and wise. Who can doubt the sincerity of the judges who condemned Joan of Arc to be burned at the stake, or of Caiaphas, whose persuasiveness helped to bring Jesus to trial and crucifixion? Today's top-ranking Communists are probably quite sincere in their faith in Communism.

The importance of sincerity will vary according to the character of the speaker, his subject, his central purpose, and the occasion. Obviously, it is much more important in speeches of persuasion than of entertainment or information. Certainly there are various levels and types of sincerity, and to these we shall give some attention.

First, there is the sincerity, or perhaps we should say the insincerity, of the *opportunist*. The opportunist is quick to fit a phrase or expression to the expediency of the moment, or to make statements to promote or sell something for a momentary gain. This type of sincerity may also be observed in friendly, nondirected "bull sessions." Here a person may engage in a sort of sophistry which takes sides on a disputed point just to engage in a mental exercise or to spark an idea which will sharpen the clash of opinion. Such verbal encounters often deal with moot or hypothetical questions, and the argument is often more for fun than to come to grips with reality. Salesmen often sell products which they do not support with personal convictions. We cannot help but wonder, too, about the sincerity of the glamorous personalities who endorse pills, cereals, cigarettes, soap, and what have you over radio and television. Surely the world champion Olympic pole vaulter does not really believe we will all have strong, healthy bodies just by eating a certain brand of breakfast food. Some commercials, of course, sound more sincere than others, and program sponsors undoubtedly are aware that this makes them more effective.

The discriminating listener gives a dubious ear to someone whose speech exploits an opportune moment for personal gain. Fortunately, the words of the sophist and the glib phrases of salesmen, advertisers, and vendors often fail to give the authentic sign. Their sincerity would have a low credit rating.

A second type of sincerity, which might be called *academic* or *intellectual,* concerns the reasoning side of our nature rather than the emotional and volitional. Truth is ascertained by the process of reason rather than by the application of any scale of human values, qualities of character, or motivational attitudes. This type of sincerity often characterizes college debaters. They may argue back and forth over some disputed point in squad discussions, taking first one side of the argument and then the other, yet maintaining a relative amount of sincerity. Their objective is to discover the valid arguments related to the point in question. But this sincerity is primarily intellectual, requiring a degree of personal detachment and adherence to the rules of logic and evidence. In an earlier period in both English and American universities, intellectual exercises called "syllogistic disputations" were very common. In this type of forensic activity personal detachment in argumentation was even more pronounced than it is in contest debating today. Similar types of intellectual sincerity may sometimes be found in legal discourse in which legal technicalities are made to outweigh considerations of wisdom and justice.

A third type of sincerity, *person-reality,* here concerns us most. It grows out of the character of the speaker and his basic philosophy and gives guidance and direction to his behavior. Out of the sum of all our experiences we develop ideals, attitudes, and fundamental beliefs which give us strength. Human values and ideals become the props that support our total being. Anything which touches or threatens these props causes us to react strongly. Subjects which concern the family, filial love, national welfare, religion, friends, education, health, income, personal honor, or death are matters in which we have a big stake. When we talk about things as close to us as these we have a sense of urgency, and herein lies the *authentic sign*.

HUMILITY. Humility is the opposite of cockiness, arrogance, and conceit. If not carried to extremes, it has a charm all its own. Usually we think of it as a positive attribute, most frequently among the kind, compassionate, and charitable.

> Humility, that low, sweet root
> From which all heavenly virtues shoot.

The speaker who appears to be humble is disarming to his listeners. Mark Antony demonstrates this in *Julius Caesar* when he faces a mob whose sympathies lie with the conspirators who killed Caesar:

> I come not, friends, to steal away your hearts;
> I am no orator, as Brutus is;
> But as you know me all, a plain blunt man,
> That love my friend; and that they know full well
> That gave me public leave to speak of him.
> For I have neither wit, nor words, nor worth,
> Action, nor utterance, nor the power of speech,
> To stir men's blood: I only speak right on;
> I tell you that which you yourselves do know . . .

Humility should not be confused with indecision, lack of confidence, or shirking of responsibility. A humble person can know how to "walk with kings, yet keep the common touch." Lincoln's greatness was marked by humility.

PERSONAL VALUES. We do not propose to offer here a detailed set of values which you must make your own. Our point is that it is better that one's reach "exceed his grasp," better to strive after some ideals than to have none at all. The average healthy person has the power to develop a set of values which will stabilize his character and "fertilize" his mind so that constructive thoughts can grow from it. He can devise a framework of values based on concepts of charity, justice, human dignity, and faith—the faith that moves mountains, the faith that goodness can prevail over evil. It would probably also defend knowledge over ignorance, good manners over barbarism, honesty over stealing, freedom over slavery, kindness over cruelty, and courage more desirable than cowardice. Any man has the free-

dom to make choices that will bring order to his life. With a set of
values based on positive choices, any speaker can have the authentic
sign.

EMOTIONAL CONTROL.   We often hear it said that "man is his own
worst enemy." Karl Menninger, the renowned psychiatrist, writes in
his book, *Man Against Himself,* that man is forever destroying himself bit by bit. He digs his own grave with his teeth, overindulges in
alcoholic beverages and tranquilizing pills, and is forever hurting
those he loves most, all because he does not know how to manage his
frustrations. We all admire and respect the person who can maintain
his equilibrium when under great emotional strain. The Scriptures
tell us that "he who is master of his own spirit is greater than he who
taketh a city."

Self-mastery is especially important when making a speech. It may
call for self-discipline more demanding than that of the Spartans or
the physical culture faddist with his diets and exercises, or the religious zealot who prays by the clock or the calendar. The speaker
must have at all times the strength and courage to control his inner
feelings by both word and action. This may mean the ability to keep
his mouth shut at the right moment, "to sheath the sword in a fit of
temper." It may mean withholding verbal blows aimed at an enemy,
or having the courage to speak up for a cause that one is alone in
believing right. It may mean the ability to remain calm in the face of
personal fire. The speaker who has control of his emotions usually has
the *authentic sign.*

Personality

Closely related to the image of the speaker's character as a factor
creating the speaker's ethos is the image of the speaker's personality.
Drs. William C. Menninger and Munro Leaf, in their book, *You and
Psychiatry,* emphasize the complexity of the personality. They tell us
that personality structure is about as difficult to explain as atomic
theory, that even if we could take a human being apart, as we do an
automobile, and lay the pieces on the table, we could not explain his
actions.

Countless definitions of personality are given by psychiatrists,
psychologists, and writers of speech texts. While it is often described
as related to character, personality is a broader term, including char-

acter, physical makeup, temperament, abilities of all kind—intellectual, physical, creative—habits of thought and action, and responses to people and things around us. Gardner Murphy, a noted psychologist, describes personality as "the social force of the individual." Another famous psychologist, Gordon Allport, sees it as "a factor of the situation, as well as the individual." Some psychologists maintain that our behavior is largely determined by basic drives, wants, and desires; others believe we act more according to what a situation means to us. For our purposes, however, it is quite immaterial whether we act because of innate tendencies or because of social pressures of the moment; the fact that matters is that we do make an impression upon others, favorable or unfavorable. And there is the rub. What kind of an impression do you make upon your audience through your speech-created personality?

The word *person* is related in Latin to the word mask. In ancient Greece, actors used masks to suggest their characters. As they spoke their lines, these masks helped create a specific stage personality. Perhaps you have heard speakers who wore a negative mask of pretense to cover up some inadequacy, such as lack of knowledge of a subject, poor preparation, or lack of a clear purpose; or perhaps the mask was meant to compensate for some emotional imbalance, and you saw a belligerent personality instead of a friendly one, arrogance instead of humility, indifference instead of earnestness, and so forth.

We concur with those who see two kinds of personality in the speaker: the *manifest* personality and the *deeper* personality of the inner self. The manifest personality, with which we must be primarily concerned, is the one of which the audience is cognizant. This manifest personality has many characteristics, some flexible, subject to alteration and modification, others more permanent. Those which have some permanence include physical aspects of the speaker: his size and figure; the shape of his head and facial features; the color of his skin, hair and eyes; his sex, race, and age; the quality of his voice, and its pitch; the rate, energy, and rhythmic patterns of his speech. The manifest personality also includes obvious types of temperament, such as the phlegmatic, energetic, excitable, bashful, intellectual, athletic, and so forth.

Aspects of the manifest personality which may be modified, as a kind of face-lifting device, are numerous and varied. Most obvious of these are characteristics such as dress and grooming which can be altered to give the appearance of neatness and general attractiveness. We are a clothes- and figure-conscious people; how often we hear such expressions as "dress well and succeed," "clothes make the man," "look the part," and that well-known female refrain, "I have nothing to wear."

The speaker's appearance, one phase of his manifest personality, can be modified and altered in countless ways: by hair-do, make-up, jewelry, a flower in the man's lapel, a corsage on a woman's shoulder. Accessories and color schemes in dress, style of clothing, and fit of dress or suit are all-important in creating an impression. On the stage, great stress is placed upon costume and make-up in creating a character; in our frame of reference, this character is the manifest personality. Innumerable life situations show how personal appearance may be remodeled for reasons of personal pride or as a badge of position and authority. Think of the army officer without his uniform, the head chef without his high white cap, the nun without her habit, or the barrister without his wig and robe.

But the speaker's outward appearance is more than a question of wearing apparel and grooming. It includes the way he walks to the rostrum, his posture, the way he moves about while talking, his gestures and facial expressions, his manner of eye contact with the audience, and every visible motion he makes. These aspects of delivery will be more fully discussed under Dimension VI, "Delivery."

Personality is also made manifest by what the listener hears. The impressions we get through the ear can be as subtle and as laden with emotion as those gained through the eye. Over the radio and the telephone the manifest personality is formed entirely through what is heard. The way in which voice and speech create the manifest personality is strikingly demonstrated by Shaw's *Pygmalion,* in which a ragged flower girl from the London slums, with thick Cockney accent and gutter nasal twang, is transformed into a well-mannered, charming, beautiful lady with a melodious voice and flawless diction. Transformed into a musical comedy, *My Fair Lady,* this play became one of the great successes in the history of the American stage.

Whereas these and other characteristics of the self are manifest to the audience, the other part of our personality, composed of innate abilities and qualities closely related to our character, lies more deeply within us. Its substance and shape are determined by the sum total of our experiences, our innermost thoughts, feelings, and desires. Although the inner man may be quite different from the outer self and may be reluctant to step out and join hands with all the outer self represents, we cannot escape the fact that the speaker's greatest potential depends upon the proper blending of this duality into one single, well-organized, fully operative personality.

The cardinal attributes of character described in the previous section—integrity, sincerity, humility, personal values, and emotional control—are strong reinforcements to speaker ethos. They give stature to the total personality. In furthering our goal of creating the ideal speaking personality in which the deeper and the manifest self complement each other, we should keep before us the following five traits: (1) enthusiasm, (2) magnetism, (3) warmth, (4) originality, and (5) good humor.

ENTHUSIASM. Emerson declared, "Nothing great was ever achieved without enthusiasm." Enthusiasm is a priceless virtue in the speaker. Without it, speaking becomes a dull, routine affair, with little pleasure for either speaker or listener. Furthermore, enthusiasm is contagious, sometimes irresistible. Even adults get excited around holiday time as they listen to the excited chatter of children about Santa Claus and Christmas.

Enthusiasm in the speaker is best when it is generated by his natural interest in the subject and his sense of urgency, but it can also be deliberately manufactured. College cheerleaders are often called upon to do exactly this when their team is hopelessly behind; even synthetic pep may be better than none at all. Enthusiasm is perhaps the foremost attribute of effective speech.

MAGNETISM. The magnetic personality is not easy to describe, although such terms as *sex attraction, physical energy, dynamics, spirit,* and *animation* give clues to its nature. Magnetism should not be confused with enthusiasm; it is largely innate in the speaker and independent of speech substance. It is something which radiates through the speaker's delivery, in both a vibrant pleasing voice and a vital animated body. It is something you have or don't have. If you have it, even in small amounts, take care not to smother it or to fail to put it to good use. Most people have at least some personal charm or magnetism. Try to discover your strong points and cultivate them in your speaking.

WARMTH. *Friendliness, cordiality,* and *humanity* are words used frequently to describe warmth. Warmth is the opposite of aloofness, iciness, and sullenness. Earlier we mentioned that an abundance of this quality twice helped elect Dwight D. Eisenhower to the Presidency. It was certainly one of the valued assets of Will Rogers during his long career as a public entertainer and speaker. Fortunately, this quality is not limited to a few people. Anyone can create a little warmth now and then with a smile, a twinkle in the eye, or a sudden lighting of the face.

ORIGINALITY.   An original painting or document is more valuable than its copy or reproduction. Primary sources are more authentic and more highly regarded than secondary sources. Of course, the content of a speech cannot always be original; the speaker must often draw liberally upon facts, opinion, and information outside of himself to compose his speech. Yet he can be original in the way he puts ideas together and gives expression to them.

Elements of originality identified within the speaker's personality are important to the listener. Originality as reflected by accompanying eccentricities and peculiarities often give charm and color to a speaker. There is something real, something genuine, refreshing and stimulating about being original.

GOOD HUMOR.   To be good-humored does not necessarily mean to be funny. In using the term here we are talking, not about the manufactured laugh but about a person's disposition. A good-humored person is patient and agreeable and adapts himself easily to any situation. He is the opposite of a snob, and there is a certain down-to-earthness about him. A good-humored person knows how to take a practical joke; "he's a jolly good fellow." The quality of good humor enhances the speaker's ethos, for it appeals to listeners.

TAILORING THE MANIFEST PERSONALITY.   The manifest personality may be adjusted or tailored to some degree to meet the needs of a specific occasion. For instance, a speaker's posture before a group in the back room of a beer hall should be quite different from that of a minister in the pulpit on Sunday. Neither would the manifest personality you exhibit at a morning coffee conference in your student union be the same as it would be at the annual formal dinner of Phi Beta Kappa.

You may know someone who seems to be dull and mousy off-stage, but becomes a radiant, magnetic personality the minute he gets up to speak before an audience. The ability to adapt one's personality at will to suit the audience and occasion is an art worthy of earnest cultivation, for it may mean the difference between being an indifferent and a really good speaker.

Using a negative approach for a moment, let us call attention to some common patterns of speech personality which should be avoided because they undermine the speaker's ethos. Perhaps one or more of these patterns will identify speakers you have heard—maybe even yourself! If any of these categories happen to fit, ask yourself why? Are you unconsciously compensating for some feeling of inadequacy or inferiority? Have you inadvertently developed bad habits or acquired an annoying style of speaking through misconceptions of your own?

1. *Belligerent.* Overly aggressive manner, unwarranted attack upon individuals, chip on shoulder, edge of bitterness, looking for a fight, dares contradiction, arrogant.
2. *Egotistical.* Cocky, braggart, big "I" stands out conspicuously, shows conceit, crows too much.
3. *Insincere.* Artificial, too slick and smooth in manner, relies too much on glibness.
4. *Apologetic.* Negative attitude, no confidence in self or ideas, droopy posture, mostly upward inflections of the voice, often reminds audience of his inadequacies, no eye contact.
5. *Show-off.* Smart aleck, displays how clever he is, too much reliance on tricks and stunts, thinks attention is real yardstick to measure his effectiveness, anything for a laugh, too much in poor taste.
6. *Platform stylist.* Stilted manner, sounds perfunctory, artificial patterns of cadence, assumes formalities in manner, not real, poor spirit of communication.
7. *Dogmatic.* Cocksure, assumes something is so just because he says it; highly opinionated, makes many generalities without support; intolerant, not open-minded.
8. *Theatrical.* Stagey, posed manner; diction and performance stick out more than thought; not conversational, sounds unnatural.
9. *Pontifical.* Sanctimonious tone, unctious manner, reeks with self-righteousness, sense of own purity, sounds like a "do-gooder," too much moralizing.
10. *Fidgety.* Nervous squirming, pacing back and forth and shuffling

feet, meaningless gestures of same type, "uhs" and "ers," ill at ease, makes audience nervous.

Prestige

The roles of character and personality have been discussed as factors which contribute significantly to the creation of the speaker's image. The third major factor in creating the speaker's image is prestige.

We spend much of our lives trying to get others to like, trust, and respect us. Vance Packard, in his book, *The Status Seekers,* calls attention to the extraordinary things people will do in order to win admiration and social acceptance. Keen sensitivity to social stratification drives them to buy expensive clothes, houses, automobiles, and boats, as well as join clubs they cannot afford. We are always alert to give that quick glance to a diamond ring, a Phi Beta Kappa key, the kind of clothes the other person wears, or the kind of car he drives. We look at someone and subconsciously ask, "Who are you, anyway?" Others ask the same of us.

Inwardly we yearn to be able to say, "I am somebody." And if we can do this with confidence, we say we have prestige. Prestige gives us a feeling of security and power. "Whatever has been a ruling power in the world," says Gustave LeBon, "whether it be ideas or men, has in the main enforced its authority by means of that irresistible force expressed by the word 'prestige.' "[2]

The prestige of the speaker, however, is more than a question of social stratification, even of character and personality—although these factors cannot be divorced from it. Primarily prestige is concerned with the speaker's reputation, his record of accomplishments, his cultural sophistication, and his ability to establish and maintain good will.

The prestige of the speaker is most clearly operative when he is dealing with subjects about which the listener has little or no information; Aristotle thought people trust men of probity absolutely on matters unknown to them. Accordingly, it is easiest to obtain belief and action where opinions have not become fixed in the minds of the audience.

Speaker prestige obviously operates better when there is no inherent incongruity between speaker and listener. Thus a college student

[2] Gustave LeBon, *The Crowd,* Unwin, 1922, p. 147.

may be likely to experience some initial difficulty before a group of industrial managers. We can conclude that speaker prestige is always in a fluid state and may vary widely from audience to audience and occasion to occasion; it is constantly subject to wide fluctuations, even during the progress of any single speech.

Any discussion of speaker ethos in terms of prestige needs to consider the following factors: (1) general reputation, (2) fame and special achievements, (3) recognized skill in speechmaking, (4) ability to create and sustain ethos during the speech. These factors help to establish prestige before the speech is made, although the fourth is readily modified at the time the speech is given.

GENERAL REPUTATION. What determines a speaker's reputation before a speech? His reputation may come from an array of facts such as those one might find in *Who's Who*—information about institutions or organizations to which he belongs, offices held or now holding, and special duties performed in government, industry, politics, armed services, education, and so on. The listener, on either the conscious or the subconscious level, considers the speaker's educational and cultural background, and his accomplishments in science, art, letters, sports, entertainment, and the like.

Information about the speaker may come from many sources—press notices, magazine articles, radio, television, comments from those who have heard him speak, advertisements, hearsay, and introductory remarks by the chairman. The listener may have no such information about the speaker or vast amounts of it, and the reliability of the information may also range from zero to a high level of trustworthiness. The important and widely accepted fact is that the reputation of the speaker heavily influences listener acceptance and belief. No matter how worthwhile the speech or how truthful the speaker, communication is impeded whenever the audience harbors bad feeling toward the speaker. The listener tends to close his mind to the speaker he does not like and to disbelieve the one he thinks incompetent. Hovland, Janis, and Kelley have concluded from an intensive survey of research data that "The very same presentation tends to be judged more favorably when made by a communicator of high credibility than by one of low credibility."[3]

---

[3] Carl I. Hovland, Irving L. Janis, and Harold H. Kelley, *Communication and Persuasion*, Yale University Press, 1953, p. 35.

An interesting study at Northwestern University reveals that the reputation of a speaker created by the chairman in his speech of introduction may strongly influence the listener's acceptance of the speech. The investigator recorded a speech on the subject of national compulsory health insurance and played it to three different student audiences, each time with a different introduction. The first audience was told that the speaker was Eugene Dennis, Secretary General of the Communist party of America; the second audience was informed the speaker was Dr. Thomas Parran, Surgeon-General of the United States, and a few supplementary remarks were made about his qualifications and achievements; the third audience was simply informed that the speaker was a college sophomore. All listeners indicated their attitude toward the proposal of compulsory health insurance before and after the speech on a ballot designed to show shift of listener opinion. The data thus collected showed Dr. Thomas Parran to be easily the most persuasive. A far greater number of student listeners shifted from unfavorable or neutral positions toward the endorsement of the proposal they believed authored by the U.S. Surgeon-General.[4] A similar study by Hovland and Mandell produced the same results.[5]

Clearly, then, the chairman who introduces the speaker is at least partially able to control the prestige factor. Too great a build-up by the chairman, however, may be damaging to the speaker if he cannot live up to it during the speech. The audience can be led to expect too much by the chairman's introduction, as well as by the press.

FAME AND SPECIAL ACHIEVEMENT. Another type of prestige springs from unusual events and accomplishments, which may not carry Emerson's authentic sign, but which nevertheless tend to win the admiration and acclaim of the public. The first man who makes a round trip to the moon will be sure of attentive audiences, whether in college auditoriums, church parlors, or civic banquet halls. Following his solo flight from New York to Paris on that May day in 1927, Charles Lindbergh, who had rarely before made a speech, was suddenly swamped with invitations and urgent appeals to speak from a hundred cities. World Olympic champions, All-American football

---

[4] Franklyn Haiman, "An Experimental Study of the Effects of Ethos in Public Speaking," *Speech Monographs*, 6 (1949), 190–192.

[5] I. Hovland and W. Mandell, "An Experimental Comparison of Conclusion-drawing by the Communicator and by the Audience," *Journal of Abnormal Social Psychology*, 47 (1952), 581–588.

players, baseball Hall of Famers, and World Champion boxers are readily thought of as after-dinner speakers. Sergeant Alvin York, who captured 132 Germans and 33 machine guns in World War I, turned to the professional lecture platform on the basis of his spectacular achievements as a soldier.

Obviously, many persons who have fame dramatically thrust upon them may have little else to qualify them to make a speech. Their brand of prestige, often acquired more by fortune than by ability, draws willing and attentive audiences. This curious hero-worship is sometimes even transferred to the children of the great, as in the case of sons of Count Leo Tolstoi and Abraham Lincoln who used the public platform, hoping to capitalize upon their father's reputations. They lacked however, the authentic sign and their efforts met with little success.

RECOGNIZED SKILL IN SPEECH. A speaker can reinforce his prestige, during the speech, through a convincing demonstration of recognized speaking ability. Such speakers as Daniel Webster, Henry W. Grady, Woodrow Wilson, Winston Churchill, Franklin Roosevelt, and Adlai Stevenson have been publicly admired and acclaimed for their unusual craftsmanship with words and their rhetorical powers. Evangelist Billy Sunday was widely heralded for his dramatic delivery, as is Billy Graham today. Edmund Burke gained fame for his speech architecture and flawless logic. Daniel Webster and William Jennings Bryan enjoyed great prestige because of their commanding physical presence and their oratorical style of delivery. Wendell Phillips and Henry Ward Beecher gained admiration and respect for their skill in handling hostile situations. These examples illustrate that a speaker adds to his prestige by mastery of the speaking skill.

Either by accident or design, some speakers utilize a particular mannerism or eccentricity by which they become identified and which ultimately serves as a trademark of their personality. Thus Theodore Roosevelt and Judge Kennesaw Mountain Landis, czar of professional baseball for many years, were known for their peculiar dramatic gestures with the index finger. Franklin Roosevelt was known for his jutting chin and his long cigarette holder, Will Rogers for his casual slouch, Jimmy Durante for his long nose and husky voice, Wendell Willkie for his tousled hair, and Clarence Darrow for his crumpled trousers and mobile face; Winston Churchill's cigar and Dwight Eisenhower's flashing smile are also trademarks.

CREATING AND SUSTAINING ETHOS DURING THE SPEECH. "This trust, however, should be created by the speech itself, and not left to depend upon the antecedent impression that the speaker is this or that kind of a man," observed Aristotle in his penetrating discussion of speaker ethos.[6] Until now we have been dealing with factors that determine speaker prestige prior to the speech. However, prestige can grow out of the speech act itself. For the speaker must not only guard what prestige he may have at the time he begins to speak, but seek to reinforce it during the progress of his speech.

First, he should think about his appearance. Much has already been said about this prestige-shaping factor; we must also negatively bear in mind the penalizing power of unfavorable appearance. What is your own reaction to a male student who faces an audience with unkempt hair, unshaven face, dirty shirt, necktie askew, wrinkled trousers, soiled shoes, sloppy posture—and all this capped perhaps by a surly look? You inevitably downgrade him, less for incompetence than for inconsideration. If the speaker is a woman with uncouth manners and untidy, slovenly appearance, the penalty will be even more severe. There is seldom an excuse for poor showing in the matter of dress, grooming, and posture.

Since space does not permit us to explore thoroughly the many ways of building prestige during the speech, we shall instead list, with brief descriptive comments, some specific ethos-building items. The first column presents positive boosters to prestige and the second negative qualities which diminish prestige. Both, however, concern what the audience sees and hears.

POSITIVE	NEGATIVE
Poise and Confidence	
Self-assured, in full command of self, subject and occasion. Cool, calm and collected. Knows what he wants and where he is going.	Uncertain, ill at ease, nervous, wavering about what to say and do. Seems uncomfortable, embarrassed, distressed about it all.
Physical Life and Energy	
Vibrant with life and animation, bodily health and vigor.	Weak, lifeless, anemic, droopy, lackadaisical, pepless, lacking in vigor.

[6] *The Rhetoric of Aristotle,* Cooper (trans.), *op. cit.,* pp. 8–9.

Mental Alertness

Active mind, smart, well-informed, keen, quick and agile in his thinking. Mental processes keep clicking.

Dull, sluggish mind, slow to react, ignorant. Mind hopelessly blank. Mental lethargy.

Spirit of Fair Play

Shows sportsmanship, asks no favors, seeks no unfair advantage. Shuns exaggeration, tends toward understatement. Gives credit where credit is due. Never gets personal.

Seeks unfair personal advantage, tends toward exaggeration and overstatement, often gets personal. Slow to give credit to others.

Emotional Balance and Control

Remains calm, never gets unduly excited, keeps inner poise. Behaves like a mature person, maintains dignity. Never loses temper. Always sees issues, not people.

Quick to lose temper. Raves and rants, acts like a spoiled child. No sign of a mature mind. Emphasizes personalities rather than causes and principles.

Decisiveness

Has a clear, definite purpose. Develops a point with decision. Always knows where he stands. Positive tone in voice, gestures are emphatic and precise. Does not confuse you.

Vacillating, hesitant, negative manner of speech. Makes statement with too many qualifications, leaves too much open to doubt and questions. Never knows where he stands. Listener mixed up and confused.

Good Taste and Propriety

Conforms with established customs and good manners. Sensitive to cultural values. Does not try to harass or embarrass listeners.

Looks and acts like a beatnik. Likes to shock or embarrass listeners. Lacks sense of cultural and moral values. Manner is boorish, uncouth, off-color or in poor taste.

Desire to Communicate

Wants to contact listener and share ideas with him, sense of urgency to tell the audience. Has both physical and mental directness. Good eye contact.

Attitude of indifference toward audience, doesn't care whether listener hears or understands. Poor eye contact. Doesn't try to sense audience reaction.

Easy Fluency

Ideas seem to flow, speech doesn't drag, listener feels he is getting somewhere. Speech seems effortless, restful to audience.

Hesitant cluttered speech. Ideas drag along. Too many "uhs" and "ers." Thought progression seems painful and labored, tiring to the audience.

Materials Well in Hand

Ideas are carefully thought through in advance, speaker ready to talk, well prepared. Speech hangs together. Materials arranged to give clarity and save time.

Speech not prepared. Wasteful arrangement of material, much groping for words, speech lacks unity and coherence. Haphazard jumping from point to point.

Thought Commands Speaker

Speech more thought-centered than speaker-centered. Thought seems more consequential than speaker, what is true or wise of more concern than who is talking. Speaker lets thought compel him, surrenders to what he says.

Speech more self- than thought-centered. Listener more conscious of speaker than his cause. Audience tends to remember speaker and forget what he has to say.

Any of the following factors can help increase the speaker's aura of expertness and trustworthiness. They are all compositional techniques—that is, they are conerned with the construction of the speech —and are listed here because they help us understand the concept of speaker ethos.

1. *Identification.* The speaker establishes common ground by revealing speaker-audience relationships: similarity of background, beliefs, sentiments, attitudes, regard for heroes, and so forth. The mere mention of the right symbols often creates much good will for a speaker.
2. *Deistic reference.* Since antiquity, deistic reference has been used in speeches. A proper reference to the Deity and such expressions as "Last Sunday on my way to church" enhance the speaker's prestige with most American audiences.
3. *Credentials.* The speaker can demonstrate "expertness" by revealing his credentials to the audience. He may tell them of his training, his experiences, and his activities. Sometimes wise use of technical jargon or foreign terms will demonstrate authoritativeness for listeners.
4. *Points of agreement.* The mere fact that a speaker begins with a point

with which the audience emphatically agrees enhances his "expertness" and "trustworthiness." The audience then feels that the speaker is a man of keen discernment.

5. *Apparent objectivity.* If a speaker shows awareness of the opposing arguments, or perhaps even admits that they have some merit, the audience will tend to view him as fair and objective—two important ethos factors.

6. *Reference to authorities.* Use of authorities not only gives credibility to the message but also affects the speaker's ethos.

7. *Reference to the speaker's record.* If a speaker can point to his wise and honest decisions of the past, he has the record in his favor.

8. *Praising the audience.* The speaker can praise the audience for their special achievements, patience, regard for truth, and so forth. People, at least privately, tend to think someone who praises them a person with peculiar insight.

SUMMARY

Dr. Charles Mayo used to insist that the guiding rule of the Mayo Clinic be to serve the whole man, since the health of the patient is not confined to the physical body alone. Likewise, the student of speech must know that man communicates best with his whole self. He must find and release this total self, composed of character, reputation, and personality. Of what use is it for the mind to know wisdom and truth when the facilities for sharing these virtues with others cannot function because the self remains enslaved by groundless fears and tensions? The release from stage fright can be the door by which the whole person becomes free and wholly communicative.

In a larger sense the whole person represents more than a free, confident human being. He is the endorsement of his own message, the underwriter of everything he says. He carries in his character, his personality, and his personal prestige the quality of authority which will be measured by his audience. The listener is always saying, like the caterpillar to Alice in Wonderland, "You! Who are you?!" If the answer is not forthcoming, directly or indirectly, from the speaker himself or from what others say of him, the listener will supply answers of his own; such is the nature of the listener-speaker relationship. The listener is willing to listen and believe the speaker in direct ratio to the speaker's ethos. In the mind of the listener, the speaker always remains a person, a "who"; yet the "who" is interwoven with the spoken word. Our society is one where people touch each other by the lives they live and by the quality of their personality and character as well as by facts, laws, customs, and traditions. Who says it gives meaning to what is said. The speaker's image is an integral part of his speech.

PROJECTS AND EXERCISES

For speaking projects see Part Three.

1. *Speaker Image Evaluation Chart.* This chart may be used by the individual student for evaluating his own image. The chart may also be mimeographed and used by the entire class for the purpose of rating one another. Make a separate check in the proper square for each individual. 1 = excellent; 2 = good; 3 = fair; 4 = poor.

	1	2	3	4	
Poise and confidence					
Warmth and friendliness					
Life and animation					
Originality					
Sincerity					
Integrity					
Ability to take criticism					
Expertness on speech subject					
Cooperative attitude					
Objectivity on controversial topics					

2. What categories would you like to add to the above rating chart? Add them, and evaluate as above.
3. Rank in the proper column the three factors of prestige as they apply to each of the individuals listed. Use 1, 2, and 3 to indicate first, second and third. For example, take a three-year-old child. You will probably "like" him more than you "respect" or "trust" him; therefore, place a

1 in the box under "like." You will also tend to "respect" him more than you "trust" him, so you would place a 2 in the box for "respect" and a 3 in that for "trust." Do the same for the other individuals.

	Like	Trust	Respect	
Winston Churchill				
Edward R. Murrow				
Nikita Khrushchev				
Your family doctor				
Your high school principal				
An eminent scientist				
An attractive movie star				
Harry S. Truman				
Richard Nixon				
John F. Kennedy				

Now check to the left of the name the individuals you think rank high in all three categories.

4. Make a list of methods other than those mentioned in this chapter by which the speaker may enhance or reinforce his prestige at the time and place the speech is being made.
5. Make a list of ways other than those mentioned in the chapter by which a speaker can impair or weaken his image.
6. Rank in order the following items which you consider most damaging to speaker ethos. Give (1) to first, (2) to second, and so on.

_____ The apologetic attitude   _____ Careless use of loaded words
_____ Poor preparation   _____ Lack of propriety and poor
                                          taste
_____ Unkempt, untidy appear-
        ance   _____ Insincerity
_____ Cockiness in manner

Compare your rankings with those of other members of the class.
7. Study Henry Grady's famous speech, "The New South." Note all ethos factors in the speech.

8. Attend a campus lecture or speech and note all the ethos factors of the speaker. Which seem to be the dominant ones?

TOPICS FOR DISCUSSION

1. Is ethos, as presented by Aristotle, synonymous with the speaker's image?
2. What do you think Emerson meant by "the authentic sign"?
3. What do you think are the most important ethos factors?
4. Which is the more important quality in the speaker, expertness or trustworthiness?
5. To what extent is age an ethos factor? Intentions of the speaker? Social status?
6. How do the speaker's associations—friends, organizations, religious— affect his ethos?
7. Does the speaker actually have to be honest, or can he merely appear to be honest, in order to enjoy high ethos?
8. What is the importance of "image" building in presidential elections?
9. Can you as a listener tell whether or not a speaker is honest? If so, how?
10. On the basis of your experience, would you say that speakers should use humor more often to enhance their ethos?

ADDITIONAL READINGS

Brembeck, Winston, and Howell, William S., *Persuasion,* Prentice-Hall, 1952, chap. 24.

Brigance, W. Norwood, *Speech Composition,* rev. ed., Appleton-Century-Crofts, 1953, chap. 5.

Hovland, Carl I., Janis, Irving L., and Kelley, Harold H., *Communication and Persuasion,* Yale University Press, 1953, chap. 2.

Mills, Glen E., *Composing the Speech,* Prentice-Hall, 1952, chap. 15

Minnick, Wayne C., *The Art of Persuasion,* Houghton Mifflin, 1957, pp. 113–135.

Oliver, Robert T., *The Psychology of Persuasive Speech,* 2nd ed., Longmans, Green, 1958, chaps. 4 and 8.

Oliver, Robert T., and Cortright, Rupert L., *New Training for Effective Speech,* rev. ed., Dryden, 1951, pp. 50–60.

Packard, Vance, *The Hidden Persuaders,* David McKay, 1957, chap. 17.

Smith, Raymond G., *Principles of Public Speaking,* Ronald, 1958, chap. 8.

Thonssen, Lester, and Baird, A. Craig, *Speech Criticism,* Ronald, 1948, chap. 13.

The Audience

🦋 3 🦋
Adapting to the Audience

The audience is the *sine qua non* of speech. A speech is given for the benefit of one or more auditors who, the speaker hopes, will respond in accordance with his purpose. The speaker is one half of the speech communication process; the audience may be called the other half—the receiving half. Thus speech is social behavior, the audience being the judge of its effectiveness. Every public speaker should therefore understand the nature and characteristics of an audience, as well as basic procedures for audience analysis. As far back as Plato, rhetoricians have emphatically declared that the speaker must adapt his message to his particular audience. Unless he does, it may be reported after the speech, in the words of Walter de la Mare, "Never the least stir made the listeners."

THE NATURE OF AN AUDIENCE

Audiences assemble in different ways and for different reasons. The orator speaking from a soap box in the city park is addressing people who, in all likelihood, just happened by and out of curiosity stopped to hear the speaker's words. The members of this audience have little in common and are little more than a collection of passing pedestrians. At the opposite end of the continuum is the highly organized and regimented audience such as the sporting team or military unit. Such an audience has gathered for a common purpose and expects to be directed by the speaker, who may be a coach or a colonel. In between are the types of audiences which most speakers address, and which Hollingworth calls "the selected audience" and "the concerted audience."[1]

The *selected audience* assembles for a common purpose, but its members are not necessarily sympathetic either with one another or with the speaker's point of view and aim. Commencement audiences, most political gatherings, and PTA groups represent this type of audience in that they gather for a common purpose but do not necessarily agree with the views of other members of the group. The *concerted audience,* on the other hand, has an active purpose, a mutual enterprise in which it is engaged. Most highly organized, but not regimented, audiences are concerted. A civic club is likely to become a concerted audience for the purpose of conducting business. Whether or not an audience is concerted depends upon the mutuality of its interests.

Audiences can also be classified according to their attitudes toward the speaker and his subject. Generally, an audience will tend to be (1) favorable, (2) neutral, (3) apathetic, or (4) hostile. Probably most audiences are neutral, which means that they are at least mildly interested in the speaker and are willing to give him a fair hearing. The favorable audience is very friendly toward the speaker and highly motivated to listen to his speech. The apathetic group, while not actually hostile to the speaker, suffers from inertia and indifference. It has little interest in the speaking situation and needs to be "jarred" to attention, perhaps by a startling introduction. The hostile audience strongly dislikes the speaker and/or his topic. Before persuasion can take place in this situation, the hostility has to be lessened.

Not only do audiences differ, but every audience is unique. Moreover, an audience is seldom so highly polarized[2] that it will act as one body. The audience also varies internally. Sometimes it is all of one sex, of one religion, and of equal educational background; usually, however, it is highly diverse. An audience consists of separate individuals with personal behaviors and attitudes. Each brings

---

[1] H. L. Hollingworth, *The Psychology of the Audience,* American, 1935, p. 24.

[2] A polarized audience is one which reacts as a group, in which individuals, have to some degree lost their individuality and respond as the group responds.

his own frame of reference to the speaking situation; each has had different life experiences, has conceptualized these experiences, and probably has developed positive or negative attitudes toward them. It is not uncommon for a speaker to address an audience consisting of Jews, Roman Catholics, and many kinds of Protestants, to say nothing of agnostics and atheists; of carpenters, merchants, salesmen, teachers, and lawyers; Republicans, Democrats, Independents, and perhaps even Prohibitionists; old men, young men, rich men, poor men, and the typical American who has a huge mortgage on his house and automobile and charge accounts at half a dozen stores.

Despite these differences, the speaker can expect a degree of interaction among listeners which will often make them respond as a group. Most members of an audience respond to each other as well as to the speaker. This is why television producers often scatter paid "laughers" or "applauders" in the audience who, at specified times, laugh loudly or clap vigorously: those sitting nearby will usually follow the lead, and soon a swell of applause or laughter is under way. This phenomenon is commonly called *social facilitation*. Certain external factors also affect audience interaction, as noted in the following pages.

External Factors

THE MEETING HALL. The type of meeting hall affects audience response. An old auditorium with an extremely high ceiling has a cold and austere atmosphere, whereas an attractively decorated, more intimate, room tends to be cheerful and friendly. Lighting of the hall is another factor; have you ever tried to tell a joke in the dark? Furthermore, a display of certain symbols—such as a flag, a club charter, or group insignia—will tend to polarize an audience and intensify response. Ventilation and seating may also affect the speech situation. An uncomfortable audience will find listening difficult.

SEATING ARRANGEMENT. If people are seated close together or are standing in a tight mass, more "elbow rubbing" occurs. Laughter will swell rapidly and emotional reactions be encouraged as a result of mutual stimulation. Adolf Hitler used this technique to great advantage. His public speeches drew vast throngs of people who were jammed together as tightly as possible. When *der Fuehrer* extended his arm upward for the famous *sieg heil,* the crowd responded en masse. The next time you are a member of a widely scattered audience in a large auditorium, observe how difficult it is for the speaker to get an enthusiastic response—be it applause, emotional reaction, or laughter. If you yourself should have the misfortune of speaking to a scattered audience, try to get them to move in together. Before you begin your speech, either you or the program chairman can ask the listeners to move down front and sit in a group.

GROUP ACTIVITY.   Group activity may affect the speech. Music especially stimulates audiences and induces group response. This is why an after-dinner speaker likes to speak immediately after a "community sing." Service clubs usually open a program with a brief community sing. One of the reasons for having a band at sporting events is that it stirs and excites feelings. Hitler used stirring march music to arouse and stimulate the German masses. Group recitations, such as of the organization's creed, will also make the audience more concerted.

Emotion and Reason in an Audience

Man's salient trait is his ability to reason, a power which distinguishes him from lower animals. Yet by and large people are guided more by emotion than by reason, and when they are part of a group they become even more suggestible, succumb even more readily to emotional appeals, and ignore logic more than ever. To some degree individuals lose identity and blend with the group; a catalysis takes place; each surrenders some sovereignty to the group as a whole.

Audience members tend to conform to group standards in belief and action. "If we are to retain our status in the group," Ewbank and Auer assert, "we do what the others do. If our fellows put money in the collection plate, sign the pledge, or cheer the speaker, we tend to conform to the group standard which they set."[3] Limited objectivity is characteristic of all men, the wise as well as the unwise, but an individual's prejudices tend to become highly operative in a crowd. A lynch mob or any other mob illustrates this all too well.

Audiences Tend to Be Friendly

The speaker should view his listeners as customers to be served; they are in a priority seat and have a right to expect a worthwhile message. Anyone who rises to speak assumes this responsibility. If

[3] Henry Lee Ewbank and J. Jeffery Auer, *Discussion and Debate, Tools of a Democracy,* 2nd ed., Appleton-Century-Crofts, 1951, p. 213.

the speaker has a well-prepared message and treats his listeners with proper respect, they invariably will be a friendly force. At least this is true of the average American audience, as well as those in other genuinely democratic societies. It is in harmony with the democratic tenet of "the right to speak and be heard." Most audiences, in fact, will share the speaker's triumphs and failures. Empathy, or "identity with," is usually so strong that if the speaker is embarrassed the audience will be embarrassed. Although many beginning speakers view a speech class audience as composed of terrifying and cynical fiends, ready to show derision and make caustic jests, nothing could be further from the truth. Most speech class audiences are even friendlier than other audiences. They are pleased by the success of one of their members and uncomfortable in the presence of failure. Their empathy is strong, inasmuch as they know that they too will soon be called upon to address the group.

AUDIENCE ANALYSIS

The speaker must orient his performance to his audience. He should select his purpose, his subject, his materials, and his language with his listeners in mind. Even his delivery should be keyed to his immediate auditors. Norman Thomas, a veteran of many speech engagements, writes that "successful speech requires a speaker to come to proper terms with his audience as well as his subject."[4]

To assure such adaptation a speaker should seek answers to the following questions: (1) What is the nature of the occasion? (2) What are the general characteristics of the audience? (3) What is their attitude toward the speaker and toward his subject?

The Nature of the Occasion

WHY HAS THE GROUP ASSEMBLED? For classroom speeches your audience will be fellow students who have assembled because they are enrolled in the same course. Most other occasions are considerably more complex, though as a rule some motivating force has pulled the people together and united them for a moment. Rotary, Kiwanis, Sertoma, and Lions clubs, for example, feel compelled to attend club meetings because of member loyalty. Commencement audiences come

---

[4] Norman Thomas, "Random Reflections on Public Speaking," *The Quarterly Journal of Speech*, April, 1954, p. 148.

to see a son, daughter, or close friend or relative graduate from an academic institution. People come to a public lecture, perhaps, to satisfy their curiosity about the speaker, or because the announced speech title has sufficiently aroused their interest. The potential speaker must consider carefully why his audience will come together and to what degree it will be organized. He then may be able to determine the group's anticipations. In other words, as a speaker you should try to answer the question: What do I have to do to satisfy the audience's expectations? If you are able to meet its demands, your speech will be a definite success.

WHAT CONDITIONS WILL PREVAIL? Find out when your speech is to be given and if there will be other events on the program. Will your speech be given after a heavy meal? After music? A business meeting? After a long program? After another speech? All these factors can influence your own speech. You may want to refer to other events on the program in your opening remarks, since this will tend to increase interest in your speech. Also, these events may warn you to be prepared to cut your speech drastically, for they are only too likely to run overtime. A speaker with no advance plans for emergency cutting of his speech may face a difficult speaking experience.

Furthermore, try to obtain information about the rules and prevailing customs of the speech occasion. Does the audience customarily ask questions after the speech? What degree of formality will the meeting have? Will the speaker be expected to acknowledge certain people or to refer to some special person or feat during the course of his remarks?

The physical conditions are also important. What is the auditorium or meeting hall like—large or small, high or low ceilinged, dark or well-lit? Will you speak from a platform? A rostrum with a lectern?[5] What will be the seating arrangement? Is the audience likely to be large enough to fill the room? Will there be a public address system?

General Characteristics of the Audience

Before you prepare your speech, apply to your audience the check list given below. Your answers should have considerable influence upon

---

[5] Confusion exists about the terms *lectern, rostrum,* and *podium.* Frank E. X. Dance, in an article, "Go to the Lectern," *Today's Speech,* February, 1961, p. 20, writes that "of all the choices given us, a *lectern* most closely resembles the stand we commonly find on stages and in classrooms." A rostrum is any elevated area from which a speech is made.

your composition. Try to identify the audience's common traits and principal differences. Your task is simplified if a high level of common ground exists among its members. If, for example, they are all of one age group, they will remember most of the same historical events. On the other hand, when great dissimilarities exist among the audience, you must try to determine the level at which you should aim. For example, if the educational training of the audience varies widely, your speech will probably fail if you gear it toward either the upper or lower educational level—the average or slightly below average level will usually prove more effective. Your problem is to make your materials simple enough for the least educated but interesting to all.

The following factors should therefore be considered in your audience analysis:

I. Sex
   A. All men
   B. All women
   C. Evenly mixed
   D. Predominately one or the other
II. Social characteristics
   A. Race and ethnic groups
   B. General social structure of group
   C. Group affiliations
III. Economic status
   A. Occupations
   B. Economic structure of group
   C. Current material needs and desires
IV. Education
   A. General intelligence
   B. Academic background
   C. Professional affiliations
   D. Reading habits
      1. Periodicals
      2. Newspapers
      3. Books
V. Cultural interests
   A. General cultural level
   B. Entertainment habits and interests
      1. Reading
      2. Sporting
      3. Dramatic

4. Radio and television
5. Musical
VI. Beliefs, attitudes, and opinions
   A. Political
   B. Religious
   C. Economic
   D. Social
   E. Educational

The Audience's Attitude Toward the Speaker and His Topic

ATTITUDE TOWARD THE SPEAKER.   The attitude of the audience toward the speaker depends upon its mental image of him, as explained in the preceding chapter. If the listeners know him well, like him, and respect him, their initial response, at least, is likely to be favorable. On the other hand, if the audience knows little about the speaker, its attitude may be one of "wait and see." In such a case, it is especially important for the speaker to gain the listeners' good will at the outset. His introduction, accordingly, may have to be longer and replete with more interest and ethos-building devices. The speaker will have to create an image of himself as a friendly, trustworthy, expert individual. As we noted earlier, the image-building process begins when the speaker first appears on the stage; it includes how he is dressed, how he walks, and how he sits and listens to his introduction by the emcee. If, at the start, the audience has a slightly negative feeling toward the speaker, he has the task of overcoming this hostility before he launches the major portion of his address. In short, his introduction should contain material that will help build good will. For a further discussion of the introduction, see Chapter 9, "Designing the Speech," pages 201–233.

In preparing his speech the speaker will finally do well to ask these and other similar questions:

1. How well does the audience know me?
2. What image do they have of me?
   a. Do they like me?
   b. Do they trust me?
   c. Do they feel that I am an expert on this subject?
3. Do they disagree with me on some basic issues?

ATTITUDE TOWARD THE SUBJECT.   It is important to ask the question: *How much and what kind of information does the audience have on my subject?* The speaker must draw the line between what the audience already knows and what he needs to explain. Even if the audience has a great deal of information on the subject, it is often wise to begin with a brief review of what they already know—but such a review must move rapidly and be made as interesting as possible.

Secondly, ask the question: *What will the audience accept and what must be proved to them?* It is pointless, boring, and a waste of time to pile up supporting materials for a point which listeners already accept. The speaker can assume that the audience will not ask for proof on most relatively obvious points; he must not, however, make unwarranted assumptions, for if he does his speech may be a failure. Before making a speech, always try to discover the audience's general attitude toward the subject—including what points they already accept and what points they will want documented.

Gaining Information About the Audience

If you are familiar with the characteristics of the audience you are to address, you can make your own analysis; simply call to mind an image of your potential listeners and apply to it the above audience analysis factors. Most audiences you will address can be handled in this way.

Sometimes, however, you may be scheduled to speak to an audience about which you know very little. How will you gain information in such cases? First, you may contact the program chairman, or whoever asked you to speak, and question him concerning the make-up of the audience. See him in person, call him on the phone, or write him a letter in which you set forth selected questions. As a rule, this person will be most helpful. If you are addressing an organized audience, you may also want to get in touch with the chairman (or other officer) of the group and enlist his aid in providing information about the audience you will address. The library is another potential source of useful information. Many libraries have newspapers from other towns in the state, and an investigation of a few recent issues should give you information about important happenings in the community. Such information will invariably contribute to the success of your speech. Another source is the chamber of commerce of the city in which you are to speak. Most chambers have prepared a large amount of material about their city and are ready and eager to mail it to an interested party.

CIRCULAR RESPONSE

Although the audience can control the speech situation to a degree, it is largely the speaker who is in the maneuverable position. If he has prepared his speech in accordance with sound audience analysis procedure, he will usually be prepared to meet the audience's interests and expectations. Frequently, however, he will find it necessary to make minor adjustments on the spur of the moment, and sometimes he may have to make drastic revisions. What revisions are required hinge upon the audience's *feedback,* or overt reactions.[6]

Listeners transmit or communicate reactions to the speaker in various ways. If the speech is extremely dull, they may get up and leave the meeting; if it is very irritating, they may vocalize their reactions by heckling or booing the speaker—when they are extremely upset they may go so far as to hurl eggs at the speaker. On the other hand, if they like the speech they may show obvious approval by applauding, laughing, or nodding their heads in agreement.

Most audience reactions, however, are more subtle. Someone who cannot hear the speaker adequately may turn his head slightly. Someone who has failed to comprehend a thought may look somewhat puzzled; perhaps he will frown or place his hand to his chin. Thus the audience silently speaks back to the speaker, and the speaker must read these signs and adapt to them.

When the speaker observes audience feedback and adapts his performance to it, *circular response* occurs. The speaker conceives an idea. His mind sends nerve impulses to the physiological speech mechanism, which in turn produces sounds that form meaningful words and phrases. These sounds are carried through the air as wave patterns to the ear of the listener, who (if he understands the speaker) recognizes the language, attaches meaning to it, and reacts, usually covertly but sometimes overtly. He may nod his head in agreement, shake it in disgust, raise his eyebrows slightly, or edge forward in his seat. The alert speaker notices the listeners' reactions and gauges his speech accordingly.

[6] It is altogether possible that the speaker will hear a piece of important local news just before he speaks. He should adapt to this eventuality by at least a show of awareness.

Such circular response demonstrates that effective speech is communication, not mere expression, and that the speaker must never forget the communicative process. His subject matter, his language, and his action—in fact, everything that goes into the speech-making process—must be audience-centered. This is not to say that a speaker should let the audience dictate his subject or the materials or proofs he uses in his speech; but it does say that his particular approach to the subject and his presentation of proofs should be audience-oriented.

PROJECTS AND EXERCISES

For speaking projects see Part Three.

1. Draw up an analysis for a possible speech to be given before your local Kiwanis Club, the League of Women Voters, and a campus religious group. Be sure to determine the audience's attitude toward the speaker and his subject.
2. Attend a campus speech and make notes on how the speaker adapted or failed to adapt his speech to his listeners.
3. Make an analysis of your class. Discover leading traits and characteristics which will help you adapt your speeches during the semester.

TOPICS FOR DISCUSSION

1. Explain and discuss the process of audience "polarization."
2. How can the physical surroundings affect the speech situation?
3. Define: feedback, empathy, circular response, social facilitation.
4. What use should a speaker make of the circular response concept?
5. What are the different types of audiences?
6. How important is audience adaptation in a speech situation?

ADDITIONAL READINGS

Brembeck, Winston Lamont, and Howell, William Smiley, *Persuasion,* Prentice-Hall, 1952, chap. 17.

Bryant, Donald C., and Wallace, Karl, *Fundamentals of Public Speaking,* 3rd ed., Appleton-Century-Crofts, 1960, chaps. 18 and 19.

Crocker, Lionel, *Public Speaking for College Students,* 3rd ed., American, 1956, chap. 21.

Dickens, Milton, *Speech, Dynamic Communication,* Harcourt, Brace, 1954, chap. 11.

Eisenson, Jon, *The Psychology of Speech,* Appleton-Century-Crofts, 1938, chap. 13.

Ewbank, Henry Lee, and Auer, J. Jeffery, *Discussion and Debate,* Appleton-Century-Crofts, 1951, chaps. 3, 12, and 13.

Gilman, Wilbur E., Aly, Bower, and Reid, Loren D., *The Fundamentals of Speaking,* Macmillan, 1951, chap. 19.

Gray, Giles Wilkeson, and Braden, Waldo W., *Public Speaking: Principles and Practices,* Harper, 1951, chap. 5.

Hollingworth, H. L., *The Psychology of the Audience,* American, 1935.

McBurney, James H., and Wrage, Ernest J., *The Art of Good Speech,* Prentice-Hall, 1953, chap. 11.

Mills, Glen E., *Composing the Speech,* Prentice-Hall, 1952, chap. 5.

Monroe, Alan H., *Principles and Types of Speech,* 4th ed., Scott, Foresman, 1955, chap. 9.

Oliver, Robert T., *The Psychology of Persuasive Speech,* 2nd ed., Longmans, Green, 1957, chap. 4.

Sarett, Lew, Foster, William Trufant, and Sarett, Alma Johnson, *Basic Principles of Speech,* 3rd ed., Houghton Mifflin, 1958, chaps. 13 and 14.

Smith, Raymond, *Principles of Public Speaking,* The Ronald Press, 1958, chap. 4.

White, Eugene E., and Henderlider, Clair R., *Practical Public Speaking,* Macmillan, 1954, chap. 2.

❧ 4 ❧
Effective Listening

It is the province of knowledge to speak and it is the privilege of wisdom to listen.

—OLIVER WENDELL HOLMES

In the previous chapter we discussed types and characteristics of audiences and how the speaker can adapt his speech and his manner to them. Our point of view, however, was that of the speaker. In the present chapter we shall consider you as a listener who is part of the audience.

LISTENING FOR COMPREHENSION

Importance of Effective Listening

Just as reading complements writing, so listening is the other half of talking. Both transmission and reception are essential to any act of communication. A message transmitted orally becomes, by definition, a complete communication only when it is received and comprehended by someone engaged in listening. If listening is viewed in this way, its importance in speech communication can easily be appreciated. A vivid illustration of the importance of listening is shown by the following incident.

A few years ago a manufacturing firm hired some new employees to work with a forge used for heating tool steel. The new workers were verbally told how to use grappling irons. They were instructed always to hang hot irons on the wall to the *right* of the forge, moving them to the other side as they cooled, and that an employee starting to work at the forge must always take an iron from the left wall. Not long after this instructional session, a worker hung a hot iron on the wrong wall. As though directed by fate, a second worker immediately came along and grabbed the hot iron. The scorching metal stuck to his hand and there was considerable difficulty in getting it loose. The burns were so severe that the man's ability to work was permanently impaired. Ralph Nichols, reporting this incident, says:

> At a hearing after the accident, the man who had placed the iron on the wrong wall swore that he hadn't heard anybody say hot irons were to be hung to the right of the forge. However, other employees testified he was present when the instructions were given.
>
> I'm sure the guilty man was telling the truth—that although he attended the meeting, his mind was somewhere else at the critical moment.[1]

The malady of not listening is a common one. Most of us suffer from it at one time or another. As early as 1923, H. E. Jones of Columbia University conducted studies that showed that Columbia University freshmen listened with only 25 or 30 percent efficiency. The average person retains only about half of a communication immediately after he hears it. After a delay of two months, the amount remembered fades to about 25 percent of the major ideas originally heard. Even Shakespeare's Falstaff admitted to the Lord Chief Justice that he was afflicted with "the disease of not listening."

Poor listening is especially appalling when we consider the amount of time we spend in listening—or in not listening. An early research study in listening by Paul Rankin[2] revealed that 70 percent of the waking day of the people he studied was spent in some form of verbal communication. The largest portion of this time, 45 percent, was spent in listening; 30 percent was spent in speaking, 16 percent in reading, and 9 percent in writing. Donald E. Bird[3] repeated this study much later with Stephens College girls, and had similar results:

---

[1] Ralph Nichols, with Leonard A. Stevens, "You Don't Know How to Listen," *Collier's*, July 25, 1953, pp. 16–19.

[2] Paul T. Rankin, "Listening Ability," *Chicago Schools Journal*, January, 1930, pp. 177–179.

[3] Donald E. Bird, "Teaching Listening Comprehension," *Journal of Communication*, November, 1953, pp. 127–130.

listening, 42 percent; speaking, 25 percent; reading, 15 percent; writing, 18 percent. It is understandable that college students should do more writing than adults in general, as reflected by a comparison of the Rankin and Bird studies; in both studies, however, listening clearly outranks the other phases of communication. Nichols and Lewis, in *Listening and Speaking,* estimate further that we probably hear at least twenty times as many speeches as we deliver, a ratio which probably exists in your speech class right now.

People are slowly becoming aware of the importance of good listening. Business and industry instituted a number of special programs to improve listening, when they began to realize the dollar value of having employees competent in listening. Frank E. Fischer, director of the communications course of the American Management Association, has said: "Efficient listening is of such critical importance to industry that, as research and methodology improve, I feel that training departments will have to offer courses in this field."[4] Interest in effective listening in colleges and universities has been less dramatic than that in business and industry; nevertheless, special training programs are offered in a number of leading institutions.

GOOD LISTENING HELPS COLLEGE STUDENTS LEARN BETTER.   Good listening is essential to us if we wish to develop ourselves fully, for we receive much of our education through listening. Since many college courses are taught by the lecture method, the student must be an efficient listener if the lectures are to be of value to him. The failure of a large number of college students is directly attributable to poor listening habits. We can pick up much worthwhile information by being alert listeners, out of the classroom as well as in. As a speech student you can considerably broaden your general knowledge by listening carefully to the speeches of your classmates—many of their talks will contain useful information. Through efficient listening to news broadcasts on radio and television we can become better-informed citizens. Sometimes even casual conversations yield worthwhile bits of knowledge. Difficult or dry speeches which require much listening effort may none the less contain valuable information. The first reason, then, why we should be good listeners is that it helps us to develop intellectually.

---

[4] Ralph G. Nichols, "He Who Has Ears," *National Education Association Journal,* January, 1956, pp. 15–16.

GOOD LISTENING HELPS IN PERSONAL DEVELOPMENT. Good listeners are usually well liked. It is well known that women who listen well are attractive to men; Ambrose Bierce, the famous satirist, keenly defined a bore as a person who talks when you want him to listen. "The art of living with dignity," Joseph Mersand writes in the *English Journal,* "has always been identified with the art of gracious listening. The age of the great conversationalists was the age of the great listeners as well as the great talkers." Calvin Coolidge was called Northampton's "champion listener." It has been jestingly said, but with a note of truth, that he "listened his way into all the offices the town would give him."

GOOD LISTENING HELPS MAKE BETTER SPEAKERS. If we listen well, the principles of effective speaking become vividly apparent to us; they become part of our personal equipment. You may observe that the best speakers in class usually are also the best listeners.

Successful and dynamic speech communication depends upon co-operation between listener and speaker. Proper interaction or circular response is a stimulant to both; a good listener inspires the speaker. Actors used to like to act with Ethel Barrymore because she had a mystic ability to inspire them to great heights by making them feel on the stage that she was really listening to what they said. From your own experience you probably know that you seem to speak better when the audience is listening intently. So the next time you hear an exceptionally poor speaker, listen to him with interest and respond to his speech encouragingly, and you will perhaps inspire him to give a better account of himself and make listening to him easier. Listeners and speakers can both share the profits of good listening.

Important Misconceptions About Listening

People tend to develop faulty notions about things they do not understand or about which they know little. This seems to be particularly true about listening. Compared to the skills of reading, writing, and speaking, listening suffers much from a neglect due largely to misunderstanding and lack of knowledge of its true role in the communication process. Among the numerous misconceptions about listening, the following are especially prevalent: (1) hearing and listening are the same; (2) a brilliant mind is an essential factor in effective listening; (3) reading ability is associated with listening ability; (4) what we read influences our decision and action more than what we hear; (5) listening is a set, unalterable skill provided by nature. Since any of these false notions may be a hindrance to listening improvement, we will seek to dispel each in the order mentioned.

Hearing and listening are not the same. Sharp hearing acuity by no means assures good listening, nor is poor listening necessarily a matter of poor hearing. Only 6 percent of our school population suffer hearing impairment, and only 3 percent have disabilities severe enough to handicap them in the classroom.[5] Yet a far greater percentage of our school population are notoriously poor listeners. Sometimes children are thought to have hearing disabilities because they never seem to be listening. Often a child who can hear perfectly well simply does not listen; possibly for some emotional reason the habit of not listening has become ingrained.

A brilliant mind is not an essential factor in effective listening. A teacher sometimes dismisses a child as being too stupid to be a good listener. After all, he reasons, we cannot raise a child's intelligence, so why be concerned about his inability to listen effectively? Unquestionably there is a correlation between intelligence and ability to listen, just as intelligence to a degree limits all thought processes. Research at the University of Minnesota, however, fails to demonstrate a close relationship between listening ability and intelligence. Studies by the World Book Company also show relatively low correlation between intelligence and good listening. If you are not the most intelligent member of your class, take heart, for you can probably be as good a listener as the person at the head of your group, especially if you sharpen your listening skills.

Actually, listening ability may be determined more by personality traits than by intelligence. Haberland reports that listening ability seems to correlate somewhat with two measures on a personality scale. In a research study he found that "vigorous" and "reflective" personalities showed the highest degree of correlation with good listening.[6]

Reading proficiency does not produce listening proficiency. Read-

[5] Ralph G. Nichols, "Factors in Listening Comprehension," *Speech Monographs,* 15 (1948), 154–163.
[6] John A. Haberland, "Listening Ability in College Freshmen," *School and Society,* December 22, 1956, pp. 217–218.

ing proficiency may be an indication that a person is a good listener; for one highly skilled in reading usually is able to concentrate intently, and this is an essential factor in listening. However, research generally shows that the most effective way to develop a skill is to provide training designed directly to improve that skill. As an *English Language Arts* manual points out, "Good listening habits are taught, not caught." Major research findings indicate that listening is a phenomenon clearly separable from reading, and skill in one does not assure skill in the other. Listening requires a complex of skills other than those involved in reading.[7]

Human behavior is not influenced more by reading than by listening. A research study of the influences that determine people's voting patterns found that the persons studied received 58 percent of their political information from radio and television and only 27 percent from newspapers and magazines.[8] These figures may well reveal that people's reading habits leave much to be desired, but they also show that listening influences more people than reading. Hitler was well aware of this phenomenon. He berated the pen as a means of influencing human behavior, proclaiming in *Mein Kampf* that it is the spoken word that from time immemorial has started the greatest avalanches in history.

Listening can be taught. A large number of theses and research projects positively demonstrate that listening ability can be significantly improved by training; work at the University of Minnesota is especially convincing. Nichols and Lewis point out that in no instance has a group which has been given training in listening failed to average less than 25 percent gain in listening proficiency and that some groups have shown as high an increase as 40 percent.[9] A study at the University of Kansas seems to indicate that even a short unit in listening in a fundamentals of speech class can positively affect listening proficiency.[10] In other words, proper training coupled with

[7] A number of studies support this contention. For an excellent summation see Paul W. Keller, "Major Findings in Listening in the Past Ten Years," *The Journal of Communication*, March, 1960, pp. 29–38.

[8] Ralph G. Nichols and Thomas R. Lewis, *Listening and Speaking*, Wm. C. Brown, 1954, p. 9. The section on misconceptions is largely based on this.

[9] *Ibid.* p. 6

[10] Kim Giffin and Larry Hannah, "A Study of the Results of an Extremely Short Instructional Unit in Listening," *The Journal of Communication*, September, 1960, pp. 135–139.

a proper attitude produces results. These facts should be encouraging to anyone who is interested in improving his listening ability. If you consider yourself to be a poor listener, don't be discouraged: you need not be afflicted with this malady for the rest of your life.

The Listening Process

"Pay attention!" "Listen!" "Open your ears!" How many times as a child did you hear these or similar words? People quite often think of listening as "paying attention." However, listening is a much broader concept than merely this.

Effective listening consists of a six-fold process of aural assimilation: hearing, concentration, comprehension, interpretation, reflection, reaction. (1) We hear sounds transmitted to us by air waves. (2) We concentrate our attention upon these sounds. (3) If the speaker is speaking a familiar language, we recognize and attach meanings to the oral symbols he is using. The meanings we attach to the words depend upon our past experience. Though we may learn the definitions of words from a dictionary, it is as we encounter them in life experiences that they assume real meaning for us. If a speaker is using a foreign tongue or terminology we do not understand, we cannot listen to his message. The best we can do is pay attention. We must be able to recognize language before we can comprehend it. (4) We interpret the speaker's message. We ask questions such as: What is the true meaning of this message? Are there any hidden meanings? What are the speaker's intentions? (5) We evaluate the speaker's communication. If we are listening effectively, we will measure the message with the critical tools discussed later in this chapter. Very often, however, reflection gives way to signal reaction. We tend to react without critical evaluation to oral symbols which have highly emotional meanings to us. One can, of course, listen without making critical judgments, but such listening can scarcely be called effective. (6) We react to the communication. Whether or not we react overtly—i.e., by clapping, cheering, smiling, scowling, and so forth—depends upon the impact the message has upon us. Sometimes a communication touches our emotional nature and we respond by cheering loudly; at other times we show logical insight through certain facial expressions.

The process of aural assimilation-interpretation makes listening an active, holistic process. Effective listening can never be passive, for it involves more than mere reception of sound. We sometimes hear music and even whistle or sing along with the tune without actually concentrating upon it. Only the fringe areas of our concentration are paying attention to the music, and we have little perception of or personal involvement in the sound transmitted to us. Sometimes we receive oral communication in the same way. Perhaps you recall a time when you were told to fetch three items from the store; when you got there you could remember that you were supposed to get something but had no idea what it was. This is hearing without listening. Listening requires concentration of our senses. To be effective listeners we must listen with all our attitudes, beliefs, intuitions, and rationality. Efficient listening is hard work.

Barriers to Effective Listening

Lack of training is the foremost barrier to effective listening. Beginning in the first grade and throughout our school careers, we receive instruction in reading and writing, since reading and writing are essential skills in modern society. Some students receive speech training in high school, either in a speech class or in interscholastic debate or discussion. However, very few receive any kind of instruction in listening, for it is assumed that if students can hear and will pay attention, listening will take care of itself. Admittedly, hearing and concentration are basic to effective listening, but the other four steps in the listening process need attention also.

A few specific factors can be isolated and identified as listening barriers. Proper knowledge of them is a positive aid to efficient listening. We have grouped these barriers under five broad categories: (1) concentration barriers, (2) personality barriers, (3) emotional barriers, (4) environmental barriers, and (5) physical barriers.

CONCENTRATION BARRIERS. We must actively want to be good listeners, or we will be unable to train ourselves in effective listening. Unfortunately, many of us are too lazy to make the effort; it is easier to be semi-alert than fully alert. Lack of mental discipline is the major reason for poor listening. The undisciplined mind usually can find some excuse for not concentrating: either the subject is too dry or the speaker is bad—his mannerisms are distracting, his voice unpleasant, or his articulation unclear. True, these factors make listening difficult sometimes, but the well-disciplined mind will cut through them and concentrate on the message.

Three problems make concentration difficult. First, the mind can give complete attention to any given stimulus for a few seconds only. Full attention for an extended period of time is impossible. Since the mind moves in spurts, focusing on one thing at a time, we must, in listening, seek to *sustain* our attention. We approach sustained attention when the mental spurts are in a continuum, with one stimulus remaining foremost in our minds. If the audience is highly motivated to listen and the speaker is extremely interesting, sustaining attention is relatively easy. However, if neither factor is strong, most people can sustain adequate attention only for a 15-minute speech; from that point on their attention tends steadily to diminish. Poor communication usually results from a speech that lasts 45 minutes or more, though a listener may find it more difficult to sustain attention for a dull five-minute speech than for an interesting one that lasts an hour.

A second concentration problem is the speaker's rate of speaking. Most speakers speak only 125 to 150 words a minute, yet the listener's mind can think much faster—generally at a rate equivalent to 400 or 500 words a minute—and some highly trained readers can read and comprehend at least 1,200 words a minute. The problem is obvious: the mind can work much faster than the speaker can talk. This means that the mind has considerable opportunity to get diverted. It will stray to another subject and then come back and try to pick up what the speaker is saying. After each mental excursion, it becomes increasingly difficult to return to the speaker's message, until finally we get so far away that we have lost track of his chain of thought and find it useless even to try to resume attention. Unless the listener uses his spare listening time in reflection and interpretation of the speaker's message, he will soon become hopelessly lost.

A third factor which makes sustained attention difficult is the many tensions of our modern, multidirectional way of life. Busy schedules and complex activities are a constant drain upon our ability to sustain attention. Did I pay last month's phone bill? Did I turn off the gas before leaving home? What shall I wear to the dance? How can I best approach the boss for a raise? These and a thousand other questions are vying for the attention of our minds. The more complicated our lives become, the more difficult total concentration becomes.

This multiorientation gives rise to private planning. While someone is speaking we permit our minds to dart off and plan what we are going to do over the weekend, how we are going to approach the term paper in history, how we are going to finance the car we just purchased, or how we are going to reply to a controversial point the speaker is making. Preoccupation with self is an enemy of effective listening. When you go to hear a speech, you must forget yourself, if you want to sustain adequate attention to make the listening experience profitable.

PERSONALITY BARRIERS. Earlier in this chapter it was pointed out that there may be a definite correlation between good listening and the personality traits indicated by the words *vigorous* and *reflective*. Some personality traits, however, act as barriers to effective listening. The following three are especially detrimental.

Self-effacement. Dominick Barbara, in *The Art of Listening*, appropriately calls self-effacing listeners "compulsive nodders."[11] These listeners agree to everything the speaker says. Always attentive, nice, sympathetic, and compliant, they nod approval and in a conversation insert "that's right," or some variation thereof, every few minutes. Such a person almost leads one to cry out with Cicero, "By the gods, disagree with me, so that there can be two of us!" These listeners can accurately be characterized as the "yep" listeners, since they say "yep" to everything that is said. They seldom engage in diligent reflection and fail to listen from any position of conviction or assertion. Their principal concern is giving the impression of being attentive and agreeable. Sometimes they are so concerned with their "yeps" that they miss out on what actually is being said.

The effective listener does more than merely nod agreement to everything the speaker says. He searches out his own convictions and brings them to bear upon the speaking situation. He evaluates critically, always testing the accuracy of the speaker's statements. The "yep" listener, on the other hand, omits the "reflection" step in the listening process. Avoid self-effacement, for people generally disrespect weak personalities.

Argumentativeness. Argumentativeness is the opposite of self-effacement. The argumentative personality listens in a defensive and aggressive manner. He cannot afford to be enthusiastic about what anyone says, let alone positively agree with him. In conversation, discussion, or debate he spends most of his time thinking of what he is going to say as soon as he gets a chance. He seldom reflects upon the

[11] Dominick A. Barbara, *The Art of Listening*, Charles C Thomas, 1958, p. 113.

ideas of others but merely gets cues from the speaker which trigger his own lines of argument. Listening to a speech is difficult for him because it never gives him a chance to speak himself. This, however, does not keep him from debating the speaker. Silently he questions everything the speaker says and goes off on thought tangents of his own. He is thoroughly distrustful of anyone else's point of view.

Avoid debating the speaker on every point, for this defeats the communication process. Listen with an open mind, and, after the speaker has finished, evaluate his ideas carefully.

Daydreaming. Many people find daydreaming a pleasant and convenient escape from reality; James Thurber's Walter Mitty has some great moments through this vicarious device. The daydreamer escapes into fantasy because his mind is undisciplined or because he is disturbed emotionally and seeks a release from his problems. Yet everyone is given to daydreaming occasionally. Perhaps a certain amount of it is time well spent—for it may be relaxing—but an excessive amount is wasteful. The time spent in daydreaming can more wisely be spent in serious reflection or creative thinking.

When listening to a speech that is especially dull, it is extremely easy to slide off into a daydream. It is pleasant, relaxing, and indeed tempting. But the listener must realize that daydreaming is the archrival of effective listening.

EMOTIONAL BARRIERS. People listen not only with their ears but also with their emotions, their prejudices, their beliefs, and their entire background of information. Our minds have emotional filters through which everything that enters has to pass. These filters are categorizations of our past experiences. As a child we may have touched a hot stove and from then on categorized all stove-like contraptions as hot. We may have had nothing but pleasant experiences with dogs, so we have classified all dogs as desirable. Some of our categories are shaped by what others tell us. A child is not concerned by racial differences until adults make him aware of them, but from that time forward he judges people by color or nationality. Categorization, however, is a useful device, since it permits us to make abstractions. Verbal communication would be cumbersome, indeed, if we could not use such a relatively abstract word as *chair* in our speech and feel reasonably certain of accurate communication. Abstractions are short cuts. Without them we would have to spend considerable time in expressing an idea. Yet improper categorizations, or categorizations that run counter to reason, act as major listening barriers.

Prejudice is hardened categorization. Some of our categories become so rigid that when we have a new encounter with one of them we react without reflection. Usually we attach labels to our hardened categories, the mere mention of which triggers a series of emotional reactions in our minds. *Socialist, Communist, Republican, Democrat,* and a long list of other labels invariably evoke emotional responses.[12] We all carry in our minds a long list of labels—emotion-laden words and phrases which, when we hear them, make effective listening difficult.

Emotional filters are not limited to negative or hostile attitudes but function similarly with emotionally charged concepts which we favor very strongly. Our critical faculties cease to operate at the mere evoking of these concepts, and we enthusiastically embrace the speaker's ideas. In such a case attention is no problem.

The prestige levels of speaker and listener can be an emotional barrier. The status or position of the speaker often will determine our regard for him. If we respect the person thoroughly, we may listen without adequate critical reflection, but if we feel superior to him we may disregard everything he says or tune him out completely. Business and industry have come to realize that status factors can be major barriers to effective communication. Executives often fail to listen to workers simply because they have lower status in the company. The effective listener must learn to break down such emotional barriers and consider the merits of the speaker and his message objectively.

ENVIRONMENTAL BARRIERS. The speaker and listener are often quite dissimilar in background and environment. The speaker may have spent most of his life in Brooklyn, for example, whereas the listener was born and raised on a farm. The speaker may currently be a university professor, whereas the listener is president of a farmers' cooperative. Such differences can be definite barriers to listening, for background and environment affect our thinking; we listen from a point of view and a position in life. Too often these environmental barriers prevent the minds of speaker and listener from meeting. The listener may pay attention to what is said but will totally misinterpret or bluntly refuse to accept the speaker's thoughts. For communication

---

[12] For further discussion of this point, see Chapter 10, "Language in Life."

to be effective, both speaker and listener must strive to overcome the environmental barrier. They should approach each other with open minds. The speaker should try to adapt his remarks to the listener's ·xperience, and the listener should take environmental differences into consideration and concentrate on the special merits of the speaker's ideas.

Differences in background and environment also frequently produce language barriers. We refuse to listen to someone because he is "not talking our language"—he doesn't talk "right." If he speaks with a slightly different dialect, if he uses considerable technical jargon or uncommon words, the listener may misconstrue his remarks. Vague words such as *democracy* can be interpreted many different ways, and the listener may easily supply the wrong meaning. The best way to overcome this listening hurdle is to become a student of language. Read the chapter in this book on "Language in Life" carefully and then reflect back to this problem of listening.

PHYSICAL BARRIERS. Poor ventilation, distracting noises, bad acoustics, and uncomfortable seats are barriers to listening. Often these matters are difficult for the listener to overcome, since he usually has little control over them. The speaker and the program chairman should be alert to eliminate all such barriers before a meeting starts. The problem of effective listening is great enough without external distractions.

The great danger of physical barriers to the listener is that he will use them as an excuse for tuning out the speaker. He may, for instance, ask himself why he should strain to listen over the rustling of the audience or the din of babies crying when the speaker is dull anyway. Whenever physical barriers exist, marshal all your listening powers and concentrate doubly hard.

We Can Listen Effectively

Listening habits are developed early in life. If parents are good listeners, their children tend to be good listeners also. Adults need to listen to children and hear them out, for good and bad listening are both contagious. The earlier a child receives training in listening, the better are his chances of developing into an adult with effective listening habits. We do not become better listeners merely by growing older. In fact, the passage of time reinforces poor listening habits and makes them worse than ever. If you have reached adult-hood with ineffective listening habits, it is especially important that you work hard at listening now. Approach each listening experience with interest; it is important that you *want* to listen. Good listening begins before the speech and continues after it is over. You must prepare to listen, you must practice good listening habits, and you must review what you have heard after the speech is over.

PREPARE TO LISTEN.   Try to look forward to a listening experience. Search for motivation for listening; think how this speech may be of possible benefit to you. Develop an "anticipatory set"—think about the topic and try to anticipate what the speaker might say about it. Anticipation of what is to come, according to Brown's research, sig-nificantly improves a person's listening ability.[13] Secondly, develop a "favorable set." Instead of approaching the speech with a highly critical attitude, try to appreciate the speaker's position and look upon the subject favorably. Give him and his subject the benefit of the doubt. A "favorable set" may be a definite asset to listening—in Con-boy's research, listeners with a favorable attitude were able to recall significantly more content after the speech than those with an un-favorable one.[14] At any rate, be sure to approach the speech with an open mind. Check your emotional filters and make certain that they do not screen out ideas before you have reflected properly upon them.

It is helpful to find out something about the speaker before the speech begins. Who is he? What has he done? What are his prin-cipal interests? What is his position on controversial issues? Also learn something about his topic. If he is going to speak on semantics, for example, be sure that you discover what is meant by this discipline and what some of its important teachings are. And if the speaker has written a book on this subject, try at least to skim through it before you go to hear his speech.

Attempt to cope with as many physical barriers to good listening as you can before the speech. Go early enough to get a good seat. Try to seat yourself where you will find it easy to hear the speaker.

---

[13] Charles T. Brown, "Studies in Listening Comprehension," *Speech Monographs,* 26 (November, 1959), pp. 288–294.

[14] William A. Conboy, "A Study of the Retention of Speech Context as Measured by Immediate and Delayed Recall" (dissertation abstract), *Speech Monographs,* 22 (June, 1955), 1943.

Get as comfortable as you can under the circumstances. Finally, always keep in mind that how you are prepared to listen to a speech can sometimes be as important as the listening itself.

PRACTICE GOOD LISTENING HABITS.   Study the following suggestions for effective listening and try to practice them assiduously.

1. *Look directly at the speaker.* Eye contact is as important for the listener as it is for the speaker. Attention is less likely to waver so long as it is focused on the speaker. You may also obtain important meanings through visual aspects of the speaker's delivery. Facial expression or a certain type of gesture may give a fine shade of meaning you would miss if you did not have eye contact with the speaker. It also is easier for the speaker to speak if he knows that his listeners are looking at him.

2. *Resist all distractions.* If noises are made by the audience or by some external agent, listen all the harder. Double your efforts to concentrate. Also, do not permit yourself the luxury of observing the lady's hat in front of you. Think about the speaker's topic. Nervous fidgeting by the speaker or any other repeated mannerisms can be distracting, but the effective listener will not permit himself to tune out simply because the speaker is not a finished orator. Tell yourself that it is his message that is important.

3. *Keep an open mind.* Too many listeners hear a few lines of a speech, decide that it is going to be dull, and stop listening. Resist this temptation. Search for items that might be of possible interest to you. Speeches often are dull only if you think of them as being dull. Also check your emotional filters. Try to recognize your emotional feelings about the speaker's topic and make certain that they do not monitor the speech unfairly. If there is a status problem between you and the speaker, remind yourself that the viewpoint of someone from another station in life can greatly broaden your outlook.

4. *Look for the speaker's purpose.* Is it to inform, to persuade, to entertain? Also, determine the specific purpose of the speech. Exactly what is the speaker trying to achieve? Keep in mind that what a speaker may tell you is his purpose may not be his real purpose at all. Since underlying purposes are often most important, try to discover the speaker's actual motivation.

5. *Look for the speaker's central idea.* If the speaker does not state his thesis early in the speech, try to determine what it might be. This will help you to understand the speech better. Moreover, you are less likely to be fooled by a clever persuader if you discover his central thought early.

6. *Concentrate on main points.* Identify the speaker's main points clearly in your mind. If he has not clearly organized his speech, do it for him. Construct a skeleton of the speech of your own. Avoid being sidetracked by details. Improper attention to details may cause you to lose proper perspective on the talk as a whole. Avoid what Nichols and Stevens call "I-get-the-facts-listening." These authors advise:

"Memorizing facts is not the way to listen. When people talk they usually want you to understand their ideas. The facts are only useful for constructing the ideas. Grasping ideas is the skill on which the good listener concentrates. He bothers to remember facts only long enough to understand the ideas that are built from the facts. But then, almost miraculously, his grasping an idea will help the good listener to remember the supporting facts more effectively than does the person who goes after facts alone."[15]

7. *Periodically review the progress of the speech.* After each main point is concluded, it is helpful to think back over the rest of the speech. This review will help fix main ideas in your mind and allow you to see the speech as a whole. Since you can think faster than the speaker can speak, use your spare time effectively. If you do not use it for reviewing the speech, you will tend to tune out and stop listening.

8. *Check the speaker's support of his ideas.* Is his reasoning sound? Is there evidence to support his stand? Does he rely upon emotional appeals?

9. *Look for hidden meanings.* This is sometimes called "listening between the lines." Try to determine if the speaker means everything literally. He may be speaking figuratively or implying something entirely different from what the surface meanings of his words indicate. Observe also his delivery habits. Does he seem to be especially worked up about something? Keep asking yourself if you are interpreting the speaker accurately. Observe also that a speaker's silence on a point may indicate that this is a particularly sore spot for him.

REVIEW THE SPEECH.   After the speech is over, mentally summarize it. What was the speaker's central idea and how did he develop it? Was his logical development sound? Did he have adequate support for his ideas? Did he achieve his purpose? Above all, try to determine what you heard in this speech that you especially want to make a part of your storehouse of knowledge and opinion. Repeat the review the next day. Firmly implant the ideas in your mind that you want to remember. Call them to mind occasionally in days to follow.

[15] Ralph G. Nichols and Leonard A. Stevens, *Are You Listening?*, McGraw-Hill, 1957, pp. 106–107.

CRITICAL LISTENING

Before we can discuss important concepts of critical listening, we must first understand what we mean by critical listening itself. Certainly it does not imply challenging—silently or aloud—every word, phrase, sentence, documentation, or idea of the speaker. To do so would seriously impair comprehension, distort the speaker's message, and generally break down the communication process. One should listen first for comprehension and then should make a critical evaluation. The critical listener measures the validity of the ideas and evaluates them, only after he fully understands the speaker's message. That is critical listening.

Tools for Critical Listening

Effective critical listeners ask four important questions about the speaker and his speech: (1) What do you mean? (2) Why are you so concerned about this? (3) Why should I believe this? (4) Why is this important? An easy way to remember these questions is to apply the words *meaning, motivation, support,* and *importance.*

MEANING. Meaningful language must be used to make an idea clear and specific. It is of utmost importance that a listener critically evaluate a speaker's language so that he may discover the real meaning. A speaker may have perfectly good and honorable intentions but misfire with his intended meaning because he is using language that is too technical, too vague, too scholarly, and so forth. Or the speaker may not really be sure himself exactly what he means, either because he does not understand it properly or because he has not thought it out carefully enough. Thus in this first step our search is for the true meaning regardless of motives or worthiness of substance. If the speaker's meaning is obscure, we should search for probable reasons for his not making his meaning clear.

A propagandist commonly bamboozles his listeners with abstract terms that are unclear and often inaccurate. Seldom is he specific. He fails to use *names, numbers, dates,* and *places,* but relies on generalities such as *truth, freedom, the people's will, progress, honor,* and *the democratic way of life.* Most of these expressions mean vastly different things to different people, but the propagandist never specifies the sense in which he is using them. He hopes his listeners will provide their own interpretations and assume that the propagandist means the same thing. The Communists are masters of this type of deceit. They often exploit such terms as *the people's party, republic,* and *the workingman's government.* A student of Soviet culture points out: "We must remember, of course, that Soviet communists, like all communists, use words in unusual ways. It is well known, for example, that the word 'peace' in Soviet usage means, as Lindley Fraser observes, 'the state of affairs inside a communist country.' And yet it is a major objective of Soviet policy to persuade noncommunists that, when communists use the word peace, they give it the same meaning as do noncommunists."[16]

Hitler, in his rise to power, spoke of such nebulous things as *lebensraum* and the super-race. What, for example, did he mean when he told the Germans, "For 15 years we were the irresolute and helpless object of international exploitation which, in the name of democratic ideas of humanity, belabored our people with the whip of sadistic egoism"?

You may have already detected that most of the generalities of the propagandist are *loaded terms.* Loaded terms are expressions with a high degree of emotional connotation. The traditional appeal to "motherhood" and the "family dog," for example, can be used by anyone for any kind of purpose.

When you hear a speaker using abstract terms, ask yourself if he really means what he seems to be saying. Try to discover his real purpose. Many people joined the Communist party during the 1930's because the party's stated principles were appealing. Yet most of these people were quickly disillusioned when they discovered what the Communists really had in mind. Don't be deceived; always expect the speaker to be concrete—to specify with names, dates, places, and numbers.

Beware of slogans and sayings. Such expressions as "Every man has his price," "You can't teach an old dog new tricks," "Throw the rascals out of office," or "Honest government for honest Americans" are never specific and rarely accurate. They are an extreme form of generality. The listener has a right to expect that the speaker specify what he means by them.

[16] Frederick C. Barghoorn, *The Soviet Cultural Offensive,* Princeton University Press, 1960, p. 13.

MOTIVATION. The speaker's motivation for speaking tends to explain why he takes a certain position on the point at issue. This is why it is wise for the listener to keep asking, "Who are you?" "Why are you so concerned about this?" "Why do you feel as you do?" A person may give the semblance of objectivity but in reality be speaking from a basic position of bias due to a vested interest. It is not wrong, of course, for someone to speak for his own best interests, but knowledge of the speaker's motivation helps the listener detect sham objectivity.

Many people think emotionally but pride themselves on their logicality. Speakers, especially propagandists, sometimes exploit this trait by giving an impression of objectivity by accentuating a few "facts" and passing them off as "typical." They may even recognize an opposing argument in order to carry through the semblance of objectivity. All the while, however, they may be engaging in card-stacking, which they accomplish by using distorted facts and figures and arguing from them to establish a point or by emphasizing unimportant or irrelevant aspects instead of the central issue.

The critical listener must try to look beyond the speaker's apparent objectivity by alertly checking if a speaker is expressing a subtle bias, if he is accentuating a few facts and passing them off as typical, or if he is distorting facts and figures.

SUPPORT. A speaker supports his ideas with logic and evidence. These are the tools which satisfy the listener's question, "Why should I believe this?" One does not have to be an expert logician to test a speaker's reasoning. Knowledge of formal logic may indeed be helpful in critical listening; yet most of the tests for logical adequacy can be made by anyone. Not every speaker who makes logical errors is necessarily an unscrupulous propagandist: logical errors are sometimes made inadvertently by the sincere and innocent. But regardless of the speaker's intentions, detection of logical inadequacies by the listener is of great importance.

The two most common logical fallacies are *false causes* and *hasty generalizations*. The speaker commits a false cause fallacy when he ascribes something as the cause of an effect when in reality it is not the cause at all. He may tell his listeners that we have to curb labor unions because the growth of labor unions has brought with it considerable unemployment. No real causal relationship may exist between labor unions and unemployment; in reality, a general business recession probably caused the rise in unemployment. A hasty generalization is the result of jumping to a conclusion on the basis of too little evidence. We may know of several artists who led immoral lives; we therefore jump to the conclusion that all artists are immoral. Our sampling in this case is wholly inadequate to warrant a universal conclusion. Causal reasoning and the processes of logical generalizations are discussed in some detail in Chapter 7, "Developing an Idea." Read that section of the chapter carefully and make the tests of these logical inadequacies important tools in your critical reasoning repertoire.

A critical listener will not accept controversial assertions unless they are grounded in evidence. This is not to say that the speaker should have to cite all kinds of figures and quotations for every point he makes. But certainly some support should exist for his main thesis, and if this support is not common knowledge he should be expected to document his arguments.

"Does this point need more proof?" is a question you should keep asking during a persuasive speech. If the answer is yes, ask yourself if the speaker has sufficient and pertinent evidence; ask if it is reliable and valid. Statistical data, analogy, specific instances, and expert authority are four sources of evidence. They are discussed in detail in Chapter 7, "Developing an Idea"; various tests of types of evidence are also given at that point.

Despite the obvious importance of evidence in speech, we must warn against being overawed by facts. *Ideas* are important, not a simple listing of facts, but many people have an uncritical respect for facts and for anything that resembles objectivity. Commercial advertisers exploit this trait fully. "Science proves" or "eight out of ten doctors smoke Brand X cigarettes" are pseudo-facts frequently seen in ads and heard on television. Another great danger of overvaluing the scientific orientation is that it tends to make us ignore the importance of judgments, sentiments, emotions, and creative thinking.

The twentieth-century American is especially awed by statistics. Sarett, Foster, and Sarett, in *Basic Principles of Speech,* express the problem thus: "A kind of fact often insidiously persuasive is that which can be phrased statistically. Statistical methods are valuable tools in the analysis and measurement of data in many fields. But in the layman's fascination with averages and percentages, he sometimes overlooks the possibility that statistics say something about what *has* happened or is *likely* to happen, but nothing at all about what *should* happen."[17] Statistics can be juggled to prove almost anything. The old maxim, "Figures never lie but liars can figure," can hardly be repeated too often. The listener should be careful to test a speaker's statistics with the checks of statistical reliability presented in Chapter 7, "Developing an Idea."

IMPORTANCE. Debaters have for years used a device known as the "so what" technique. It consists of questioning the importance of the opponent's arguments. One side may have carefully developed a point but failed to demonstrate its significance in the larger issue being debated. If the affirmative says that we need to abolish capital punishment because it was opposed by the greatest criminal lawyer of all time, Clarence Darrow, the negative may justifiably ask, "So what? How is this important?"

The "so what" technique is equally useful in critical listening. A speaker may develop a point with meticulous care but fail to demonstrate that it has any real significance. Most commercial testimonials certainly should receive the "so what" treatment. "Mickey Mantle smokes Camels." (So what?) "Bob Richards eats Wheaties." (So what?) "Marilyn Monroe wears bikini bathing suits?" (So what??)

In listening to a persuasive speech, keep asking yourself if the speaker's ideas are really important. If a question and answer period is held and some of the speaker's ideas have failed to pass the "so what" test, ask him to demonstrate their importance.

Special Propaganda Devices

A propagandist seeks irrational action through various clever devices. The critical listener must be alert to this kind of persuasion.

SCAPEGOATING. How many incidents can you recall when some misfortune befell you and your first inclination was to pin the blame on the nearest person? The desire to blame someone else for one's troubles seems to be a natural human instinct. Take, for example, a domestic scene. The baby has gone unwatched for a moment and has broken expensive dishes. The husband blames the wife for not watching the child, and she in turn at once blames her husband. Later, in a

[17] Lew Sarett, William Trufant Foster, and Alma Johnson Sarett, *Basic Principles of Speech,* 3rd ed., Houghton Mifflin, 1958, pp. 20–21.

calmer moment, they will probably realize that it was the fault of neither one.

The propagandist exploits people's inclinations to rationalize illogical actions by providing a scapegoat for their misfortunes. History is replete with examples of scapegoats, the most appalling one being Hitler's attack upon German Jewry. He made the Jews the scapegoat for every social, political, and economic problem of the nation. The propagandist usually selects his scapegoat on the basis of race, nationality, political affiliation, or religion. Critical listening is needed to avoid being duped by this kind of unscrupulous attack.

INVECTIVE. The propagandist uses invective to attach a stigma to the object of his attack. With derogatory terms such as *fellow-traveler, pink, cold, calculating politician,* or *imperialist exploitation,* he tries to get people to form negative judgments of the persons, causes, and ideas which he denounces. He hopes listeners will react so emotionally that they will not ask for evidence in support of his stand. His name-calling may be blunt or extremely subtle. Note how the *New Masses,* April 9, 1946, reported then Secretary of State Byrnes' role in the United Nations Security Council: "Jimmy Byrnes, the American Secretary of State and sharp little lawyer with a cold smile and a hard mind, ran the proceedings of the Security Council with the contemptuous assurance of a county political boss." The critical listener will accept no such invective without evidence.

ASSOCIATION. The propagandist sometimes tries to establish a psychological connection between his ideas and some object, person, or cause. The hope is that the listeners will transfer their attitude from one thing to the other. The speaker, for example, may casually reveal that the characteristics of a person are similar to those of an enemy. Note how one newspaper used this device in the early 1940's: "There are two kinds of speakers, one appeals to your emotions, the other to reason. Roosevelt is the kind that works your emotions, the same as does Hitler, and the masses blindly follow to the bitter end."[18] Those of you who recall the McCarthy era will remember how the Senator from Wisconsin established guilt by association by identifying people with questionable organizations or individuals. An especially good example of guilt by association is the following

[18] *Omaha World-Herald,* October 8, 1944.

passage from a speech by Congressman Murray of Tennessee, May 25, 1943: "Why is it that the Communists, the Socialists, the radicals, and those who want to overthrow our democratic system of government are unanimously in favor of the repeal of the poll tax? Why is it that all those with strange ideas, philosophies, and doctrines that are inimical tᴏ our form of government favor the repeal of the poll tax? Why it is that the clamor and demand for the repeal comes from those people outside the States requiring poll tax rather than from the citizens within such States?" Guilt by association is one of the most vicious forms of propaganda, and alert, critical listening is its worst enemy.

BLACK OR WHITE.   Hitler divided people into Aryans and non-Aryans—one good, the other bad. He created a two-valued situation out of one which in reality is multivalued. Such black-or-white reasoning is sometimes appropriately called "totalitarian logic," as it involves the "allness" concept. A propagandist divides persons, things, or countries into two mutually exclusive groups, and labels one good and the other bad. Never does he admit that most of these concepts are relative, that they need not be black or white but might consist of varying shades of gray. Stuart Chase[19] reports that after Bishop Sheil of Chicago criticized Senator McCarthy in 1954, letters such as the following began appearing in newspapers: "Destroy all Communists in America—it's either them or us!" "I am aware that some highly respected personalities have joined in the attack on McCarthy, but in my book, regardless of their big names, anyone who seeks to discredit McCarthy is sympathetic to the Reds."

The anti-poll tax bill of 1943 produced considerable irrational discussion. Congressman Manasco presented this argument on May 24: "If you want to destroy private enterprise, if you want to turn our country over to those who openly admit they hate everything American, if you want to open the gates to all the people of the earth and destroy our immigration laws, if you want to destroy our Republic, if you want every heartbeat controlled from Washington, vote for this bill. On the other hand, if you still believe in the principles of States' rights, if you still believe that our country is the greatest Nation on earth, if you still believe a republic is the best form of government, vote against this bill."

[19] Stuart Chase, *Guides to Straight Thinking*, Harper, 1956, p. 138.

Whenever a speaker poses a black-or-white argument, the critical listener will check if it is truly a two-valued situation or if what seems like a dilemma is actually relative or multivalued.

BANDWAGON. The bandwagon device is a "follow the crowd" appeal: "everybody's doing it." The speaker who uses this device is trying to give a sweep or scope to his arguments which will carry the audience along. The political speaker often seeks to create a bandwagon. He asks you to get on his side and sweep to victory with millions of other Americans in November. Thomas E. Dewey used this appeal in 1944 in a political speech on October 25: "Since I was last here in June, a great campaign has gained force daily to restore honesty and competence to our government. All over the country that movement has taken hold until now it has become an irresistible tide, sweeping on toward victory for a free America in November. The strength of that movement does not lie in any individual. It springs from an urgent conviction in the minds of our people."

Such an appeal in a political campaign may not be especially unscrupulous, but when the "everybody's doing it" approach causes people to surrender individuality and unhesitatingly bow to conformity it leads to a regimented society. In such areas as women's fashions or automobile design, the appeal may not have genuinely ill effects, but when it is used in the domain of ethics it must certainly be classed as one of the most insidious kinds of persuasion.

The critical listener will not blindly follow the crowd. Whenever you are tempted to do so, call to mind the story of the Pied Piper who was able to get all the rats to follow him into the water and the children to follow him into the side of the mountain; the rats plunged to their destruction—the children were never heard from again. The bandwagon may be appealing and glamorous, but noise and glitter do not necessarily lead to wise courses of action.

Responsible Speaking and Listening in a Free Society

Responsible speech communication, the lifeline of a free society, requires the joint effort of speaker and listener. Much of the following discussion, therefore, applies to both phases of speech communication. We include it at this point to emphasize that the listener has at least as great a responsibility in a free society as the speaker. Responsible listening is integral to wise decision-making. It is just as essential for the listener to look for and detect the truth as it is for the speaker to be free to speak it.

Hitler once cynically observed, "It is in their listening that people are the most vulnerable." This statement by history's greatest demagogue highlights the importance of effective listening. If we are to preserve our cherished freedoms, we must have a discriminating citizenry. Too many of us, even the informed and the educated, gullibly accept the utterances of unscrupulous demagogues, lobbyists, radio and television advertisers, and supersalesmen. We either lack the ability to be discriminating or else we are too apathetic and unsuspecting to expend the effort. Wendell Johnson pinpoints the problem: "As speakers, men have become schooled in the arts of persuasion; and without the counter-art of listening a man can be persuaded . . . to eat foods that ruin his liver, to abstain from killing flies, to vote away his right to vote, and to murder his fellows in the name of righteousness. The art of listening holds for us the desperate hope of withstanding the spreading ravages of commercial, nationalistic, and idealogical persuasion."[20]

Responsible citizens in a free society must be willing to accept the basic responsibilities of communication. When people shrink from these duties demagoguery and totalitarianism make insidious gains. In order to perpetuate our democratic way of life, we should accept the following responsibilities:

UPHOLD THE RIGHT TO SPEAK. Our precious right of free speech is based upon the First Amendment to the Constitution: "Congress shall make no law . . . abridging the freedom of speech. . . ." The framers of our government believed man to be endowed with the inalienable rights of life, liberty, and the pursuit of happiness, not the least of which was the right to formulate and express opinions freely. They wished the government to permit and even encourage dissemination of public opinion without threat of reprisal. This condition is essential for a democratic government to flourish. It is platitudinous to say that our government is government by talk, but it is still true. The ablest and wisest decisions are usually made after intensive discussion of issues. "Men are never so likely to settle a question right," wrote Macaulay, "as when they discuss it freely."

[20] Wendell Johnson, "Do You Know How to Listen?" *ETC*, 12 (Autumn), 1949, p. 3.

It is the freely expressed ideas of able thinkers that produce laws for the common welfare. John Stuart Mill in his essay *On Liberty* succinctly expressed the need for free speech: ". . . the peculiar evil of silencing the expression of an opinion is that it is robbing the human race; posterity as well as the existing generation; those who dissent from the opinion, still more than those who hold it. If the opinion is right, they are deprived of the opportunity of exchanging error for truth: if wrong, they lose, what is almost as great a benefit, the clearer perception and livelier impression of truth, produced by its collision with error."

It is our responsibility to uphold the right of everyone to air his views. We must guard our sacred trust of freedom of speech zealously by always giving people a fair hearing, and a good place to begin this practice is in your classroom. Show a proper respect for ideas. Don't close your mind to controversial issues, but encourage classmates to express their thoughts fully, so long as their speech is in good taste. The critical listener must stand as guardian of wise thought and action, which, as Macaulay so wisely observed, are most often arrived at when men speak their minds freely and openly.

LISTEN TO ALL SIDES OF A CONTROVERSIAL QUESTION. Enlightened public opinion is the dynamo of a republic. We make our best decisions when we understand the question at hand most fully, for a proper study of a controversial issue requires the probing of all sides of the question. Cicero, as a famous Roman trial lawyer, assiduously studied the other side of his cases. Aristotle listed, as one of the four purposes of rhetoric, learning the other side of the question. The more diligently speakers and listeners study the other sides of a question, the better will they understand their own sides. If we know only our side, we frequently know little of that. We will make far more rational decisions if we put aside our bias and try to understand the other person's point of view, if we suspend judgment until we understand the question fully. Indeed, the best way to acquire proper understanding is by listening to speakers who present points of view not in accord with ours. As Milton said, in his *Areopagitica,* the truth is to be discovered through the conflict of differing ideas. A truly critical listener will try to find arguments in their most plausible form, and that means hearing them from persons who actually believe them. In class as well as out, we cannot be termed responsible, effective listeners unless we demonstrate a willingness to study and listen to all sides of a controversial question. Rational choices are made by sober and critical reflection, not by long-standing biases.

LISTEN TO THE MESSAGE, NOT THE MAN.   In the chapter on the speaker's image we described the importance of the speaker's ethos in public address. It is true that on matters unknown to us, we as listeners do well to place the greatest credence in the words of the person of known integrity. On most issues, however, we should try to separate the message from the speaker. Judge the merits of the speaker's ideas, not the speaker himself. Closing one's mind to ideas simply because we do not like the speaker is listening uncritically. The same is true if we accept ideas merely on the basis of who utters them. A critical listener avoids being influenced by the speaker rather than by the merits of his message.

DEMAND HIGH ETHICAL STANDARDS.   The Greek derivatives of the word *ethics* signify character and customarily approved conduct. Broadly speaking, the science of ethics is concerned with customarily approved or disapproved conduct. As one authority says, "Its aim and guiding principle may be stated as intelligence in valuation."[21] Valuation problems span the whole of man's experiences, not just special fields or phases. Much of our conduct is morally neutral, being neither good nor bad. However, the problem of honesty and dishonesty is always latent.

Just as in other phases of life, the problem of ethics also presents itself in speech communication. As potential speakers and listeners, sooner or later we all will have to make ethical decisions. When this happens, we should be prepared to act with responsibility. To be able to do so, we must find the best available answer to the question: what are the ethics of speech in a free society?

Machiavelli in *The Prince* and Hitler in *Mein Kampf* were interested only in getting results, not in what is morally justifiable. No responsible speaker can use this approach; what works must be limited by what is ethical. Yet it is difficult to list in one-two-three order the ethical obligations of a speaker. Ethical concepts are so relative to situations that they almost defy such identification. Nonetheless, it is helpful to try to isolate as many unethical practices as possible.

Historically there have been two approaches to judging the ethics

21 Radoslav A. Tsanoff, *Ethics,* rev. ed., Harper, 1955, p. 4.

of speech: (1) the *end* sought by the speaker and (2) the *methods* used by the speaker. Both approaches, as Minnick ably points out,[22] have limitations. If we are to use the "end" of the persuader as our guide, who is to answer the question whether or not the end is justifiable? And if we set apart certain methods as inherently unethical, then are we never justified in using them—for instance, in telling a white lie?

Despite these problems, most writers on the subject feel it important that we try to differentiate between unethical and ethical practices and set down relatively useful criteria for judging ethics in speech. The present authors choose to present a code concerning the ethical responsibility of a public speaker prepared by an honors class in Fundamentals of Speech at the University of Kansas. Each semester one author divides his class into committees which prepare and submit to the class a resolution concerning ethics in speech. The class hears these committee reports and then tries to adopt a code which they will use as an ethical guide for classroom speeches as well as for speech in society. The most recent class adopted the following resolution:

Whereas, in modern society, due to technological developments in the field of communication, public speech has become one of the major means of disseminating ideas, and

Whereas, the opinions of men are influenced mainly by the words of public speakers, and

Whereas, all communication presupposes a premise of ethical participation, and

Whereas, the audience cannot always have at hand the facts necessary to distinguish distorted or biased materials,

BE IT RESOLVED that the public speaker should recognize his ethical responsibilities and conduct himself accordingly, these responsibilities being as follows:

1. That he examine his motives to assure that they not be harmful to society;
2. That the idea he wishes to promote likewise not be harmful to society, that he be responsible for the consequences of his idea, and that he recognize the limitations of his own perception;
3. That he seek a productive end (such as sharing valid information,

[22] See Wayne C. Minnick, *The Art of Persuasion,* Houghton Mifflin, 1957, pp. 276–286.

helping to solve common problems, and to lift the spirits of his fellow men), and not merely to manipulate and exploit his listeners;

4. That he use emotional appeals to prove his point only if the appeals have a logical basis;

5. That he truly have something worthwhile to say and have convictions of his own, and not merely speak glibly without thought or parrot the ideas of others;

6. That he avoid methods which would distort, falsify, or misrepresent the truth, or would personally devaluate his opposition instead of his opposition's arguments, or would make himself (the speaker) appear as an authority on the subject when in reality he is not, or would attempt to conceal his motives or the interests he represents, *but instead employ methods which never reject or attack the value of human beings.*

Both speakers and listeners must assume responsibility for ethics in speech. Since most people sooner or later find themselves in both roles, everyone has the obligation to develop definite standards. Ethics are usually lowest when people have no concept of what they should be. But if the majority of people have formulated ethical principles and have the courage to proclaim them and seek adherence to them by people engaged in communication, then the ethical level can be raised.

The audience, probably more than the speaker, determines ethical standards of speech communication in a free society. Listeners have freedom of choice and can accept or reject both the speaker's message and his practices. This freedom of choice brings with it the responsibility of independent thinking. Too often people find it easiest to let others make their decisions for them. This usually is due to apathy, but sometimes it is because people are afraid to stand alone. They fear nonconformity and do not have the strength to be free. Such fear of freedom is a dangerous threat to democracy.

The enlightened listener who through his critical faculties is able to detect unethical practices or specious reasoning has a moral obligation to speak out and expose it. Silence is not always golden; it can be gross irresponsibility. As one author states it, "Speaking out against what one thinks wrong is more than a citizen's privilege in a free society, it is his bounden duty."[23]

Ethics of speech should begin in the classroom. As a speaker you

[23] Theodore Clevenger, Jr., "The Teacher of Speech and Freedom of Speech," *The Speech Teacher*, March, 1956, pp. 91–101.

have the obligation to speak ethically, and as a listener you should expect your classmates to observe high principles. If a speaker is distorting facts or is plagiarizing materials, you should make this known. As a responsible listener outside of the classroom you need be even more vigorous in demanding high ethical standards. The demagogues America has known have been successful only because they had undiscriminating and apathetic listeners. Speakers in a free society will be as ethical as listeners force them to be. Apathy and an uncritical attitude foster a lack of scruples.

PROJECTS AND EXERCISES

For speaking projects see Part Three.

1. Prepare a list of what you consider are your greatest barriers to effective listening.
2. Read Ralph G. Nichols and Leonard A. Stevens' *Are You Listening?* and write a two or three-page review of the book.
3. Take a standard listening test and determine your level of listening comprehension. We suggest the *Brown-Carlsen Listening Comprehension Test*, Yonkers-on-Hudson: World Book Co., 1951; or Beery, Althea, *et al.*, *Listening Comprehension Tests*, Educational Testing Service, Princeton, New Jersey, 1957.
4. Check your listening habits. Attend a campus speech and fill in the charts below:

Did you do any of these things?	Not at all	A few times	Frequently
1. Daydream			
2. Debate the speaker			
3. Nod compulsively			
4. Listen with your emotional filters			
5. Private planning			
6. Become interested in physical distractions			
7. Listen for facts only			
8. Judge delivery instead of content			

Did you do these things?	Yes	No
1. Capitalize on thought speed by thinking ahead and reviewing		
2. Look for the speaker's purpose		
3. Look for his central idea		
4. Listen for main ideas		
5. Prepare for the listening occasion by thinking about the speech ahead of time		
6. Review the speech after it was over		
7. Keep an open mind		
8. Look for hidden meanings		

5. Plan a detailed report of Stuart Chase's *Guides to Straight Thinking.* Have students report on chapters of the book.
6. Read Rudolf Flesch's *Art of Clear Thinking* and write a two or three-page review of it.
7. Read John Stuart Mills' essay *On Liberty* and prepare a report of his ideas on freedom of speech. Comment on them.
8. If you were to draft a resolution concerning the ethical responsibility of the public speaker, would you make it different from the one on pages 114–115? If so, prepare a revised report.
9. Read carefully pages 15–22 and Chapter 2 of Sarett, Foster, and Sarett, *Basic Principles of Speech,* and come to class prepared to discuss the concepts.

TOPICS FOR DISCUSSION

1. How can family environment be a stimulus or impediment to the development of good listening habits?
2. What is the difference between listening and hearing?
3. How is listening more than simply "paying attention"?
4. Do you consider the fact that listeners can think much more rapidly than speakers normally speak a reason for the speaker to speak more rapidly? If your answer is yes, what new problems might the increased rate produce?
5. Explain what Nichols and Stevens mean by "I-get-the-facts" listening.
6. What particular listening techniques have you found especially helpful?

7. Which of the listening barriers do you find the easiest to overcome? The most difficult?
8. What special "emotional filters" affect your listening?
9. Are all emotional appeals unethical? Why or why not?
10. What is meant by "critical listening"? Does "critical" always mean making a negative judgment?
11. What are some of the more common propaganda devices used by the Communists?
12. What is a "fact"? Are the words *fact* and *evidence* synonymous?

ADDITIONAL READINGS

Barbara, Dominick A., *The Art of Listening,* Charles C Thomas, 1958.

Borchers, Gladys, and Wise, Claude M., *Modern Speech,* Harcourt, Brace, 1947, pp. 284–299.

Brembeck, Winston L., and Howell, William Smiley, *Persuasion, A Means of Social Control,* Prentice-Hall, 1952, chap. 24.

Brigance, William Norwood, *Speech, Its Techniques and Disciplines in a Free Society,* Appleton-Century-Crofts, 1961, chap. 5.

Chase, Stuart, *Guides to Straight Thinking,* Harper, 1956.

Chase, Stuart, *Power of Words,* Harcourt, Brace, 1953, chap. 15.

Ewbank, Henry Lee, and Auer, J. Jeffery, *Discussion and Debate,* Appleton-Century-Crofts, 1951, chap. 9.

Flesch, Rudolf, *The Art of Clear Thinking,* Harper, 1951.

Gray, Giles Wilkeson, and Braden, Waldo, *Public Speaking,* Harper, 1951, pp. 13–22.

Meiklejohn, Alexander, *Political Freedom,* Harper, 1960, pp. 1–89.

Minnick, Wayne C., *The Art of Persuasion,* Houghton Mifflin, 1957, chap. 12.

Nichols, Ralph G., and Lewis, Thomas R., *Listening and Speaking,* Wm. C. Brown, 1954, chaps. 1–6.

Nichols, Ralph G., and Stevens, Leonard A., *Are You Listening?,* McGraw-Hill, 1957.

Oliver, Robert T., *The Psychology of Persuasive Speech,* 2nd ed., Longmans, Green, 1957, chap. 2.

Oliver, Robert T., Dickey, Dallas C., and Zelko, Harold P., *Communicative Speech,* Dryden, rev. ed., 1955, chap. 4.

Sarett, Lew, Foster, William Trufant, & Sarret, Alma Johnson, *Basic Principles of Speech,* 3rd ed., Houghton Mifflin, 1958, chaps. 2 and 3, pp. 15–22.

ഇ ഇ ഇ ഇ DIMENSION III ഇ ഇ ഇ ഇ
Thought and Content

ഇ 5 ഇ
Thought and Speech

THOUGHT AND HUMAN AFFAIRS

Thought Rules the World

Man's behavior is determined by his ability to think logically and creatively. His powers of thought give him a great capacity not only to adjust to his physical and social environment, but also to alter and create new circumstances. Basically man is a learning animal. While in a limited way this may be true of other animals, there is an important difference: man's learning feeds on itself. The more he learns, the more he is able to learn. The more he knows, the greater his capacity to accumulate more knowledge and put it to fruitful uses. The remarkable phenomenon of the human mind is its capacity for growth and development during the entire life span of the individual.

Modern nations increasingly emphasize education, and publicly supported grade school education is now compulsory in many countries. We go to school to improve and develop the mind in order that we may know more, think more clearly, and judge more discriminately. It is man's nature constantly to revolt against ignorance and mental stagnation. His energetic mind, like his heart, works incessantly. He is a restless creature, always seeking and yearning for some kind of fulfillment which will bring him greater happiness and new satisfactions.

Modern man has a great advantage over his distant ancestors. He has access to a vast stockpile of ideas which other people before him have accumulated through ages of thinking and experience. Although his forward progress may have been painfully slow and he may have slipped backward three steps for every four he has gone forward, his ability to think has saved that one step of his forward momentum.

Ideas Are Productive

Ideas, translated into action, are brilliantly reflected in the chronicle of man's achievements. At one time he feared and worshipped fire; later he learned how to control it and make it his powerful and benevolent servant. As a result, today 60 million automobiles speed along highways in the United States alone at a mile a minute, powered by controlled fire. Fourteen thousand airplanes streak the sky every second of the day, some exceeding the speed of sound, all powered by the same means—fire. Countless ships are steered across the seas, thousands of trains and millions of trucks and busses across the continents. Man has also penetrated the mysteries of electronics and the ether waves to create light by which to pierce the darkness, send his voice around the world by radio, and his facial expressions across vast spaces by television. Such are the products of ideas.

Thought an Indestructible Force

Thought at various times becomes an indestructible force, an armor which bullets cannot penetrate or bombs destroy. Nor can it be confined by iron bars. Autocratic rulers, from Herod to Hitler, are keenly sensitive to the power of thought. Hitler realized its importance and set up a separate ministry of propaganda in his government to control and direct the flow of ideas, both into and out of Germany. Since World War II many nations have come to look upon thought control as their first line of defense. Battle lines for the control of peoples' minds are formed and reformed. We spend millions of dollars trying to communicate Western ideas to people under communistic rule, and the Russians promptly retaliate by jamming the air channels and policing receiving sets to keep the ideas of the free world from reaching their people. Rulers who fear the force of ideas become experts at thought control, propaganda, and brainwashing.

Philosophers, scientists, artists, literary men, and spiritual leaders often make poor soldiers, but they determine the currents and cross-currents of thought in the great sea of civilization. The works of a Caesar, an Alexander the Great, a Ghengis Khan, a Napoleon, a Hitler are basically much less influential than the works of a Plato, a Saint Francis, a Leonardo da Vinci, a Michelangelo, a Newton, a Galileo, an Einstein, a Locke, and a Shakespeare. Who can measure the impact of Harriet Beecher Stowe's novel, *Uncle Tom's Cabin,* upon the emancipation movement during the decade before the Civil War? How can we measure the total effect of the works of Karl Marx upon the political and economic theories and practices of nations during the past century? The total influence of the Bible upon a large portion of the globe exceeds our imaginative grasp.

THOUGHT IN SPEECH

The foregoing chronicle of the role of ideas in human affairs is part of the rationale for our belief that thought and substance should be the speaker's first and greatest concern. We do not expect you to bring forth world-shaking ideas in the speeches you will make in this class, but we do expect you to remember that the purpose of the speech class is not merely to learn to speak, but to speak about something worthy of time and attention. In this class a well-said nothing is a violation of your basic responsibilities.

Thought and substance thus represent the core of all the dimensions of speech-making. National speech authorities place them first among all the factors in the speech-making process. (See summary of survey in the Appendix.) One well-known text states it as follows:

It is inevitable . . . that the public speaker or the student of public speaking must have something of consequence to say. This means that the man who knows most about most things and most people—he who has thought most, has read most, has experienced most, has observed most, has become most familiar with the minds and hearts and manners of his fellow men, and has retained most completely the knowledge and insight thus gained—this man, if he has also learned the principles of public speaking and has cultivated the will to communicate, will be the best speaker.[1]

[1] Donald C. Bryant and Karl Wallace, *Fundamentals of Public Speaking,* Appleton-Century-Crofts, 1960, p. 13.

Meaning of Thought and Content

A man building a house must have materials with which to construct it—lumber, stone, nails, and so forth. The speaker also needs basic materials, or ideas, from which to fashion a speech. Speech substance, however, is more elusive than lumber and nails, for ideas change in value from one day to the next and from one speech occasion to the other.

Although the terms *thought* and *idea* are often used interchangeably, thought usually refers to the process of thinking, meditation, and reasoning, whereas an idea is the product of that process and as such may represent a point of view, an impression, an opinion, a description of a person, an object, an event, or an alleged fact. An idea thus may be the product of the mind by which a variety of materials is synthesized by reflective thinking. When you say you have an idea about an orange, you mean you have a mental image of it. This may include its size, shape, color, smell, texture, and taste—images you acquire through the senses. You may also have a mental image of something you want or desire, such as going to a party or going on a trip; or you may have an impression that someone doesn't like you. When you say you have a notion, a concept or a perception of a thing, a person, a plan of action, a proposal, or a desire, you have indicated that you have an idea.

The Dynamic Center of a Speech

We have noted earlier that thought and substance are the core of all the dimensions of speech; there can be no substitute for content. Make thought and content your first concern, for here is where your speech gets its life and texture; this is how to reward your listeners and make your speech effective. Having something worthwhile to say produces a reaction which aids the other five dimensions, while substance in turn becomes more meaningful to the audience if skillfully presented. The point is that substance must be present before the interaction can take place. Therefore, *substance becomes the dynamic center* of the entire speechmaking process.

Observe how substance reacts upon the other areas of speech communication. Adequate subject matter helps build confidence and establish speaker ethos. Being well prepared and having something worthwhile to say is probably the greatest single source of self-assurance, for substance generates a kind of motivation in the speaker which cannot be found or manufactured by any other means. Having a worthy product for the audience helps to trigger the inter-action between speaker and listener which is so essential before real communication can take place. Thus substance becomes the means by which the speaker can most readily command listener interest and attention.

All phases of organization become easier when there is pertinent, suitable, and worthwhile content. Thought and substance are especially helpful toward more effective language expression. The more one knows about a subject and the more one has to say about it, the easier it is to find suitable words to make the idea clear, believable, and persuasive. Finally, what the speaker has to say can obviously be a great aid to his delivery. Good substance encourages him to respond with animated voice and action. It gives him a sense of urgency to share his ideas with others which can produce spontaneity, naturalness, enthusiasm, and fluency. And as the speaker surrenders to the full meaning, he naturally speaks in more vibrant tones and with more pleasing, colorful vocal modulation. In other words, when thought is adequate, delivery becomes much easier.

Ideas Are the Basis of Creative Effort

A basic idea underlies every creative effort to communicate, whether by poetry, sculpture, architecture, painting, music, dance, or public speaking. The exact shape and details of the completed thought image may not be initially present in the creator's mind; yet he must have as an objective some clearly defined notion of what he wants to create. We must, however, remember that by itself thought does not make a speech; nor can an idea, no matter how good, be the sole criterion of speech effectiveness.

The value of thought is determined in large measure by the way it is fashioned for communication purposes. It takes on form and tex-ture and—therefore—qualitative value in a variety of ways. The steps in the development of the central thought in a speech and the manner of its organization are discussed in detail in subsequent chapters. At this point we are concerned only with showing how the raw substance in a speech may be treated by two parts of creative thinking: systematic mental labor, and vision or inspiration. Depend-ing upon their temperament, some speakers rely predominantly on

one or the other of these approaches, while others use a combination
of both. The nature of the subject matter and the speaker's central
purpose also in part determine which method is more useful.

IDEAS BY SYSTEMATIC MENTAL LABOR.   Some ideas used in a speech
may be put together piece by piece like bricks in a wall or like the
pieces of a jigsaw puzzle. The labor lies in finding the right pieces
for the right places, a type of creative thinking which is rarely emotional and requires much concentration. Here logic is the creator's
principal tool. He becomes a kind of craftsman, a contractor in ideas
who goes about his job in a deliberate, methodical way. Eliot D.
Hutchinson in his book, *How to Think Creatively,* quotes an English
historian, Joseph McCabe, as follows: "Inspiration seems irrelevant
to my work, which is largely *intellectual* and *systematic. My health is
consistently good, and my method such that so-called artistic moods
rarely occur.* I can work with good results at all times."[2]

Thomas A. Edison's remark that "genius is 99 percent perspiration
and one percent inspiration" is often quoted. Gamaliel Bradford
quotes him as saying: "But when it comes to problems of a mechanical nature, I want to tell you that all I have ever tackled and solved
have been done by *hard, logical thinking.* . . . I speak without exaggeration when I say that I have constructed three thousand different
theories in connection with the electric light, each one of them
reasonable and apparently likely to be true. Yet in two cases only did
my experiments prove the truth of my theory."[3]

Will Durant describes his method of writing history as follows:

I spend a good deal of time making notes and gathering materials. Each
item is on a separate slip, so that it may be shifted around from one position to another. The notes so made are first classified according to the chapters of the projected book, and the notes for one chapter are classified under
an outline that usually contains some six hundred headings; then the notes
under each heading are arranged in an apparently logical order, and the
whole business is then typed for me and presented to me as the raw material for a chapter; *the rest is up to me and solitude. . . . I am never
inspired by a big idea; ideas form in me very slowly* if at all. Still I do
believe in genius—that is, in people to whom *sudden revelations* come.[4]

2 Eliot T. Hutchinson, *How to Think Creatively,* Abingdon Press, 1949, p. 13.
3 Quoted in *Ibid.,* p. 15.
4 Stanley J. Kunitz, Howard Haycraft, and W. C. Hadden (eds.), *Authors Today
and Yesterday,* H. W. Wilson, 1933, pp. 214–215.

This method of systematically hammering out substance on the anvil of the mind to give thought its temper and shape is probably the most workable and useful method for creative effort in a college speech class. Your success in the course will hinge upon how well you perform this task.

Problem-solving thinking, sometimes called *directed* or *reflective thinking,* can usually be broken into four steps:

1. Carefully identifying or locating the felt need or problem.
2. Exploring the problem by assembling pertinent data.
3. Examining and testing possible or suggested solutions to the problem.
4. Choosing the best solution.[5]

In the preparation of problem-solution speeches, this pattern of directed thinking should be especially helpful, for it tends to assure orderly thought processes.

IDEAS BY VISION OR INSPIRATION. We often hear people tell about a sudden moment of inspiration—how after struggling with a problem for some time the answer came to them "like a bolt out of the blue." This may at first sound like an easy or lazy way of handling a problem, but really it is not. The key to this kind of creative experience is insight. Such a flash of revelation is a kind of breakthrough in thinking made possible only by the most rigorous and sometimes agonizing previous mental efforts. The two methods of creative thinking should not be compared with a view to selecting the easier; they simply represent two different types of creative thinking. Each has its merits for certain persons and certain speech purposes. Occasionally, the moment of inspiration marks the beginning of long and arduous labors, as with Milton. In his youth he seized upon the notion of *Paradise Lost* but spent his lifetime developing his conceptions—completing his work as a blind old man. Goethe had the vision of *Faust* as a young man but did not bring his dream into reality until he was 60.

Little is known about how to devise a reliable formula for creative thought by the inspirational method. There is some evidence, however, supporting the thesis that creative minds in art and science experience assistance by a sudden moment of insight: "In a question-

---

[5] A modification of John Dewey's reflective thinking pattern as set forth by H. L. Ewbank and J. Jeffery Auer, *Discussion and Debate,* 2nd ed., Appleton-Century-Crofts, 1941, p. 70.

naire sent out by the American Chemical Society—a group naturally suspicious of anything undefined in methods of discovery—regarding the frequency of insight in scientific problems, 83 percent of 232 directors of research laboratories and American men of science— chemists, mathematicians, physicists, biologists, men of standing generally—admitted assistance from this experience."[6]

Before the moment of insight takes place, certain conditions usually transpire which seem to contribute to the mind's fertility. First, there must be a careful and thorough study of the problem as to its essential characteristics, its scope, and its vital importance. The difficulty must be understood and its significance realized. Then the creator usually goes through a period of puzzlement, bafflement, and even frustration. He is like one who has come to a stone wall, not knowing which way to turn. And, finally, there must be a strong inner desire, a sense of compulsion, that a solution be found. When these conditions prevail, the subconscious mind stands by to be of assistance; the flash of insight therefore most readily occurs when the person is relaxed and free from fatigue.

In the process of creative thinking you may sometimes find the visionary technique helpful in varying ways. Often more insight may be gained by setting a thought aside for a period of time, then returning to it again. Or the speaker may have long had ideas in his mind but never analyzed them or attempted to shape them for use in a speech. Oliver Wendell Holmes, in his *Autocrat of the Breakfast Table,* offers some helpful hints on this situation:

I will tell you my rule. Talk about those subjects you have had long in your mind, and listen to what others say about subjects you have studied but recently. Knowledge and timber shouldn't be much used till they are seasoned. . . . Put an idea into your intelligence and leave it there an hour, a day, a year, without ever having occasion to refer to it. When, at last, you return to it, you do not find it as it was when acquired. It has domiciliated itself, so to speak—become at home—entered into relations with your other thoughts, and integrated itself with the whole fabric of the mind.[7]

We have presented the thesis that an idea is the basis of creative effort. Much can also be said to support the thesis that creative thinking makes the idea more communicable. While creative thinking may not change the essence of the raw material, it can make it more meaningful, more forceful, more attractive, and more durable for the listener. A mousetrap is only a mousetrap, but when it becomes better than any other the world starts beating a path to the door of its maker.

Creative imagination can take knowledgeable ideas and facts and reshuffle them into new relationships with one another, creating new and different concepts and points of view. Knowledge alone, then, is not enough. Actually, knowledge is almost completely useless unless one knows how to interpret it and use it. It becomes power only when it is effectively applied. In short, knowledge of the subject is not the sole criterion of speech effectiveness.

Sources of Thought and Substance

The first source of speech substance lies in the realm of your own experience—your home life, the people you have known, the things you have done, the schooling or training you have had, the attitudes, opinions and beliefs you have developed. Every sensory experience and all the psychic reactions you have had make up part of your present fund of experience. By the time you are 20 years old, over 200,000,000 words have flickered impressions upon your mind, by means of the four modes of communication—reading, writing, speaking, and listening. Important also are the endless and varied mental excursions you have had: your private planning, your daydreaming, your visits with yourself, and your dreams while asleep. In other words, your first source lies within yourself.

The second major source of substance lies outside yourself and is reached by investigating what others know. It is done by reading, observation, conversation or interview, and listening to speeches. Radio and television can be fertile sources, although the bulk of this substance is in the form of printed matter such as newspapers, magazines, pamphlets, and books. The library, the heart of the university, is usually the best place to go. Here, in an orderly, systematic fashion, are stored vast amounts of useful materials prepared by able minds and representing billions of hours of mental endeavor.

Common Sources of Printed Material

A few suggestions may be helpful as you dig for materials from printed matter. Read selectively, with a definite goal in view. Read critically, but with an open mind. Read with the purpose of achieving wide scope and getting plenty of material to enrich the distilled speech substance. Take notes to amplify and supply the central thesis, and record sources accurately. Record the name of the author, the title of the work, and—if it is a magazine—the name of the journal, publication date, and page numbers.

The following is a list of helpful sources for speech materials.

INDEXES. *Reader's Guide to Periodical Literature, Poole's Index* (for periodicals between 1802–1907), *The International Index to Periodicals, Education Index* (for educational journals), *Agricultural Index, Catholic Periodical Index, Index to Legal Periodicals, Occupational Index, Industrial Arts Index, Engineering Index, Biography Index,* and *Art Index. The Public Affairs Information Service* is a special subject index in the fields of political science, sociology, and economics, and indexes books, government documents, and current periodicals. Certain newspapers also have special indexes and are fertile sources of speech materials. *The New York Times Index* and the *London Times Index* are perhaps the best known and the most extensive.

YEARBOOKS AND STATISTICAL ABSTRACTS. *The World Almanac, The Information Please Almanac, The Statesman's Yearbook, American Year Book, Britannica Book of the Year, Statistical Abstract of the United States, The United States Census Reports.*

ENCYCLOPEDIAS. *The Encyclopaedia Britannica, The Encyclopedia Americana, The International Encyclopedia, Collier's Encyclopedia, Encyclopedia of the Social Sciences, Encyclopedia of Religion and Ethics, Cyclopedia of American Government, Monroe's Cyclopedia of Education.*

BIOGRAPHICAL SOURCES. *Who's Who, Who's Who in America, Dictionary of National Biography, Webster's Biographical Dictionary, Twentieth Century Authors, Current Biography, The Dictionary of American Biography, National Cyclopedia of American Biography, Who's Who in Commerce and Industry, International Who's Who, Dictionary of American Scholars, American Men of Science.*

GOVERNMENT PUBLICATIONS. *The Congressional Record, Document Catalogue, Monthly Catalogue.* Most Congressmen are glad to send government pamphlets concerning vital issues upon request.

OTHER HELPFUL SOURCES. *The Congressional Digest* presents the pros and cons of important controversial issues; *The Reference Shelf* series has many volumes devoted to the pros and cons of controversial topics. Each issue of *Current History* gives extensive coverage of a single topic. Sometimes books of quotations are helpful to one preparing a speech. The *Oxford Dictionary of Quotations* and *Bartlett's Familiar Quotations* are best known.

As you are doing your research, keep in mind that some materials have more value than others. Primary material is always better than secondary. An actual speech text, for example, is a better source than a report on the speech by a magazine. Government documents themselves are similarly preferable to a newspaper report on them.

Other questions about the materials should be raised: Is the author biased? If so, from what point of view does he speak? Does the date of publication affect the validity of the material? Is the material based upon sound evidence, or is it mere opinion? If it is research material, does the author sufficiently explain his methodology? Always make a careful check of any materials before you use them in a speech. It may save embarrassment later.

What to Talk About

This is always a troublesome and sometimes a baffling problem. We can offer no magic formula for its solution. You must realize that selecting a subject is entirely your responsibility, unless you have been asked to speak on a particular topic. The difficulty of choosing a subject is frequently aggravated by speech students when they look for something easy, something which requires little preparation. It often happens that no matter what subject you choose you will not be perfectly satisfied with it. This is natural, since you want a subject which will both meet the central objective of the class assignment and offer you the best possibility for success.

The best source of speech subjects, as we have said, is the speaker himself. Therefore ask yourself a succession of questions: What experiences have I had that can be of interest and value to this audience? What have I read that could profitably be the basis for a speech? What peculiar knowledge and abilities do I have? What vocational interests? Is there anything in the nature of the occasion that suggests the speech subject? What are the special interests of the group I am to address? What would they most like to hear me discuss? What subject would be most profitable for this audience?

Keep two major considerations in mind when choosing a subject: (1) the quality of the substance and (2) its suitableness and manageability.

QUALITY AND VALUE OF SUBSTANCE. Your first responsibility is to offer the listener worthwhile substance—real merchandise, so to speak, not trash. It may be something which brings him joy, delight, information, or a new point of view; provokes his thinking, alters or strengthens his belief, stimulates his interest, or moves him to action. You should give the listener something which will make him richer in mind or spirit for having heard you.

What stands out for the listener as significant is determined by what you are able to elicit from your topic. If a speech seems trivial, gossipy, or inconsequential, the trouble may be the way you developed your subject; you may have failed to relate your materials to some principle or philosophical concept.

It should hardly be necessary to say that you should avoid substance that is too sensational or emotional; above all, avoid anything that may be embarrassing to you or your audience. Finally, avoid insignificant and trivial subjects. What you talk about should be a worthwhile addition to the listener's fund of knowledge. Any speech subject you choose should pass this test.

THE SUBJECT THAT IS SUITABLE AND MANAGEABLE. Qualifications for what is suitable and manageable overlap somewhat with the criteria for quality and value. Use the following principles as guides in the selection of a speech subject:

1. Choose a subject appropriate to your audience.
2. Choose a subject appropriate to the occasion.
3. Choose a subject appropriate to yourself as speaker.
4. Choose a subject appropriate to your general purpose.
5. Choose a fresh, timely subject.
6. Choose a subject which can be adequately developed in the available time.
7. Choose a single, definite subject.
8. Choose a subject on which you can obtain adequate information.
9. Choose a subject which is in good taste.

Some Methods of Hunting for a Subject

Perhaps the easiest way to find a topic is to draw one out of a hat, but this is not the best way. Since we know of no single best way, we can only suggest some possibilities: (1) Try "brain storming." Spend 20 or 30 minutes combing your mind for any subjects which may fall within the prescribed area of consideration. Don't evaluate or judge these topics at this point—work for quantity first, then ferret out and evaluate later. (2) Jot down ideas at the moment the assignment is first made. Make written notes of flashes of insight as to both possible subject and subpoints. You may thus find the germ of an idea which will develop into a full-grown plant. (3) Go browsing and shopping for ideas. Glance through newspapers, magazines, and lists of suggested topics offered by your instructor and in Part Three of this book. (4) Talk to others. Discuss possibilities for a speech subject with your roommate, your classmates, your boy or girl friend, your instructor, or anyone who will give a sympathetic ear. (5) Keep a notebook and use it as a kind of personal diary for jotting down any burst of inspiration you may have at any place or any time.

Requirements for Developing a Sound Idea

Substance should deal only with related matter. When your material is organized, as is explained later, the relationships of all ideas and subpoints should be clear and obvious. There should be a central thought line, and all materials used should serve to amplify or reinforce it. All matter leading off on tangents and byways which are not clearly related to the central thesis should be avoided.

Substance must contain only reliable and accepted matter. This is another way of saying that the speaker should never use fraudulent or misleading materials. The public platform is no place for a hoax. Although the speaker may talk about controversial issues, he should be careful to use accurate and reliable materials to support his views. He should carry in the back of his mind the thought that should hecklers question the accuracy and reliability of his statements, he must be prepared to defend himself.

Substance should rest upon logical adequacy. The conclusions and inferences made in the speech should meet the tests of sound logic and methods of reasoning.

Substance should suit the total situation. Thought should be appropriate to the audience and the occasion and in keeping with the spirit and purpose of the group. The substance should not be too deep, too technical, or too foreign for the speaker to handle, or too complex for him to give it reasonable treatment in the time allotted.

PROJECTS AND EXERCISES

For speaking projects see Part Three.

1. We hear much about the influence of the culture and thought of the ancient Greeks upon our society. Compose a list of their contributions, and identify these as they are reflected in the course offerings of your university.
2. Prepare a brief statement of what you consider the most original idea you have had for a speech. Explain, if you can, how you discovered the idea, how it grew, and how it took final shape.
3. Identify some idea or ideas you gleaned from a book, theatrical performance, member of the family, minister, or close friend which influenced your attitude toward some personal or social problem. Try to make up a short list of such ideas and name the probable source of each.

TOPICS FOR DISCUSSION

1. At the time of the Korean War the Chinese Communists found that among the prisoners of war the Americans were the easiest to brainwash. Do you think this is because Americans lack ideals? What relationship is there between these matters and "thought and human affairs"?
2. What is philosophy? What is its special concern? What relationship can you see between philosophy and speech?
3. Why is it important to consult more than one source in preparing a speech?
4. Is it plagiarism for a student to take one article and make a speech from it without acknowledging his source?
5. The beaver and the human being can both build dams. How does thought give man the advantage as a dam builder as to (a) types of dams, (b) habit patterns in building dams, (c) design of dams, (d) reasons for building them.

ADDITIONAL READINGS

Arnold, Carroll C., Ehninger, Douglas, and Gerber, John C., *The Speaker's Resource Book, An Anthology, Handbook, and Glossary,* Scott, Foresman, 1961.

Baird, A. Craig, *Argumentation, Discussion, and Debate*, McGraw-Hill, 1950, chap. 3.

Black, Edwin, and Kerr, Harry P., *American Issues, A Sourcebook for Speech Topics*, Harcourt, Brace & World, 1961.

Courtney, Luther W., and Capp, Glenn R., *Practical Debating*, Lippincott, 1949, chap. 5.

Dewey, John, *How We Think*, D. C. Heath, 1910.

Dickens, Milton, *Speech, Dynamic Communications*, Harcourt, Brace, 1954, chap. 5.

Ewbank, Henry Lee, and Auer, J. Jeffery, *Discussion and Debate*, Appleton-Century-Crofts, 1951, chaps. 3 and 12.

Gray, Giles Wilkeson, and Braden, Waldo W., *Public Speaking: Principles and Practices*, Harper, 1951, chap. 7.

Hutchinson, Eliot, *How to Think Creatively*, Abingdon, 1949.

Sarett, Lew, Foster, William Trufant, and Sarett, Alma Johnson, *Basic Principles of Speech*, 3rd ed., Houghton Mifflin, 1958, chap. 3.

Thonssen, Lester, and Finkel, William L., *Ideas That Matter, A Sourcebook for Speakers*, Ronald, 1961.

Winans, James Albert, *Public Speaking*, Century, 1917, chap. 11.

❧ 6 ❧
Shaping Thought for a Purpose

THE ENDS OF SPEECH

Speech teachers and textbook writers categorize the ends of speech in different ways and in different terminology. Some classify all purposes of speech in three categories: to entertain, to inform, to persuade. Persuasion here includes speeches designed to secure belief, impress the listener, and secure action. Others use a fourfold classification—to interest, to inform, to stimulate, to persuade—and still others use five classifications. Some call the speech to interest a speech to entertain; others call the speech to impress a speech to stimulate, and so on. In this text we shall use the most common terminology and a fivefold classification: to entertain, to inform, to convince, to impress, and to actuate. The last three types are all persuasive speeches and can be placed under the general classification of persuasion, if the student so desires. It is largely for academic convenience that we list them separately.

Obviously, any speech with one of the five above aims may have in varying degrees the elements of other aims within it. No speech is likely to be pure information or pure conviction or pure anything else. Thus we cannot think classified speech purposes in the same way that we think of five different kinds of fruit in a basket—where an apple is all apple and a peach is all peach. A speech, no matter what its central aim, is likely to have fringe benefits from other aims.

The Speech to Entertain

In simple terms, the speech to entertain is designed to give the audience an enjoyable time, to send the listener on his way saying, "That certainly was a delightful talk." We ought not to consider this type of speech as designed to make the audience roll in the aisles with laughter, or as a sort of vaudeville act; nor should we think of it as something entirely "off the cuff." The speech to entertain should, like any other speech, be carefully planned and organized to stand up as a creative piece. Like any other speech, it should have underlying, stimulating ideas.

The speech to entertain is commonly characterized by the speaker's originality, his charm, his inventiveness, and his sense of humor. Wit and humor are among the speaker's best tools, but wit is the sharper tool. Wit is humor geared to wisdom; it combines laughter and thinking. It is a way of using ideas like barbs to prick the mind. The speech of entertainment which features wit and humor is a special type of speech for which most people have limited ability. However, age and experience will do much toward improving one's ability to use humor effectively. Actors in the area of the theater say, "Tragedy is for youth, but a sense of comedy comes only with the mellowness of age." And when humor is present, its effect is largely a matter of degree. Generally, one should not try too hard to be funny. Humor is best when it seems effortless. Avoid stale jokes, long drawn-out stories, difficult characterizations or impersonations, and stories which have nothing to do with the point you are trying to make or with the spirit of the occasion. (For further discussion of humor see the next chapter.)

Speeches of entertainment often occur at banquets and on the public platform. After-dinner speeches are very common. By lore and tradition there is a festive mood; at any rate, the occasion usually calls for something not too somber or solemn. However, the prevailing mood of cheerfulness and intimacy does not preclude sensible, serious thought, if it is made delectable by the charm and imaginative touch of the speaker.

Some speeches may be delightful, interesting, and have much entertainment value without necessarily being loaded with humor.

Many travelogues and speeches of demonstration which use visual supports that create a spectacular or dramatic effect are partly informative, yet predominantly entertaining.

The Speech to Inform

The informative speech is the most common of all. It predominates in the classroom, the lecture hall, at the Armed Service training centers, industrial training centers, civic clubs, women's clubs, in shops, and on guided tours of all sorts. It is the most essential tool in the educational process. Even when informing is not the primary purpose of a speech, informative materials are usually present. In varying degrees they are blended into almost all other kinds of speeches— speeches to entertain, to convince, to impress, and to persuade.

There are two broad types of informative speeches, those designed to give instruction and those designed to impart worthwhile factual knowledge. The instructional type gives directions on how to do or make something. It prescribes a sequence of steps or line of action to be followed, such as in how to saddle a horse, throw a baseball, run a typewriter, train a dog, conduct an experiment in chemistry or physics. Such demonstrational speeches are more fully explained in the section dealing with assignments, pages 351–353.

Other informative speeches of the same type are those involving more or less abstract theories or principles which may be clarified by means of numbers, diagrams or graphs. Examples would be speeches on how to set up a corporate organization or how to organize a toastmasters' club in your town.

The second type of informative speech—that which is primarily concerned with factual information—is more common. Recall the many books you read in grade school on The Story of Coal, The Story of Wool, The Story of Cotton, and so on. These books tell in story form the uses, kinds, and methods of processing these products. They use story technique as a method helpful in making the subject matter interesting and alive.

The informative speech, as the term implies, must inform the listener; that is to say, it must give him something new, something he did not know before. The speaker's purpose is either to impart new knowledge or to give new light and deeper insights into something of which the listener may already have some knowledge. The informative speaker should always keep in mind the major goals of clarity, richness of substance, and high level of audience interest. The matter of clarity is dealt with later in this chapter. How to use the informative speech in class is more fully explained in the section dealing with assignments, pages 357–364.

The Speech to Convince

The speech to convince is concerned with making an idea believable or acceptable to the intellect. Its central purpose is to establish the truth—or at least to reveal what is most probably true. It may or may not cause the listener to change his mind. It may motivate him to action, but action is not the central aim. If there is action, it is a by-product. The speaker giving a speech to convince seeks mental agreement. His appeal is to the intellect by means of reliable facts and sound reasoning.

The speech to convince springs from areas of thought where there are doubt, dispute, disagreement, clash of opinion, and variations in point of view. Here the verdict at stake is in the listener's mind. The appeal is to the listener as a judicious, critical judge who wants to ascertain what is desirable and true, based upon the evidence and the application of logic.

The process of reasoning may also be a part of a persuasive speech in which the manipulation of the motives which determine action is the central objective. The persuader's methods are both logical and psychological, but the listener's behavior is his first concern, whereas in the speech to convince logical considerations are primary and whatever may be psychological is secondary or incidental. In conviction the central issue is what is true, whereas in persuasion the central issue is a future course of action. A lawyer arguing a case before a single judge in court will place more reliance on the tools of conviction than when facing a jury, in which case he will use more of the weapons of persuasion—the assumption being that the experienced, trained judge will base his verdict largely upon evidence, and logic, whereas the jury will be more susceptible to sentiment, desires, and prejudices. Speeches of conviction occur in high school and college competitive debate, in law courts of all kinds, in special reports before Congressional investigating committees, in speeches by executives of corporations, and in many other situations.

The predominant form of composition when the primary end is to convince is argumentation, whereas exposition and description commonly prevail in the informative speech. Subject matter in the speech to convince usually stems from three types of questions or propositions: the question of value, as, "Is honesty a greater virtue than cleanliness?" "Does science contribute more than art to society?" —the question of fact, as, "Did Mr. X murder Mr. Y?" "Was Shakespeare the author of *Othello?*";—and the question of policy which involves a proposal for change and is by far the most common form of the speech to convince. The question of policy, properly phrased, objects to the status quo. It calls for some change, as, "Should there be a national amendment giving 18-year-old citizens the right to vote?" "Should Congress enact legislation providing for a program of national health insurance?" Most questions of policy involve issues of need, desirability, and practicality. The essential characteristics of a policy question are the problem and its solution.

The Speech to Impress

The speech to impress is designed to vitalize and emotionalize a belief that is already established, at least to some extent, in the listener's mind. Here the speaker usually deals with old, established truths and burnishes them to glow with new luster. Old ideas then are more fully appreciated, concepts of long standing become more meaningful, and old faiths are renewed and strengthened. Sermons, memorial speeches, eulogies, speeches of welcome and farewell, and commemorative addresses fall in this category. Such speeches may have in them elements of conviction, but those of persuasion are more prevalent. The speech to impress is usually characterized by lofty ideals, elevated language and delivery, and various techniques to ennoble the thought. The impressive speech is inspirational; it is concerned more with feeling than with logical thinking. Its audience is nearly always receptive and friendly. Some of the finest prose in American speech literature falls in this category. Robert Ingersoll's oration at his brother's grave, Theodore Roosevelt's "Strenuous Life," and that masterpiece known to every schoolboy, Lincoln's "Gettysburg Address," are examples.

The Speech to Actuate

Brembeck and Howell define persuasion as *"the conscious attempt to modify thought and action by manipulating the motives of men toward predetermined ends."*[1] According to this concept persuasion is designed to influence the volition and behavior of others and is accomplished more often by appealing to human wants, desires, and emotions than it is by the processes of logic. We use the term *the speech to actuate* for speeches of persuasion in which action is the central aim and motivational appeals the central technique. Man, being essentially an emotional creature, is governed more by feeling than by pure reason; it is often said, "He persuades best who argues least." In the speech of persuasion, the question is, "What will the listener do?"

The persuasive speech is a dynamic tool of democracy. In our free, competitive society, the highest premium is placed on the man who can get the most votes, get the most people to sign on the dotted line, or to support his cause, his movement, or his program. Both our political and our economic systems are based upon the persuasive process. Persuasion and the American way of life are bedfellows.

Like dynamite, persuasive tools in the wrong hands can be the means of destruction and evil-doing. Thus the question of ethics and morality comes into sharper focus in the persuasive speech than in any other. Whether persuasion serves for good or evil is determined by the character of the speaker and the critical thinking ability of the listener.

Political spokesmen for Russia, China, and other communist nations have demonstrated again and again their mastery at handling the weapons of persuasion. The same is true of demagogues and dictators with the lust for power, no matter what country or form of government they represent. We, as members of the general public, need to know and understand the modes of persuasive speech not only as speakers but as listeners. This knowledge is important as a matter of self defense, for the same fire that can destroy us can also serve as a shield to protect us.

Persuasion, or Persuasive Speech, is ordinarily an advanced course in the curriculum of speech communication. In this text we can devote only a few pages to a subject about which entire books are written, and we shall therefore concentrate on three essential ways to reinforce and implement the persuasive process: (1) by creating

[1] Winston L. Brembeck and William S. Howell, *Persuasion: A Means of Social Control,* Prentice-Hall, 1952, p. 24.

and holding audience interest and attention, (2) by motivational appeals, and (3) by applying laws of suggestion. Some of these factors, especially those pertaining to attention and interest, apply to all types of speeches.

ATTENTION AND INTEREST

The words *attention* and *interest* are often used together; although they are not synonymous, they have interlocking and overlapping meanings. We pay attention to what interests us, and what interests us commands our attention. Sometimes a distinction is made that attention responses are more elementary and primitive than interest responses, which are dependent upon cultivated and learned behavior. Attention is the door to the mind. Attention awakens the senses; interest stimulates the mind and inner feelings. Attention and interest form the first link in the communication chain between the speaker and his audience. Without this link the speaker talks to himself.

In attention, the mind holds still and comes to a specific focus. A child walking along may suddenly come across a dead bird in its path; he stops, looks transfixed at what he sees, and perhaps stoops to pick it up by its tail feathers. There is a moment of concentration and a general state of tenseness, while his consciousness is drawn for a moment toward a focal point. The mind does not focus upon a single thing very long, however—usually not for more than a few seconds. The psychologist Walter Dill Scott described this as thinking in spurts: "All of our thinking is done in 'spurts,' which are uniformly followed by periods of inactivity. We can think of nothing consecutively for any great length of time. What we have called constant or fixed attention is simply spurts of attention. Do what we will our attention will not stay fixed, and if we desire to hold it for a longer period of time on an unchangeable object, all we can do is to keep pulling ourselves together repeatedly, and avoid as far as possible all competing thoughts or counterattractions."[2] The speaker's problem is to keep on triggering new spurts of attention from his listener and to revitalize waning interest.

Another characteristic of attention lies in its selectivity. The listeners' field of attention and interest is as wide as the universe. The

[2] Walter Dill Scott, *Psychology of Public Speaking*, Noble and Noble, 1926, pp. 112–113.

speaker's problem is to get the audience to tune in with him on a particular thought channel. The speaker is the selector. Not only must he seek a clear channel for projecting his thought, he must cope with interferences and counterattractions extraneous to the subject matter he wants to convey. The first step is to avoid interferences as much as possible and control counterattractions which intrude upon the business at hand. The speaker almost inevitably faces some competitive disturbances, certain of which he may generate himself by gaudy, or sloppy dress, annoying mannerisms of voice and gesture, or nervous, irritating habits. Outside disturbances include banging doors, flapping curtains, honking automobile horns, crying babies, people talking in undertones, inadequate lighting, and so on. A good rule is to ignore such interferences as much as possible, unless they are so violent that communication is impossible. In that case, pause and wait until the interference subsides, or do something to control or remove the disturbance.

Kinds of Attention

The first kind of attention to note is *involuntary*. A fire siren goes by or somebody accidentally drops a book in the classroom and we give involuntary attention. Speakers can elicit this type of attention—with discretion—by means of strong vocal emphasis, clapping hands, exaggerated inflections, or striking physical gestures that catch the eye. A second type of attention, that involving effort, is *voluntary*. If the subject we are to attend to holds little interest for us or is presented in a dull manner, we have to work hard at attention. If, however, the speaker is talking about something that is extremely interesting, paying attention may require no effort at all; it then becomes *nonvoluntary*. The attention we give to ideas linked to our strong desires or special interests is almost second nature. The speaker discussing them will not have to pound on the table to keep us awake.

Basic Factors of Interest and Attention

The speaker should develop an awareness of basic factors which help to gain and hold the attention and interest of an audience and should learn how to season his speech liberally with them—remembering, however, that the elements of attention and interest should serve only to make the speech more effective. Firecrackers, noisemakers, and blaring bands are all right for certain celebrations but can be very obnoxious at other occasions. Similarly, a speaker who uses attention devices which are obviously out of harmony with his ideas or with the spirit of the occasion may fail miserably as a speaker, even though he holds the attention of his audience. Attention alone is not a good yardstick by which to judge a speech. The best attention and interest arise naturally from challenging ideas, new information, discussion of timely, vital topics, and use of effective language and delivery.

Attention and interest factors should be viewed as means for reinforcing thought and making it more communicative, nothing more. As you read and study the following list of factors, also do not think of them as distinct, separate items to be applied one at a time, independently of each other. You may tell a story, cite a fact, refer to an incident, or have an expository paragraph while employing two, three, four or more of the factors listed here.

ACTION. Moving pictures and television rely on the principle of action. Attention is caught by anything moving—trains, meteors in the heavens at night, floating clouds, rolling ocean waves, flying birds, flickering lights, and so on. A circus is all action, and its monkey cage is something no one wants to miss. A speaker can use a blackboard, objects, visual aids, or gestures to describe or give emphasis to thought through action.

SUSPENSE. Theaters are crowded because people come to them to cry, to laugh—and to anticipate. Will the handsome hero finally win the heroine? Suspense keeps us up late reading stories to the end and in our seats at ball games until the final play. The speaker can utilize the factor of suspense by narrating and describing examples vividly, by developing points with increasing clarity, and by accumulating force in the use of supporting evidence.

THE VITAL. Deep human hungers always enlist our attention and interest. Anything connected with our basic drives is of vital interest to us. Self-preservation, sex, family, ego preservation, and bodily demands such as hunger and thirst are strong motivational forces. Generally speaking, we are interested in anything which touches upon our honor, our loyalty, our sense of patriotism, our freedom, our children, and our personal belongings.

THE NEW AND FAMILIAR.   The main business of a newspaper is to communicate news. We are always asking what is new and what is latest. A new hat, a new car, a new house, a new recipe are of interest to friends and neighbors. The speaker holds attention by imparting new knowledge, new bits of information, or by making reference to the latest striking bit of news. We are also interested in the old and familiar: the old home town with its familiar places and sights, the old songs we used to sing and the hit tunes we used to know, and other old memories which hold a nostalgic interest. One speaker who talked about railroads began his speech in this manner, "How many of you remember when you were a child on the farm and what a thrill it was when the train went by, how you would run to the fence on the high ridge and wave to the engineer and he would wave back and perhaps blow his whistle? Do you remember?" A speaker should strive to present the old in a new manner and the new in familiar garb.

CONFLICT.   People have always been interested in fights and conflicts. The amphitheaters of ancient civilizations give testimony to this. Modern athletics represent conflict in controlled, sublimated form. The debates between John F. Kennedy and Richard Nixon in the Presidential campaign of 1960 had great public appeal. A speaker who takes a statement from the press or from another speech and says, "I deny this," or "I object to this," or "I will attack this for the following reasons," will elicit the interest of the audience because he demonstrates a conflict of opinion.

THE UNUSUAL.   Robert Ripley found fame and fortune as a collector and publisher of bits of the unusual. His widely syndicated column, "Believe It or Not," was world-renowned for more than two decades. Something strange, extraordinary, or different captures our attention. A speaker making an informative speech about bees, whales, wild geese, space travel, big game hunting, digging oil wells a mile deep 10 miles out in the ocean, and countless subjects featuring unusual materials is able to arouse our interest.

VARIETY.   Life is a long struggle against monotony, and what is more boring than a monotonous speaker? The speaker can incorporate the element of variety in his speech by variation of moods, language expressions, styles of physical delivery, and change in the pitch, tempo, and force of his voice.

HUMOR.   A good laugh from the listener is the sign of some kind of attention. But humor does more than claim the attention and interest of the audience; it provides "comic relief," giving listeners release from emotional tensions.

THE REAL AND THE CONCRETE.   The desire for what is real and tangible is the underlying appeal to souvenir hunters. We are interested in visual tokens of ideas; thus objects and visual aids are valuable attention devices. Mark Antony demonstrated the attention-holding power of the concrete as he threw back the cloak which covered the corpse of Caesar to show the wounds made by the conspirators. This was indisputable, concrete evidence of the crime, which even the Roman mob understood. President Eisenhower, in one of his television speeches reporting on our progress in space exploration, showed his viewers a cone tip which was recovered from outer space. This visual object served not only as proof of our achievement but as an effective attention and interest device. Look for opportunities to use visual supports in your speech. In addition, be sure to express statistics in concrete form. Instead of simply citing some huge, meaningless figure, break it down in terms of the individual listener.

THE HUMAN.   What is more interesting to us than people? Shakespeare is a great playwright because his characters are human. People have been reading and studying the character of Hamlet for more than 300 years, saying to themselves, "Why, I have felt just like that." But even comic strips in our metropolitan newspapers have wide human interest appeal. As we read them, we identify the oddities of human nature in ourselves and in the people we have known. Television programs featuring the candid camera technique have become very popular. President Roosevelt's dog Fala and Senator Nixon's dog Checkers were intentionally introduced into Presidential campaigns as human interest factors. Take advantage of human interest. Whenever possible, talk about single, specific people. As E. B. White once wisely observed, "Don't talk about man, talk about a man."

Observe the attention and interest factors employed by a speaker at the turn of the century, in a story illustrating the importance of dependability as a character trait:

Listen to the story of the 20th Century Limited. It is midnight at La Salle Station in Chicago. Standing on the tracks headed for New York is the 20th Century Limited, filled with passengers. All are aboard except one sailor on leave standing by the platform gate. At exactly 12:02 a.m. the conductor waves to the engineer who calls out in a ringing voice, "All aboard!" The sailor passionately kisses his sweetheart goodbye in one last embrace, turns, runs, steps aboard the train which has already started to move. It creeps along, clicking across the rails as it slowly threads its way out of the yards and moves into the night past dimly lighted settlement districts, industrial areas, the suburbs of the city, its outskirts, and at length past the steel mills of Gary, Indiana. As the Limited roars through the dawn and morning hours, people of the countryside regulate their chores by a train running on schedule. At high noon a farmer, cultivating his fields, hears the deep-throated whistle of the 20th Century Limited and his horses perk up their ears and quicken their pace for they know when they reach the end of the row they'll go home for a brief rest, for oats and hay. As the train roars on its way over the plains of Ohio late in the afternoon, two women stand gossiping across the garden fence when suddenly they pause and one of them says, "Goodness sake, its five-forty, time to fix supper! I must go now." For in the distance they hear the whistle of the 20th Century Limited. As the train roars on its way into the night, far in the hills of eastern Pennsylvania an old man lies in his bed, his body racked with pain. For him the sleepless hours drag by like years. "Oh, God," he moans, "will the morning never come?" Finally he gives a sigh of relief as he hears in the distance the deep-throated whistle of the train. "Thank the good Lord," he murmurs, "it is five-fifteen. Morning at last!"

The 20th Century Limited is more than a railroad train. It is a symbol of dependability—a cardinal virtue in the formation of character.

This story employs at least seven of the attention and interest factors listed above and illustrates how a speaker may weave them into his materials. He may also, of course, further intensify the effect by his manner of delivery.

IMPORTANT MOTIVATIONAL FORCES

The persuasive speaker's first concern is to chart the phenomena of human behavior. He must be sensitive to the deep motivating forces which cause people to act as they do, for he may use these forces as motivational devices in his speech. Among the forces, needs, and drives which a speaker may use motivationally are: (1) sex and family, (2) self-preservation, (3) religion, (4) feeling of self-importance, and (5) curiosity. In simpler terms, we want to be loved, we want to live, we want to believe, we want to be recognized, and we want to learn.

Sex and Family

The sex motive is strongly intertwined with the biological behavior pattern of species reproduction; the deep hunger to have a home and family has biological roots. However, the love experience of man and woman goes far beyond this, including the satisfactions of companionship and the mutual fulfillment of each other's physical, mental, and spiritual needs. Love stimulates our creative efforts; it refines and sublimates everything we do. Is it any wonder, then, that the love theme is eternally expressed in poetry, song, drama, the novel, and all other creative arts? Successful speakers frequently appeal to home, family, and the theme of love.

Self-Preservation

The will and desire to live also has biological roots. Our American forefathers were aware of this basic motive when they put *"life,* liberty, and the pursuit of happiness" in the preamble to the Constitution. The Israelites, after their flight from Egypt, cried for food, and the Lord provided manna from heaven. The Lord's commandment, "Thou shalt not kill," is respected throughout the civilized world. Wars have long been fought for economic reasons: food, clothing, and shelter. An army fights on its stomach, prison riots are born in the mess hall, and hunger is a breeding place for communism. We will pay our last dollar to the doctor who saves or prolongs life. Money has a strong appeal for us because it represents freedom from want. Political candidates win elections by talking about their plans for reducing taxes, security for the aged, better medical care, and strong national defense. All these appeals strike directly at our longing for self-preservation.

Religion

"Man does not live by bread alone." There are three sides to his nature: body, mind, and soul. His spiritual needs and hungers are historically demonstrated by the many religions he has founded and by his responses to them as manifested in architecture, painting, literature, and music. Some of his most significant triumphs among the arts have been inspired by religious motives. This same motive has also been a guiding force behind crusades, colonization movements, and bloody wars. Tyrants have attempted again and again to stamp out or suppress the religious motive, but their efforts have almost always been in vain.

Speakers are not usually as obvious in utilizing this motive as others; yet in varying degrees religion is reflected in speeches from the pulpit, at church gatherings of all sorts, lodge meetings, Boy Scout and Girl Scout activities, and fraternal organizations. It is present in the Declaration of Independence, in the war messages of Woodrow Wilson and Franklin Roosevelt, and in most Presidential inaugural addresses. Reference to deity is abundantly reflected among the orators of ancient Greece. Although the occasions to use the religious appeal in a speech class may be limited, it is important that we understand its dominant influence in lives of some people and its governing force in our society in general.

Feelings of Self-Importance

Man is a proud creature. It is difficult for us to realize how self-centered we are, how firmly the sense of ego is tied with everything we do. The sound of our own name is usually music to our ears. Think of the time and money we devote to dress and appearance because we covet the approval of others. Barbershops, beauty parlors, clothing stores, and reducing diets are constant reminders that we must look attractive.

How we crave honor and recognition! Think of the work and furor which revolves around intercollegiate athletics! And what is it all about? Pride and honor. Oscars, Nobel prizes, Congressional medals, and trophies of all sorts are common fixtures of pride. At one time we fought duels to vindicate pride. Millions of dollars are presented to institutions to perpetuate the names of the donors. We want peace, but always peace with honor. It is difficult to estimate our total output of thinking and energy as "status-seekers" and "status-keepers." This motive helped our colonial forefathers write the Declaration of Independence and fight the War of Independence. It gave birth to the Bill of Rights in the Constitution. It gave us our rugged individualism and private enterprise. For Patrick Henry, the choice was "liberty or death"—he chose liberty, a concept born of the feeling of self-importance.

Curiosity

Man is a learning animal. His mind remains restless for growth and expansion. It is impossible to imagine what valuable results the motive of curiosity has had through all the history of man. Think of the countless days and years men have looked through microscopes and telescopes and bent their backs over test tubes in laboratories and risked their lives on uncharted seas in all kinds of weather—all because they were curious about something that wasn't understood. The questioning urge which is so strongly manifested in the curious child really never leaves him. The hunger to learn and know is never completely satiated.

SUGGESTION

Suggestion is the act of planting a thought in someone's mind by means of a hint that something exists or has happened or that it might, could, or should occur. In suggestion there is no coercion, browbeating, or coaxing to get a response. When suggestion affects a person, he is seldom aware of the process, usually assuming that his decision and action are of his own free will and initiative. The crux of the matter lies in the ability of the suggester to turn the mind of the observer or listener in a certain direction and keep it constantly there until belief or action takes place—provided the individual is capable of such belief or action. Suggestion implies a possible or probable response with little concern as to its logical basis. If you say, "I suggest we stop at the Union for a cup of coffee," and are turned down, you will probably respond, "Okay, it was only a suggestion." Psychologist Kimball Young wrote that we are moved far more effectively by emotions and feelings than by rational ideas, and therefore "the most far-reaching effects of suggestion are produced by appeals to those emotionalized images, sentiments, and attitudes which rest upon previous conditioning."[3] Jon Eisenson, an authority on the psychology of speech, says suggestion is "the uncritical ac-

3 Kimball Young, *Social Psychology*, Appleton-Century-Crofts, 1944, p. 110.

ceptance of an opinion as the basis for belief or action." A characteristic of suggestion, then, is that it ordinarily is effected without careful thought analysis. Its influence springs from hunches, flash opinions, snap value judgments, and impulses which are not based upon rationalized concepts.

Direct and Indirect Suggestion

BUY BONDS, NO SMOKING, and SIGN HERE are examples of direct suggestion—simple, explicit, and straightforward. Indirect suggestion is less obvious; it is subtle and reaches the mind by the back door, so to speak. Its roundabout nature can be illustrated by an incident that happened in a college speech class. The assignment was a speech of demonstration calling for the use of objects and visual aids. A premedical student with a knack for cartooning chose for his topic, "You, Too, Can Cartoon." Equipped with easel, charcoal pencils, and all the necessary accoutrements, he showed how to create various effects with simple lines to make eyes, noses, and mouths. As he went along, he tore off the completed charts. The last and final chart he had carefully sketched in detail the night before. It was a friendly, humorous caricature of his instructor who up to this moment had been little concerned about the matter of girth control. This sketch, with its cartoon exaggeration, reminded him so vividly of the equatorial region of his anatomy that he proceeded at once to go on a diet and managed to take off twenty pounds in ninety days. No word about weight control had been said in the speech.

Positive and Negative Suggestion

We think of positive suggestion in connection with affirmative statements. "Thou shalt" seems stronger than "Thou shalt not." "I will" is a key phrase in wedding vows and for public officials taking the oath of office. It reduces doubt to a minimum. In a sense, negative suggestion is positive suggestion in reverse. Sometimes people are inclined to do the very opposite of what they are told. The suggester, perceiving this situation, will therefore suggest a course of action contrary to his purpose. If a person is told several times not to do a certain thing, he may be inclined to try it out just to discover what the results will be. A letter stamped in several places, "Do not open if you are not the addressee," might prompt someone to tamper with another's mail, whereas he normally would not think of it.

Rendering an Audience Suggestible

The effectiveness of suggestion as developed by the speaker is a matter of degree, ranging from extreme mildness to great force, and its effect varies widely from listener to listener. Suggestion comes somewhat into play in any type of speech, but it is most consequential in speeches designed to motivate the audience. In the remainder of this chapter we shall designate several ways by which the strength of suggestion may be increased within the audience itself.

UNITE THE AUDIENCE.   Your audience is usually made up at first of many separate units, or listeners. It becomes united when members of the audience react upon one another, as if by an electric current, causing the characteristics of the individual listener to be merged or welded with that of the group. The methods of uniting an audience are many. It was advised earlier that if the audience is widely scattered in a big room you have the members move forward in a compact huddle close to the speaker. Get the audience to respond together as a team by having them sing, stand, cheer, laugh, or raise their hands together. Create the feeling of togetherness, of having something in common: a common purpose, a common cause, a common mood, a common action. Unite the audience to think, feel, and behave as one; then responses to suggestion are easy.

GET ON COMMON GROUND WITH THE AUDIENCE.   Help the audience to feel that you are one of them. Charlie Weaver, on a Jack Paar television show, makes capital of the phrase, "These are my people!" Our most effective ambassadors in foreign lands are the ones who talk the language of the people and try to show sympathy for their customs and ways of life. The old saying, "When in Rome, do as the Romans do," is in point here. Henry Ward Beecher was unhappy with the success of his early preaching efforts until he took a hint from the sermons of the Apostles.

And I studied the sermons until I got this idea: That the apostles were accustomed first to feel for a ground on which the people and they stood together; a common ground where they could meet. Then they heaped up a large number of the particulars of knowledge that belonged to everybody; and when they got that knowledge, which everybody would admit, placed in a proper form before their minds, then they brought it to bear upon them with all their excited heart and feeling. That was the first definite idea of taking aim that I had in my mind.

"Now," said I, "I will make a sermon so." . . . First I sketched out the things we all know . . . And in that way I went on with my "you all knows," until I had about forty of them. When I got through with all that, I turned around and brought it to bear upon them with all my might; and there were seventeen men awakened under that sermon. I never felt so triumphant in my life. I cried all the way home. I said to myself: "Now I know how to preach."[4]

GUARD YOUR AIM OR PURPOSE. Approach from the blind side of your listener. Don't rush or crowd your audience too abruptly or be too obvious about your intention before you have reached the punch line by which you seek response. Suppose you have what you consider a sure-fire humorous story, but you tell your audience in advance that you are going to make them laugh with a very funny story. You have labeled your intention in advance and spoiled the whole effect. The audience knows what is coming and braces itself against it. It puts up its mental guards, saying, "Go ahead and tell your story—we dare you to make us laugh." Or suppose you have a dramatic story filled with pathos and you announce that you are about to say something that will make them cry. Again, you have "called your shot," and you will probably hear snickers before you get to the most pathetic parts. Give the audience no cause to suspect you and hence to say, "Look out, we're about to be tricked!" Mark Antony, in the well-known funeral scene in *Julius Caesar,* begins his speech before an aroused mob thus: "I come to bury Caesar, not to praise him." Had he announced his true intentions he probably would have been torn apart on the spot.

OTHER WAYS TO ENHANCE THE POWER OF SUGGESTION. Many other factors influence the listener's suggestibility and deserve consideration here. Some of them are listed below with a few amplifying comments:

1. Use repetitions and refrains—a common device in nursery rhymes, ballads, choruses of songs, and radio and television commercials.
2. Use simple language. It was effectively used by Marshal Pétain in World War I when he said, "They shall not pass," and by General MacArthur, in World War II, with "I shall return." This is a basic tool in political campaign slogans and commercial advertising.
3. Use glorified testimony. Commercial advertisers use endorsements of

---

[4] Henry Ward Beecher, *Yale Lectures on Preaching,* The Pilgrim Press, 1902, p. 11.

movie stars, athletic heroes, and famous men and women from public life. Speakers may seek good company by quoting Scriptures, passages from popular classical literature, revered documents like the Constitution, and beloved national figures, such as Washington, Franklin, Jefferson, Jackson, and Lincoln.

4. Use imagery for central idea. Examples in political history are: a chicken in every pot, square deal, new deal, fair deal, new frontiers. Examples in speeches: acres of diamonds, cross of gold, happy warrior, the plumed knight.

5. Use timely, well-selected humor. Well-placed and well-chosen humor, especially face-saving humor, breaks up tensions and disarms opposition. It was an effective persuasive weapon of Benjamin Franklin and Abraham Lincoln.

6. Use courtesy, friendliness, and charm—that phase of personal prestige by which the listener develops a liking for the speaker. They enhance the power of suggestion and help keep the listener's mind open.

7. Use delivery reflecting positive attitudes. Delivery interprets and gives emphasis to what is said. It is a potent tool for creating positive moods and impressions. Every gesture and vocal inflection can have the power of suggestion.

PROJECTS AND EXERCISES
For speaking projects see Part Three.

1. Indicate which kind of attention—voluntary, involuntary, or non-voluntary—would arise from the following instances:
   a. Relatives gathered at the opening and reading of a wealthy uncle's will.
   b. A bright flash of lightning followed by a clap of thunder.
   c. The speaker says early in his speech, "I am going to tell you how to make a million dollars."
   d. Your history professor announces at the close of his lecture that there will be a quiz tomorrow on chapter 5.
   e. A teamster cracks his whip over a team of mules. (From the viewpoint of the mules.)
2. Make a list of ten polarizing devices you have observed speakers using in their speeches.
3. Read three speeches from the latest issue of *Vital Speeches*. Decide what is the end or purpose of each of the speeches. What attention factors can you discern in the speeches?
4. Identify and name seven attention and interest factors employed in the illustration which features the 20th Century Limited.

5. Select and analyze on the basis of the five major motivating forces the underlying motivational appeals of ten advertisements in *The Saturday Evening Post*. List the appeals in order of importance if it is clear that more than one is used.
6. What motive or motives are employed by each of the following slogans or statements?
   a. Join the Navy and see the world.
   b. Careless driving is kid stuff.
   c. What would Christmas be without the song, "Silent Night, Holy Night"?
   d. The life you save may be your own.
   e. In God we trust.
   f. Come to the spring formal dance.
   g. Fat people die young.
   h. They went into the Ark two by two.
   i. Ah! You can't take it, can you?
   j. Better a live coward than a dead hero.

TOPICS FOR DISCUSSION

1. Consider the speech purposes as classified early in this chapter:
   a. Which type represents the greatest total volume in your listening experience, including speeches heard in high school and college class rooms?
   b. Which type do you feel has contributed most to your growth and development as a total personality? Which has been most rewarding?
   c. Which type is the most interesting?
   d. Which do you think offers the biggest challenge from the standpoint of the speaker?
2. What is meant by the word *persuasion?* Can you distinguish between persuasion, debate, and argumentation?
3. How important are logical materials in a persuasive speech? Can logic be ignored in a speech to actuate?
4. What use do modern advertisers make of suggestions? Give examples.
5. Do most television advertisements have an attention arouser? If so, what kind of devices are used?
6. Evaluate the following statement: The speaker's ability to hold and maintain attention is not a reliable yardstick by which one should judge or measure his speaking success.

ADDITIONAL READINGS

Baird, A. Craig, and Knower, Franklin H., *Essentials of General Speech,* McGraw-Hill, 1960, chaps. 13–15.

Beardsley, Monroe C., *Thinking Straight,* Prentice-Hall, 1956, pp. 40–142.

Brembeck, Winston Lamont, and Howell, William Smiley, *Persuasion, A Means of Social Control,* Prentice-Hall, 1952, chaps. 14 and 16.

Bryant, Donald C., and Wallace, Karl R., *Fundamentals of Public Speaking,* 3rd ed., Appleton-Century-Crofts, 1960, chaps. 20 and 21.

Ewbank, Henry Lee, and Auer, J. Jeffery, *Discussion and Debate,* Appleton-Century-Crofts, 1951, chap. 14.

Gray, Giles Wilkeson, and Braden, Waldo, *Public Speaking: Principles and Practice,* Harper, 1951, chaps. 3 and 4.

Hutchinson, Eliot D., *How to Think Creatively,* Abingdon, 1949.

McBurney, James H., and Wrage, Ernest J., *The Art of Good Speech,* Prentice-Hall, 1953, chaps. 13–16.

Monroe, Alan H., *Principles and Types of Speech,* 4th ed., Scott, Foresman, 1955, chaps. 20–22, 27.

Oliver, Robert T., *The Psychology of Persuasive Speech,* Longmans, Green, 1957, chaps. 6–8.

Sarett, Lew, Foster, William Trufant, and Sarett, Alma Johnson, *Basic Principles of Speech,* 3rd ed., Houghton-Mifflin, 1958, chap. 3.

Smith, Raymond G., *Principles of Public Speaking,* Ronald, 1958, chap. 12.

ஐ 7 ஐ
Developing an Idea

Plants and animals are made up of one or more cells, each a compartment of the living organism. The basic cell from which a speech derives its essential life is called a point and represents a fragment or part of a whole. Essentially, the point is an idea that blends with or supports the central thought and purpose of the completed speech. Although it is possible for a speech to make only a single point, that is not the usual situation, and we shall therefore deal with the selection and treatment of an idea or point as if it were a segment or piece of a whole.

The matter of supporting, developing, and displaying an idea, or making a point, is the crux of speech craftsmanship. Here, where the central thought springs into being, the speech gets its life and texture. For reaching and penetrating the listener's mind is almost wholly dependent upon the manner in which points are developed and related to the central theme and purpose of the speech.

You get your best results as a speaker if you have a definite goal in mind for every point you make—a particular goal at a particular spot to fit a particular place in your speech. We are not at the moment concerned with the over-all objective of your speech, but rather with the specific craftsmanship which applies to a particular point and purpose.

There are three types of questions to ask yourself about listener

155

response with respect to a specific point: (1) Are you primarily concerned with the listener's understanding, enlightenment, and insight? In other words, do you want him to have a clear mental grasp of the point you are trying to get across? (2) Or are you primarily concerned with the listener's accepting and believing your point on the basis of rational and logical processes? This implies that you are ready and willing for the listener to test the validity of your facts, your logic, and your conclusions. (3) Or are you primarily concerned about interesting, stimulating, exciting, or motivating the listener? Do you want to impress him so strongly that he will long remember what you say, that he will be emotionally aroused to do something you want him to do?

These three questions are oriented around three major goals: (1) *Clarity,* an idea that is clear and easy to grasp; (2) *Logical adequacy,* an idea that is trustworthy and believable; (3) *Stimulation and motivation,* an idea that is interesting, impressive, appealing, or has persuasive impact. These goals are not necessarily independent of one another. Two, or even all three, goals may in some instances and in some measure be combined. But the speaker must first sharply focus his mind on his selected goal and then strive to achieve the other two as best he can. This will give added richness to the total substance.

GOAL ONE—CLARITY

Clarity is of course important in any speech, but it is of primary urgency in speeches of demonstration, instruction, factual reporting, and information. Narration, description, and exposition—the characteristic forms of discourse—must be so clear that they are readily grasped. The methods of gaining clarity are discussed below: (1) definition and explanation, (2) illustration, (3) comparison and contrast, (4) division and classification, (5) making the abstract concrete, (6) use of objects, graphs, and visual aids, (7) elements of specificness.

Define and Explain

We can clarify a point or a concept by definition, description, amplification, illustration, or elucidation. By these same means we can rectify false impressions and throw light on facts, incidents, happenings, and complicated procedures and processes.

Too often we fail to understand each other simply because we fail to explain or define what we mean by the words we use. In private conversation and informal discussion we are often asked, "What do you mean by that?" In a speaking situation where the listener has little or no chance to check what the speaker means, definition of key terms is very important, sometimes crucial—particularly when words used by the speaker have a special meaning. When we define, we set up boundaries to confine the concepts about the term within a limited area. We not only narrow the field we are viewing but also throw more light on it, thus cutting down mental confusion.

Definitions represent an attempt to make meaning clear or clearer, but they cannot always be completely definitive. Abstract thought and matters concerning theories, laws, and principles are more difficult to explain than anything concrete. Thus many common but indispensable terms such as *liberty, love, democracy, communism, socialism, success, education, God,* and hundreds of words like these often cause the worst kind of communication entanglements. Words like *apple* or *fish,* and even most technical terms, are far easier to define and explain.

Below are specific ways of revealing the meaning of a word or phrase.

Define by authority. Let the expert, the one who knows most about the term in question, explain what it means. Let Albert Einstein give us the meaning of the theory of relativity, John Dewey the meaning of reflective thinking, and General Omar Bradley the meaning of logistics.

Define by negation. Show in other words, what a term does not mean. Robert Hutchins, former president of the University of Chicago, tells us that a "university is not a kindergarten, it is not a club, it is not a reform school, it is not a political club, it is not an agency of propaganda. A university is a community of scholars."

Define by etomology. Show the origin or derivation of the word; indicate the primitive form or root upon which it is based. For instance, *transcend* comes from the Latin *transcendĕre,* to climb over to surpass.

Define by synonyms and antonyms. Although no two words have identical meanings, they do have similar meanings called synonyms. We define *competition* as *rivalry, work* as *labor, demolish* as *destroy.* Antonyms are words with opposite meanings. Thus *smart* is the opposite of *stupid, weak* the opposite of *strong, cowardice* the opposite of *bravery.*

Define by example. When we say, "Here is an example of what I mean," we try to translate meaning by presenting a concrete example which clarifies the thought. Note how *kilowatt-hour* is defined in this passage: "Kilowatt-hour (kwh). A kilowatt-hour is a unit by which electric energy is measured, just as the bushel is the unit for measuring wheat and corn, the gallon the unit for measuring gasoline, and the pound the unit for measuring butter. It represents one hour's use of one kilowatt of power. For example, one 50-watt light burning for 20 hours will use 1 kilowatt-hour of electricity. 1,000 watts is one kilowatt. 746 watts is one horsepower."[1]

Define and clarify by diagram or chart. Sometimes a diagram is the best way to clarify a concept. Observe how the following diagram gives a simple picture of the organization of Air Force operations:[2]

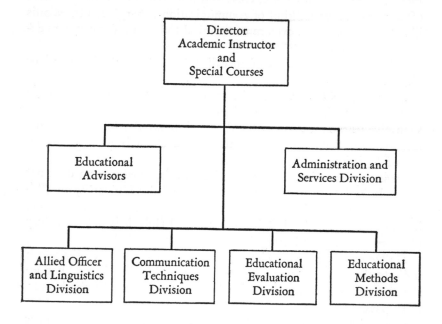

[1] E. C. Buehler, *Should the Government Own and Operate Electric Utilities?*, Noble and Noble, 1936, p. 29.

[2] We are indebted to the *Academic Instructor Course Curriculum*, 1959, Air Command and Staff College, Air University, Maxwell Air Force Base, Maxwell, Ala., p. ix, for this diagram.

Illustrate

Man has no doubt illustrated his ideas since he first learned to speak; the value of an illustration for making ideas clear is immeasurable. We have all been influenced by illustrative stories we heard in grade school and from our parents. Fairy tales, fables, and parables are effective tools for developing an idea; for instance, Jesus explained the idea of who is your neighbor by means of a parable.

"And who is my neighbor?" Jesus replied, "A man was going down from Jerusalem to Jericho, and he fell among robbers, who stripped him and beat him, and departed, leaving him half-dead. Now by chance a priest was going down that road, and when he saw him he passed by on the other side. So likewise a Levite, when he came to the place and saw him, passed by on the other side. But a Samaritan, as he journeyed, came to where he was, and when he saw him, he had compassion, and went to him and bound up his wounds, pouring on oil and wine, then he set him on his own beast and brought him to an inn, and took care of him. And the next day he took out two denarii and gave them to the innkeeper, saying, 'Take care of him, and whatever more you spend, I will repay you when I come back.' Which of these three, do you think, proved neighbor to the man who fell among the robbers?"

Compare and Contrast

Comparison and contrast mean setting two objects, ideas, events, or concepts side by side or one against the other. We are all familiar with the advertiser's trick of showing the difference between old and new, before and after—with movies and television westerns that contrast the hero and the villain, the bully and the timid soul. Thomas W. Phelps explained the problem of buying common stocks with this use of contrast: "When you play football you belong to one team and you stay on that team until the end of the game, win, lose or draw. But when you go into the stock market your sole object is to decide in advance which side is going to win, and to join that side. If any time thereafter you think the other side is going to win you change sides as fast as you can. The object is to be on the winning side as much of the time as you possibly can."[3]

[3] Given before the Bond Club of Buffalo, N.Y., January 28, 1948, in *Vital Speeches*, May 1, 1948, p. 430.

Note how Stuart Chase clarifies the principle of soil erosion by an apt illustration containing the element of comparison:

Here is a sloping cellar door. Take a watering can and sprinkle a quart of water on the top of the door. Measure the amount which slides off. Except for a little evaporation, the whole quart will be at the bottom, and it gets there almost instantly. Now tack a piece of thick carpet on the door; to cement it on would be still better. Fill the can and pour a quart of water on the carpet. Your measuring trough at the bottom will be lucky if it receives the merest trickle at the beginning. Observe that the trickle continues for a long time as the water slowly filters through the mat.

This is the story of water erosion in its simplest form. The cellar door is any land with a slope; the canful of water is rainfall; the bare boards are bare fields, or fields cultivated between the crop rows with the rows running down the slope; the carpet is a natural cover, either grass or forest. In the first case, most of the water comes down, dissolving the topsoil and taking it along. In the second case, the cover absorbs the water, puts much of it into ground storage to be slowly released over periods of scanty rainfall. Almost no soil comes down.[4]

Divide and Classify

This is an age-old device of sorting out ideas and arranging them in separate piles or categories, so that the mind can pay attention to one division at a time. The method helps us to remember the three branches of our government, Moses and the Ten Commandments, and Shakespeare and the Seven Ages of Man. It also is the basis for arranging the processes of speech-making into the Six Dimensions with which this text is concerned.

Suppose you are making a speech about democracy. You will have made a start toward clarity by dividing your speech into three divisions—namely, political democracy, economic democracy, and social democracy. During World War II there was much talk about the various fronts. The total war effort became clear to the average citizen when the United States Bureau of Information, through its press releases, spoke of the four fronts—the military front, the economic front, the political front, and the home or psychological front. Note how a college student bases an approach to the subject of racial differences between Negro and white children upon five considerations: "Much has been written on racial differences from many angles, in-

---

[4] Stuart Chase, *Rich Land Poor Land: A Study of Waste in Natural Resources of America*, Whittlesey House, 1936, p. 83.

cluding anthropology and sociology. I will base my discussion upon five differences which seem to be uppermost in the minds of white parents everywhere. These are health, home environment, marital standards, crime, and intellectual capacity."

Transform the Abstract into the Concrete

The average listener finds it difficult to pay attention to abstract thought, no matter how noble it may be. The abstract is vague, but the concrete is vivid and appeals to the senses. Death is abstract; "dead cat" is concrete. Cold is abstract; frost-bitten ears concrete. Beauty is abstract, but a beautiful rose is concrete. A vivid, concrete image of the Southern soldier is dramatically portrayed by Henry W. Grady in the following excerpt from his famous speech, "The New South."

Dr. Talmage has drawn for you, with a master's hand, the picture of your returning armies. He has told you how, in the pomp and circumstance of war, they came back to you, marching with proud and victorious tread, reading their glory in a nation's eyes! Will you bear with me while I tell you of another army that sought its home at the close of the late war—an army that marched home in defeat and not in victory—in pathos and not in splendor, but in glory that equaled yours, and to hearts as loving as ever welcomed heroes home. Let me picture to you the footsore Confederate soldier, as, buttoning up his faded gray jacket, the parole which was to bear testimony to his children of his fidelity and faith, he turned his face southward from Appomattox in April, 1865. Think of him as ragged, half-starved, heavy-hearted, enfeebled by want and wounds; having fought to exhaustion, he surrenders his gun, wrings the hands of his comrades in silence, and lifting his tear-stained and pallid face for the last time to the graves that dot the old Virginia hills, pulls his gray cap over his brow and begins the slow and painful journey.[5]

Use Objects and Visual Aids

There is an old Chinese proverb about one picture being worth ten thousand words. Many psychologists tell us that learning is usually easier through the eyes than the ears, that visual images are remembered longer than auditory ones. Studies by H. E. Nelson and A. W. Vandermeer show that film instructions supplementary to

[5] Henry W. Grady, "The New South," delivered at 81st Anniversary of the New England Society, December 22, 1886, in James Milton O'Neill (ed.), *Models of Speech Composition*, New York Century, 1921, pp. 579–580.

lecture materials are more effective than lecture alone. They conclude: "The proportion of learning that is attributable solely to listening to the commentary is significantly smaller than that which is attributable to viewing the film with both picture and sound."[6] We learn best, in other words, when seeing and hearing are combined at the same time.

The main purpose of visual aids, and the one with which we are now concerned, is to provide clarity. But they also serve as effective interest and attention devices, enhance the listener's memory, and often help the speaker to relax and control his tensions. There are many types of visual aids: pictures, graphs, maps, charts, objects, and mechanical devices; live models such as people, animals, insects, and reptiles; and printed hand-out materials. Fairs, exhibitions, and tours are types of visual aids.

How to use objects and visual supports in the speech of demonstration is discussed later, on page 352; we shall limit our attention here to charts and graphs as aids to clarity. The four most common graphs are the pie or circle graph, the picture graph, the lined or curved graph, and the bar graph. Examples of these are shown in Figures 1 through 4.

The following suggestions should help to make your graphs more useful:

1. Keep the graphs as agents of communication while you talk. What they have to say should blend with what you have to say—the graphs should help you and you should help the graphs. When you have finished with the ideas related to them, and have more material to cover, remove the graphs; otherwise, they become counterattractions and stand as your silent competitors in communication.
2. Each graph should have one simple, easy-to-grasp idea. Don't crowd too much on one graph or give the impression that the materials are cluttered.
3. Be sure the graphs are large enough for all to see and that all essential matter is legible to everyone in the audience.
4. Keep your audience in your line of vision. Refer to your charts with eye glances as necessary but be careful not to pin your eyes upon your visual aids in such a fixed manner that the audience gets the impression you are talking more to the charts than to the group.

[6] "The Relative Effectiveness of Several Different Sound Tracks Used on an Animated Film on Elementary Meteorology," *Speech Monographs*, 20, no. 4 (November, 1953), 267.

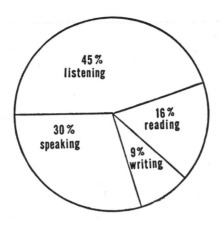

FIG. 1. Pie Graph of Communication During the Waking Day (research by Paul Rankin, "Listening Ability," *Chicago Schools Journal*, January, 1930, 177–179).

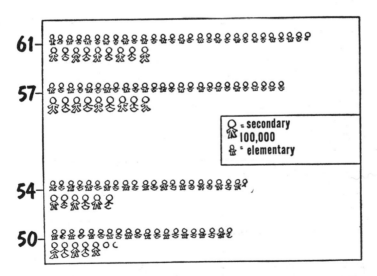

FIG. 2. Picture Graph of Students Attending Public School, 1950–1961 (based on facts and figures from *National Education Association Research Bulletin*, October, 1959, 74–77).

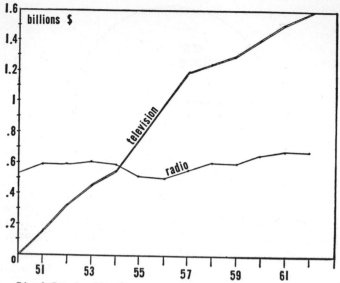

FIG. 3. Lined Graph of Radio and Television Advertising (based on a graph from *The Wall Street Journal*, April 24, 1961, p. 1).

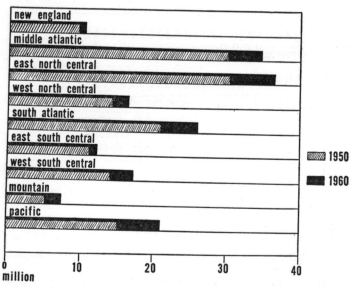

FIG. 4. Bar Graph of United States Population Trends (based on a graph from *The Wall Street Journal*, April 17, 1961, p. 1).

Be Specific

Modern newspaper reporters are schooled to stress the specific. Science closely observes all details and pays the strictest attention to specificity. This is the secret of modern crime detection, too, for criminals are caught by fingerprints, loops in their handwriting, and dust specks on their shoes. Note the clarity Dr. Menninger achieved in the following passage by his specific instances:

Accident proneness got to be a widely used term some years ago. It was noted that some people seemed to have more than their share of accidents. Here is a clipping about a Californian who spent every tenth birthday during the past fifty years recovering from some major injury suffered in accidents happening on or just before the anniversary. Here is the record: 1890—badly crushed right hand; in 1900 lost a leg in a train wreck; in 1910 hospitalized for five weeks due to an explosion; in 1920, he got into a fight, got knocked out, had the other leg amputated. On his 50th birthday he was arranging a deal in his print shop, and while he was handing a pen to the customer to sign the contract, the pen dropped. He stooped to reach for it, missed, and caught his hand in the printing press

. . . . .

But, even the healthy-minded person can become a little unhealthy-minded from all sorts of things—weariness, fatigue, a series of disappointments. There isn't one of us who hasn't had days when we have thought—"One more thing and I'll bust, or bust somebody!"

I recall the case of a father who was going to take his family on a little outing. Everything was going happily. He went out to pack the car and discovered a flat tire. He groaned, but he fixed it. While doing so, he hit his finger with a wrench and got a badly bruised hand. He came in the house, quite upset and mad. He went to put a bandage on his hand—knocked over a table which crashed into some china. This series of minor catastrophes struck one of the children as amusing, as well it might, and the little daughter laughed. This was the last straw. Without a word to any of them, he went to the basement and hanged himself.

This is a true story. Another father might have struck the child, and then felt guilty all day. Still another might have been mentally healthy enough to have joined his daughter in the laugh. But there is a limit to everybody's absorption powers.[7]

[7] Karl Menninger, "Mental Attitudes and Safety," *Vital Speeches*, March 1, 1959, pp. 312–313.

GOAL TWO—LOGICAL ADEQUACY

All speech points should have an adequate logical basis. In the development of some points, of course, psychological factors will be heavily stressed. But if a speaker wants to make a point especially trustworthy, to satisfy the listener's intellect more than his desires and emotions, the premium is upon clear, straight thinking and evidence, with a maximum degree of personal detachment.

The principal methods for gaining logical adequacy are the following: (1) statistical evidence, (2) analogy, (3) specific instances, (4) expert authority, (5) causal relationship, (6) inductive and deductive reasoning.

Statistical Evidence

It is often said that statistics are dull, but this is true only when they remain isolated and unrelated to something. Actually, facts and statistics are an exciting and important phase of living in our complex society. Almost every action or policy in commerce, government, the armed services, science, and social welfare rests to a considerable extent upon statistics. Certain statistics are reported by the year, quarter, month, or day—even by the hour, on the New York Stock Exchange. Buy insurance, open a bank account, get married, have children, and you come face to face with statistics.

Although statistical material is a common mode of proof, several tests should be applied to its use.

1. What is meant by the key words used to describe a unit tabulated? In other words, what is meant by six million *unemployed?* Who is an unemployed person? Words like *juvenile delinquency, criminals, drunkenness, amateur athletics,* and many others used in connection with statistics need definition.

2. Are cited facts taken from competent sources? That is, is the person, institution, or organization supplying the data likely to represent an unbiased source of information? Or is the compiler a promoter? Does he have an "axe to grind"?

3. Are the statistics cited relevant to the point to be proved? Suppose a speaker cites figures indicating that in a given year the incidence of sickness among 500,000 civilians is twice as great as among 500,000 men in the Armed Services and concludes it is

healthier to be a soldier than a civilian? Such a comparison is not valid because the healthy and physically fit make up the Army population, whereas civilian life includes all Army rejects, the aged, and the physically unfit.

4. Do the statistics cover sufficient cases and length of time? Data covering corn production for only one year, or coal production from only one mine for a period of two months, or the batting average of a ball player for thirty days are too limited and unrepresentative to permit drawing sound conclusions.

5. Is the data based upon typical units of the whole group? During the political campaign of 1936, when Alf Landon was the Republican candidate for president and Franklin Roosevelt headed the Democratic ticket, the *Literary Digest* conducted a nation-wide poll covering more than a million would-be voters, upon the results of which it confidently predicted a sweeping Republican victory. Instead, the Democrats emerged with their greatest landslide in history. The *Digest* poll failed to include a representative share of typical voters. Its samples were limited to names found in telephone directories, but during the severe economic depression of the 1930's the heavy Democratic support came largely from people who didn't have a telephone because they couldn't afford one.

Statistical evidence represents only one mode of proof. Although in many instances it provides the speaker with his strongest means of support, it should not be overused. Facts should be carefully selected to fit a specific disputed point. Remember, it is not the isolated fact that counts, but the way we use it and make it serve as an agent of proof.

Analogy

There are two kinds of analogy, literal and figurative. The former is used as a case in point and an element of proof in an argument; the latter serves to clarify an idea or make it more impressive and is often a short cut to understanding a point in question. The *literal analogy* draws comparisons between objects, things, principles, happenings, and concepts which—in their essentials—are similar. For instance, a student argues for a unicameral form of legislature for his state and cites Nebraska as a successful example. He carefully demonstrates that the conditions in his state are similar to those of Nebraska and that a unicameral legislature should therefore prove successful in his state. Or he may argue for government-controlled radio and cite the British Broadcasting Corporation as an analogous example. Patrick Henry, in the debate on the adoption of the Federal Constitution, argued from analogy to prove that the American colonies did not need a strong central government:

The history of Switzerland clearly proves that we might be in amicable alliance with those states without adopting this Constitution. Switzerland is a confederacy, consisting of dissimilar governments. This is an example which proves that governments of dissimilar structures may be confederated. That confederate republic has stood upwards of four hundred years; and, although several of the individual republics are democratic, and the rest aristocratic, no evil has resulted from this dissimilarity; for they have braved all the power of France and Germany during that long period.[8]

In using literal analogies, it is important to keep in mind that there must be no important differences between the factors compared. True, we cannot expect the cases to be identical, but what differences there are must have no significance to the point under discussion.

The *figurative analogy* is a hypothetical illustration based on metaphor. It cannot be classified as evidence, since it is fictitious. It can be used to clarify a point and to make it seem realistic. Figurative analogy was used effectively by Willy Brandt, Mayor of Berlin, in this manner: "Regardless of which side of the Atlantic we live on, we are all sitting in the same boat. We should constantly check our course and our stroke. We must adjust to every weather and every rise of the waves. If the wind is against us, we shall have to tack, but we must also know that anyone is lost who leaves the boat. Alone no one can reach the shore for which we are headed."[9]

Specific Instances

Much of our reasoning is by example. We develop an idea and support it by citing specific instances which demonstrate our point. We may argue, for example, that the quarter system has certain inherent advantages over the semester system by pointing to several universities which have found this to be true. Or we may argue that foreign governmental officials resent direct American economic aid and then

[8] Ernest J. Wrage and Barnet Baskerville (eds.), *American Forum*, Harper, 1960, p. 20.

[9] Willy Brandt, "Gabriel Silver Lecture," delivered at Columbia University, March 17, 1961, in *Vital Speeches*, April 1, 1961, pp. 381–384.

quote several important foreign leaders to this effect. Specific instances are a fast, efficient way of supporting a point.

Expert Authority

The speech situation makes use of three kinds of opinion: that of the speaker, the listener, and authorities quoted or referred to in the speech. Where the speaker's mission is to make what he says believable and acceptable to the judicious listener, expert testimony plays an important role. It is a common tool of the college debater and the courtroom lawyer. It has the advantage of forcing the opposition to attack the ideas of the expert instead of the speaker. The completely perfect expert, however, probably does not exist, and we must therefore seek the best authority possible.

The worthiness of an authority may be tested by asking the following questions: (1) Is the authority free from prejudice, or does he seek some personal gain or benefit from his testimony? (2) Is he a specialist, a qualified expert in the field in which he is quoted? (3) Is he in a position to know all the essential facts? That is, has he had the opportunity to obtain the necessary knowledge and insight affecting the matter on which he is quoted? (4) Is his testimony likely to be accepted by listeners who have an open mind? In other words, will the audience look upon him with a feeling of trust and respect?

In the following example a member of the Supreme Court quotes another member to support his point: "Free and honest elections are the very foundation of our republican form of government. Hence any attempt to defile the sanctity of the ballot can not be viewed with equanimity. As stated by Mr. Justice Miller in Ex Parte Yarborough, 110 U.S. 651, 666, 'the temptations to control these elections by violence and corruption have been a constant source of danger in the history of all republics.' "[10]

Spruille Braden, in a speech on nonintervention, used a quotation from the Secretary of State to support his contention.

Secretary of State Acheson, on July 4th of this year, declared before the Brazilian Chamber of Deputies that: "The essence of the inter-American system is collective responsibility plus *absolute non-intervention* in the affairs of other states. The United States intends *to abide* by both the

[10] Justice Douglas, "Supreme Court Address," U.S. Supreme Court, 1940, in Jasper Berry Shannon, *Toward a New Politics in the South,* University of Tennessee Press, 1949, p. 35.

letter and the *spirit* of these inter-American commitments." This appears to be a concise and categorical enunciation of a noble and humane policy. It is in keeping with our inter-American, United Nations and other obligations.[11]

Causal Relationship

Nothing in this world, we are told, exists purely by chance—there is a cause for every effect. The establishing of causal relationships is one of our most common and widely used reasoning devices. History, social science, medicine, geology, and many other fields are essentially oriented to facts and happenings and their consequences. *Why* is the key word. Why the economic recession? Why the crime wave? What caused the disease? What was the motive for the murder? Why can't Johnny read? What caused the accident or fire? Why did John lose or Jim win the election? And so on, ad infinitum.

The two basic types of causal reasoning are from cause to effect and from effect to cause. By nature they are based on similar assumptions: that the same cause will produce the same effect and that the same effect will result from the same cause. The difference lies in time relationship: when we look for the cause, we look backward; when we seek the effect, we look forward. One concerns what probably has happened, the other what probably will happen.

EFFECT TO CAUSE. We must be mindful of one outstanding characteristic in the matter of causal relationship: namely, its complexity. For any given effect there are usually many causes—some major, some minor, some barely contributory—acting on one another in the manner of a chain reaction. Another characteristic to keep in mind is that causal investigation is a probing tool; ultimate cause must often remain undiscovered.

Note how tricky the thought operation is as you figure out why you are a college student. Can you tell us in one single sentence why you are in college? Probably not. Your list of reasons may include many of the following:

1. My parents wanted me to go to college.
2. I didn't know what else to do.
3. I wanted to be a doctor or a lawyer, and one needs a college degree for this.

[11] Spruille Braden, "Non-intervention," delivered in Chicago, October 13, 1952, *Vital Speeches,* December 1, 1952, p. 102.

4. Education is something no one can take away from you.
5. I wanted to have a good time for four years.
6. I wanted to get married and felt here is a good place to look for a mate.
7. I was intellectually curious; I wanted to know more.
8. I wanted the prestige of a college degree.
9. I can't get a good job without a college education.
10. All of my friends are going to college.

The above examples illustrate how complicated the evidence may become when we say, "because." Our goal should be to put a finger on the cause which contributes most to produce the effect; our search is for the strongest and most probable cause. We can best test this process by asking two questions: (1) *Is the alleged cause adequate to produce the effect?* If the cause is merely a possible one, the argument is weak. If the cause is highly probable, the argument is much stronger but still not conclusive. It is difficult to find an absolute cause to make an argument conclusive. Suppose an apple falls from the tree and you reason that it was caused by the law of gravity. The gravity pull would be sufficient to produce the effect. But this is only a link in the chain of reasoning. What conditioned the apple so it would become detached from the tree? Was it ripe, was it loosened by the wind, or did someone shake the tree? In human affairs such as politics, wars, economics, social conditions, causal relationship becomes far more complicated than this. There may be a score or more causes for a war: an economic depression, a political occurrence, and so on.

A weakness in effective causal argument may be shown by establishing a more probable cause than the one cited. The second way, therefore, to test effect to cause reasoning is to ask, (2) *Could other causes produce the known effect?* Suppose you reason that the New York Yankees won the American League pennant because the team had Roger Maris, who led the league in home runs and in runs batted in. Another speaker might say the Yankees won because they had superior pitching and reserve bench strength, which is a stronger cause than the batting power of just one player. The soundness of the argument from effect to cause rests largely upon the probability that no other causes could have produced the alleged effect. When there are many causes, we should be careful not to omit a cause greater than the one singled out as principal.

Arturo Frondizi, in a Washington speech, made this statement based on effects to cause reasoning: "The American Continent is a community of nations united by geographical facts, by history and by a spiritual identity. Precisely because they believe that the destiny of man is a spiritual destiny, the peoples of this Hemisphere belong, from the historical viewpoint, to the cultural world of the West, where the principles of human dignity and universal brotherhood were born."[12]

CAUSE TO EFFECT.   In a sense, we become prophets when we reason from cause to effect. We start with a condition or circumstance and try to establish a probable outcome. Suppose the country is in a mild economic recession and we argue the federal government should do something about it. We recommend a program of establishing public works in depressed areas, lowering income taxes, speeding up road construction, lowering interest rates for home builders, and a number of other things. Our support for these measures is based on the argument that they will have the effect of improving our economy.

The following tests are applicable to this form of reasoning: (1) *Is the cause sufficient to produce the alleged effect?* Many approaches, for example, can be used to slow down a trend toward inflation. The government may enact more stringent laws to control labor unions, but whether this measure will be sufficient actually to slow down an inflationary trend may be disputable. (2) *Is the cause prevented from producing the alleged effect?* The problem of farm surpluses has long plagued the federal government. In the 1950's the soil bank plan was devised as a sure method of controlling the supply of grain produced. The farmer would be paid for taking 20 percent of his land out of production. It was assumed that acreage reduction would reduce grain production. The plan was not successful, however, for two reasons: first, the farmer tended to set aside 20 percent of his poorest land; and second, he heavily fertilized the balance, and raised more in total than ever before.

Note how Marvin McLain, in a speech delivered at the National Council of Farmer Cooperatives, used cause to effect argument to good advantage in opposing farm price supports: "When price supports are set at uneconomic levels, uneconomic consequences are certain to follow. Artificially high supports are a stimulus for farmers

---

[12] Arturo Frondizi, "The Miracle of America," delivered in Washington, D.C., January 21, 1959, *Vital Speeches,* February 1, 1959, p. 230.

to push the possible gains from research improvements too soon and too far. They are an assurance under which the farmer is encouraged to pour more capital investment and attention into the production of crops which may already be in surplus."[13]

Inductive and Deductive Reasoning

Factual evidence alone is often easy to find, but serious reasoning is required to use it in reaching sound conclusions. In inductive reasoning, thinking proceeds from the particular to the general. In deductive reasoning, the thinking process leads from the general to the particular. An American visitor, traveling in England, notices he is served orange marmalade at breakfast in London, again in Manchester and Liverpool, and concludes the English always have marmalade for breakfast. This is inductive reasoning—from specific instances a conclusion is reached. The deductive process is the reverse. Our tourist has generalized that English restaurants serve marmalade for breakfast; if he is to eat breakfast in Leeds he now assumes that he will be served marmalade.

INDUCTION. Inductive reasoning is in a limited sense a form of scientific investigation. It is a process of collecting, examining, analyzing, and interpreting specific facts and instances in an effort to establish a general rule, law, or condition. In the "perfect" induction, the conclusion is based on thoroughly established facts: water freezes at 32 degrees Fahrenheit and boils at 212 degrees; the earth revolves on its axis; ocean tides are at regular intervals. These are conclusions based on well-tested experience. The "imperfect" induction, in which the facts are less thoroughly established, concerns the speaker most. It attempts to establish the greatest probability that something is true. The pattern of reasoning in both kinds of induction, commonly known as *generalization,* is widely used in medical science, in all kinds of laboratory experimentation, in estimating risks in casualty, health, and life insurance, and countless other human undertakings.

The validity of a generalization may be tested by asking four questions about it: (1) *Have enough specimens been examined to warrant the conclusion?* A visitor to your speech class notices that four girls in the class are wearing white bobby socks and concludes that all girls in your class wear bobby socks. This is a *hasty generalization.*

13 *Vital Speeches,* February 15, 1959, p. 279.

The unobserved part of the total group is too large to warrant such a conclusion. (2) *Are the specimens fair samples of the total group?* If you collect a dozen or more snowflakes upon a cold mirror, you may have fair specimens of the kind. But if you buy a basket of peaches and inspect only the nice ones on top, concluding that the entire basket is the same, you may have generalized falsely. The few specimens you examined are not necessarily typical of the class. (3) *Are there exceptions to the rule?* The mind of the scientist is always looking for exceptions to the rule. It is the exception which may cause serious trouble for the researcher who seeks final proof for his hypothesis. The white whale, the black sheep, the red ear of corn, and the barkless dog are all exceptions to the rule. We should extend our investigation beyond the limited area upon which the generalization is based in search of possible exceptions. (4) *Does the conclusion from generalization check with other known existing facts and information?* A generalization must be consistent with the laws of causation. A savage who contracts poison ivy infection from a vine without suspecting the real cause of his affliction may generalize that he is suffering because he has displeased the gods. He must, therefore, fast and pray more that his heart be pure and his body whole. His conclusion does not reconcile itself with the known fact of poison ivy infection.

DEDUCTION. Deduction is based upon syllogistic reasoning. The syllogism is not an end in itself but a device for orderly reasoning and the testing of logical relationships. The three main types are (1) categorical, (2) conditional or hypothetical, (3) alternative or disjunctive.

The *categorical syllogism* consists of two premises and a conclusion. The premises set forth an unqualified principle or law. If the principle is not universally distributed, then the best we can do is draw "probable" conclusions; no positive deduction can be made. The minor premise, in order to form a valid deduction, must either affirm the subject of the major premise or deny the predicate. And if one of the premises is negative, then the conclusion must be negative also. The two syllogisms below serve as examples:

Major premise 1. All professional ball players play for money.
Minor premise 2. John is a professional ball player.
Conclusion 3. Therefore, John plays for money.

Major premise   1. All professional ball players play for money.
Minor premise   2. John does not play baseball for money.
Conclusion   3. Therefore, John is not a professional ball player.

It is difficult to establish many universals, especially on the basis of the topics of most speeches. The speaker commonly deals with probable truths; hence we say he tries to establish a high degree of probability. Furthermore, people rarely talk in formal syllogisms. The *rhetorical syllogism,* as an alternative possibility, serves to present deductions in other than strictly syllogistic style. As a rule, it omits one of the three statements. The speaker presents a probable truth to the audience, and the rhetorical syllogism is completed if the listeners make the proper inference.

The *hypothetical syllogism* presents a condition determined by the word *if.* If one contention is true, then another contention follows. If we get more rain, the river will overflow. If Congress raises taxes, industry will stop producing. In these instances, the major premise— the antecedent "if" clause—sets up a condition. Suppose you say, "If the sun shines today, we shall pick flowers." The phrase "if the sun shines today" is the antecedent; "we shall pick flowers" is the consequence.

Major premise   1. If we get more rain, the river will overflow.
Minor premise   2. It is raining.
Conclusion   3. Therefore, the river will overflow.

A valid hypothetical syllogism can also be constructed by denying the consequence, such as:

Major premise   1. If we get more rain, the river will overflow.
Minor premise   2. The river is not overflowing.
Conclusion   3. Therefore, we have not gotten more rain.

In the *disjunctive syllogism* the qualifying words *either, or* occur and offer a choice of possibilities. The major premise introduces the possible choices, one of which the minor premise negates or affirms. The conclusion is determined by the process of elimination.

Major premise   1. The man is either married or single.
Minor premise   2. He is not married.
Conclusion   3. Therefore, he is single.

or

Major premise	1. The man is either married or single.
Minor premise	2. He is not single.
Conclusion	3. Therefore, he is married.

GOAL THREE—STIMULATING AND MOTIVATING

This goal covers a broad area and concerns making a point impressive, emotional, entertaining, stimulating, or motivational. The method of proof in such cases is more psychological than logical. The speaker goes beyond fact and logic to make the ordinary appear extraordinary, the casual exciting, the dull interesting, the neutral colorful. His ability to attain this goal depends in large measure upon his creative imagination, his originality, his sensitivity to human values, and his emotional balance. Those who strive to win success by means of this goal should take caution, however, not to sacrifice naturalness, sincerity, integrity, and similar virtues for the sake of the sensational. The dramatic must never be overdone; good taste and a sense of propriety must govern the temptation to exploit human sentiments and feelings. The methods for making an idea appealing and motivational are discussed in the remaining pages of this chapter.

Glorified Testimony

Statements and opinions from popular heroes, both living and dead, usually have a benign effect upon the listener. Such testimony falls in two broad classifications: First, there are those persons we respect because of their position or their power, such as prime ministers, kings, queens, and presidents. The second group includes other persons of the past for whom we have a feeling of reverence or at least high esteem, such as Thomas Jefferson, Daniel Webster, Walt Whitman, Thomas Edison, Henry Ford, Frank Lloyd Wright, Henry Ward Beecher, and hundreds more. These may come from many fields—science, art, literature, politics, religion, and so forth. This halo type of authority may extend beyond personalities and include documents and institutions such as the Constitution of the United States and the International Red Cross. Advertisers today make extensive use of glorified testimony. Popular figures endorse all kinds of cigarettes, and much is presented in the name of "science." The speaker who employs personal testimony should exercise discretion.

Dramatic Narration and Description

The dramatic story is one of the most effective devices for sharpening listener interest and making the point memorable. Note the penetrating effect gained in the following dramatic narrative:

When the picture [Wild Strawberries] opens, it is on the eve of his departure for the University from which he once graduated, and where he is now to receive an honorary degree for his long years of service. He goes to bed and dreams. He dreams that he arises and walks out into the streets of his native city. All is deserted, there is no sound, save the clap, clap of a shutter upon a window. He can see no one. He turns his head and looks up at the town clock. The hands are gone. He looks at his watch, there are no hands. Of course symbolism lends itself to many interpretations, but in this case, the symbolism that Bergman is speaking of is that of a man who does not know what time it is, and a man who symbolized a world that does not know what time it is. All of the machinery is moving, the springs and wheels are awhir, but there is no direction. There is the condition of modern man. Much activity, little direction.[14]

Appeal to Basic Human Motives

The deep longings of the human heart come into play in almost any persuasive speech that you may read or hear. Patrick Henry, in his "Call to Arms" speech, appealed to personal liberty. Winston Churchill, in many of his wartime rallying speeches, appealed to both personal liberty and the motive of self-preservation. Franklin D. Roosevelt, in his "Four Freedoms" speech, appealed to self-importance, religion, self-preservation, and national security. President John Kennedy, in his inaugural address, January 20, 1961, pointed to liberty in one paragraph and to self-preservation in another.

Let every nation know, whether it wish us well or ill, that we shall pay any price, bear any burden, meet any hardship, support any friend, oppose any foe to assure the survival and the success of liberty. . . .

Now the trumpet summons us again—not as a call to bear arms, though arms we need—not as a call to battle, though embattled we are—but a call to bear the burden of a long twilight struggle year in and year out, "rejoicing in hope, patient in tribulation"—a struggle against the common enemies of man: tyranny, poverty, disease and war itself.[15]

[14] John P. Leary, as delivered to students and faculty of North Montana State College, Havre, Montana, February 21, 1961, in *Vital Speeches,* April 1, 1961, p. 359.

[15] "For the Freedom of Man," *Vital Speeches,* February 1, 1961, pp. 226–227.

The speaker's appeal may be to many different motives: curiosity, fear, independence, loyalty, personal comfort and enjoyment, power and authority, pride, reverence, sex attraction, companionship, and so forth. However, it is best to select one basic appeal for a speech and make all others cluster around it. The strongest appeal often seems to be one of "threat"—based upon man's fears concerning his basic drives or motives. It does not necessarily follow, though, that the stronger the threat is the stronger the appeal will be. The optimal level of effectiveness of the threat appeal probably varies with the subject, the audience, and the occasion.[16] This is how President Kennedy used the threat appeal in his inaugural address: "To those new states whom we welcome to the ranks of the free, we pledge our word that one form of colonial control shall not have passed away merely to be replaced by a far more iron tyranny. We shall not always expect to find them supporting our view. But we shall always hope to find them strongly supporting their own freedom—and to remember that, in the past, those who foolishly sought power by riding the back of the tiger ended up inside."[17]

The Personalized Story

In some instances the personalized story can be highly effective as a means for bringing the speaker and the audience closer together. Personal words are realistic, direct, and intimate. The poignant beauty and power of the words of Abraham Lincoln, as he said farewell to friends and fellow townsmen at Springfield, Illinois, following his election, is a classic of simplicity and sincerity in American speech literature:

My Friends: No one, not in my situation, can appreciate my feeling of sadness at this parting. To this place, and the kindness of these people, I owe everything. Here I have lived a quarter of a century, and have passed from a young to an old man. Here my children have been born, and one is buried. I now leave, not knowing when or whether I may return, with a task before me greater than that which rested upon Washington. Without the assistance of that Divine Being who ever attended him, I cannot suc-

[16] For a thorough discussion of the scientific data available concerning "fear arousing appeals," see Carl I. Hovland, Irving L. Janis, and Harold H. Kelley, *Communication and Persuasion,* Yale University Press, 1953, chap. 3.

[17] John F. Kennedy, "Inaugural Address," *Vital Speeches,* February 1, 1961, pp. 226–227.

ceed. With that assistance, I cannot fail. Trusting in Him who can go with me, and remain with you, and be everywhere for good, let us confidently hope that all will yet be well. To His care commending you, as I hope in your prayers you will commend me, I bid you an affectionate farewell.[18]

Striking Comparisons and Contrasts

Comparison and contrast should be part of the stock in trade of any speaker, no matter what his goal may be. We are accustomed to thinking in terms of relationships, as we compare the present with the good old days, the house we now live in with the one we lived in before, the present French teacher with the previous one, and so on. The sharper or more striking the contrast, the deeper and more lasting the imprint upon the mind.

Comparison as a compositional device can serve many purposes. Robert Ingersoll used it effectively in comparing the life of Napoleon with that of a French peasant. The following is a portion of Ingersoll's soliloquy as he leaned over the balustrade at the tomb of Napoleon and mused about the accomplishments of this military genius.

I saw him in Egypt in the shadow of the pyramids—I saw him conquer the Alps and mingle the eagles of France with the eagles of the crags. I saw him at Marengo—at Ulm and Austerlitz. I saw him in Russia, where the infantry of the snow and the cavalry of the wild blast scattered his legions like winter's withered leaves. . . . And I saw him at St. Helena, with his hands crossed behind him, gazing out upon the sad and solemn sea.

I thought of the orphans and widows he had made—of the tears that had been shed for his glory, and of the only woman who ever loved him, pushed from his heart by the cold hand of ambition. And I said I would rather have been a French peasant and worn wooden shoes. I would rather have lived in a hut with a vine growing over the door, and the grapes growing purple in the kisses of the autumn sun. I would rather have been that poor peasant with my loving wife by my side, knitting as the day died out of the sky—with my children upon my knees and their arms about me—I would rather have been that man and gone down to the tongueless silence of the dreamless dust, than to have been that imperial impersonation of force and murder, known as "Napoleon the Great."[19]

[18] "Farewell Address at Springfield," in Wayland Maxfield Parrish and Marie Hochmuth (eds.), in *American Speeches*, Longmans, Green, 1954, p. 305.
[19] C. H. Cramer, *Royal Bob, The Life of Robert G. Ingersoll*, Bobbs-Merrill, 1952, pp. 57–58.

Statistical material can be impressively presented by comparison, especially since facts and figures are meaningless unless they are brought into close relationships with other known facts. A Farm Bureau representative speaking to a group of Midwestern farmers about the problem of a boxcar shortage brought out the fact that more than a million freight cars are in constant use. But the bald fact of a million freight cars owned by the railroads by itself means little or nothing to an audience—so the speaker made this figure more meaningful by adding the following: "Suppose you couple all these cars together and make up one long single freight train. That train could go roaring through your city at sixty miles an hour and it would be a month before you would see the lights of the caboose."

A student speaking on the subject of the high cost of taxation realized that rattling off statistics about billions of dollars of federal taxes and percentage schedules and income brackets would make dull listening; he hit upon the following device which startled and impressed the class audience: "Today is Good Friday, April 20. While you are at home over Easter Sunday, I hope you will be especially thoughtful and kind toward your parents. Your dad, especially, will need a little sympathy, for he will not see a single penny he will earn from this day until the 4th of July. For two months and twelve days every red cent will be taken from his paycheck by someone else, and that person is the tax collector, federal, state, and local. This is the way your dad will pay this year's tax bill."

Repetition and Refrain

We drive a nail into wood, not by a single stroke, but by repeated blows of the hammer. In the same manner, ideas are made to stick in the mind. Here is an example of Winston Churchill's use of repetition: ". . . we shall not flag or fail. We shall go on to the end, we shall fight in France, we shall fight on the seas and oceans, we shall fight with growing confidence and growing strength in the air, we shall defend our island, whatever the cost may be, we shall fight on the beaches, we shall fight on the landing grounds, we shall fight in the fields and in the streets, we shall fight in the hills; we shall never surrender. . . ."[20]

In the same manner, another speaker emphasizes "togetherness":

[20] Winston Churchill, "Miracle of Dunkirk," June 4, 1940, in *A Treasury of World's Great Speeches,* Simon and Schuster, 1954, p. 780.

"Together we cut the hay; together we spread the hay; together we raked the hay; together we drew the hay; together we planted the corn; together we hoed the corn; together we cut the corn; together we husked the corn. Together was another factor in that home."[21]

Rhetorical Questions

This is a good way to channel your thought into the lap of the listener. In a sense, it involves shifting the burden upon him, challenging him to make his own decisions and initiate his own actions. The speaker is not expected to answer a rhetorical question in voice, directly and specifically. Rather, it is a means of emphasis and dramatization, a way to prod the listener to think, to feel, to act. Patrick Henry used it effectively:

They tell us, sir, that we are weak; unable to cope with so formidable an adversary. But when shall we be stronger? Will it be the next week, or the next year? Will it be when we are totally disarmed, and when a British guard shall be stationed in every house? Shall we gather strength by irresolution and inaction? Shall we acquire the means of effectual resistance by lying supinely on our backs, and hugging the delusive phantom of hope, until our enemies shall have bound us hand and foot? Sir, we are not weak, if we make proper use of the means which the God of nature hath placed in our power.

Wit and Humor

Humor is a subtle but potent weapon of persuasion. The technique of the typical traveling salesman who tells a funny story before he gets out his order book may seem a bit crude, but it apparently gets results. A good laugh at the right time, whether when making a sale or a speech, may be worth a dozen facts and the most irrefutable logic. A hearty laugh produces an immediate psychological effect, often quickly changing the whole atmosphere of an occasion from one of apprehension or dissatisfaction to one of pleasant anticipation. Laughter levels out the edges of anxiety, gives radiance to the countenance, and cools hot tempers.

Abraham Lincoln knew the value of laughter. At a moment of crisis in the Civil War, when the Union army met an important setback, Congressman Arnold of Illinois called upon President Lincoln

---

[21] Hon. Woodbridge N. Ferris, "Give American Youth a Chance," *Executive Speeches,* October 7, 1927, p. 461.

and found him reading a book by the humorist, Artemus Ward. Arnold was horrified that at this crucial hour the President should spend his time so frivolously. Lincoln saw the disgust on his visitor's face and said, "If I could not get momentary respite from the crushing burden I am constantly carrying, my heart would break."

Humorous incidents, well related and aptly applied, catch the attention of the audience and serve as "memory hooks" on which to hang an important point. Such points, furthermore, will be remembered longer than others by the audience. Psychologists tell us we retain ideas longer when they are associated with a pleasant experience.

However, humor in a speech has its limitations and pitfalls. Stories that do not advance a point usually should be left untold, unless it is an occasion when rounds of storytelling are in order for the sake of general merriment. But for the speaker to break away from his central theme just to drag in a joke which has nothing to do with his subject is a waste of time and a violation of the law of unity. Furthermore, once a speaker gets the reputation of using humor only for its own sake, he soon becomes known as a funnyman, a clown.

One of the best laugh-makers is a good story. The point of the story should be perfectly clear; if it isn't, the story is not a good one to use. Further comment or explanation of the point should never be necessary, for this spoils its effect. Nor should a humorous story reflect discredit upon a person, group, or race. Humor should be clean, spontaneous, refreshing, and in good taste.

The elements that produce humor are varied and elusive. While laughter may be universal, a sense of humor is personal and individualistic; a speaker whose attempts at humor may bring roars of laughter from one audience may get only stony silence from another. Psychologists and people in show business have written volumes in the attempt to explain the phenomenon of laughter. The subject is far too complex to discuss here in detail—we can abstract only a few essential characteristics of humor as it concerns the speaker.

Laughing at yourself. Many comedians and humorists make themselves the butt of their jokes. In this way, they can make others look like heroes, but never themselves. As they poke fun at themselves, they come out "on the short end of the stick."

Appropriate humor. Although stinging, bitter irony or sarcasm may provoke laughter, it may also make listeners uncomfortable. Low, bawdy humor also has little place on the public platform. Humor must be suitable to the audience, to the occasion, and to the speaker.

Humor with an undercurrent of pathos. When the listener does not know whether to laugh or cry but ends up laughing, he usually laughs harder than he would have otherwise. A dignified, elderly man slipping on a banana peel brings laughter, but if he breaks his leg we are sad. Clowns, with their sad faces, know how to blend impending disaster with the struggle for triumph and success. This poignant type of humor is demonstrated in some of the writings of James Thurber and Mark Twain and in the moving pictures of Charlie Chaplin.

The ludicrous and incongruous. What is normal or near perfect is not funny. A man riding down the street on a beautiful, spirited, well-groomed horse draws no laughter. But, when he rides a swaybacked, long-haired, mangy, balky old plug, people are amused. We smile at someone who makes glaring grammatical errors and mispronounces common words. A very stout woman and a very slight man entering a room together may provoke mirth—and will, when he begins to order her around.

Situational humor. Perhaps the best type of humor is that which grows out of the speaking situation and is therefore created spontaneously. This is usually original and natural humor which can be made to serve the speaker and his cause. The following speech by Will Rogers at a bankers' convention effectively illustrates situational humor, but it would take a Will Rogers to "get away" with it:

Loan Sharks and Interest Hounds: I have addressed every form of organized graft in the United States excepting Congress. You are without a doubt the most disgustingly rich audience I ever talked to with the possible exception of the Bootleggers Union Local #1 combined with enforcement officers. Now I understand that you hold this convention every year to announce what the annual gyp will be. I have often wondered where the depositors hold their convention. I had an account in a bank once and the banker he asked me to withdraw it—he said I used up more red ink than the account was worth.

I see where your wives come with you. You note I say come, not were brought. I see where your convention was opened by a prayer. You had to send outside your ranks to get somebody that knew how to pray. You should've had one creditor there. He'd a shown you how to pray. I noticed in the prayer, the clergyman announced to the Almighty that the bankers

were here. Well, it wasn't exactly an announcement, it was more in the
nature of a warning. He didn't tell the Devil as he figured he knew where
you all were all the time anyway.

I see by your speeches that you're very optimistic of the business conditions of the coming year. Boy, I don't blame you—if I had your dough,
I'd be optimistic, too.

Will you please tell me what you all do with the vice presidents the
bank has? I guess that's to get anybody more discouraged before you can
see the main guy. The United States is the biggest institution in the world
—they've only got one Vice President. Nobody's ever found anything for
him to do.

I've met most of you as I come out the stage door at the Follies the other
night. I want to tell you if any of you that are capitalized at under one
million dollars needn't hang around there. Our girls may not know their
Latin and Greek but they certainly know their Dunn and Bradstreet.

You have a wonderful organization. I understand you have ten thousand
here and with what you have in the various federal prisons brings your
membership up to thirty thousand. Goodbye, paupers. You're the finest
bunch of Shylocks that ever foreclosed a mortgage on a widow's home.[22]

Imagery

An image is a sense picture created in the mind of the listener.
Figures of speech are common tools for picturing ideas. The speaker
can use an image to impress the listener with a sharp picture or to
drive home a major point in his speech. Abraham Lincoln was effective with the words, "a house divided against itself cannot stand."
Robert Ingersoll nominated Colonel Blaine as candidate for the
presidency with the image created by the phrase, "the plumed
knight." Franklin Roosevelt nominated Alfred Smith upon the image,
"the happy warrior." William Jennings Bryan electrified a Democratic Convention and the general public with the famous phrase,
"You shall not press upon the brow of labor this crown of thorns.
You shall not crucify mankind upon a cross of gold." During World
War II President Roosevelt captured the imagination of the country
following Italy's declaration of war on France with a dramatic image,
"The hand that held the dagger struck it in the back of its neighbor."
Winston Churchill stirred our imagination in an hour of war crisis
when he said, "Give us the tools and we will finish the job!"

[22] Will Rogers, "Speech to the Bankers," taken from a recording.

PROJECTS AND EXERCISES

For speaking projects see Part Three.

1. The speaker can do much to make pertinent statistics stick in the listener's mind by translating them into striking percentages and comparisons. How might you make the following figures impressive if you were to use them in a speech?

   a. There are 70,000,000 words spoken in one session of Congress.
   b. The annual automobile traffic toll in the U.S. is 38,000.
   c. The population of China is 600,000,000.
   d. The area of Texas is 263,513 square miles.

2. Speakers and listeners should always search for the real cause and/or the important contributing causes of a problem. Try to do this with the topic, "automobile accidents." Below is a list of frequently mentioned causes of car accidents. Can you rank them in order of importance? Do you have any evidence to support your ranking? Are they all causes? Take any one of the causes listed below and make a thorough investigation of it in which you determine how important it is as a cause of automobile accidents. Report your findings to the class.

a. Poor roads	e. Juvenile drivers
b. Alcohol	f. Driver carelessness
c. Mechanical failure	g. Inadequate laws
d. Speed	

3. Complete the sentences below with one of these terms: *probably not, possibly, perhaps, probably, almost certainly, certainly.* What types of materials would you probably use to support these assertions if you made them in a speech? Investigate any one of the topics and try to determine if the evidence supports your judgment as to the certainty of the statement. Report your findings to the class.

   a. Nixon was _____ defeated in the 1960 election because of the labor vote.
   b. The United States should give official recognition to Red China, for this would _____ decrease international tensions.
   c. Safety belts should be made standard equipment of all automobiles because this would _____ reduce the number of fatal accidents.
   d. The federal government should have a national academy of diplomacy, for this would _____ improve our relations with other nations.
   e. We should abolish the direct primary, for doing so would _____ _____ enable us to elect better men.

f. Extracurricular activities are _____ the cause of poor grades of many college students.

g. We should have more hydroelectric power plants similar to T.V.A., for this would _____ give the public cheaper electricity.

TOPICS FOR DISCUSSION

1. How important is the use of humor in a speech? What criticism do you have of most of the humor you hear in speeches? How can humor spoil what otherwise would be a good speech?
2. Distinguish between induction and deduction as methods of reasoning. Give two examples of each.
3. Does a speaker normally speak in syllogisms? If not, explain how a speaker usually presents a deductive argument.
4. What are some of the major fallacies in causal reasoning?
5. What relationship does evidence have to logic?
6. Are all forms of support evidence? If not, what is evidence? What is a fact?
7. What role does probability play in public address?
8. What is a dilemma?
9. What is meant by fallacious reasoning?
10. What is a value judgment?
11. What are some common methods of making an idea clear and vivid?
12. Can you be both logical and interesting?
13. Why are illustrations interesting to the average listener?
14. What evidence can you cite that conflict is a factor of audience interest?
15. Can you define wit?
16. To what extent are quotations evidence?
17. It has been said that there are no dull subjects—just dull speakers. Do you believe this to be true?

ADDITIONAL READINGS

Baird, A. Craig, and Knower, Franklin H., *General Speech,* 2nd ed., Mc-Graw-Hill, 1957, chap. 15.

Beardsley, Monroe C., *Thinking Straight,* Prentice-Hall, 1956.

Braden, Waldo W., Gehring, Mary Louise, *Speech Practices,* Harper, 1958, chap. 5.

Brigance, William Norwood, *Speech, Its Techniques and Disciplines in a Free Society,* Appleton-Century-Crofts, 1952, chap. 10.

Courtney, Luther W., and Capp, Glenn R., *Practical Debating,* Lippincott, 1949, chaps. 6–8.

Crocker, Lionel, *Argumentation and Debate,* American, 1944, chaps. 5–9.

Dickens, Milton, *Speech: Dynamic Communication,* Harcourt, Brace, 1954, chap. 17.

Foster, William Trufant, *Argumentation and Debating,* 2nd rev. ed., Houghton Mifflin, 1945, chaps. 4–7.

McBurney, James H., and Wrage, Ernest J., *Guide to Good Speech,* Prentice-Hall, 1955, chap. 15.

Monroe, Alan H., *Principles of Speech,* 4th ed., Scott, Foresman, 1958, chap. 6.

Smith, Raymond G., *Principles of Public Speaking,* Ronald, 1958, chaps. 10–12.

Thouless, Robert H., *How to Think Straight,* Simon and Schuster, 1950.

Weaver, Andrew Thomas, and Ness, Ordean Gerhard, *The Fundamentals and Forms of Speech,* Odyssey, 1957, chap. 9.

White, Eugene E., *Practical Speech Fundamentals,* Macmillan, 1960, chaps. 10 and 11.

Organization

🙈 8 🙈
Planning the Speech

THE IMPORTANCE OF ORGANIZATION

There could be no useful creation without form. From the intricate pattern of the snowflake to the vast shape of stars orbiting in space, all physical nature testifies to form, order, and plan of creation. Thus organization is one of nature's primary characteristics; the parts of the universe function in a smooth, systematic manner in which nothing is left to chance.

The speaker needs to take an example from nature and shape his speech materials into a carefully integrated whole. If he fails to do this, his speech will be "without form and void"; chaos will be the result and failure the reward. Quintilian expressed it this way:

. . . speech, if deficient in that quality [arrangement], must necessarily be confused, and float like a ship without a helm; it can have no coherence; it must exhibit many repetitions, and many omissions; and, like a traveller wandering by night in unknown regions, must, as having no stated course or object, be guided by chance rather than design. . . . just as it is not sufficient for those who are erecting a building merely to collect stone and timber and other building materials, but skilled masons are required to arrange and place them, so in speaking, however abundant the matter may be, it will merely form a confused heap unless arrangement be employed to reduce it to order and to give it connexion and firmness of structure. . . .[1]

Good organization yields many rewards for the public speaker. First, it helps to *make ideas clear*. Rhetoricians from Aristotle onward insist that the most important aspect of good speech style is clarity. Some ways of attaining clarity were discussed in the last chapter, but Herbert Spencer, in *Philosophy of Style*, goes to the heart of the matter. He asks the speaker to so present ideas that the listener can comprehend them "with the least possible mental effort." Effective organization is the first step toward achieving such clarity.

Second, good organization helps to establish the speaker's *central idea*. An unorganized, confused mass of material frequently conveys no message at all, whereas a carefully constructed discourse usually communicates at least the main idea.

Third, good organization helps to *maintain interest and attention*. Jon Eisenson, in *The Psychology of Speech*, notes:

> The more definite, the more sharply defined the object, the more likely it is to attract attention. A small, definitely shaped cloud is more attractive than a wide expanse of cloud without sharpness of outline. The arrangement of heavenly bodies into forms gives us such constellations as the Big and Little Dippers, and Orion. These arrangements are attractive and win our attention when we gaze at the sky. The moon, having greater definiteness of shape, easily attracts our attention whenever it can be observed. Sounds assume definiteness of form when they are arranged into patterns which we call music. The simple tune or jingle represents an elementary type of well-defined sound. The motif of a symphony stands out, wins our attention, and is remembered.[2]

So it is with speech. Speeches with a clear design have much greater attention value than those without it.

Fourth, good organization is an *aid to the speaker's memory*. Most speakers fear forgetting. A sure way to transform such fears into reality is to have a careless arrangement of speech materials. If ideas are arranged in a logical pattern, however, one idea readily leads into the next. Good organization makes the difference between order and

---

[1] H. E. Butler (trans.), *The Institutio Oratoria of Quintilian*, Harvard University Press, MCML III, Book VII, Pr., 2–3.

[2] Jon Eisenson, *The Psychology of Speech*, Appleton-Century-Crofts, 1938, p. 217.

chaos, clearness and haziness, beauty and ugliness, force and weakness, efficiency and waste.

Plan with Subject and Purpose in Mind

Organizing a speech is always a unique problem, since it varies with the subject, the purpose, the audience, and the occasion. A simple comparison will illustrate this point: a good basketball coach surveys his material before he decides upon the style of play he wants to use. If he has a small, fast team, he may extensively use the fast break; if he has tall, slower players, he may play a ball control type of game. Thus it is with the speaker; he should first carefully survey his materials before deciding on a method of organization.

The purpose of the speech must also be considered. When we build a house, we have a definite purpose in mind before we begin. If we are principally seeking beauty, we may build a colonial style house; for comfort and rustic atmosphere we might choose a rambling cottage; for endurance, a two-storied, native stone house; for economy, a small, modern ranch house. Similarly, a speech whose purpose is to inform may call for a different organizational approach than a speech which seeks to stimulate action; the former might emphasize ease of comprehension, whereas the latter would build to a climax with an impelling emotional experience.

The skillful speaker also adapts his method of organization to the audience and the occasion. A trainer may walk directly to a tamed lion; however, if he is wise, he will use a more circuitous approach to a hostile one. He may carefully circle the latter, looking for an opportune moment of approach, or he may first feed the beast to soothe its temper. Similarly, it is reasonable that the speaker approach a hostile audience differently than an extremely friendly one. With the hostile audience, the speaker may want to begin with points of agreement before he speaks about his main proposition, whereas such an approach would be a waste of time when addressing a friendly audience.

In other words, the successful speaker always tailors his organization for each speaking situation. He does not choose a mode of organization first and cram his materials into the chosen framework; he begins with his materials, purpose, audience, and occasion, and—in the light of these factors—chooses an organizational vehicle. Through such a procedure he is likely to achieve the most effective logical and psychological arrangement of his materials.

STEPS IN PREPARATION

Organizing a speech is inextricable from the entire process of preparing to deliver it. Your preparation should, in fact, be as well organized as your speech. To help make it so, we shall offer, not a rigid plan to fit every type of speech equally well, but some steps that are commonly essential to preparing for the major speech.

Survey and analyze the occasion and the audience. The speaker should always begin with his audience. Speech is for the purpose of communication and eliciting response; the best way to achieve this purpose is to determine what kind of people are going to listen to the speech, in what kind of setting, and on what kind of occasion. Such knowledge will help you to choose your subject, determine your purpose, and adapt your remarks to the audience. The more thoroughly you analyze the speech situation the easier it will be to prepare your speech.

Determine the general purpose of your speech. It is not enough merely to center your speech on some general topic; you must also know what message you wish to communicate *about* that topic. Decide what general response you wish to elicit from your audience. Select one of the basic speech purposes: to inform, to entertain, to convince, to impress, or to actuate. Remember that persuasive speeches may well, and perhaps should, contain a great amount of information and also be interesting. But keep your basic purpose clear and definite.

Select your subject. Usually the task of preparing a speech is relatively simple once the "right" subject is found. Review the section on "choosing a subject" in Chapter 5, pages 129–131.

Limit your subject to a specific purpose. It is not enough to pick a general purpose and subject for your speech; you must also select a specific purpose. To do this you must bring your primary objective into sharp focus and limit your subject accordingly. The statement of the specific purpose might read something like this: "To get the audience to appreciate the importance of ethics in advertising to the point where they will reject all products advertised unethically," or,

"To explain the functions of the Federal Communications Commission."

Gather materials.   Review the discussion of gathering materials in Chapter 5, "Thought and Speech," pages 127–129. Keep in mind that the more materials you gather, the easier it will be to compose and organize your speech.

Arrange your materials and construct an outline.   The following chapter deals with this step.

Phrase and word your speech.   This may entail anything from mentally thinking through the thoughts of your speech to writing a complete manuscript. Even when speaking extemporaneously—or especially when speaking extemporaneously—this is an important step; for unless the speaker thinks his ideas through several times, phrasing them in his mind, the actual presentation is likely to find him groping for words, sentences, and even thoughts.

Practice your speech.   This is the last important step of your speech preparation. Commit the *skeleton* of your speech to memory and speak it through, either in your mind or aloud, until the words flow smoothly and easily. You will almost never memorize the exact language to be used, but rather the ideas and their rough development. Careful rehearsal provides the confidence that the average speaker needs.

A GOOD TITLE OFTEN HELPS

Do not confuse the title of your speech with its thesis. The thesis is what the speech is about, whereas the title may be a catchy phrase which tells little about the speech itself. Follow these guides in choosing your title:

Make it attention getting.   A speech title should arrest the casual observer's attention when he reads it in a newspaper or sees it posted on a bulletin board. The title of Russell Conwell's famous "Acres of Diamonds" speech must have stirred considerable interest in the minds of the people who went to hear it.

Make it imaginative.   All good speech titles appeal to the imagination; they stimulate thinking and arouse curiosity, suggesting various lines of thought which the speaker might be expected to explore in his speech. Good titles do not tell all; they merely suggest. "Tomahawks, Reservations, and Destitution" is certainly more imaginative and catchy than "A Need for a New Indian Policy."

Keep it short and simple. Avoid all complex statements for titles of your speech. Word it simply.

Avoid triteness. The danger of being trite is always a real one when selecting a speech title. For a commencement speech, for instance, "The Challenge of the Future" is surely trite. Search for a fresh, original title—one which has personality of its own.

Make it appropriate. The title should be relevant to the content of the speech. In fact, something in the speech should point up the real meaning of the title. If the meaning does not become apparent to the listener, the title is an ill-chosen one.

The following examples from *Vital Speeches* illustrate qualities of a good speech title:

Title	Subject
"The Year of the Rat"	Epidemic cynical selfishness.
"The Indispensable Sale"	Selling an industry to the public.
"The Challenge of Africa"	The new Africa and the United Nations.
"Your Story Must Be Told"	What is meant by communication?
"The Meaning of Lincoln Today"	The need for a national dialogue in overcoming discrimination.
"Have Trade, Will Compete"	The Latin America export-import situation.

Here are some imaginative titles of older addresses: "The Rise and Fall of the Mustache," "Walking Dust," "Veterans of Future Wars," "Acres in the Sky," "The Nailed Hands vs. the Mailed Fist," "The Crime of Poverty," "A House Divided," "The Forgotten Man," "The Message of Jesus to Men of Wealth," "The Man with the Muck Rake," "Nebraska Boy Over Japan," "Which Knew Not Joseph," "The Cooing Dove." How many of these titles can you identify?

THE DIRECT APPROACH TO SPEECH ORGANIZATION

Ordinarily, when people think of speech organization they think in terms of "introduction, body, and conclusion." Certainly these factors, constituting the *rhetorical order* of a speech, are integral to the speech. However, it is vitally important to realize that there is more to organizing a speech than mere preparation of an introduction, body, and conclusion.

A basic decision concerns the type of structural design to be used. Building a house involves more than simply constructing a front entry, the basic structure, and a back porch. An elementary decision is the type of structure to be built—should it be ranch style, Dutch colonial, split-level, or Spanish adobe? These homes have much in common yet are vastly different. So it is with speeches; they have common elements but vary in strategy and form. Basically, the approach to speech organization can be either direct or indirect. Each of these approaches has advantages and disadvantages; it lends itself to some speech situations and not to others. Which to use must be determined by analysis of the audience, subject, and occasion.

If a speaker chooses a direct approach to his speech subject, he establishes interest in his speech in the introduction, lays down his proposition or states his thesis, and then proceeds to divide his thesis into main points or issues which are then taken up in a clear and precise order. He may either state his topic and then forecast his development, or he may state his topic and let the main points unfold as he gets to them. For practical purposes we will call the former the "forecasting" method and the latter the "unfolding" method.

The Forecasting Method

The forecasting method of speech design involves five steps: (1) introduction, (2) statement of thesis, (3) partition and forecast of main points, (4) development of the points (body), (5) conclusion. At the close of the introduction the speaker must make a transition into the thesis, which he states explicitly. Immediately after disclosing his thesis, he announces his main points to the audience. If, for example, you were to speak on the subject, "How to Play Tennis," at the close of the introduction you might say:

So this morning I shall discuss the subject, "How to Play Tennis." I shall deal with this subject from three standpoints: first, the rules of the game; second, the fundamentals of the game; and third, the strategy of the game.

The rules of tennis . . .

The following is an example of forecasting at the end of the introduction in a speech to convince: "Because of this I feel compelled this evening to speak against the proposal that we admit Communist China to the United Nations. Two reasons for not admitting Communist China are readily apparent: (1) Admission of Communist China to the United Nations violates basic principles of the U. N. Charter. (2) Admission of Communist China would contribute to greater instability of world relations."

ADVANTAGES OF THE FORECASTING METHOD. *Forecasting main points increases the clarity of the speech.* Since the principal issues are clearly outlined in advance, the listener knows in what direction the speaker's thinking will go. He is thus able to picture the speech as a whole and to see clearly where the parts fit in. Clarity is always an aid to understanding.

Forecasting aids retention. It has of course long been known that repetition assures a high degree of retention.[3] Since forecasting involves reiteration of main issues, it should give reasonable assurance that the listener will retain at least the skeleton or basic structure of the ideas of a speech.

Forecasting is impressive. The mere act of listing several reasons for or against something impresses the average listener. An enumeration of points tends to have a cumulative effect; each point builds upon the others.

Forecasting gives the impression of fairness. If a speaker announces his points early in the speech, the element of fair play stands out; there seems to be nothing deceitful about his approach.

Forecasting is an aid to appreciative listening. Most people like to know how far they have come and how far they have yet to go when they are traveling. This knowledge tends to diminish the fatigue of a traveler, or, in the case of a speech, of the listener. Forecasting provides road signs which tell the listener how far the speech has progressed. To know how much remains, Quintilian wrote, "stimulates us to fresh effort over the labour that still awaits us. For

---

[3] See Arthur T. Jersild, "Modes of Emphasis in Public Speaking," *Journal of Applied Psychology,* 12 (1928), 611–620; Ray Ehrensberger, "An Experimental Study of the Relative Effectiveness of Certain Forms of Emphasis," *Speech Monographs,* 12 (1945), 110–111.

nothing need seem long, when it is definitely known how far it is to the end."[4]

DISADVANTAGES OF FORECASTING. *The forecasting approach lacks flexibility.* Important points which the speaker may have omitted in his forecast may occur to him during delivery of the speech. In such a case he is faced with a dilemma: if he strays from his announced partition, it will seem as though he is digressing; if he does not insert the point that comes to his mind, he may be omitting important material. Moreover, it is difficult to make "on-the-spot" adaptation to the audience if the skeleton of the speech has been outlined already. Then, too, a point which a speaker has forecast may suddenly escape his memory, and many listeners may notice that he has omitted it. The speaker will thus appear to be careless. Finally, whenever a strict time limit is placed on a speech, the forecasting approach lacks the flexibility needed to end a speech on time. If the speaker does not get to the final point he has promised his listeners, they may rightfully feel cheated.

A forecast of ideas may arouse passive hostile listeners. When addressing a hostile group, it is usually best to begin with points of agreement and gradually lead into the area of disagreement. If disputable points are forecast, hostile listeners may immediately begin to refute them in their minds without listening to the speaker's reasoning and documentation.

A forecast of ideas may seem to be anticlimactic. With this approach no important points are held in abeyance to be sprung upon the listener as clinching arguments. Although the speaker's specific development of his main points is unknown, yet the general direction of the speech is clear to the listener.

Forecasting may cause listener impatience. Quintilian explained: ". . . there is in every case some one point of more importance than the rest, and when the judge has become acquainted with it, he is apt to disdain other points as requiring no notice." The same author provides us with a useful example. If a speaker were to say, "I will not say that the character of my client is such as to render him incapable of murder, I will only say that he had no motive for murder and that at the time when the deceased was killed he was overseas,"[5] the judge

[4] Bk. IV, V. 23.
[5] Bk. IV, V. 9.

might well become impatient; for if the last point can be proved, then everything else is immaterial.

In summary, forecasting is a good, basic organizational approach for a speech to inform or to secure belief when the audience is either favorable or neutral to your speech subject. For both types of audiences, clarity, impressiveness, and factual materials are cardinal virtues, and forecasting permits of emphasizing these matters, although with some psychological losses.

The Unfolding Method

The unfolding method is the second type of direct approach to basic speech design. Its only essential difference from the forecasting method is that the speaker does not openly partition and announce his major points after he has introduced his subject for discussion; that is, he omits the forecast. He merely states his thesis and proceeds immediately into the development of point one; it is thus accurate to state that the speaker lets his ideas "unfold."

The advantages of the unfolding method correspond essentially to the disadvantages of forecasting, and *vice versa*. Increased flexibility is the chief advantage of the unfolding method. The speaker does not commit himself in any way and can better adapt to audience reaction, time limit, and spur of the moment inspiration.

The unfolding method is useful for many types of speeches. However, if the audience is predominantly hostile, it is more effective to use an indirect route to persuasion. The direct approach is didactic; it sets out to teach the listeners. And the hostile audience does not wish to be taught.

THE INDIRECT APPROACH TO SPEECH ORGANIZATION

Unlike the direct approach, the indirect method does not present generalizations before it presents support. Instead, the speaker begins with concrete examples, and not until the supporting framework has been carefully constructed does he spell out his stand or proposal. For example, he might start with a historical review of his subject, describe the current circumstances, and only then make inferences based upon the material cited.

When General MacArthur spoke to Congress after his recall from Japan in 1951, he first examined "Asia's past and the revolutionary changes which have marked her course up to the present" and then interpreted the character of the contemporary scene. Finally, he ended with his main point: the admonition not to "scuttle the Pacific."

Popular agitators often use a *screened* attack, an excellent example of which is found in the funeral oration of Mark Antony in Shakespeare's *Julius Caesar*. Although Antony definitely came to praise Caesar and arouse the citizens to mutiny against Brutus and his associates, he gives not the slightest hint of his intentions in the early part of his speech; for to the mob, Brutus was a hero, and Caesar a tyrant. Cautiously Antony begins. He proceeds skillfully, using such expressions as "noble Brutus," "an honorable man," "all honorable men," "I speak not to disprove what Brutus spoke," "I will not do them wrong," "let me not stir you up," and "I am no orator, as Brutus is." So cleverly is the main aim guarded that the oft-repeated phrase, "honorable men," becomes to the mob of citizens bitter irony without their knowing it. The impact of accumulated emotion, drama, and evidence makes the very same mob which seemingly muttered, "He had better not say anything against Brutus" suddenly do a complete about-face, to the extent that it is bent upon killing Brutus.

The screened attack can be used for noble as well as for ignoble purposes. Patrick Henry developed his "Liberty or Death" speech indirectly. Only at the very end did he conclude that the colonies have no alternative but to fight. Many other eminent speakers have used the indirect approach effectively.

A special kind of indirect approach is seen in the *allegorical* speech. The speaker puts his ideas into story form, and the narrative structure supplies evidence by implication. Some of Christ's most important teachings, for example, were by implication through parables. The story may be fact or fiction, as long as the implication is clear to the audience. Joan Graham, a University of Kansas student, in a short speech on college "conformity," ably demonstrated her point by an extended story of a rabbit attending Rabbit University. Pete the rabbit found that at R.U. it was strictly taboo to be anything but "Brer College." Being a weak, naive bunny, he soon succumbed to the pressure: "By the end of the spring semester, Pete was a pretty slick college rabbit—and pretty superior about it. He could chain smoke, talk a unique brand of funny bunny talk, and gulp a fifth of distilled 90 proof Keg and Keg in one pre-party. Positive proof of his collegiateness were his gradepoints—they vanished altogether.

Now Pete realized his dates must be sharp, all have white paws, and preferably come from a family whose patriarch owned many, many carrots."

A variation of the allegorical speech is the extended story speech, which relates the story and then makes the application. Although this procedure loses some of the dramatic impact of the story, it at least assures application of the theme.

Which is more effective, to let the audience draw its own conclusions or to make the application specific and direct? The best available answer is a study by Cooper and Dinerman, of reactions to an anti-prejudice film. One of the important messages in the study was explicit, whereas the other depended upon audience inference. The study revealed that the implicit message influenced only the more intelligent members of the audience.[6] It would seem, then, that the answer to the above question rests with the intellectual level of the audience and, we assume, with the dramatic impact of the story.

Which approach to speech organization should the speaker use, the direct or indirect? Generally the direct method is advantageous; however, in certain persuasive speaking situations where the audience is predominantly hostile, indirect development will prove more effective, for it forces the listener to listen to evidence on the matter before his prejudices and attitudes become operative.

PROJECTS AND EXERCISES

For speaking projects see Part Three.

1. Analyze the speech titles found on pages 192–193. Do they all fulfill the criteria established in the chapter?
2. Take a recent issue of *Vital Speeches* and examine the titles. Try to state the central thought of the speech from the title.
3. Read three speeches from a recent issue of *Vital Speeches* and decide what basic organizational approach the speaker used: direct (unfolding or forecasting) or indirect.
4. Check the speech subjects below which you think are too broad for a five to seven minute speech.

How a Steam Shovel Works	Riddle of the Sphinx
How to Make Steel	Major League Baseball
The Art of Emceeing	How to Train a Dog

---

[6] Eunice Cooper and Helen Dinerman, "Analysis of the Film 'Don't Be a Sucker'; a Study in Communication," *Public Opinion Quarterly*, 15 (1951), 243–264.

History of Labor Law	American Rivers
Woman Suffrage Movement	Steamship Travel on the Mississippi
Marriage Customs in Foreign Lands	What is Progressive Education?
The Social Security Laws	Raising Minks
Music Therapy	Tidal Waves

TOPICS FOR DISCUSSION

1. How important is the title of a speech?
2. What advantages and disadvantages can you see to the indirect organizational approach?
3. How can good organization be an aid to the speaker's memory?
4. Distinguish between the general purpose and the specific purpose of the speech.
5. Which of the organizational approaches would you use for a speech to convince a relatively hostile audience that "Socialized medicine is to be preferred to our present system"? How would you change your speech for a favorable audience? Neutral audience? Apathetic audience?

ADDITIONAL READINGS

Brembeck, Winston Lamont, and Howell, William Smiley, *Persuasion, A Means of Social Control,* Prentice-Hall, 1952, chap. 15.

Monroe, Alan H., *Principles and Types of Speech,* 4th ed., Scott, Foresman, 1955, chaps. 7 and 8.

Oliver, Robert T., *The Psychology of Persuasive Speech,* 2nd ed., Longmans, Green, 1957, chap. 15.

Smith, Raymond G., *Principles of Public Speaking,* Ronald, 1958, chap. 4.

Soper, Paul L., *Basic Public Speaking,* 2nd ed., Oxford University Press, 1956, pp. 34–48.

❧ 9 ❧
Designing the Speech

The earliest classical rhetoricians maintained that a speech should have a beginning, a middle, and an end. "Every discourse, like a living creature," Plato wrote in the *Phaedrus,* "should be so put together that it has a body of its own and lacks neither head nor feet, a middle or extremities, all composed in such a way that they suit both each other and the whole." Aristotle thought that only two parts of a speech were indispensable, "the statement of the case and the proof," but added that there may be four: the introduction, statement of the case, proof, and the conclusion. Other classical writers added numerous parts, some listing as many as seven rhetorical parts of a speech. The concept of rhetorical order, or divisions of a speech, has survived the test of time and is still taught by modern rhetoricians. Although different terms are frequently used, twentieth century speech theorists consider the introduction, the body, and the conclusion as the three basic parts of a speech. A few would add a fourth and include a statement of the thesis. Our discussion in this chapter will be cast in the framework of the three traditional parts, the thesis being handled as a final function of the introduction.

THE INTRODUCTION

There are two basic reasons for using an introduction in the structure of your speech: (1) It prepares the audience for the subject to

201

be discussed. The introduction can enlist the interest and good will of the audience and prepare its mind for understanding and appreciation of the subject. In other words, the introduction should pave the way for the fullest communication of the speaker's thought and purpose. (2) An introduction contributes to the artistic creation of the speech. A good speech is a creative piece which should give the impression of an aesthetic whole. Aristotle thought that a speech introduction "answers to the prologue in poetry, or to the prelude in music for the flute." This alone may be sufficient reason for utilizing the three traditional parts of a speech, even if analysis of the audience reveals that their interest is so great that no more than a statement of the case and the ensuing development is needed.

The introduction of a speech should perform certain basic functions, described below. This is not to say that an introduction cannot be successful if it omits one or more of these functions, but it does say that on most subjects and for most audiences the speaker can profit from an introduction which fulfills these five principles: (1) establishes contact with the audience, (2) establishes the speech as being interesting, (3) establishes the authentic sign, (4) establishes a need to listen, (5) discloses and clarifies the subject.

Establish Contact with the Audience

The very fact that a speaker walks in front of an audience, pauses, and looks at them establishes contact. Verbal contact, however, still needs to be made. Some speakers like to do this through a formal greeting, such as "Ladies and Gentleman," "Members of the Board," or "Mr. Chairman and Fellow Delegates." Often, especially when dignitaries are sitting on the stage with you, it is almost mandatory that you recognize them with a formal greeting. However, except for acknowledgment of the chairman, it is usually well to avoid a formal greeting; for not only do greetings tend to be trite but they also detract from the emphasis of the opening sentence.

The opening sentence is so important that it should be prepared with special care. Make it short and make it say something that will arouse intellectual curiosity. It is usually well to memorize the first two or three sentences in order to assure a smooth start and well-thought-out wording. A speaker should never grope for words at the very beginning of his speech.

Establish the Speech as Being Interesting

Different methods of arousing the audience's interest and attention may be used, so long as, in Cicero's words, the opening renders "auditors well disposed, attentive, teachable." Of the many possible interest-getting devices, the following are most common.

REFER TO THE IMPORTANCE OF THE OCCASION. Making the occasion seem important not only establishes the need to listen but also helps to create interest in the speech. Ernest Gruening, in his Independence Day address after Alaska was admitted to statehood, used this device effectively.

It is a rare privilege that you have accorded me in asking me to address you on this occasion, or, perhaps, to use the English language more precisely, a unique privilege.

For this is no ordinary Fourth of July.

This is an Independence Day ceremony which, in several important respects, is unprecedented—and therefore, unique.

We are celebrating the admission to the Union of the largest state in American history.

We are celebrating the admission of an area larger than ever before admitted to the Union in any one year—an area one-fifth as large as the older forty-eight states.

We are celebrating the admission to the Union of a state that extends American dominion and full citizenship, and all concomitant blessings that American citizenship implies, to America's farthest west and America's farthest north.

Thus, we are celebrating the extension, for the first time in history, of the Union north into the Arctic and west into the Eastern Hemisphere. This is new terrain for the family of states.

We are celebrating the admission to the Union, for the first time, of a non-contiguous area—this is the first time that we have taken into the family of states territory which did not touch the rectangular block that hitherto has constituted the Union.

We are celebrating the admission of a new state after forty-six years without such evidence of growth and expansion. Thirteen years was previously the longest interval between the admission of states.

These geographical and historical data imply a great deal more than their mere recital reveals. Behind these physical facts lie far more important symbolic and spiritual connotations. These are, first, that the

United States is not static, not limited, not complete; but, on the contrary, is dynamic, growing, and on the march.[1]

REFER TO HISTORICAL EVENTS. Important historical events usually are strong interest factors, and if the historical incident is related to the subject, the occasion, or the audience addressed, an effective appeal to the audience's pride results. A speaker making a commencement speech might, for example, refer to the first commencement ever held in this academic institution. James B. Carey, addressing the Pennsylvania Industrial Union Council, CIO, evoked considerable interest and pride in his listeners with this introduction:

This, the twentieth and last regular convention of the Pennsylvania State CIO, is both a solemn and portentous occasion.

I am extremely proud of having had the opportunity of addressing both the first convention of the Pennsylvania State CIO and its last convention. And if, in this final convention, we are inclined a bit toward sentimentality that indulgence is not only justified but appropriate. We would be less than human and we would be unfeeling toward our own hectic history if we did not, during these two climactic days, glance backward over the long, long path we have traveled during the past two decades. It would be surprising if we didn't look back even with a touch of nostalgia to the excitements and turbulences of our early years.

Those years have already started to take on something of a rosy, romantic glow. It's an astonishing thing but today, looking back over the receding years, it somehow doesn't seem so terrible that we had our heads clobbered by Pearl Bergoff goon squads or took beatings efficiently administered by Pinkerton thugs. The pain somehow seems to have disappeared from our recollections of broken arms and legs handed out by Baldwin-Felts professional strikebreakers. Today we look back on bloody noses given us by Railway Audit detectives or by Chowderhead Cohen almost as the equivalent of a merit badge or a distinguished service medal.[2]

REFER TO TOP NEWS EVENTS. People are generally interested in important happenings, whether of world or of local significance. Wendell Willkie, in 1940, skillfully referred to world affairs in his speech, "Why Are You Unemployed?"

Winston Churchill, in whose hands rests the fate of England, and for that matter perhaps the fate of all Europe, was installed as prime minister

[1] *Representative American Speeches: 1959–1960*, The Reference Shelf, The H. W. Wilson Company, 32, no. 4 (1960), 31–32.
[2] *Ibid.*, 30, no. 4 (1957–1958), 97–99.

only a few months ago. His first speech in Parliament sounded a strange note. Mr. Churchill made none of the usual promises. He did not offer the people higher incomes. He did not offer them bread and circuses as the old Roman emperors used to do. "I have nothing to offer you," he said, "except blood, tears, toil and sweat."

It is a tragedy, I think, for England and for all the rest of the world, that no honest statesman was able to step forward sooner and say these words or something like them. It is a tragedy that England had to wait to hear those words until the invader was at her door and her sons were being slaughtered in the struggle in Flanders. Those words, or their equivalent, and their acceptation, spoken a few years ago might have saved Britain and France from the desperate case in which they now find themselves. But during the last seven years, during the rise of Hitler in Germany, the people in England were led by men who preferred compromise to the forthright truth. And the French people have been in the same fix. In the hands of a so-called liberal government, the French people were given promises of shorter hours and higher pay. The French government played financial football with the franc, industry became demoralized, and the people were kidded into believing that they were safe. How deeply must French mothers now regret those wasted years; those years of promises and those years of illusion; those demogogic years during which the statesmen of France toyed with the destiny of their country!

We in America have not escaped this fatal weakness of democracy. We too have been living by fair promises.[3]

CITE A QUOTATION.   A short, provocative quotation, appropriate to the speech topic, is an effective opening device. Keep in mind, however, that quotations are not inherently interesting; it is only when they are short and provocative that they hold considerable listener interest. Arthur Larson, in an address to the International Association of Industrial Editors, effectively quoted from Shakespeare.

Man has been endowed with many gifts, but prophecy is not one of them.

This obvious fact has never, however, proved to be the slightest impediment to this most engaging of all human games—guessing the future. Whether the game is carried on with tea leaves or Univac machines, whether the "future" consists of the outcome of the fifth at Pimlico or the sixth of November, we never tire of asking, as Banquo asked of the three witches, "If you can look into the seeds of time, And say which grain will grow and which will not."

Of all the branches of vaticination, the most fascinating is the exercise

[3] *Ibid.*, 14, no. 1 (1939–1940), 307–308.

we are undertaking at this conference: picturing how the world will look many years from now.[4]

BEGIN WITH A STARTLING STATEMENT.   "All hell's full of booze" is how Billy Sunday began one of his most famous revival sermons. This astonishing thought arouses interest. Startling statistics, and statements such as, "Tonight I am going to talk to you about murder," attract attention, at least until the listener discovers the specific topic of the speech. A word of caution, however. There is a tendency to overwork this particular type of opening; too often the "startling statement" is nothing but a trite expression. Be sure that you achieve a high degree of originality if you use this device.

ASK SEVERAL RHETORICAL QUESTIONS.   A rhetorical question is not directly answered by the speaker; it is asked rather to provoke thought. Two or three well-phrased questions presented at the outset of the speech arouse considerable intellectual curiosity, although this device is also frequently overworked. Jo Mohri, a speech student, began a tribute to Helen Keller with a series of questions:

Did you see how beautiful and green the campus looked this noon as you came to class? Did you hear the bells of the campanile telling you the time? Have you ever stopped to think what it would be like not to be able to enjoy these things—to live in a world of darkness, a world of silence? Some time close your eyes and plug your ears for a while. Intensify this feeling many times and you have the feeling one of the most remarkable women alive today has all the time. Helen Keller, now 81, has been deaf and blind since she was two.

RELATE A PERTINENT ANECDOTE.   Both true and hypothetical narratives can be effective, so long as they are relevant to the subject and help you to disclose the subject in an effective and interesting manner. Factual illustrations, if you can find them, are usually the best. This is how a truly great rhetorician, the late President Franklin D. Roosevelt, opened his appeal for the purchase of war bonds:

Once upon a time, a few years ago, there was a city in our Middle West which was threatened by a destructive flood in a great river. The waters had risen to the top of the banks. Every man, woman, and child in that city was called upon to fill sandbags in order to defend their homes against the rising waters. For many days and nights destruction and death stared

[4] *Ibid.*, 29, no. 3 (1956–1957), 115–116.

them in the face. As a result of the grim, determined community effort, that city still stands. Those people kept the levees above the peak of the flood. All of them joined together in the desperate job that had to be done—businessmen, workers, farmers, and doctors, and preachers—people of all races.

To me that town is a symbol of what community cooperation can accomplish.[5]

USE PERSONAL EXPERIENCES. These often constitute the most effective opening. Search in your storehouse of past experience for related material. Dorothy Thompson opened a 1937 commencement address at Russell Sage College on a personal note.

It is more than twenty years since I sat where you are sitting this morning. The year of my own graduation was a portentous year; a fateful and fatal year. It was 1914. Hardly was I out of college when the World War broke out, and from that day to this the world has never been remotely the same place that it was before.

I suppose that I have been asked to speak to you this morning because I have lived those twenty-odd years more intensively, perhaps, than most people. It has been given to me to live in many parts of the world, to see many of the events of my times—my times, which are also yours, for there is no break in the continuity of history, no real break. One may say, as I have just said: In 1914 the World War broke out, and since then nothing has been the same. But the World War was only the crystallization of what had been done up to that time. Wise men saw its shadow darkening the world long before the first shot was fired. And out of the war, directly out of the war, opened other phases of history, quite logically, although never inevitably. It is customary now to say that the generation of 1914 was "fated." Some people have said it was "lost." But the generation of 1937 is no less fated, and whether or not it will be lost depends upon you.[6]

USE A BIT OF HUMOR. Humor undoubtedly is one of the most effective attention-getting devices, as we indicated in an earlier chapter (p. 144). It not only arouses interest in the listeners but also can gain considerable good will for the speaker. Note, however, that not all speeches should begin with humorous stories. Far too many speakers seem to have the idea that one cannot safely begin a speech without first telling the latest joke. Not everyone can relate humorous

<hr/>

[5] *Vital Speeches,* September 15, 1943, p. 706.

[6] Lew Sarett and William Trufant Foster (eds.), *Modern Speeches on Basic Issues,* Houghton Mifflin, 1939, pp. 185–186.

anecdotes effectively, and, worse yet, far too often the stories aren't funny. But humor arising out of the occasion and humor directed at the speaker himself usually are effective opening devices.

Henry W. Grady, in the introduction of his famous speech, "The New South," uses humor not only to arouse interest but also to secure good will.

. . . I ask an indulgent hearing from you. I beg that you will bring your full faith in American fairness and frankness to judgment upon what I shall say. There was an old preacher once who told some boys of the Bible lesson he was going to read in the morning. The boys, finding the place, glued together the connecting pages. [Laughter.] The next morning he read on the bottom of one page: "When Noah was one hundred and twenty years old he took unto himself a wife, who was"—then turning the page—"one hundred and forty cubits long [laughter], forty cubits wide, built of gopher-wood [laughter], and covered with pitch inside and out." [Loud and continued laughter.] He was naturally puzzled at this. He read it again, verified it, and then said: "My friends, this is the first time I ever met this in the Bible, but I accept it as evidence of the assertion that we are fearfully and wonderfully made." [Immense laughter.] If I could get you to hold such faith tonight I could proceed cheerfully to the task I otherwise approach with a sense of consecration.

RELATE THE HISTORY OR BACKGROUND OF THE PROPOSITION. This often is an effective way of opening an argumentative speech. Choose your information carefully so that it will clearly present the history of the case and develop a high degree of interest in your subject.

Establish the Authentic Sign

Since the best speeches usually contain some personal elements, the speaker will do well to relate himself in some manner to his subject, to establish the *authentic sign* discussed in Chapter 2. A personal anecdote is a good method, for it arouses interest and relates the speaker to the subject. An example is the personal illustration used by Dorothy Thompson in the preceding section, although personal illustrations are appropriate throughout your speech—not just in the introduction.

By identifying himself with the subject, the speaker is able to present himself as an authority. If you can show your listeners in your introduction that you have had considerable experience or training that peculiarly qualifies you to speak on this subject, your prestige will be enhanced. The listeners will pay closer attention and believe you more readily, for everybody likes to get his information from an authority. If, for example, you are discussing how to train dogs, and you have been doing it for years, it will be to your advantage to reveal your practical experience to your audience.

Arthur G. Trudeau, in an address on "Morals and Missiles," carefully reveals his qualifications for speaking on the subject.

It is a great pleasure for me to be here this evening and to join with you in honoring our Army Missile Men. Let me congratulate those who have just received the awards. More and more in these crucial days, the battlefield leans heavily on industry and what it is able to produce. Nowhere is this more clearly seen than in the missile business. Here, industry teamed with the Armed Forces forms a major front of national defense and a bulwark to our freedom.

The thoughts I would like to bring you tonight are those of an American who has been privileged to serve our nation for more than 35 years in posts of increasing responsibility in the realm of national defense. My work, especially my experience as a former Chief of Army Intelligence, has provided me unusual opportunities to perceive and appreciate the challenges which face our great Republic and the Free World today, tomorrow and in the foreseeable future.[7]

The speaker can also establish the authentic sign by *identifying* himself with the audience, their stereotypes and strong beliefs, their heroes, and the community in which he is speaking. A skillful speaker usually establishes some common ground with his listeners. Thus, when addressing a group of manufacturers he will speak of his own interests in business. Observe how Winston Churchill in a speech before Congress at the outset of World War II identifies himself with America and our American ideals.

The fact that my American forebears have for so many generations played their part in the life of the United States and that here I am, an Englishman, welcomed in your midst makes this experience one of the most moving and thrilling in my life, which is already long and has not been entirely uneventful. I wish, indeed, that my mother, whose memory I cherish across the veil of years, could have been here to see

[7] *Vital Speeches,* April 15, 1960, pp. 404–405.

me. By the way, I cannot help reflecting that if my father had been American and my mother British, instead of the other way round, I might have got here on my own. In that case, this would not have been the first time you would have heard my voice. In that case I would not have needed any invitation, but if I had it is hardly likely that it would have been unanimous. So, perhaps, things are better as they are. I may confess, however, that I do not feel quite like a fish out of water in a legislative assembly where English is spoken. I am a child of the House of Commons. I was brought up in my father's house to believe in democracy; trust the people, that was his message. I used to see him cheered at meetings and in the streets by crowds of workingmen way back in those aristocratic Victorian days when Disraeli said, "The world was for the few and for the very few." Therefore, I have been in full harmony with the tides which have flowed on both sides of the Atlantic against privileges and monopoly and I have steered confidently towards the Gettysburg ideal of government of the people, by the people, for the people.[8]

Political speakers usually begin by praising the audience, the community, and the people's heroes. American politicians, to put it facetiously, try to get on the side of God and Abraham Lincoln.

Establish a Need to Listen

You must have a justification for addressing your audience on a certain subject at a given time. Reveal this justification to your listeners by building up the significance of your subject. Point out that it is important to social welfare or individual security, or whatever. Try to identify it with listener motives. Perhaps you can promise them a tangible reward, such as a saving on income tax, if they have the knowledge you are about to present; or you may be able to suggest a penalty if your advice is not heeded. At other times you may be able to arouse intellectual curiosity in your listeners. You can show them, during the course of your introduction, that your speech will be intellectually stimulating.

A student in a speech class, speaking on the importance of soil conservation, tried to build a need to listen with this introduction:

It was two o'clock in the afternoon, but the sun's rays were beginning to lose their luster. The sun gradually turned into a red ball and appeared no longer to possess the needed energy to light and sustain the earth. The red spot grew dimmer and dimmer, until it disappeared al-

8 "Here We Are Together," *Vital Speeches*, 1941–1942, p. 197.

together. The sky became grayish-orange and visibility was limited to a few hundred feet.

The cows turned their noses upward and sniffed the impure, dusty air in a perplexed fashion. The small boy and his somewhat older sister, herding the animals, were struck by fear. They placed handkerchiefs over their noses to filter the dust. Leaving the cattle unattended, they started for home, walking rapidly; soon they were trotting, and then they were running—panic was their propulsion. Following the fence line, they reached the farm home safely.

The orange colored dust grew so intense that night had come in the afternoon. Home alone, with their parents in town, the terror-stricken children huddled in a closet. The boy, in childish naïveté, thought that the world was coming to an end. It was the first dust storm that he had experienced.

Today, as I recall that dark, dusty day of the '30s on our Kansas farm, I think it most ironic that as a lad I should have linked the idea of the world coming to an end with a dust storm—the depleting of our soil upon which we depend for life-giving food.

Fairfield Osborn, President of the New York Zoological Society, says: "Forests, grasslands, soils, water, animal life—without one of these the earth will die, will become dead as the moon. Each part is dependent upon another, all are related to the movement of the whole. . . . Parts of the earth, once living and productive, have thus died at the hand of man. Others are now dying. If we cause more to die, nature will compensate for this in her own way, inexorably, as already she has begun to do."

Disclose and Clarify Your Subject

Aristotle says that the principal function of the introduction is "to make clear the end and object of your work," but he did not attach undue importance to this step. The introduction should clear the way for what is to come; it must not be misleading. Far too often a speaker uses an interest-arousing introduction, but fails to show any relation between it and his subject; worse yet, there sometimes is no relationship. Another common failing is when a speaker uses an appropriate introduction but fails to make an adequate transition from it to the statement of his subject. Transitions are always important, perhaps more between the introduction and the statement of the subject than anywhere else in the speech. Always show a definite tie up between your introduction and your topic; make your introduction truly clarify "the end and object of your work."

Note how Oveta Culp Hobby, in a speech on "Citizen Responsibilities," uses her introduction to disclose and clarify her subject:

I think most of us are aware of the growing tendency in this country to blame our problems on a completely fictitious monster which we identify quite simply as "they."

"They could be doing things differently down there," we say—with an airy wave of the hand in the general direction of Washington or Springfield or City Hall.

"They ought to do something about this . . . They need somebody with brains in that office . . . They don't know what they're doing down at the school board . . . or at the tax office . . . or in the highway department . . ."

Who is this "they" that we talk about? If we acknowledge that we live in a republic which is governed by its citizens through their elected representatives, aren't we obliged to concede that the much-maligned "they" is more accurately pronounced "we"?

Don't we, then, have to take responsibility for what happens in Washington and Springfield and downtown in the Mayor's office? Don't we have to look to ourselves when we discover that the school our children attend is overcrowded or that the highway we take to the lake on Friday evening is a death trap?[9]

The *thesis* to be clarified is the central idea of a speech. Sometimes it is called the "theme" of the composition or perhaps the "topical statement." When a speech is argumentative or persuasive its thesis is usually called a "proposition." Regardless of the name used, the thesis is always a concise summary statement of what the speech is about. It is a formal wording of your specific purpose. You will certainly not want to state your specific purpose to every audience, but if you do it should be carefully worded in the form of a thesis.

The following examples illustrate the difference between the title, subject, general end, specific purpose, and thesis of a speech:

Title: "The Measure of a Man"
Subject: Personal development
General end: To stimulate thought
Specific purpose: To impress the listeners that it is important not only to earn money for paying the bills but also to build a satisfying life's experience
Thesis: You must make a life as well as a living.

[9] *Vital Speeches,* December 15, 1954, pp. 905–908.

Title: "Will the Foot Ruler Continue to Rule?"
Subject: The metric system of measurement
General end: To secure belief
Specific purpose: To convince the audience that the metric system should replace our current American system of measurement
Thesis: The metric system of measurement is vastly superior to the American system.

If your speech is organized to include a statement of your thesis, this will come at the end of your introduction, and you will then proceed to the development of the body of your speech. A more indirect method is to withhold your exact thesis until the end, disclosing only your general subject as you move into the body of the speech.

Whether or not it is stated explicitly in your speech, word the thesis carefully and make it as concise as possible. Avoid long, complex sentences and be sure that the statement contains only one main idea. Use a complete sentence, but make it a simple sentence, free from wordiness. *Try to make your thesis memorable.* Strive for headline or slogan value. If the listener remembers anything at all about your speech, it should be your thesis. The following are examples of thesis statements taken from student speeches: "He who travels for wealth and glory never goes very far or sees very much," "There are no gains without pains," "We must curb nuclear weapons development or face inevitable annihilation," "Appeasement in Berlin is tantamount to ruin."

When Should the Introduction of the Speech Be Prepared?

Cicero emphatically declared that the introduction should be prepared last, after the body and conclusion have been carefully worked out. Most modern textbook writers concur, but this is far from a hard and fast rule. Once you have determined the thesis and specific purpose of your speech, you may want to proceed to your introduction; sometimes key ideas for the body of your speech will grow out of it.

How Long Should the Introduction Be?

The answer is obvious: it should be as long as necessary. In other words, its length should be governed by the subject, purpose, audience, and occasion. Usually a relatively short introduction will be sufficient. As a rule, it should not take more than one-tenth to one-sixth of your allotted time. Sometimes, however, it is wise and expedient to use as much as half of your time preparing your audience for your subject; you may wish to alleviate hostility in order to make your listeners receptive.

Common Faults of Speech Introductions

(1) The speech introductions of student speakers tend to be too short and fail to make difficult subjects clear. (2) Conversely, the introductions of adult speakers tend to be too long and too replete with irrelevant jokes. (3) Introductions do not adequately pertain to the speech and therefore give a false lead. (4) Introductions tend to be overly dramatic and too sensational. Interest can be obtained without standing on your head!

THE BODY OF THE SPEECH

Main Points of the Speech

The body of the speech consists of a development of one or more main points. Sometimes these main points are called "issues," but since that term is applicable only to persuasive or argumentative speeches, we use the term *main points* throughout. The speaker must always study his topic, break it down into main points, and then decide which points to use in the speech.

Only very rarely should you have more than four or five points. A large number of main points are hard for the listener to remember. It is much easier to remember and recall the development of two or three broad topics than it is to remember seven or eight. If you have broken down your topic into more than five main points, you can usually cluster some of them under a broader classification so that you have only three main points, the others being subpoints.

Main points should have parallel structure. This implies two things:

1. *They should be similar in significance.* In other words, they should all be on the same level of generalization or classification. Suppose you listed the following main points on the topic, "How to Play Tennis":

1. The history of tennis
2. The rules of tennis

3. The backhand drive
4. The strategy of tennis

A cursory examination reveals that the third main point, "The backhand drive," is not on the same level of generalization as the other three. Point number three, if you want four points, might be, "The fundamentals of tennis."

2. *They should be similar in form.* If one main point is a question, make them all questions; if one is a short phrase, make them all short phrases. Complete statements are probably the most desirable form. Once you have decided what your main points are to be, try to state them with similar rhythm, length, and phraseology. Note the lack of parallelism among these three points:

1. Is a change to the metric system really needed?
2. A change to the metric system is practical.
3. Changing to the metric system of measurement would not cost as much as most people think.

These points could easily be recast thus:

1. A change to the metric system is needed.
2. A change to the metric system is practical.
3. A change to the metric system would be inexpensive.

Obviously, not all topics can be broken down that handily; however, a large measure of parallelism can be achieved—as one speaker did on the subject of capital punishment:

1. Capital punishment is barbarian revenge.
2. Capital punishment sometimes kills the innocent.
3. Capital punishment is not a deterrent to crime.
4. Capital punishment does not permit rehabilitation.

Main points should also be worded concisely. If possible, they should be expressed in terms of listener interests. In a persuasive speech, the statement that "Federal aid to education will assure high level education for your children," is more effective than "Federal aid to education improves learning."

There are four steps to the development of a main point: (1) state the point, (2) explain and develop it, (3) use supporting materials, such as evidence or illustrative materials, (4) terminate the point—round it off—before going on to the next one.

A matter of special concern in speech organization is that of bridging the gap between main points. Since good transitions increase the coherence of your speech, work them out carefully. Transitions between main points normally terminate the preceding point and forecast the next, with some indication of an interrelationship between the points. In some persuasive speeches you will want to reveal that your points are cumulative, each building on top of the others.

The words *and*, *now*, and *so* are inadequate thought bridges. So is the dull repetition of the same word or phrase. Search for new and varied bridges. Rhetorical questions frequently make good transitions: At the close of a point you can ask a question which leads into the next point—which in essence will answer the question. For example, one might conclude a point by asking: "But can courage do it alone? Obviously not. Imagination is also needed." The next point then is imagination. Sometimes a brief restatement of preceding points will provide an adequate thought bridge, as in the following: "Having thus reviewed the rules of tennis and the basic fundamentals of the game, let's move on to another important consideration, the strategy of the game." Often a simple statement of termination of a point and an introductory statement of the next will be adequate. Below are four examples:

Thus it is apparent that our city faces an impelling problem. My solution to the problem is a simple one.

Having thus seen three specific reasons for the proposal, let's move on to the fourth and final one.

That is the past. Now let's look at the present.

The results of the first experiment are obvious. The second experiment involves a different principle.

Methods of Arrangement

After you have isolated the main points for your speech and have decided upon the basic organizational approach, you will need to arrange your main points in some effective manner—and the manner you select is largely determined by your analysis of the subject. You will soon discover that some topics can easily be broken down in certain stock ways. For example, if one were to speak on the subject of the United States government, one might have three main points: the executive, the legislative, and the judicial branches. In the following there are suggested various methods of arrangement which will both aid in your analysis of the topic and help to give the body of your speech a definite design or form.

TEMPORAL ARRANGEMENT. Many subjects can best be developed by a time sequence. You might, for example, break down the subject, "The Story of the Airplane," into four phases of development.

1. Wilbur and Orville Wright's flying machine at Kitty Hawk demonstrated man's ability to fly.
2. World War I saw the advent of the airplane as a war machine.
3. World War II brought rapid advances in airplane development.
4. The postwar era produced the faster-than-sound jet plane.

In giving simple instructions, we often employ a time sequence—telling our listeners what to do step by step. A special type of time sequence is the stock "past, present, future" pattern. A speaker using this approach will trace the history of a topic, survey existing circumstances, and forecast the future. A political speaker often uses a past-present-future design. He extols his former party leaders and their achievements, praises the good work the party is presently doing, and then claims that his party will benefit the listener most in the future.

A temporal plan of development is well adapted to a biographical speech or eulogy. The speaker discusses his subject's growth and development, recounts what he or she accomplished in life, and then perhaps predicts what influence these achievements will have upon the future.

SPATIAL ARRANGEMENT. This is a useful method for arranging certain types of informative materials. In a speech of description you may, for instance, be able to arrange your materials geographically, such as from east to west, north to south, bottom to top. Specifically, in discussing the development of the American frontier, you might want to arrange your materials something like this:

1. Settlers moved beyond the Appalachian mountains.
2. A few hardy souls pushed on to Kentucky and the midwestern regions.
3. Free land brought many settlers farther west to the Great Plains.
4. The California gold rush bridged the continent.

5. The mountainous regions between the plains and California became the last frontier.

Note how this speech on the development of the American frontier combines temporal and spatial relations into a logical pattern or design.

TOPICAL ARRANGEMENT.   Some speech subjects can best be broken down by classifications, types, or categories. For example, cattle can be classified as dairy and beef, horses as race, riding, and draught; these natural classifications can then be used as topics or main points in a speech. Other stock topical designs are: local, state, national, international; theory, practice; heredity, environment; structure, function; political, economic, social; background, characteristics, accomplishments; resemblances, differences; physical, mental, emotional, spiritual; symptoms, cure, prevention; and so forth. The words *who, what, why, when, how,* and *where* can often be successfully used as the basis for a topical analysis and arrangement.

Speeches to secure belief usually are arranged topically, for they tend to cite reasons "why" a person is for or against something. A speaker may present three reasons why he feels that "A Democratic Form of Government Is Best," such as:

1. It guarantees legitimate freedom to the individual.
2. It reflects the will of the majority.
3. It deepens the citizen's feeling of responsibility.

In most types of arrangement, certain points naturally come first, others second, and still others last. This, however, is not true of a topical speech; the speaker must somehow decide which point to place first, which to place second, and which to place last. Cicero emphatically advised: "Let the arguments of most weight be put foremost; yet . . . some of superior efficiency be reserved for the peroration; if any are of but moderate strength . . . they may be thrown into the main body and into the midst of the group."[10] At another point he maintained that of the orator's "own strongest arguments, some he will place in the van, some he will employ to bring up the rear, and the weaker ones he will place in the centre."[11]

A modern researcher, Harold Sponberg, concludes from a study

10 *De Oratore* II, lxxvii.
11 *Orator,* XV.

testing "The relative effectiveness of climax and anticlimax order in an argumentative speech" that if two or more main points differ in amount of material, *the longer one should be presented first.*[12] A study by William J. McGuire showed that placing communications highly favorable to the listener in a primary position, followed by those less desirable, produces more opinion change than the reverse order.[13]

In light of Sponberg's evidence, and considering the fact that the audience's attention usually is highest at the outset of the speech, we are inclined to agree with Cicero that the strongest argument, as a rule, should be placed first. On the other hand, if points of agreement are to be presented, they should precede controversial issues. No matter what the order of arrangement, never end the speech with a weak point, since the ending leaves the final impression upon the audience.

CAUSAL ARRANGEMENT. A speaker who uses a cause-effect development begins by identifying certain forces and follows this with an explanation of their effects. Conversely, he may move from effect to cause, describing conditions or events first and identifying the causes later. An example of a causal relationship speech is the topic, "How was militant nationalism a cause of World War I?"

PROBLEM-SOLUTION ARRANGEMENT. This method of arrangement is used in persuasive speaking. The speaker begins by describing a problem and then proposes, outlines, and advocates a solution. In making an analysis of this type of speech subject, the following stock questions are often helpful:

1. Does a need or problem actually exist?
2. Is the proposed solution a workable one?
3. Will the benefits of this solution be greater than its disadvantages?
4. Is this solution better than any other plan or policy which could be proposed?

You may not want to deal with all four of these questions in your speech, but a consideration of them will give you a sound analysis of your subject and will help you discover the essential arguments. It is

---

[12] *Speech Monographs*, 13 (1946), 35–44.
[13] Reported in Carl Iver Hovland, *et al., The Order of Presentation in Persuasion,* Yale University Press, 1957, chap. 7.

important in this type of speech that you describe the problem vividly, clearly outline a solution, and demonstrate that there is a high degree of probability that your solution will solve or alleviate the problem.

It usually is extremely effective if at the end of the speech you can get the listener to visualize the solution. Stimulate his imagination with these three approaches: (1) Get him to picture the many benefits of your proposal. How will it profit him or his family? Use imagery so he can plainly see the advantages. (2) Use a threat appeal. Make graphic for him what will happen if your solution is not accepted. Picture how the problem will affect his life. (3) Use a method of contrast. Get the listener to visualize first what things will be like under your plan, and then trigger his imagination about how bad things will be without your plan.

Dr. Robert F. Goheen, President of Princeton University, used a visualization step in a speech asking for adequate support for the total university enterprise.

Here in conclusion, I am forced to point out that unless there is developed adequate understanding and adequate support for the total university enterprise, any one of these tensions can get out of hand, with the result that the bowstring may snap and even the bow.

Great Conceptions are not themselves enough to give our arrows flight, nor our lyres music. It takes input to get output. It takes money —far more money than as yet we Americans have been willing to devote to higher education.

Quality-quantity, teaching-research, internal national needs-international responsibilities, science-humanism, and detachment-involvement; this battery of vital, counterstraining forces within the modern university constitute, when in balance, both its strength and its promise. To fire each engine in this potent cluster we must grasp the importance to the total assembly of each of these antitheses, and match this understanding with the support required to ignite and sustain their effective interplay. The forward thrust will not be felt in the universities only but in our entire country, whose historic mission is as a force for human freedom.[14]

A special type of problem-solution arrangement is the so-called *this-or-nothing* speech. Here, as in any problem-solution speech, you first describe the problem and then itemize and analyze suggested solutions to it. Point out that three or four courses of action can be

14 *Vital Speeches*, February 15, 1961, p. 283.

used in solving this problem and that you want to analyze them and try to determine which is the most advantageous. Carefully eliminate alternative proposals by demonstrating that they will not work or have too many inherent disadvantages; then reveal that there is only one course of action remaining—yours. Hence, "this or nothing" must be done, and almost anything is better than nothing.

The *this-or-nothing* approach is effective when there are a number of outstanding proposals. In such a case it is almost imperative that you deal with and eliminate the alternative proposals.

Research has offered the following conclusions concerning "presenting one or both sides" of a question:

1. Presenting both sides is more effective for listeners who are initially opposed to the stand taken; conversely, the one-sided speech is more effective for listeners initially favoring the stand taken.
2. Presenting both sides is more effective with better educated listeners; presenting one side only is more effective with the less educated.

The researchers conclude that the first difference in effectiveness "may be reversed for the less educated men and, in the extreme case, the material giving both sides may have a negative effect on poorly educated men already convinced of the major position taken by a program." They offer this important advice: "From these results it would be expected that the total effect of either kind of program on the group as a whole would depend on the group's educational composition and on the initial division of opinion in the group. Thus, ascertaining this information about the composition of an audience might be of considerable value in choosing the most effective type of presentation."[15]

Since there is a similar relation between presenting both sides of the question (advantages-disadvantages) and discussing alternative proposals in the form of the *this-or-nothing* arrangement, the conclusions of the above research findings can apply there too. In the final analysis, whether or not the speaker should present one or both sides of the question or use the *this-or-nothing* technique may depend upon the time allowed for the speech. Presenting and discussing several alternative solutions takes time, and, if the time limit is too short to permit adequate treatment of a number of proposed solu-

15 Carl I. Hovland, Arthur A. Lumsdaine, Fred D. Sheffield, *Experiments on Mass Communication*, Princeton University Press, 1949, p. 215.

tions, it may be wise to use a simple *problem-solution* arrangement rather than a *this-or-nothing* type.

You are not limited to one or another arrangement sequence in a speech. Sometimes you may find it helpful to combine two methods; or you may want to use different arrangement methods in developing main points. In a problem-solution speech, for example, you might develop the problem temporally or spatially.

CONCLUSION

Speeches should not just end; they should be brought to a carefully planned conclusion, ending on a note of completeness and finality. The conclusion should round out the creative piece and perform three principal functions:

1. *Re-emphasize the central idea.* The entire purpose of the conclusion is to focus attention upon the theme of your speech and, in the process, leave your listeners with the most favorable impression possible. Hence, it is usually well to restate your thesis as you lead into your conclusion.

2. *Summarize or crystallize your main ideas.* Sometimes you will want to summarize your points by restating them one by one. If it is important that your audience remember your main points, a simple restatement of them will probably be the best procedure, since research has amply demonstrated that restatement of points in a speech is a positive aid to retention. As a rule, it is more effective to draw together or crystallize the content of your speech without a routine itemization of your main points. Tie the threads together so that the pattern of your speech is clearly revealed. In summarizing your ideas, be sure to observe Quintilian's warning that the final recapitulation be as brief as possible: "For if we devote too much time thereto, the peroration will cease to be an enumeration and will constitute something very like a second speech."

3. *Dramatize and ennoble your central idea.* In an informative speech there is no need for this step, but in any persuasive speech success may hinge upon how capably you end it. Your final appeal should lift the persuasive speech to a climactic close and should motivate your audience. Some emotion usually needs to be used to accomplish this.

The following conclusion taken from a student's speech of tribute to J. Sterling Morton, founder of Arbor Day, illustrates the functions of the conclusion. He uses a summary as a lead-in to his conclusion, follows with a short quotation, and then seeks to ennoble his subject and lift the speech to an effective close.

Courage, industry, imagination. These were the qualities that caused the *Chicago Tribune* in eulogizing Morton to remark: "The qualities which characterized him . . . are not so frequently met with among public men that young men can afford to neglect to study his life."

Today as the traveler drives through Nebraska City on Highway 73, at the west edge of the city he sees Arbor Lodge, Morton's home, which has been preserved for posterity. Around the magnificently kept house the traveler sees beautiful flowers and shrubbery, and trees of many species shading the spacious lawn. At the entrance of the estate stands a large statute bearing the simple inscription: "J. Sterling Morton—1832–1902—AUTHOR OF ARBOR DAY."

Thousands of forest trees and fruit trees, shrubs and vines owe their existence to this true Johnny Appleseed. Arbor Day is no doubt the thing for which Morton will be longest remembered, and this seemingly complies with his wishes, for in the conclusion of his Arbor Day Address at the University of Nebraska in 1887, Morton directed: "If you seek my monument, look around you."

Useful Devices for Ending a Speech

A TERSE, PROVOCATIVE QUOTATION. Any quotation used in the conclusion of a speech should be short; when possible, one sentence is often best. Jo Mohri, the freshman speech student quoted above, ended her tribute to Helen Keller with a quotation:

I feel it is through her extremely great courage and unlimited determination that Helen Keller was able to learn to speak and help others who were handicapped in the same way as she was. The things she has accomplished are almost incredible. She learned Italian merely so she could read Dante and Petrarch in their own tongue—quite a feat for anyone, to say nothing of one who can neither see nor hear. She summed up her attitude of her life well when she compared herself to the sea.

"The dark, too," she says, "has its deep silent currents and dangerous reefs, its monsters, its creatures of beauty, its derelicts and ships. In the dark, too, there is a star to steer by, and no matter how far I travel there are always before me vast oceans of experience I have not yet explored."

A SHORT, PERTINENT VERSE. A poetic quotation or even a verse of your own construction can be an effective way of terminating your speech. Too often, however, the verse is really not relevant to the central idea of the speech, or, at best, is only vaguely relevant and will therefore not produce the final punch needed.

Dr. Rufus E. Clement, President of Atlanta University, speaking in Denver at the annual convocation of the United Negro College Fund, concluded his speech with a personal anecdote and an ending verse.

In conclusion, I would have you remember that these colleges are training students for "inclusion" in American life. Ours is no "separatist" movement. We are not training leaders for a fifty-first state. We are training people who want to contribute to America. These colleges desire and hope and work for a stronger America. We do not believe that America can afford to ignore, to ill-train, to cast aside, one tenth of its strength in the decisive decade which is in front of us. To do so, in our opinion, would be most disastrous. These colleges teach loyalty to the highest and finest ideals of this republic. We, too, sing "America."

I think that this was never so strongly borne in upon me, personally, as when one month ago today, the twenty-seventh of February, I was sitting before my television screen watching the Squaw Valley telecast of the hockey game between the teams representing the Soviet Union and the United States of America. Finally when the decisive goal, hockey goal, had been scored by an American . . . I found my elation mounting so high that I suddenly discovered that I was standing, and to my utter amazement there were tears streaming down my face. As this happened, I stopped and my other self said to me, Are you a fool? Why do you weep? Why, why, why are *you* so glad? There isn't a single Negro on the Winter Olympics team. These are not your people, this is the United States of America and has nothing to do with you. And just as suddenly I put down all of this riotous, turgid voice within me and said, This *is* my team, this is *America*, I *am represented there, this is my country also.*

> Honest work for today,
> Honest hope for tomorrow
> Are these worth nothing
> Save the hands they make weary, the hearts they leave dreary?
> Hush! The seven-fold heavens are telling:
> He that overcometh will all things inherit!

"How would you have us?"[16]

[16] *Representative American Speeches,* The Reference Shelf, 32, no. 4 (1959–1960), 187–188.

A SHORT ANECDOTE.   Concluding a speech with a pertinent illustration can be as effective as beginning the speech with one. The illustration used should dramatize and ennoble your theme. It should tell the whole story of your speech in a few short lines. Unless the speech is one to entertain, however, humorous anecdotes probably should be avoided in the conclusion, for they may detract from the central thought. The preceding example from a speech by Dr. Clement is an excellent example of a conclusion with a personal anecdote.

A CONCLUDING THOUGHT BY THE SPEAKER.   A speaker usually will do well to conclude with his own ideas and his own words. One effective method of doing this is to refer back to the introduction, especially if it contained an anecdote. The speaker thus may be able to point out things that would have been different for the person or persons in the story if his solution had been in effect.

The way in which Abraham Lincoln ended his First Inaugural Address is an example of an excellent speech conclusion; it rounds off the speech splendidly and ends on a sublime note.

In your hands, my dissatisfied fellow-countrymen, and not in mine, is the momentous issue of civil war. The government will not assail you. You can have no conflict without being yourselves the aggressors. You have no oath registered in heaven to destroy the government, while I shall have the most solemn one to "preserve, protect, and defend" it.

I am loath to close. We are not enemies, but friends. We must not be enemies. Though passion may have strained, it must not break, our bonds of affection. The mystic chords of memory, stretching from every battlefield and patriot grave to every living heart and hearthstone all over this broad land, will yet swell the chorus of the Union when again touched, as surely they will be, by the better angels of our nature.

In discussing speech introductions, we placed considerable stress upon the first sentence of the speech. The last sentence is even more important. It is your final statement to the audience and should, therefore, carry considerable impact. Make your ending reach for sublimity of thought, if this is appropriate. Almost always try to make your final sentence terse and simple: it should place a period at the end of your speech. In a persuasive speech this is most important.

A good example of an ending both sublime and full of impact is

Winston Churchill's: "Let us therefore brace ourselves to our duty and so bear ourselves that if the British Commonwealth and Empire last for a thousand years, men will still say 'This was their finest hour.' "

MAKING AN OUTLINE

The composition of a speech is facilitated by a carefully prepared outline. Such an outline should help the speaker view the speech as a whole unit of thinking, make relationships clear, and arrange materials to give proper balance and emphasis to the central thesis. It also should help to insure accuracy and, especially, relevancy of materials.

Not every speech will require a detailed outline. Short talks can sometimes be constructed and delivered from a few simple notes. But a blueprint is almost always needed in constructing an effective major speech.

Since outlining is part of the work of organization, it must serve a specific individual goal. An outline, like a speech, may be developed in logical or psychological order; or it may serve primarily for clarification purposes.

Important Principles of Outlining

1. Use complete thought phrases or complete sentences.
2. Use only one idea in each statement.
3. Be consistent in the use of symbols. The following system is more widely used than any other:

    I.
       A.
          1.
             a.
                (1)
                (2)
             b.
          2.
       B.
    II.

Not every heading needs to be divided as often as in the above illustration, the symbols you use should appear in this order: I, A, 1, a, (1).

4. Be consistent in using complete sentences or key words. A complete sentence outline usually is better since it phrases ideas more clearly and specifically. A key word outline should be adequate, however, for most speech subjects with which you are well acquainted.

5. Use a logical sequence of ideas. Your materials should have cohesiveness and a logical flow from point to point. Be sure your outline makes sense as you go down from one symbol to another. Here is an example of completely illogical arrangement:

I. Lou Gehrig is an example of baseball's greatest heroes.
   A. Baseball is justly called "America's National Pastime."
      1. Players perform heroic feats, even in the face of great odds.
      2. Babe Ruth devoted considerable time to visiting sick children.
   B. Players demonstrate remarkable skill.
   C. Pitched ball may travel over 90 m.p.h.
      1. Sentiment is an important part of the game.
      2. Special plays such as the double play require perfect timing.

At various points of your outline, you should pause to check the logical support and audience appeal of your materials. For example, Points A and B in the full outline which follows contain statistics which help to support the main point. The subpoints under C contain statistics, and also a direct personal and familial appeal to the listener. When you have completed your outline, check the logical support and audience appeal of each point, as well as of the speech as a whole. If your instructor requires an outline for your speeches, he may want you to identify your supports and appeals in the left-hand margin, as in the following:

	I.
	A.
Statistics	1.
Analogy	2.
Appeal to fear	3.
	B.
Explanation	1.
Specific instance	2.

Included here is a student's detailed outline for a speech on public health insurance. Study it carefully. Go through it and analyze the supports and appeals used to develop each major point. Evaluate the wording of the points and decide if the statements are phrased effectively. What criticisms can you make of the concepts and their supports?

INTRODUCTION

I. The health of the American people is appallingly bad.
   A. In World War II, 8 out of 10 men eligible for the draft had physical defects.
   B. In the Korean War, 15 percent of eligible draftees were rejected for medical reasons.
   C. Dental problems are even greater—for children and adults alike.
      1. If your child is average, by the time he is 17 he will have 7 decayed, missing, or filled teeth.
      2. And if you are over 30, the chances are 8 in 10 that you will sometime have some form of pyorrhea.
II. Unexpected medical costs can work a hardship on the stricken families.
   A. My family last year learned the magnitude of a health problem when my mother became an invalid as a result of a cerebral hemorrhage.
      1. The illness was sudden and unexpected.
      2. The hospitalization and medical costs are extremely high and promise to be so for perhaps several years.
   B. Each year thousands of other people are confronted with the same problem.
III. A system of federal health insurance is urgently needed. (Thesis—may be stated at this point or withheld until later in the speech.)

BODY

I. The high cost of medical care is a principal reason for our nation's medical problems.
   A. Illness rates are highest among the poorer classes.
      1. Low income groups have twice as high an illness rate as the middle income class. (E. Wight Bakke, "The Debate on Socialized Medicine," *Connecticut Medical Journal*, 6, October, 1942, 784.)
      2. Many poor people usually have to omit preventive medical care and periodic checkups; they often follow the diagnosis of friends.
      3. Low income groups cannot afford to pay for adequate medical care or for private health insurance.
   B. Rising costs of medical care have made it difficult for people in other income groups also.

    1. Per family medical costs are 42 percent greater than in 1953 and five times as much as in 1940. (*New York Times,* February 15, 1960, "Talk About Medical Costs—They're Not Only for the Old People." And *United States News,* 43, July 5, 1957, 34.)

    2. The rate of increase of medical costs is much greater than the general cost of living. (Jerry E. Bishop, "Health Insurance," *Wall Street Journal,* 154, August 27, 1959, 1.)

II. Voluntary health insurance does not provide adequate protection.

  A. Coverage of Blue Cross insurance is inadequate.

    1. Hospital costs represent only a small portion of our medical bills.

      a. 90 percent of all physician services occur outside of a hospital.

      b. Insurance covers only part of hospital costs.

    2. The aged are poorly covered by Blue Cross insurance, for most Blue Cross plans have age limits.

  B. Commercial insurance plans have most of these same pitfalls, some even worse.

III. A plan of compulsory health insurance could provide adequate medical care for all people.

  A. All patients could be given the care they really need, regardless of cost.

  B. Stress could be put on the prevention of disease.

  C. Medical costs would be distributed according to ability to pay.

CONCLUSION

I. Health is a public concern.

  A. The annual cost of illness is a handicap to our national efficiency.

    1. We need a strong, productive America to fight the Red menace.

    2. The Russians are much more conscious than we of the importance of national good health.

  B. Patients suffering from communicable diseases are a direct menace to neighbors.

    1. By insuring the good health of someone else, you help insure your own.

    2. A communicable disease may prevent you from working long enough to cause an appreciable loss of income.

II. Health is a moral matter.

  A. Christian ethics dictate a right to the best possible health.

  B. You may be the next to be stricken with a serious health problem.

C. Urge your Congressman to act upon a system of federal health insurance.

NOTES FOR SPEAKING

After you have completed your outline, you will probably need to prepare notes to take with you to the speech lectern. These notes, which serve merely as an aid to your memory, need take no special form. Actually, the form most usable for you is the best. Perhaps the biggest pitfall of the beginning speaker is an inclination to prepare an elaborate set of notes, more than likely in sentence form or even something which resembles a manuscript. Avoid this temptation and limit your notes to key or "trigger" phrases. Detailed, voluminous notes will almost certainly be difficult to follow, and you will either become confused and spend awkward moments looking for the next thought or will follow your notes too carefully and so lack directness and eye contact.

Put your notes on cards rather than sheets of paper, which tend to be too flexible to manage. Usually 4 x 6 inch cards are the most functional; you cannot get enough on smaller cards, and larger ones tend to be awkward.

Try to limit yourself to three cards at most, with notations *on one side only*. Number your cards; then if you drop them or get them mixed somehow, it will be easy to rearrange them swiftly.

Notes can be either "content" or "descriptive." Content notes consist of key phrases, sentences, and visual aids, all of which give the exact materials to be used. Descriptive notes merely give reminders as to what comes next. Thus descriptive notes might simply say, "Give statistics," whereas content notes might say, "50,000 get inadequate care." For especially difficult and unfamiliar subjects you may want to make key sentence notes; the sentences may help you word your speech more fluently on the platform.

Write large enough so that you can read your notes easily. Typed notes are best. Double space between main points and perhaps even between important subpoints, for your eyes can pick up a key heading more easily if a blank space precedes it.

During the delivery of your speech, do not try to conceal your notes by holding them behind you. There was a time when the speaker was advised to make very small notes which could be hidden in the palm of the hand, with the hope that the audience would be deceived into thinking that he was speaking without notes. This is poor practice. In the first place, the audience will notice your attempt at deception all too easily; and, second, the notes will necessarily be so small that you will have a hard time reading them. If you are speaking from a lectern, you may want to lay your notes on it; but if the lectern is low and your notes difficult to see, pick them up and hold them at a more useful height. Notes skillfully used are not distracting to an audience. Feel free to hold them up in your hand so that you can read them without effort. Do not press the cards tight against your body so that you have to peer past your nose and down your chest to see them. In fact, feel free to gesture with the hand which holds them.

It is true, however, that a speaker achieves maximum effectiveness when he is able to speak without notes. Eye contact is extremely important in speaking, and every time a speaker looks at his notes he breaks contact with his audience. However, unless you feel completely sure of yourself without notes, it is better to use them. They will be less of a handicap than awkward mental blocks or omission of major points. And even if you decide to speak without notes, make a set to place handily in your pocket or on the lectern, just in case you should need them.

PROJECTS AND EXERCISES

For speaking projects see Part Three.

1. Analyze the introductions and conclusions of the speeches in a recent issue of *Vital Speeches*. Note the techniques employed. List which introductions and conclusions you think effective, and why?
2. Prepare a careful analysis of the organization of a speech found in *Vital Speeches*. Identify the basic approach and the patterns of arrangement. Evaluate the logical progression and coherence of the speech.
3. List, in order, three to five of the most common weaknesses you have observed in speech introductions.
4. Imagine you are going to make a 20- to 30-minute informative speech before a local civic club about your college or university. What would be the dominant pattern in the arrangement of your materials?
5. Which of the functions of speech introductions seem to you to be most important in these speech situations?
   a. The preacher in his church.

  b. A high school commencement speaker.
  c. You, making an informative speech in class.
  d. A professor giving a lecture.
  e. A soapbox orator on the street corner.

TOPICS FOR DISCUSSION

1. Distinguish between the title, thesis, and specific purpose of a speech.
2. Read Chapter 16, "Organizing the Complete Speech: The Motivated Sequence," in Alan H. Monroe, *Principles and Types of Speech,* Scott, Foresman, 4th ed., 1955. Compare this method of speech organization with what you just read in this chapter. For what types of speeches can "the motivated sequence" be used most effectively?
3. What determines the number of main points you will have in your speech?
4. This chapter presents five basic functions of a speech introduction. Does any one of them stand out as being most important?
5. Do you think that the thesis of a speech should always be clearly stated?
6. What is meant by the "ending note"? How important is it to a speech? How does the speech purpose affect its importance?
7. What is meant by "building a need to listen"?
8. Are the words *arrangement* and *organization* synonymous?
9. How does the importance of a summary in the conclusion vary with the speech purposes?
10. Look up the meaning of the word *disposition.* Can it mean *organization? Arrangement?*
11. Is it ever advisable to have more than one central idea in a speech?
12. What is your opinion of the suggestion to prepare your introduction last?
13. Many speech authorities state that when making short talks it is wise to bring out your strongest and best points first. What is the reasoning behind this advice?

ADDITIONAL READINGS

Baird, A. Craig, and Knower, Franklin H., *General Speech: An Introduction,* 2nd ed., McGraw-Hill, 1957, chap. 5.
Braden, Waldo W., and Gehring, Mary Louise, *Speech Practices, A Resource Book for the Student of Public Speaking,* Harper, 1958, chap. 3.
Brembeck, Winston Lamont, and Howell, William Smiley, *Persuasion, A Means of Social Control,* Prentice-Hall, 1952, chap. 19.

Brigance, William Norwood, *Speech: Its Techniques and Disciplines in a Free Society,* Appleton-Century-Crofts, 1952, chaps. 11, 12, and 14.

Bryant, Donald C., and Wallace, Karl R., *Fundamentals of Public Speaking,* 3rd ed., Appleton-Century-Crofts, 1960, chaps. 9, 10, and 22.

Crocker, Lionel, *Public Speaking for College Students,* 3rd ed., American, 1956, chap. 17.

Gray, Giles W., and Braden, Waldo W., *Public Speaking: Principles and Practice,* Harper, 1951, chaps. 13–15.

McBurney, James H., and Wrage, Ernest J., *The Art of Good Speech,* Prentice-Hall, 1953, chap. 12.

Monroe, Alan H., *Principles and Types of Speech,* 4th ed., Scott, Foresman, 1955, chaps. 14–17.

Thonssen, Lester, and Baird, A. Craig, *Speech Criticism, The Development of Standards for Rhetorical Appraisal,* Ronald, 1948, chap. 14.

❧ ❧ ❧ ❧ DIMENSION V ❧ ❧ ❧ ❧
Language

❧ 10 ❧
Language in Life

THE MIRACLE OF LANGUAGE

Language is the principal medium used for transmitting ideas in speech communication. Before we give our full attention to the role of language in a speech, however, let us first explore its role in human experience.

We come to know our world, its past and present, and to conceive of its future by means of language. Language gives us the tool by which we think, speak, learn, and give shape to our lives. Language creates for us our real world, for words prescribe in part the very horizons about us.

The structure of language as we know it is intricate and complex. In the functional sense, language is the system by which we attempt to symbolize meaning for each other and for ourselves. How language was first originated is not certainly known, although there are a number of theories about it. The invention and development of the alphabet, however, represented the great breakthrough in devising a science of languages; before that, a system of pictographs and hieroglyphics was used.

But not until the invention of the printing press, in comparatively modern times, did we have a means of recording and pooling the knowledge and wisdom of the past on a broad scale. This was a truly revolutionary development, by which words were given new power to bind people and generations together. Men die but their thoughts and deeds are preserved by the printed word. Its power is ably described in the following statement by S. I. Hayakawa, a well-known authority on language:

Language, that is to say, is the indispensable mechanism of human life —of life such as ours that is molded, guided, enriched, and made possible by the accumulation of the *past* experience of members of our species. . . . The cultural accomplishments of the ages, the invention of cooking, of weapons, of writing, of printing, of methods of building, of games and amusements, of means of transportation, and the discoveries of all the arts and sciences come to us as *free gifts from the dead*. These gifts, which none of us has done anything to earn, offer us not only the opportunity for a richer life than any of our forebears enjoyed, but also the opportunity to add to the sum total of human achievement by our own contributions, however small.[1]

Language and Learning

Language is the chief medium for basic learning procedures. From kindergarten to graduate school, words must serve us as we learn about history, art, literature, science, law, and philosophy. Yet, in spite of the many required courses that are devoted solely to the improvement of language skills—reading, writing, speaking, and listening—we hear loud complaints that Johnny can't read and that the college student is woefully deficient in English composition.

Words can be your gateway to learning, college or no college. You need words to cultivate your mental powers and invigorate the mind. The way you use words is to a large degree the measure of your mind. You need words to live with yourself—it has been said that an educated man is one who can wait for a train that is four hours late at two o'clock in the morning in a strange railroad station without being bored. You need words to crystallize your ideas. In reflection, you force your brain to digest an idea as you carefully phrase it into words. Words, then, can be used as tools with which you sharpen your own mind and develop your perceptual powers.

How Language Comes to Us

An infant's acquisition of language is high on the ladder of accomplishments in his struggles to communicate. At first he communicates by means of action—kicking, reaching, squirming, and

---

[1] S. I. Hayakawa, *Language in Action,* Harcourt, Brace, 1941, p. 14.

batting his arms about—and by various types of vocalization—crying, screaming, cooing, and other utterances. Finally, after a year or so, he learns to associate a few sounds with objects, or with things he can or cannot have and do. Adults encourage him, and as the child repeats the same sounds the identification of sound and object becomes stronger. He now rapidly learns other words from adults. This process represents his initiation into a world of language and meaning. Reading and writing come last on the ladder of his communication skills, usually not until he starts to school. In many backward areas of the world these skills go undeveloped during the individual's entire lifetime.

Language as Clothing for Thoughts

We hear such expressions as "the speaker clothed his ideas in effective language" or "words are the garments of the mind." The analogy has some merit as we strive to understand the nature and function of language. We wear clothing and use language for three main reasons: (1) We do so for utilitarian purposes. Clothing makes us comfortable; it keeps us warm in winter and cool in summer. Similarly, language gets things done, sells services, leads people, explains processes, and so on. The great bulk of our language is devoted to practical undertakings. (2) We wear clothing for purposes of *adornment,* to please our sense of the aesthetic. Likewise, we use language to beautify, glorify, and emotionalize ideas—in song, sermon, oratory, and literature. In such communications we have portraits of thought, rather than the casual snapshots of a candid camera.

Some speeches contain more than just the surface of thought; they also symbolize the deep emotions and sublime aspirations of the heart. These speeches go beyond what is merely practical; they reach inner realities and are therefore thought beautiful. Note, for instance, what Shakespeare does in the last scene of *Hamlet.* After the Prince has died from the poison-tipped sword, his lifelong friend, Horatio, does not pronounce him dead in any literal, factual manner. He does so figuratively: "Now cracks a noble heart. Good night, sweet prince, may flights of angels sing thee to thy rest."

The Declaration of Independence impresses us with its literary value as well as its ideas. Suppose this document had been worded in a casual, colloquial and ultra-informal manner, yet with the factual substance essentially retained. The following excerpts provide an interesting comparison. The first one is the opening of the Declaration of Independence as Thomas Jefferson penned it:

When in the course of human events, it becomes necessary for one people to dissolve the political bands which have connected them with another, and to assume among the Powers of the earth, the separate and equal station to which the Laws of Nature and of Nature's God entitle them, a decent respect to the opinions of mankind requires that they should declare the causes which impel them to the separation.

We hold these truths to be self-evident, that all men are created equal, that they are endowed by their Creator with certain unalienable Rights, that among these are Life, Liberty and the pursuit of Happiness. That to secure these rights, Governments are instituted among Men, deriving their just powers from the consent of the governed. That whenever any Form of Government becomes destructive of these ends, it is the Right of the People to alter or to abolish it, and to institute new Government, laying its foundation on such principles and organizing its powers in such form, as to them shall seem most likely to effect their Safety and Happiness. . . .

Now compare this with a paraphrase of these words into the vernacular by H. L. Mencken:

When things get so balled up that the people of a country got to cut loose from some other country, and go it on their own hook, without asking no permission from nobody, excepting maybe God Almighty, then they ought to let everybody know why they done it, so that everybody can see they are not trying to put nothing over on nobody.

All we got to say on this proposition is this: first, me and you is as good as anybody else, and maybe a damn sight better; second, nobody ain't got no right to take away none of our rights; third, every man has got a right to live, to come and go as he pleases, and to have a good time whichever way he likes, so long as he don't interfere with nobody else. That any government that don't give a man them rights ain't worth a damn; also, people ought to choose the kind of government they want themselves, and nobody else ought to have no say in the matter. That whenever any government don't do this, then the people have got a right to give it the bum's rush and put in one that will take care of their interests. . . .[2]

(3) We wear clothing and use language to express our *individuality and personality*. Your language differs from that of every other per-

[2] H. L. Mencken, "The Declaration of Independence in American," in Dwight Macdonald (ed.), *Parodies, An Anthology from Chaucer to Beerbohm—And After*, Random House, 1960, pp. 442–443.

son. It is part of your unique personality; it reflects your early home life, your associates, the jobs you have had, the books you have read, your sense of security or insecurity, your temperament, and your attitude toward the world about you. Your choice of words and the way you form your sentences are aspects of your individuality. The style of Will Rogers contains in a large measure the secret of his charm and popular appeal. This, in varying degree, is true of Webster, Bryan, Ingersoll, both Roosevelts (Franklin and Theodore), Churchill, Stevenson, and many others. No doubt you have known college professors whose unique expressions reflected and enhanced their personalities.

Note, however, that clothes do not make the man—they express and reveal him. Words also do not make the thought—they symbolize and represent it.

Language and Democracy

Language is perhaps the most democratic institution in the world. The real authority as to the worth of a word, at least an English one, rests with the people. The way they write and speak makes a profound difference in the English language you eventually use. Dictionaries are merely systematic indications of what is probably good or preferable word usage: how, at that time, the people are using words.

Language and the people who use it in speech and writing play a unique and vital role in a democracy. The price of freedom, says Lord Bryce, is eternal vigilance. This vigilance must first come from the habit of fighting for and regaining again and again the blessings of liberty, by responsible choices supported by responsible speech. Freedom of speech and action places directly upon our shoulders the responsibility of shaping and formulating the kind of society in which we choose to live. These choices and responsibilities do not exist among totalitarian governments, whose rulers fear freedom of speech. Such governments use language, but communication works only one way, from the top down. Language is an instrument of power in the form of directives, slogans, and decrees, telling the people what they can and cannot do. Democracy, on the other hand, cannot exist without freedom of speech. And freedom of speech means more than the license to talk: it means to share fully at all times the responsibility of energizing and communicating ideas among the citizenry in order to have wise and efficient government.

Words Around Us

We are born into a sea of words which create our culture and shape our personal destinies. We are bombarded every day with words—from radio, television, newspapers, magazines, billboards, junk mail, books, lectures, conversations, committee discussions. We speak as many as 25,000 words in a single day and hear many more. Our vocabularies grow larger and larger, our dictionaries thicker and thicker. During World War II some five thousand new words were added to the English language each year; and the United States Air Force alone prepared a dictionary of nearly 600 pages containing more than 16,500 words and phrases which have special meaning for people in this service.

THE WORLD OF WORDS

Symbols and Things

Words are the symbols of things and ideas. The child may learn the meaning of the word *doggie,* after hearing it repeated many times, by associating the sound with the furry pet he plays with. Then, when he sees and feels another furry object—perhaps a Teddy bear—for the first time, he may by association call it a doggie, too. His frame of reference is narrow and limited, but later in life he will discover that Teddy bear and doggie are not the same and that, furthermore, there are many kinds of doggies.

This is a simple illustration of how words come to us. Faced with a complicated system of symbols, we learn to master the intricacies of language gradually and slowly. Language appears in the form of patterns to the ear and eye. Words are in sequence, in combinations to which we become accustomed as we express ideas and wants, and we come to understand others by learning to recognize similar symbolization.

We must always remember that the word is not the thing itself; it is a symbol. You cannot stroke the word *cat* or eat the word *popcorn.* A glass jar filled with peanut butter does not become applesauce by changing the label on the jar. Shakespeare knew this when he said, "A rose by any other name would smell as sweet." Yet people tend to form such firm habits of identifying the symbols with the thing to which the symbol refers that disturbing breakdowns in communication result. This also happens when they assume that the meaning or reference is inherent in the symbol.

The Strange Power of Words

Words, however, have the power of objects. Lord Byron, a master craftsman of words, said of them:

> But words are things, and a small drop of ink
> Falling like dew upon a thought, produces
> That which makes thousands, perhaps millions, think.

When we talk about simple objects or items which can be measured or numbered, we experience little difficulty in communication. When you and your friend agree to meet for dinner tomorrow at seven o'clock at the Deluxe Cafe at Eighth and Locust, there probably will be no breakdown in communications. But when we use abstract terms which have special meanings to masses of people or different segments of society, we have, as Lord Byron points out, something which may make millions feel and think. The engineer can build a bridge, using many men, stacks of blueprints, and vast amounts of mathematical data with comparatively few communication snarls. But human engineering is fraught with endless communication problems. Pass a law, change a city ordinance, run for office, investigate a crime, carry out the duties of an ambassador for your country and you come to grips with words, their meanings, and their tyrannical power.

When Nikita Khrushchev said to us, "We will bury you," he aroused the fears of hundreds of millions of people. When Hitler said, "Germany must march eastward," all Europe stirred uneasily. However, in *The Tyranny of Words,* Stuart Chase, writes that "language is apparently a sword that cuts both ways. With its help man can conquer the unknown; with it he can grievously wound himself." We see benevolent power in the words of Lincoln, "With malice towards none and charity for all"; of Webster, "Union now and forever, one and inseparable"; of Wilson, "Make the world safe for democracy"; and of Churchill, "We shall never surrender."

Many ordinary words convey more than ordinary meanings. We classify such words in two broad categories: those which connote what seems good and those which connote what seems bad. Our common fallacy is to structure meanings that are all-inclusive, that embrace the *allness* of evaluative attitudes under one single term. The immature mind tends to make a judgment covering all cases of a class or category from only a few specific samples. A high school girl discovers that her boy friend is dating another girl and she reacts with the comment, "Men are all alike. They are all fickle." One man in office turns out to be corrupt and people may say, "What can you expect from a politician? They are all a bunch of grafters." This is the fallacy of calling something all white or all black, 100 percent good or 100 percent evil. Listed below, with terse descriptive comments, are six words which register good qualities and six which suggest evil. In one column their conventional values are given. A parallel column raises questions designed to delete the *allness* concept from these words. Note that these are abstract terms, loaded in varying degrees with emotional and implied meanings.

GOOD OR HALO WORDS

1. *Progress*

Everything done in the name of progress must be good. Who dares interfere with the march of progress? Infers improvement, something better. We want a progressive nation, progressive faculty, progressive community, progressive person.

Can we equate change with progress? Who is to judge it? Did the Greeks and Romans believe in it? Are all wars, inventions and scientific discoveries a sign of progress?

2. *Justice*

Has sound of "righteousness." Stands for fair play and equal rights. Judges and juries are noble, upright people. Justice a blessing from the gods. The goal of all mankind.

Justice by the book or law? Who wrote the book or law? When administering justice, should the quality of mercy be considered? Can we have the same kind of justice for everyone, South, North, poor, rich? Is eye for an eye, tooth for a tooth justice? What about wars and capital punishment?

3. *Democracy*

No one should be so base as to interfere with this goal of mankind. We fight wars to make the world safe for it. The cradle of freedom, liberty, justice.

Will it work when people aren't ready for it? Can it rise above the level of the people? Do we have social, educational, economic democracy? Are there no second-class citizens?

4. Science

Can do no wrong. Draws from the secrets of nature. Can't lie. Always a blessing to mankind. Science no respecter of persons; always impartial. Basis for progress. Gives untold blessings to mankind.

Has it done more for the world than philosophy or art? If all great minds turned solely to science for 100 years and neglected the arts and humanities, would this be a good thing?

5. American

Loyal to our country, the home of the brave and the free. Stands for best of everything, freedom, high standard of living, unlimited opportunity. No flag like the red, white and blue.

Is our national abundance due to our genius or gifts of Nature? How about our "greatness" in educational methods, physical fitness of our youth, our crime rate, racial intolerance, divorce rate, widespread mental illness? Do we know how to live?

6. Efficiency

A bulwark against wastefulness of time, money, materials, and labor. Means economy and capacity of production. Blessed be the efficiency experts.

Is it always a virtue? What does it mean to the artist, the philosopher, the literary man, the spiritual leader?

BAD OR EVIL WORDS

1. Propaganda

Promotion for dubious causes by dubious methods. A slick device. Unworthy motivation. Information is misleading and unreliable.

Is the evil in the device, the men, or the cause? Should all uses for purposes of government, politics, religion, commerce be condemned? What about Radio Free Europe?

2. Dictatorship

It is tyranny. Destroys freedom. Nonhumanitarian. Enemy of democracy. Represents injustice. All dictators are power-mad, evil men. Rule by threat and force.

Are benevolent dictators possible? They may be necessary in times of crisis. Most efficient type of government. Degrees of dictatorship in any government.

3. Un-American

Disloyal to country. Threat to national security. Potential traitors. The Un-American Activities Committee a noble watchdog.

Who defines the word? Who can judge the true patriot? Most dangerous person may have most patriotic front.

4. Communism

Atheistic, anti-Christian, antidemocratic doctrine. A criminal conspiracy with apparatus to dominate the world. Enemy of human liberty and justice.

Only system that could destroy Russian feudalism of the czars—Russian masses better off now. Is communism worse than Hitler's fascism? Can communism alleviate misery and despair? Poses no threat to most European democracies with progressive social legislation.

5. Politician

An unsavory person without principles. Power-hungry. Gets what he wants by craftiness, trickery, and chicanery. An opportunist whose hands are usually soiled by graft and corruption.

Is in position to do great public service. Can be great leader for worthy causes. Examples: Moses, Lincoln, Churchill. We need them. Voters to blame for bad ones.

6. Socialistic

Enemy of free enterprise. Anti-American. Makes the able and industrious provide for the lazy and shiftless. Unfair scheme to distribute the wealth.

What about the post office, public schools, state colleges and universities, and social security? Most advanced nations of Western Europe with highest standard of living have progressive socialistic legislation.

The strange power of words is discussed in a thought-provoking article in *The Saturday Evening Post,* by Professor Stefan T. Possony, professor of international politics at Georgetown University. He points out how words divide the world, how Communists preach *disarmament, negotiation, coexistence, nonaggression,* and *peace—* all benevolent, good words that sound sweet to all ears, but that to the Communists do not mean the same as they do to us. Semantic warfare is crucial in the Communist technique. "Words can serve the same purpose as artillery barrages before an attack, preparing nations opposed to communism to accept with a minimum of protest the 'decisive' or death-dealing blow. In brief, the communists have taught themselves to use language as an instrument of conquest."[3]

Negotiation, to Communists, is merely a stalling technique to gain time, in order to get rather than give. *Agreements* according to Stalin, are "to secure future strategic advantages." The Soviets have concluded nearly a thousand treaties in 38 years and have broken almost all of them.

War, in the Communist mind, says Professor Possony, ". . . is a creative force of social development. Just wars are those which accelerate the global success of communism. In fact, all words like peace, coexistence, liberation, disarmament have meaning and inferences solely as related to the overall and ultimate goal of world communism, when there will be no resistance or opposition. Stalin laid down the rule, 'Words must have no relation to action . . . words are one thing, action another. Good words are a mask to conceal bad deeds.' "[4]

The foregoing discussion concerns the effect of words not only upon the mass mind but also in interpersonal relationships. We all know how words can hurt or cheer us up. They can cut like a knife or sting like a bee. They can soothe like syrup or rattle like a tin can. Thus most words carry meanings beyond what the dictionaries reveal. And we can use them to tear an idea to shreds, twist it around, reshape it, hide it, or bring it into a new light.

Two Kinds of Meaning

There are two fundamental kinds of meaning in words, denotative and connotative. It is difficult, however, to categorize all meanings thus, since many words have both denotations and connotations. Denotative meanings are logical, objective, and extensional; and connotative are emotive, subjective, and intensional. A denotative meaning, say the semanticists, is extensional; that is, it points beyond and outside your mind to what the word stands for. It has an explicit reference, like a section on a map which represents a definite territory.

[3] Stefan T. Possony, "Words That Divide the World," *The Saturday Evening Post,* July 9, 1960, p. 43.
[4] *Ibid.*

But the territory is not always definite. Words may also carry along implicit meanings; the intention or connotation of the word is everything that the concept implies. Such inclusive meaning may easily be misleading. It may refer to territory which exists not in the real world but in the mind and the emotions.

If the nursemaid tells the child, "The goblins will get you if you don't watch out!" what she says contains emotive intensional, but not extensional, meaning. There is nothing in the content which is verifiable; we cannot see, hear, touch, or photograph the goblins. The reference must reside in the emotions and mind of the child. Whether you believe in goblins or not, there is no way of settling the dispute by endless argument. However, if there is an argument about the height of the table in your room, the dispute will come to an end when someone measures it with a yardstick. Statements that have extensional meanings can be verified and agreements reached, whereas those containing only emotive intensional meanings afford no basis for logical agreement. In such situations individuals, institutions, and nations may find themselves involved in bitter, fruitless quarrels and conflicts.

An individual may also experience inner emotional turmoil by using affective intensional words and phrases which are self-defacing and self-wounding. When this habit becomes sufficiently aggravated, guilt and inferiority complexes are manifest. If you keep saying to yourself that no one likes you, you will probably end up believing this to be true; you anticipate the fulfillment of your prophecy. Some cases of stage fright are worsened thus. In both cases you are using affective language which has meaning and emotional value only for you.

We often associate denotative meanings with concrete words. The terms *denotative* and *concrete* are not synonymous, yet in many ways they are of the same dimension. Similarly, connotative words are often associated with the abstract, for abstract terms are particularly prone to have a variety of meanings. For instance, the words *democracy, socialism,* and *communism,* when unrelated to sensory experience, are vague and ambiguous, having different meaning for different people. The process of abstracting is the act of drawing off a common or general meaning from specific objects or things. For instance, if we point to John, a boy of twelve, we are, to a degree, specific. We may go up the ladder of abstraction by referring to John as a child, as representative of American youth, a member of the human race, a living organism. Or we may talk about pigs, horses, and cows as farm livestock and make an abstraction indicating they are domestic animals, quadrupeds, animals, and living creatures. The higher we climb the ladder of abstraction, the bigger the umbrella becomes for covering concepts, and the more general and vague are the concepts.

Newspaper editors often slant their headlines toward either denotative or connotative content. For instance, the headlines in one newspaper may read, "Holiday Traffic Total 288" and another may read, "Murder on Highways, 288 Killed Over Holiday." The first is informative only, whereas the second is both informative and affective. In his book, *Language in Action,* Hayakawa presents in parallel columns some statements to illustrate how affective connotations can be changed while extensional meanings are retained:

Finest quality filet mignon.	First-class piece of dead cow.
Cubs trounce Giants 5–3.	Score: Cubs 5, Giants 3.
McCormick Bill steam-rollered through Senate	Senate passes McCormick Bill over strong opposition.
Japanese divisions advance five miles	Japs stopped cold after five-mile advance.
French armies in rapid retreat!	The retirement of the French forces to previously prepared positions in the rear was accomplished briskly and efficiently.
The governor appeared to be gravely concerned and said that a statement would be issued in a few days after careful examination of the facts.	The governor was on the spot.

WORDS HAVE PECULIARITIES, WEAKNESSES, AND LIMITATIONS

Up to this point we have been concerned with the wonders and powers of language and its role in our culture and private lives. We know that life would be unbearable without such a system of symbolizing thought; that words, like people, have ways of doing things in the communication process. We shall now take a closer look at those characteristics of language which make true communication of ideas difficult and hazardous. Wonderful as words are at times for communicating ideas and feelings, they also at other times are awkward, unreliable, and treacherous devices which thwart the attempt to convey meaning. Words are not always reliable to carry out their intended purpose, because, as we have seen, they do not always mean the same to all people. They seldom tell all there is to tell, their meanings change, some have many meanings, some meanings are affected by the vocal tone given to the word, and some words are so heavily loaded with hidden emotions that their intended meanings go far off the mark. We shall now investigate why and how these tools often become faulty and unsuitable for their purpose.

Words Remain the Same—People Are Different

We look at things from different points of view. We see the world, not as it is, but as we are. We have different opinions, interests, motives, and beliefs. The total of our experience, thinking, feeling gives us separate abilities to conceive and grasp a concept or idea. No two people, witnessing the same automobile accident, will give identical testimony about it. A mountain means different things to a ski enthusiast, a lumberman, an artist, and a miner. The skier examines the slopes for a long gentle glide, the lumberman looks for a good spot to set up his sawmill, the artist thinks about the blue haze and how it will blend with the colors of the landscape, and the miner thinks about the "gold in them thar hills." The four-year-old boy, when asked where the sun sets, replies with assurance, "On the highway"; for his family are city dwellers and motor on highways on summer evenings. Ask twenty adults in a room to write down what each considers to be the meaning of *religion* or *happiness* or *communism* or some similar term, and you are likely to get twenty different definitions. A speaker will soon find that *segregation* does not mean the same in Minnesota as in Mississippi, nor does *unemployment insurance* mean the same to a college faculty that it does to automobile workers in Detroit. There can be no true communication unless there is a common *core of experience.*

Words Never Tell All

There is always more to know and more to talk about. We may look at a simple object, an apple. We may describe it as being round, red, juicy, good to eat, sweet, with seeds, and so forth. But we as yet have not been very definite. We have not said how red, how juicy, how sweet, where are the seeds, how many, and what is their color. And there is much more. From apples we make apple pie, cider, applejack, applesauce, apple strudel. Apples grow on trees; these trees have blossoms, are cultivated, sprayed. Apples are picked, packed, and sold. Yet there is still much more. They are important to our economy, especially in Missouri, Michigan, and Washington. Sayings about apples are common, such as, "An apple a day keeps the doctor away," "Polish the apple," "An apple got Adam into trouble." There is always more, much more. As the king of Siam said in the delightful musical, *The King and I*, "etcetera, etcetera, and etcetera!" And this is the case of nearly all words; there is always more than can be said about what the word represents.

It is this realization that gave rise to The Institute for General Semantics and later to the International Society for General Semantics, which for nearly a generation has published the well-known magazine *ETC*. This official organ of the society is widely supported by students, not only from the United States but from many foreign countries as well. Their response reflects a growing public awareness of the vital role of words and their meanings as related to human communications.

Words Are Fickle

Meanings change, although their symbols remain the same. Such words as *comrade, big brother,* and *fellow traveler* had only benign connotations two generations ago; now they have malignant ones. Not very long ago, if you looked under a *hood* you would expect to find a monk; now you find the motor of your automobile. Music that used to be considered *hot* is now *cool*. Ladies' underwear evolved from *drawers* to *step-ins* to *panties* and now has a sound of propriety —*lingerie*. Dictators *conquer* nations no more, they *liberate* them; school teachers do not get *fired*, they *resign; janitors* have become *custodians;* the *poor* are no longer with us—they have become the *underprivileged;* juveniles are never *criminals* but *delinquents*. The *saloon*, long looked upon as something beneath the notice of respectable society, lost its nasty connotation when it became a *cocktail lounge*.

Words, like coins, wear out, and new mediums of exchange are minted. The word *nice* once meant *stupid* or *ignorant; pretty* once meant *treacherous;* and *hussy* once meant *housewife*. Thus every word has a biography, a story.

Words Have Many Meanings

No two words have identical meanings. The *American College Dictionary* lists more than fifty distinct uses for the word *point,* more than 100 for the word *run.* If you say, "I am all *in,*" some one may ask, "In what?" When you are driving along a highway in your automobile and your companion shouts, "Look out!" he doesn't mean for you to look out of the window, for that is what you have been doing. Thus we translate not words, but ideas. Such words as *up* and *down* cannot always be translated literally. When a mother says, "Johnny, eat *up* your dinner," or "don't *down* your food that way," or "eat it *up* slowly," there really is no communication breakdown. Johnny knows he eats *up* his food, even though he *downs* it. And whether a house burns *up* or *down* does not matter, so long as we know it was destroyed by fire.

The word *run* can be a verb or a noun. It may be used as a run in your stocking, a run in baseball, run the man down, run for office, a deer run, the creek is running, your nose is running, the sap is running. Similarly, such words as *strike, will, deuce, racket, pipe, poll, foot, bill,* and hundreds of others have many meanings. Such words are useful, for they work overtime, but they may also cause communication failures. A newspaper reported a suicide by a man whose pockets were *full of bills,* but the meaning became clear only when the police found the bills were for money owed.

Words Have Special Meanings for Particular Purposes and People

Language may be custom tailored to meet specific needs. Special types of uniforms, caps, hats, insignia, boots, coat of arms, and the like may signify a special type of profession, service, occupation, or region. Similarly common words and phrases may have technical meanings or serve special purposes, among groups, professions, and individuals, parts of the country, organizations, and the like, as illustrated in the major's letter to the English teacher on the following page. Vocabulary may be characterized by colloquialisms, jargon, slang, and technical terms and expressions peculiar to professions or occupations. Meanings of many of the words in specialty vocabularies do not appear in our standard dictionaries and often are not understood by outsiders. Most of us would have difficulty understanding what might be strictly the language of the atomic scientist, the lawyer, the doctor, or the pharmacist. Neither would the formal language of high-level national diplomacy be quite clear to us.

There is a special type of "lingo" one hears among waiters in restaurants as they relay their orders to the kitchen, or among tobacco auctioneers, inhabitants of Skid Row, baseball players, and so on. An odd mixture of technical language and jargon develops in the branches of the armed services. Such language developments have been particularly noticeable in the Air Force, but even airmen find that jargon and colloquialisms vary from one place to another and that scores of words which are common terminology at one air base are like Greek at another. No doubt many coined expressions which are useful to this branch of service are nevertheless viewed with apprehension by college departments of English. This is illustrated by a letter from an administrative officer of major rank, USAF, to an English professor who was puzzled and disturbed by an article which appeared in a recent popular national magazine. In it an officer said that a student pilot "made four unsuccessful attempts at roosting his bird." The teacher wants to know if the expression *roost his bird* was a flight of fancy on the part of the officer or if it is familiar among airmen. If the latter is true, is the usage slangy or technical? The major's reply, quoted here in part by special permission, is most enlightening and helps us to appreciate how special jargon may develop and how it relates realistically to communication problems in the Air Force.

Roost is a colloquialism more often used with a connotation of disapproval in the inability of a student to successfully master landing techniques in an aircraft, i.e., "After crowhopping (bouncing) the length of the pad (runway) he decided to roost (land)." Many such colloquialisms are used around a Training Command Base where pilot training is the primary mission. Some have attained Air Force wide usage, as Air Force jargon, such as the following: *Fishtail*—alternating rudder pressure in order to disrupt air flow about rudder for purpose of dissipating airspeed; *Slip*—crossing aircraft surface controls in order to expedite loss of altitude; *Crab*—correction for wind drift: *Tallyo*—visual contact with target; *Splash*—target destroyed; *Pigeons*—most direct route to airfield; *Pad*—homebase; *Flame-out*—dead engine; *Stovepipe*—jet aircraft; *Truck*—cargo type aircraft.

Air Force jargon is effective in communicating only if everyone has the same common core of experience. Therefore, the Air University compiled The United States Air Force Dictionary, which is for sale by the Superintendent of Documents, U.S. Government Printing Office. . . .

I might add such jargon has been made to serve our purpose and allows us to more effectively carry out our military operation.

The point we should remember is that the main function of language is to help people understand one another. There are types of symbols which may effectively convey meaning among people with a common core of experience yet do not readily lend themselves to conventional compositional or literary treatment. So long as true and reliable communication is our goal and the symbols do not violate good taste, we should view tolerantly special language which serves special functions. Today's slang and jargon may be part of tomorrow's literature.

Some Words Have Extra Voltage

Earlier in this chapter we discussed the strange power of words and the nature of connotative meanings. We should also bring into sharper focus words commonly heard whose connotations carry "extra voltage." Language may do more than communicate information—it may be used for thinking and persuasion. The speaker or writer may find many words in common use so pregnant with thought and emotion that the reader or listener assigns new meanings to them. Such words open the floodgates for the extensions of meanings; exactness of expression in such instances may thus not be desirable for the speaker's purpose. Here, words and phrases are used for their connotation, for their appeal to private interests, or for their emotional impact.

The hidden dynamics released by such words as *Wall Street, imperialist, swine, capitalist, communist, traitor, slacker,* and the like are, however, unpredictable; they often kindle emotional fires and cause conflicts with tragic consequences. Speech may be compared to a copper wire along which may travel two currents: one of information, the other of emotion. When words become highly charged emotionally they have potential danger. Mussolini and Hitler demonstrated this at the zenith of their power when the people of Italy and Germany were led to think not with their heads but with their corpuscles.

Words of the name-calling variety aimed to damage or belittle the character or reputation of an individual can often be cruel and inhuman. In the days of McCarthyism many innocents were caught in the crossfire of the Communist-hunters and suffered severe character damage. The word *communist* became so heavily charged with feel-

ing that the courts in many parts of the country took action to protect people from unwarranted character damage inflicted by it. Words
like *wop, crook, liar, thief, nigger, scab, bastard, snob, gangster,
doublecrosser, rat,* and hundreds of this type, when directed at a
person, are emotionally loaded. Such words stop thought. They aim to
hurt, and hurt they do—often the user more than the one aimed at.

Other terms have a positive charge. *Home, mother, country, the
family dog,* and *the baby* are common examples. Some of these words
spark great emotional reaction—so much so that Joseph Conrad said,
"Give me the right word and the right accent and I will move the
world."

PROJECTS AND EXERCISES

For speaking projects see Part Three.

1. (a) Write an imaginary 100-word telegram to a high school senior you
   know, urging him or her to go to college. Be as specific, accurate, logical and impersonal as possible. Use essentially extensional words. (b)
   Write another 100-word telegram to the same person using predominately motivational, connotative and personal language.
2. Translate the following newspaper headlines into connotative language:
   (1) Senate Passes Hydro-electric Bill 55–45. (2) Football Score—
   Army 28 Navy 0. (3) Soldiers Get Leave Dec. 25. (4) Kansas Tornado
   —18 Lives Lost.
3. Look for new or unusually effective words and phrases used by your
   classmates in their speeches. Keep a notebook and write these down;
   try to find opportunities for incorporating some of them into your
   vocabulary.
4. Learn to use new words every week. Devise your own program for en-
   larging and strengthening your vocabulary. When you hear a new word,
   jot it down. Use the dictionary to find as many uses and meanings of
   the word as you can. Discuss the sense of the word with others. Finally,
   make it a point to weave the word into both your conversation and
   writing, but do so only with words which you normally come across
   in the course of your reading or listening. Keep a record of the words
   you accumulate in this manner.
5. How many meanings and uses can you think of for the following words:
   tight, foot, check, pipe, love, can, bill, fit, tongue, fast.
6. Unscramble the following list of twenty terms into matching pairs of
   concrete and abstract concepts. There are ten of each. *Mumps, finance,
   banquet, psychological complex, dog, wheel of justice. lion, foreman
   hates boss, dollar bill, cranberries, animal, medical science, city ordi-*

nance, circus, I heard a burglar, steak, Thanksgiving dinner, stop sign, cow, agriculture.

7. Define in specific and concrete language meaning growing out of two or more of the abstract terms in the table below. Bring your translation into the common core of your sensory experiences. Use no more than 150 words.

The first column contains words loaded with emotion and unfavorable associations. They carry defamatory power when applied to persons. They may place a stigma or label on them. Indicate the strength of your reaction by marking an X in the proper square: 1—no reaction, 2—mild reaction, 3—strong reaction, 4—very strong or violent reaction. Words in the column on the right suggest glorification and benevolence and give a favorable feeling. Mark an X in the proper square in like manner.

Stigma Words	None 1	Mild 2	Strong 3	Very Strong 4	Glory or Benevolent Words	None 1	Mild 2	Strong 3	Very Strong 4
traitor					honest				
liar					sincere				
slut					true blue				
social outcast					gentleman				
coward					kind soul				
communist					dependable				
doublecrosser					good American				
nigger					lady				
bastard					wonderful guy				
thief					friend				
fourflusher					good scout				
cheat					tolerant				
crook					Christian				
fool					good sport				
idiot					square shooter				
snob					jolly good fellow				

ADDITIONAL READINGS

Beardsley, Monroe C., *Thinking Straight,* Prentice-Hall, 1956, chaps. 4, 5, and 6.

Brigance, William Norwood, *Speech, Its Techniques and Disciplines in a Free Society,* Appleton-Century-Crofts, 1952, chap. 10.

Bryant, Donald C., and Wallace, Karl R., *Fundamentals of Public Speaking,* 3rd ed., Appleton-Century-Crofts, 1960, chap. 16.

Hayakawa, S. I., *Language in Thought and Action,* Harcourt, Brace, 1949.

Chase, Stuart, *Power of Words,* Harcourt, Brace, 1954.

Chase, Stuart, *The Tyranny of Words,* Harcourt, Brace, 1938.

Lee, Irving J., *Customs and Crises in Communication,* Harper, 1954.

Sarett, Lew, Foster, William Trufant, and Sarett, Alma Johnson, *Basic Principles of Speech,* 3rd ed., Houghton-Mifflin, 1958, chaps. 1 and 8.

Smith, Raymond G., *Principles of Public Speaking,* Ronald, 1958, chap. 7.

Soper, Paul L., *Basic Public Speaking,* 2nd ed., Oxford University Press, 1956, chap. 13.

Weaver, Andrew Thomas, and Ness, Ordean Gerhard, *The Fundamentals and Forms of Speech,* Odyssey, 1957, chap. 9.

Weaver, Andrew Thomas, and Ness, Ordean Gerhard, *An Introduction to Public Speaking,* Odyssey, 1961, chap. 8.

White, Eugene E., and Henderlider, Clair R., *Practical Public Speaking,* Macmillan, 1954, chap. 12.

❧ 11 ❧
Language in the Speech

Language most shows a man;
Speak, that I may see thee.
—BEN JONSON

In the previous chapter we discussed the philosophical bases of language as a medium of human communication without differentiating between written and spoken language. In this chapter we shall be concerned essentially with language as it applies to speaking and listening. Although spoken and written language have much in common and are complementary to each other, the difference between the two is much greater than is generally realized.

Centuries ago Aristotle observed that ". . . each kind of rhetoric has its own appropriate style. The style of written prose is not the same as that of controversial speaking. . . . A knowledge of both the written and the spoken style is required."[1] Thus skill in one does not necessarily mean skill in the other—celebrated authors and editors are often disappointing public speakers. Bryan's "Cross of Gold" speech, which electrified the 1896 Democratic convention and won him the presidential nomination, made poor reading when the full text appeared in newpapers. On the other hand, although Edmund

[1] Lane Cooper (trans.), *The Rhetoric of Aristotle,* Appleton-Century-Crofts, 1932, Bk. III, chap. 12.

Burke's forensic efforts were models of composition and language usage, when he spoke he often emptied the House of Commons. Yet, the next morning, members of Parliament snatched the press reports of his speeches—a case of good writing and poor speaking.

The development and widespread use of radio did much to increase our awareness of the difference between oral and written communication. Hitler was the first leader of the great powers of Europe to place heavy reliance upon radio for promoting and propagandizing the interests of the Third Reich; in fact, his skillful use of the radio was an important factor in his rise to power. The late President Franklin D. Roosevelt capitalized heavily upon radio, both to win elections and to report to the nation in his fireside chats. Radio announcers and commentators quickly learned that the style in which press releases came over the teletype was not well suited for effective oral communication, and these reports were therefore usually recast in oral language more suitable for broadcasting. Some announcers and commentators merely made notes covering the essential content of press releases and did their broadcasting extemporaneously, thus assuring themselves of a natural or direct *me-and-you* oral style.

ORAL STYLE AND INTELLIGIBILITY OF SPEECH

Although rhetoricians and students of speech have long recognized that there is a marked difference between spoken and written language, there has been relatively little study and research to determine exactly what these differences are. One significant study in this area was made by Gordon L. Thomas, Michigan State University, on the effect of oral style on the intelligibility of speech. The more common elements of oral style were arranged in the following categories: specific words, colorful words, informality and simplicity of vocabulary, figurative language, personalization, informality of syntax, questions, and direct quotations. Two versions of a short lecture of 250 words were prepared. Both versions had identical factual matter and identical arrangement of material. One, the oral version, was characterized by the above eight elements of style; in the nonoral one they were omitted. A well-trained speaker read the two versions, as nearly as possible in the same manner, before two separate but similar audiences of 250 each. Twenty minutes after the lecture, members of the audience were tested by multiple-choice questions on their comprehension of the material. On the basis of the results, Thomas reports the following conclusions: "The use of certain elements of 'oral' style definitely increases the amount of information imparted to an audience when compared to the same speech without these elements of 'oral' style. In general it can be said that the introduction of oral elements increases the intelligibility of the speech by about 10 percent." He goes on to say, "The superiority of the 'oral' style is apparent, regardless of who delivers the speech, how it is delivered (i.e., whether it is delivered in person or by means of a tape recorder), or whether the students are motivated or not."[2]

COMPARISON OF WRITING AND SPEAKING

Writing is for reading, speaking for listening; one is for the eye, the other for the ear. Out of this obvious yet basic difference grows a wide variety of communication needs which determine the style and characteristics of language. The writer and speaker start from different poles as they seek to transmit ideas. Their widely differing audiences influence the character of subject matter, the way it is shaped, and the mode of treatment. Thus the speaker and the writer, in their initial approach, are of different mind and spirit.

Psychological considerations differ widely between writer and speaker. The speaker presents his thoughts and feelings in person, seeing and sensing the immediate reactions of the audience before him (except when speaking for radio or television, and even then he usually has a studio audience). The writer presents his message in ink, knowing little or nothing about reader reaction. Speaking is thus more personal than writing. The writer uses fixed and rigid black ink marks on paper, whereas the speaker uses voice and action, which are tremendously variable. The writer must be content with fixed symbols; but the speaker uses articulation, pronunciation, quality of voice, rate, pitch, force, rhythm, gesture, posture, and bodily movements, and these provide him with a great potential for punctuating his thoughts and shading his meanings and feelings. Further psychological and physiological considerations which influence differences between written and spoken language are discussed in the rest of this section.

[2] Gordon L. Thomas, "Effect of Oral Style on Intelligibility of Speech," *Speech Monographs*, 23 (March, 1956), 46–55.

Differences in Sensory Stimuli

The sensory experiences one receives in reading are not the same as those that come from listening. What we see makes an instantaneous photographic impression upon the mind; words and phrases can be recognized and identified by flash cards in the smallest fraction of a second. Visual stimuli tend to make ideas instantly intelligible. Auditory stimuli, however, tend more toward stimulation of emotions. Music, an auditory stimulus, is the most purely emotional of all arts. The English playwright, William Congreve, about 300 years ago wrote, "Music hath charms to soothe the savage breast." Today medical science recognizes the value of music in combating both physical and mental disturbances, and it is widely used as an auxiliary agent in hospitals. To see is to know, to hear is to feel. For this reason most people find it more exciting to listen to radio newscasts than to read the same news in the newspapers. An actor must place great reliance upon his voice to create the desired dramatic atmosphere and arouse emotional response; it has been said that Sarah Bernhardt could bring tears to an audience by reciting the alphabet. In other words, spoken language tends to be a more potent emotional sensory stimulus than written language.

Differences in Methods and Means of Symbol Control

When you wish to communicate an idea in writing, you can select symbols, letters, punctuation marks, and spelling and put your choices on paper. You can then check meanings, rearrange symbols, underline, capitalize, and generally refine and revise both the thought and its composition. You have a kind of circular response with your manuscript but no direct stimulation from your reader such as the speaker gets from his listeners. When you have completed your writing, your control of it ceases; you have—so to speak—manufactured your product, packaged it, and shipped it away for use and consumption. To alter its merits is beyond your control.

Since the writer aims at an imaginary reader and because his symbols are subject to scrutiny, he generally tends to develop a more formal or literary style than the speaker. True, some writers, like Will Rogers, Mark Twain, Ring Lardner, and a few columnists, have successfully developed a casual "folksy" style. But, in general, writers avoid personalized language, colloquialisms, and provincialisms more than speakers. The speaker's language also tends to be more flexible and responsive to the local and immediate needs of his listeners. His communication is thus more realistic—a type of realism usually denied the writer. As the speaker gets feedback from his audience, he can change phraseology or give color and emphasis to his meanings by voice and gesture. In other words, he tends to develop skills in the flexible use of language to meet the needs of a variety of situations, whereas the writer tends to refine his language skills for the general reading public, in a situation more or less constant.

Differences Related to Persons and Personalities

The writer is separated from his readers. He can never be sure who will read what he writes. Furthermore, his material is read at different times and places. The speaker stands before his listeners and has direct and immediate contact with them, in part even when speaking over radio or television. He usually meets his audience face to face where he can hear and see them and sense their mood and feelings. There is something intimate and personal about this—a brushing together of personalities, a situation that is alive with human warmth. As Sir Walter Raleigh once said, "A sea of upturned faces is half the speech." Language style born of this intensified social environment will naturally be different from that of the writer's seclusion.

Differences in What Is Believable

People tend to believe more readily what they see in print than what they hear. The sharp black letters on the white page are tangible things, to which we tend to attribute authority. If someone doubts our word, we can reply with an air of finality, "See for yourself, it says so in the book." Ministers read directly from the Bible instead of reciting passages which they could confidently quote from memory, for this carries more authority than reciting the words. A man's word before the law is not as good as his bond. Furthermore, the written word stands as a permanent record for all to see, to reread and reexamine at will. It is not to be tampered with or altered. The spoken word, unless it is recorded in writing, suffers the hazards of being altered or misquoted or having its meaning fade with the passage of time.

Differences in Amount and Pertinence of Ideas Communicated

Most people can read two to four times faster than they normally speak, even when the vocabulary is more difficult. The reader can therefore cover much more ground per time unit than can the speaker. Since, however, it is not the quantity of thought that counts but its quality and relevance, the spoken word has an advantage. It can strike at the heart of a problem as no written word can. A group of men in a well-directed conference can often accomplish more in thirty minutes than they could by weeks of correspondence. Although this electronic age has seen astounding developments in the mechanics of communication, high-level statesmen depend more and more on the conference table for negotiating and settling their differences in a moment of crisis. In our private lives, probably more than 80 percent of decisions are arrived at by the spoken rather than the written word.

Differences in Accuracy and Reliability

In speech, language must be instantly intelligible. Speech is a thing of the moment, allowing little opportunity for the listener to ponder over a word or phrase. He must grasp the speaker's intended meaning now or never. Nor can he listen at his leisure or have much control over his personal comfort; he must meet tensions of the moment as best he can. A reader can, at his leisure and in comfort, reread what is not clear as deliberately and as often as he pleases. He may even take time out to look up meanings of words in a dictionary. But the listener cannot relisten. Since the speaker must therefore use only symbols that are readily and instantly understood, his style of language must be quite different from that of the writer. It should be characterized by simple, short, Anglo-Saxon words, imagery, personalized words, and sometimes even colloquialisms. His working vocabulary may be only half as large as that of the writer, but the fewer tools with which he works must serve him well.

IMPROVE YOUR ORAL STYLE FOR BETTER COMMUNICATION

So far in this chapter we have discussed some of the inherent differences in the communication goals of writer and speaker and in the reception of what is communicated by reader and listener. These characteristics of the spoken style of language did not develop without cause; they are the direct result of the speaker's needs as an effective communicator.

As a speech student, you need to think in terms of oral rather than written discourse. Your language should be essentially *tongue-born*, rather than *pen-born*. This does not mean, however, that written language has less value than spoken. Although writing and speaking are, in a sense, distinctly separate disciplines employing, to a degree, separate language styles, yet they work together. One cannot stand without the other. Peculiarly, however, writing seems to help speaking more than speaking helps writing. Writing outlines, phrases, paragraphs, parts of a speech, or even an entire speech with the listener image sharply before you will help you to hammer out points, refine them, and give shape to your substance. Both written and spoken words are tools for thinking and for formulating ideas. The act of using a pen or typewriter is helpful in getting your mind into gear—that is, you can often prepare yourself to talk by putting your pen and pencil to work. Thinking aloud as you write is a good habit for developing skills in oral language. Remember that you are not writing an essay, but preparing a speech. Actually, you are conversing in ink with an audience.

Gordon L. Thomas, in a study on the "Effect of Oral Style on Intelligibility of Speech," examined representative writers in the field of rhetoric to observe constantly recurring patterns of elements of style which these writers thought characterized oral language: ". . . accurate expression, suggestive words, specific words, vivid speech, colorful words, direct quotations, loaded words, questions, comparisons and contrasts, homely words, illustrations, informal English, simple words, short words, concise statements, figures of speech, short sentences, figurative language, direct address, personalizations, informal syntax, simple syntax, summary, suspense and climax, euphony, transitions, repetition."[3]

The choice of these elements depends on two principal approaches to the characteristics and functions of oral style: informational and psychological. As we saw in Chapter 7, the goal of an informational approach is always clarity; it thus uses elements of language which characterize: (1) the specific and concrete, (2) simplicity, (3) accuracy, (4) facts and figures, and (5) direct questions. The psycho-

[3] Thomas, *op. cit.,* pp. 47–48.

logical approach uses words to impress the listener, heighten his interest, arouse his emotions, and appeal to his motives or drives. It uses elements of language which characterize: (1) the personal, (2) the colorful and impressive, (3) the local and informal, (4) sound effect words, and (5) rhetorical questions and reiteration.

Informational Approach

BE SPECIFIC AND CONCRETE

His substance also was eleven thousand sheep, and three thousand camels, and five hundred yoke of oxen, and five hundred she asses, and a very great household; so that this man was the greatest of all the men of the East.

—Job 1:3

In order to be specific we must concentrate on details, names, dates, places, facts, and things measurable. The five W's—*who, what, when, where,* and *why*—that are basic to news-reporting, are the keys for ferreting out detailed and specific information. The term *concrete* has much in common with the term *specific.* The opposite of specific is *general;* the opposite of concrete is *abstract.* An abstract idea concerns thoughts, feelings, and attitudes not directly connected to sensory experience. Translated into the concrete it is brought into the area of sensory experience, of something that can be seen, heard, tasted, smelled, felt, or touched. Note, however, that these are all relative terms. *Animal* is more general than *cow,* and *cow* is more general than *Aberdeen Angus. Missouri Valley* is more specific than *national, Nebraska* is more specific than *Missouri Valley,* and *twenty miles due north of Omaha* is still more specific. But the relative difference matters. Beauty is abstract, but the smell of honeysuckle on a warm summer night is concrete. The general and abstract become more meaningful and real through the agency of the concrete and specific. (Also see Chapter 7, examples under *Clarity.*)

Managers of our large industrial plants wage a ceaseless campaign to get their workers, foremen, and shop supervisors to be specific in their instructions and reports as the company strives for more efficient plant operation. Here the watchword is "SPECIFY"—give the important details. An important message received by letter, telegram, or long-distance telephone can be unclear because essential details are missing. Suppose you wreck your car on a vacation trip and have to wire home for money. If your telegram reads, "WRECKED CAR SEND

MONEY," it is not very clear. It would be better to say specifically, "DAMAGED CAR SLIGHTLY IN WRECK. WIRE TWO HUNDRED DOLLARS FOR REPAIRS. DELAYED ONE DAY. AM FINE."

Observe the specific and the concrete in the following letter to parents prepared by the Atlantic Coast Line Railroad:

My eyes were focused well ahead of my car, which was moving at slow speed. As I turned a blind corner, from out of nowhere and on the wrong side of the road, pumping his pedals as though the devil were after him, came a little "shaver" on a shining red bicycle. He saw me just in time; made a desperate corkscrew turn ahead of me and zigzagged out of sight.

"Fool kid," I muttered, as my hair turned a bit whiter from the scare, "but a cute little rascal." He was at least eight years old, dressed in cowboy outfit complete with all the trimmings; and my anger eased up a bit.

"Wonder if Mary and John, my two kids, pull anything like that on their bikes? I'll talk it over with them when I get home."

Good idea to talk things over with *your* children, because this is no light matter.

Each year from four to five hundred children on bicycles are killed, and over twenty-five thousand are injured, according to a National Safety Council survey, which reveals that in four out of five cases the child is violating a law; eight out of ten victims are under 16 years of age, and nine out of ten are boys.

As a parent, see that your young cowboys and cowgirls know and obey all traffic laws, lights, and signs. Cultivate in their minds a sense of responsibility. Appeal to their pride; convince them that it takes skill and brainwork to be a safe bicycle rider, just as much as to be a safe automobile driver. Shape a safe biker today, and you're building towards a safe automobile driver for tomorrow.

The streets and highways will be buzzing with these young jet pilots who will do anything. Never expect them to do the right thing, however, for when a youngster pedaling in front of you signals a left turn, anticipate anything from a double reverse corkscrew to a figure eight curb-to-curb rock'n roll.

Small fry on a bicycle is pure happiness on two wheels. Don't be the one to shatter that happiness in a terribly one-sided collision between your sturdy car and a child's fragile bike.

Remember, it is always the season for reason. Drive carefully.[4]

USE SIMPLE WORDS. In order to do his job well a carpenter wants the most effective, easy-to-operate tools. An intricate, complex piece of machinery is hard to manage and often will not work effectively.

4 *Industrial Supervisor,* the National Safety Council, 425 North Michigan Avenue, Chicago 11, June, 1960, p. 3.

It is the same with words: vague and complicated language is a barrier to effective communication. Even one unclear word or cumbersome phrase may cause a speaker to lose his listener. Short, simple words are in general the clearest and most effective mode of communication.

Use words familiar to the listener. Saint Paul expressed the importance of this habit when he said, "Except as ye utter by the tongue words easy to understand, how shall it be known what is spoken? For ye shall speak into the air." A father, warning his eight-year-old son not to eat an apple on the table, would not say, "My lawful and legal heir, I recommend that you refrain from partaking of this fruit, for the process of decomposition has already been inaugurated." It is far better to say, "Son, don't eat that apple—it's rotten." *Rotten* is a good Anglo-Saxon word, familiar and meaningful to every eight-year-old boy.

Do not be afraid to use simple, clear language. When Winston Churchill paid tribute to the RAF after the battle for Britain had been won, saying: "Never in the field of human conflict was so much owed by so many to so few," his forceful eloquence largely rose from his monosyllabic, Anglo-Saxon words. An attempt to improve this statement by using longer words would only spoil it. The same applies to Patrick Henry's classic utterance in his most famous oration: "I care not what course others may take, but as for me, give me liberty or give me death!"

It is often said that little minds believe "big words" to signify "big ideas," but obscurity of language should not be mistaken for profundity of thought. Robert Spencer reminds us that words learned early in life seem to have stronger meanings than words learned later in life. As children we learn to say "think" instead of "contemplate," "fire" instead of "conflagration," "wish" instead of "desire," and so on. The English language itself began as Anglo-Saxon and gets most of its strength and vigor from words of that tongue. The simple word retains a power which complex, latinate words lack. It gives the speaker his best chance of being understood and offers him the best chance of being persuasive. We should, therefore, never be afraid to use simple language. Some of our greatest literature is known for its simplicity. The twenty-third Psalm contains 118 words, 92 of which are of one syllable. Of the first 118 words of Hamlet's most famous soliloquy, 99 are of one syllable; and witness the force of its first words: "To be or not to be. . ."

USE ACCURATE WORDS. Mark Twain once said the difference between the right word and the almost right word is the difference between lightning and lightning bug. Words should convey their intended meaning as accurately as possible. Inaccuracy often results from the careless use of common words with many meanings. When you use such abstract phrases and words as *love, honor, socialism, liberty, right, wrong, the American way,* and the like, without some explanation or definition of your intended meaning, you give the listener leeway to supply meanings which suit his fancy. Since these may be far different from your intentions, it is important for you to clarify meanings to indicate the sense you wish to convey. Words which have special meanings or are uncommon to the listener—such as foreign words, technical terms, jargon, idiomatic expressions, and the like—generally should not be used unless they are specifically explained and defined at once.

CITE FACTS AND FIGURES. The use of facts and figures in a speech is very common, for they represent verifiable information often scientifically collected and classified. Yet they are often used so as to give hazy and vague impressions. When expressions such as *few, many, a whole lot,* and *millions* accompany them, it may indicate that the speaker did not want to go to the trouble of finding the exact information. A boy came home from grade school one day and said, "Father, the teacher told me to ask you how much is a million." The father replied, "Son, tell your teacher that a million is a hell of a lot," thereby jumping from one ambiguity to another.

It is more exact to say, "We had one and one-fourth inches of rain last night," than to say "We had a good shower." It is better to say there were sixty-four automobile accidents in Johnson County last year than to say this county had a lot of car wrecks—still better to say that this is only half as many accidents per passenger mile as there were ten years ago and that this county has the second best safety record in the state. If you say the new building will be 500 feet high, your listener will not visualize it as well as if you tell him that it will be forty-five stories high and if laid on its side would extend one city block.

Sometimes a vague fact becomes clear when a series of examples with figures is cited. A student who says in a speech, "Many men reach success by the time they are 35 years old," leaves a weak and fuzzy image in the minds of his listeners. But such a statement becomes clearer and more impressive with this kind of follow-up: "Lindbergh made his famous New York to Paris flight when he was 25; William Pitt was prime minister of England when he was 24; Mendelssohn composed his overture to *A Midsummer Night's Dream* when he was 16; Keats had established his place in the world of poetry before his death at the age of 26."

The late Secretary of State John Foster Dulles, speaking to the American Federation of Labor in St. Louis, not only cited essential facts but translated them dramatically into realistic meanings for the laboring man by comparing what one hour of labor will buy for the American worker in New York and for the Russian worker in Moscow: "To buy a pound of butter in New York, it takes 27 minutes of work; in Moscow over 6 hours of work. For a pound of sugar, $3\frac{1}{2}$ minutes in New York, 8 minutes in Moscow; for a quart of milk, 7 minutes in New York, 42 minutes in Moscow; for a dozen eggs, 25 minutes in New York, nearly 3 hours in Moscow; for a cotton shirt, nearly 1 hour in New York, 22 hours in Moscow; for a man's suit, 3 days in New York; 47 days in Moscow; for shoes, 1 day in New York, 13 days in Moscow; and for a woman's wool suit, 22 hours in New York, 22 days in Moscow."[5]

POSE DIRECT QUESTIONS.   All children know a simple and easy way to get information—they ask questions. This often drives their parents to distraction but nevertheless is a sound device for picking up information and pinning down an idea. Socrates, the great Greek philosopher, made it his characteristic method of teaching. For the speaker, questions are particularly useful, enabling him to maneuver and adjust to the response of his listeners with amplifying questions and explanations for clarity's sake. This is an advantage the writer does not have.

Two types of questions characterize oral style: one requires an answer or explanation to clarify an idea; the other dramatizes or

---

[5] John Foster Dulles: "Organized Labor's Fight Against World Communism," delivered before the American Federation of Labor, St. Louis, September 24, 1953, in *U.S. Department of State Bulletin*, 29, 745 (October 5, 1953), 445.

makes thought impressive. The latter, called the rhetorical question, has been mentioned before and will be referred to in the following section. The former, the direct question, can be described as a question which helps to channel the thought of the listener into a specific phase of the subject; it therefore speeds coming to grips with essential matter. Direct questions can also help to classify ideas in separate categories and make the total thought picture clear to the listener. This was demonstrated by a college student, speaking on Navy Day during World War II, who had carefully prepared an informative speech to be given before civic clubs on the subject of the battleship. Through a misunderstanding he found himself faced instead with four audiences of grade school children. But this young man met the challenge of audience adaptation by telling his story about the battleship by means of a chain of questions. "What is a crow's nest?" he began, and explained how the crow's nest was the eye of the battleship. "How far is it from the crow's nest to the bottom of the ship?" He compared its height to a 12-story building. "How much does a battleship cost?" He didn't answer millions; it cost more than two hundred new high school buildings. "How long is it?" More than twice as long as the high school football field. And so for thirty minutes he took these youngsters on an exciting sightseeing tour of a battleship, using the simple device of a direct question followed by a clear, concise answer.

Psychological Approach

THE PERSONAL. The speaker's relation to his audience is almost always more intimate and personal than is the writer's with the reader. Speaking creates a kind of *you and me* environment. The speaker's language is naturally, often characterized by personal pronouns—I, we, you, yours, ours, me, and mine—which help him make a direct appeal to his listeners. In the personalized story, *I* and *we* may appear often. For example, in Lincoln's farewell speech of 144 words, 19, or 15 percent of all the words used, are personal pronouns. In many persuasive situations the speaker is in a sense in court, seeking a verdict from his listeners. The direct, personal touch can win his case. Note these lines of Mark Antony's oration in *Julius Caesar:* "If *you* have tears, prepare to shed them now. *You* all do know this mantle. . . . Oh, what a fall was there, *my* countrymen! Then *I* and *you* and all of *us* fell down whilst bloody treason flourished over *us.* Oh now *you* weep; and, *I* perceive *you* feel the dint of pity. . . . *I* come not, friends, to steal away *your* hearts. *I* am no orator, as Brutus is; but as *you* know *me* all, a plain, blunt man, that loved *my* friend and that *they* know full well that gave *me* public leave to speak of *him.*"

The word "we" appears nine times in two sentences in one of Churchill's speeches. The personal pronoun was a characteristic trademark of Franklin Roosevelt's speaking.

COLORFUL AND IMPRESSIVE LANGUAGE.   This is a broad category and provides some of the sharpest and most effective tools of the speaker—words and phrases which often carry extra power, implied meanings, sharp and vivid images, sensory and emotional responses. Such words and expressions commonly make ideas more vigorous and vivid. Shakespeare, for instance, had a genius for using powerful images to vivify a description or express an idea. In *Julius Caesar,* instead of saying that Cassius is a thin man, emaciated and treacherous, over six feet tall and weighing 140 pounds, he says:

> Yon Cassius has a lean and hungry look;
> He thinks too much; such men are dangerous.

SAYINGS AND SLOGANS.   There are many ways a speaker may make an idea vivid and memorable. Sometimes he is able to compress a vast amount of meaning into a single word or phrase. Theodore Roosevelt's expression, "Walk softly and carry a big stick," Wilson's "Make the world safe for democracy," Harding's "Back to normalcy," Daniel Webster's "Union now and forever, one and inseparable," Marshal Pétain's "They shall not pass," and General MacArthur's "I shall return" are examples. They compress a broad or big concept into a few words. They are also catchy expressions with slogan value, which have been used as potent weapons.

METAPHORS AND SIMILES.   In order to describe a thing vividly to a listener, one often contrasts it with something else. A *simile* compares two things with the use of *as, like,* or *so.* A *metaphor,* dispensing with these connective words, identifies the two things more closely. For instance, "The man paced back and forth like a tiger," is a simile. But "He is a tiger," "The fog came on little cat feet," and "The sun rose with fingers of light reaching upward" are all metaphors.

Similes and metaphors often provide powerful images. Shakespeare, in *Antony and Cleopatra,* speaks of "my salad days, when I was green in judgment." One of the most famous metaphors of our times was coined by Churchill at Fulton, Missouri, in March, 1946: "From Stettin in the Baltic to Trieste in the Adriatic, an *iron curtain* has descended across the continent." Churchill used metaphors extensively and effectively; much of his oratorical greatness lay in his ability to find the exactly right figurative language. In a single speech, for example, can be found expressions such as: "For the first time we have made the Hun feel the sharp edge of those tools with which he has enslaved Europe," "the United States . . . has drawn the sword for freedom and cast away the scabbard," "the stakes for which they have decided to play are mortal," "the long arm of fate reached out across the oceans to bring the United States into the forefront of the battle."

During World War II President Roosevelt made effective use of a metaphor in a fireside chat when he referred to the German submarines in this manner: "When you see a rattlesnake poised to strike, you do not wait until he has struck before you crush him. These Nazi submarines . . . are the rattlesnakes of the Atlantic."

ANTITHESIS. Antithesis consists in sharply contrasting an idea by parallel structure. Antony's line in *Julius Caesar,* "I come to bury Caesar, not to praise him," is an example.

PARALLELISM. Parallelism is repetition of an idea by repetition of parallel words and variation of others. For example, "Of the people, by the people, for the people," "Man made the city, God made the country, but the devil made the small town," "I came, I saw, I conquered."[6] Saint Paul's I Corinthians, Chapter 13, on the subject of "charity," contains excellent contrasts and parallelisms:

Though I speak with the tongues of men and of angels, and have not charity, I am become as sounding brass, or a tinkling cymbal.

And though I have the gift of prophecy, and understand all mysteries, and all knowledge; and though I have all faith, so that I could remove mountains, and have not charity, I am nothing.

And though I bestow all my goods to feed the poor, and though I give my body to be burned, and have not charity, it profiteth me nothing.

[6] This type of expression, characterized by the omission of conjunctive participles for the expression of vehemence or speed, is sometimes called an *asyndeton* and is a common and important rhetorical device.

Charity suffereth long, and is kind; charity envieth not; charity vaunteth not itself, is not puffed up,

Doth not behave itself unseemly, seeketh not her own, is not easily provoked, thinketh no evil,

Rejoiceth not in iniquity, but rejoiceth in the truth;

Beareth all things, believeth all things, hopeth all things, endureth all things.

Charity never faileth: but whether there be prophecies, they shall fail; whether there be tongues, they shall cease; and whether there be knowledge, it shall vanish away.

For we know in part, and we prophesy in part.

But when that which is perfect is come, then that which is in part shall be done away.

When I was a child, I spake as a child, I understood as a child, I thought as a child: but when I became a man, I put away childish things.

For now we see through a glass, darkly; but then face to face: now I know in part; but then shall I know even as also I am known.

And now abideth faith, hope, and charity, these three; but the greatest of these is *charity*.

EXAGGERATION AND UNDERSTATEMENT. Rhetoricians call overstatement *hyperbole* and understatement *litotes;* when carefully used, both can give force to your statements. If you say, "He hit the ceiling," you are using hyperbole for saying that the man was very much upset. On the other hand, if someone were to develop a process for extracting gold from seawater and you remarked to him, "I think you have something there," you would be using *litotes.*

PERSONIFICATION. Inanimate objects and abstractions are personified when they are treated as having personal attributes: "The sun smiled on us," "the car groaned," "I heard a forest praying." Stuart Chase demonstrates how the device of personification can be grossly overdone:

Here is the dual shape of Labor—for some a vast, dirty, clutching hand, for others a Galahad in armor. Pacing to and fro with remorseless tread are the Trusts and the Utilities, bloated, unclean monsters with enormous biceps. Here is Wall Street, a crouching dragon, ready to spring upon assets not already nailed down in any other section of the country. The Consumer, a pathetic figure in a gray shawl, goes wearily to market. Capital and Labor each give her a kick as she passes, while Commercial Advertising, a playful sprite, squirts perfume into her eyes.[7]

[7] Stuart Chase, *The Tyranny of Words,* Harcourt, Brace, 1938, p. 25.

STRONG NOUNS, ADJECTIVES, AND VERBS. Good tools must be strong and powerful; so must good words. In general, words which conjure up sensory impressions are always strong. In Hamlet, Shakespeare describes the night by saying, "The air bites shrewdly; . . . it is a nipping and an eager air." Try to increase your use of connotative words to make ideas vivid. For instance, *clasp* is more strongly connotative, more colorful, than *hold*. To say, "He left the meeting," is not as colorful as "He stalked out of the room." Of course, you must always be careful to reflect good taste as you seek to color your spoken language.

COLLOQUIALISMS. The use of colloquial language also requires care and good taste, for—misused—it can lower you in the minds of the audience. A few speakers of renown—Al Smith, Abraham Lincoln, Franklin Roosevelt, Clarence Darrow, Will Rogers, Mark Twain, and Theodore Roosevelt—were able to use the raw, folksy, local style to good advantage. This style is more pertinent for the speaker than it is for the writer, and when properly applied it is an effective medium for attaining directness, realism, and warmth. It is a matter of talking the language of the people, but without sacrificing personal dignity and sincerity.

SOUND-EFFECT WORDS. Even when divorced from their meaning, words have sound appeal, but they are most effective when sound and sense complement each other. They can caress and assault the ear; this is often observed in poetry, which should usually be read aloud to be fully appreciated. Sound effect words are a feature of nursery rhymes, where they frequently imitate noises: *bow-wow, meow, moo, ding dong, bang, boom,* and so forth. This use of words whose sounds match their meanings is called *onomatopoeia*.

The reaction to sound in a word is an individualistic matter. A French poet who did not know the English language called *cellar door* a pleasant-sounding phrase. Hendrik Willem Van Loon, the historian, thought *cuspidor* had melodic quality. When told of this, Walter de la Mare, an English writer, replied that *cuspidor* was nice, but he preferred *spittoon*, and so it goes. Lexicographer Wilfred J. Funk lists the following among our most beautiful words: *dawn, hush, lullaby, murmuring, tranquil, mist, luminous, chimes, golden* and *melody*. The use of such pleasant-sounding words is called *euphony*. A group of speech teachers in turn proffers the following as ugly words: *spinach, naughtiness, plutocrat, mash, sap, plump, victuals, phlegmatic,* and *jazz.* The use of such words is called *cacophony.* It should be noted, however, that ideas described by these words probably influenced the selection.

The sound effect of alliteration can often have a decided psychological effect. "54–40 or Fight," "Keep Cool with Coolidge," "I like Ike," "Rum, Romanism, and Rebellion" are examples of its use in political slogans. "Eye It, Try It, Buy It," "Be Happy Go Lucky," "Duz Does Everything" are examples in advertising.

RHETORICAL QUESTIONS AND REITERATION.   Rhetorical questions and reiteration are also effective in the oral style, often providing convenient tools for the speaker. They have already been discussed in Chapter 7, pages 180–181, and we suggest that you review these passages with their accompanying illustrations.

Other Stylistic Considerations

SENTENCES AND WORD COMBINATIONS.   The sentence should be tailored to fit the thought—never the reverse. You learned in your first English composition courses that there are three principal types of sentences: simple, compound, and complex. The simple sentence has one subject and one verb, plus modifiers; the compound sentence contains two or more clauses of similar importance; and the complex sentence contains at least one independent and one dependent clause. Neither the writer nor the speaker should try to follow a fixed pattern, using, for instance, first a complex sentence, then a compound one, followed by three simple sentences; nor should he use largely one type of sentence. Nothing can be more monotonous than a uniform pattern of sentence structure. No rules can be laid down for the speaker, but experience shows that he should generally use shorter sentences than the writer—that short, simple, declarative sentences should predominate in oral style, with enough compound and complex sentences mixed in to achieve variety.

If you want a given sentence to have power, put the verb to work. The verb propels it, makes it go. Note the strength of active verbs in the following imperative sentences: "Vote for Mr. X," "Buy Bonds," "Eat Less," "Drive Carefully," "Swat the Fly," "Ask the Man Who Owns One." As much as possible, use active verbs rather than passive. "I think" is more effective than "It is my thought." "See your doctor" is better than "Your doctor should be consulted." Lack of vigor in oral style (and written also) is often the result of using the passive too much. Develop the habit of putting the verb directly to work.

Complex sentences are either *periodic* or *loose*. Periodic sentences are climactic—that is, the qualifying clauses come first and the main thought is placed at the end. For example, "As George gazed up into the clear blue sky and watched an eagle make lazy circles overhead, he was hit by a truck." This sentence has suspense; the listener does not know what the speaker is leading up to until the very end. The loose sentence is the opposite: the main thought is placed first. The above example turned into a loose sentence would read: "George was hit by a truck as he gazed up into the clear blue sky and watched an eagle making lazy circles overhead." Periodic sentences are usually more effective than loose, but over-using them can make a person's style stilted—some loose sentences are desirable. For a vigorous, dynamic oral style use a predominance of active verbs and periodic and simple sentences.

The *balanced sentence* is a special type of sentence often employed by skilled rhetoricians. A sentence is said to be balanced when parallel clauses are similar in language, rhythm, and movement—for example, "The strong died bravely, the weak begged for mercy."

ADJECTIVES AND ADVERBS. Learn to use adjectives and adverbs effectively. The purpose of an adjective is to give a more accurate or vivid image of a noun. Its role is to modify meaning. We say "a *cold* day," "an *old* woman," "a *sharp* curve," "a *wet* cloth." When we use certain vague adverbs to qualify the adjective, we often dilute the true meaning we intend to convey. You can spoil your meaning by attaching an unnecessary *most* to such words as *unique, exceptional, extraordinary, unusual,* and *perfect*. It probably adds nothing to the meaning to place *very* before *cold, old, sharp, wet, happy, nice,* and so on. *Very* is perhaps the most overworked word in the English language.

FILL-IN AND CONNECTING WORDS. Verbs, nouns, and adjectives are like pearls on a string, giving life and luster to the thought. Yet words that hold and bind these pearls together and keep them in place can be extremely important, even though they may have little meaning. These include prepositions, conjunctions, adverbs, and relative pronouns. The "pearl" words are easy to grasp, but such "string" words as *consequently, if, and, but, however, with, what, about, for, the,* and many others cause trouble. Some of them are indispensable, but there is a common tendency to use three or four when one or two would do as well. Fowler, in his *Dictionary of Modern English Usage,* calls these clusters "compound prepositions and conjunctions." The following are examples: "in the event that (if)," "on account of (because)," "due to the fact that (since)."

We commonly use certain words, phrases, and expressions to show a transition of logical sequence or causal relation. Examples of such transitions are:

consequently	therefore	hence
because	accordingly	thus
as a consequence	on that account	since

Other transitions represent thought which is amplified, added to, or enlarged. Examples of transitions that indicate "addition" are:

moreover	furthermore	likewise
also	additionally	in addition
besides	too	another

Another group of transitions shows time relationship. For example:

later	concomitantly	at the same time
subsequently	after a while	in conjunction
afterwards	thereupon	therewith
thereafter	whereupon	earlier
simultaneously	prior to	soon
previously	beforehand	formerly

Still other words and phrases are used for further clarification of an idea. These transitions are often associated with "comparison and contrast." Examples are:

contrarily	yet	similarly
conversely	contrariwise	similar to
however	to the contrary	quite the same
inversely	more important still	congruently

APPROPRIATENESS. As we have said before, your language should always be suitable to the occasion, your audience, your subject, and your personality. Your speaking will probably be most acceptable when you use language similar to that of your listeners. Be your own censor and judge of good taste. When in doubt about the impropriety of a word or phrase, do not use it. Vulgarities and off-color language have no place on the public platform. However, slang used carefully, sparingly, and skillfully may in some instances be effective.

It is certainly in order in most pep talks, student union discussions, and "whistle stop" campaign speeches. But slang is almost never appropriate in speeches to teachers, college professors, scientists, or similar dignified audiences. Slang can give color and spice to an idea, and occasionally a slang expression like "bunk" or "cockeyed" may convey more meaning than can be put into several paragraphs. But there is always a danger of overdoing it.

Colloquial and informal language has a place in coffee cup conversations but should be used with great discretion before an audience. An effective illustration of a snatch of conversation and a formal speech on the same subject is offered by McBurney and Wrage in a recent text. The first passage is suitable to living room or office conversation, whereas the second has a more elevated and formal style suited for public speech.

(*In conversation*)
A university is not out to please customers. It's more of a busybody than a business. Its job is to poke around, sniff out facts, air them—no matter whether people like 'em or not. It ought to puncture prejudices and platitudes. Let the bigots howl. A university is a people's hairshirt.

(*In a speech*)
A university that does not lead is a university only in name. A true university diligently pursues facts amid appearances. It is a critic of what is, and a standard-bearer for what ought to be. Often it must speak as a solitary voice, championing truth against the clamor of outraged opinion and prejudice.[8]

TRITENESS AND OVERWORKED WORDS AND PHRASES. Clothing worn too long can become threadbare, or if worn too often for the same occasion or purpose can become tiresome. The same is true of words and phrases. Some speakers use stale or hackneyed expressions—expressions we have heard so often that no freshness or originality remain. Here are a few examples heard in speeches: "Now without further ado," "It gives me great pleasure," "Unaccustomed as I am," and "According to statistics." "Ladies and gentlemen" is a salutation

[8] James H. McBurney and Ernest J. Wrage, *Guide to Good Speech*, 2nd ed., Prentice-Hall, New Jersey, 1960, p. 174.

which, like "Dear sir" in a letter, is not objectionable when used only in the opening of a speech; repeated again and again in a speech it can become annoying. Certain words and expressions used repeatedly during the course of a speech can become irritating to the listener. College debaters often abuse the use of such terms as "honorable judge," "worthy opponents," "friends of the opposition," "we find," "we have proved." In daily conversation many words and expressions are overused. Some adjectives, for instance, need to be put on a quota basis: *nice, lovely, terrific, great, fine, swell, wonderful, fabulous, adorable, marvelous, fantastic,* and *cute.* College students overuse such expressions as *snowed, bombed, dig, I'll buy that, you're out of your mind, stoned,* and *neat.*

We resent some expressions in others yet seldom realize when we use them ourselves. Among these ancient similes and metaphors are the following: "mad as a wet hen," "white as a sheet," "a walking encyclopedia," "sticks like a leech," "as good as gold," "fat as a pig," "slow as molasses in January," "dead as a door nail," and "clean as a hound's tooth."

Habitual use of trite and hackneyed words and expressions reflects a lazy mind. With a little effort and a sense of pride in personal accomplishment, you can make your own language more original, more refreshing, and less monotonous.

PROJECTS AND EXERCISES

For speaking projects see Part Three.

1. Prepare a list of words which, because of their sound, are unpleasant and irritating to you. Compare your list with that of other members of the class.
2. Prepare a list of hackneyed words and expressions taken from conversation among your friends and schoolmates.
3. Explain the difference in the meaning of the following words: principle—principal; elicit—illicit; respectfully—respectively; stationary—stationery; counsel—council; capital—capitol.
4. How many words and expressions in our common vocabulary can you think of which come from frontier life? Examples: *kicking over the traces, going off half-cocked, getting hitched.*
5. Take a recent issue of *Vital Speeches* and find examples of the following:
   a. the specific and concrete

b. use of figures and facts
c. direct questions
d. colorful and impressive language
e. especially effective metaphors and slogans
f. antithesis
g. parallelism

TOPICS FOR DISCUSSION

1. Compare the types of emotional experiences of a reader and a listener.
2. Can we fight a war without a drum?
3. Discuss what is meant by "pen-born" and "tongue-born" language.
4. Why are we able to find satisfaction by reading good literature over and over again?
5. Discuss the use of slang, jargon, and colloquialisms—(a) advantages, (b) dangers and disadvantages.
6. What is "style" in speech?
7. Discuss the language style of some nationally known radio news commentators.

ADDITIONAL READINGS

Barrett, Harold, *Practical Methods in Speech,* Holt, 1959, chap. 7.

Brigance, William Norwood, *Speech Composition,* 2nd ed., Appleton-Century-Crofts, 1953, chap. 6.

Brigance, William Norwood, *Speech, Its Techniques and Disciplines in a Free Society,* Appleton-Century-Crofts, 1952, chap. 15.

Bryant, Donald C., and Wallace, Karl R., *Fundamentals of Public Speaking,* 3rd ed., Appleton-Century-Crofts, 1960, chap. 16.

Chase, Stuart, *Power of Words,* Harcourt, Brace, 1954.

Hayakawa, S. I., *Language in Thought and Action,* Harcourt, Brace, 1949.

Lee, Irving J., *Customs and Crises in Communication,* Harper, 1954.

Lewis, Norman, *Word Power Made Easy,* Doubleday, 1953.

McBurney, James H., and Wrage, Ernest J., *Guide to Good Speech,* Prentice-Hall, 1960, chap. 12.

Mills, Glen E., *Composing the Speech,* Prentice-Hall, 1952, chap. 14.

Reid, Loren, *First Principles of Public Speaking,* Artcraft, 1960, chap. 13.

Smith, Raymond G., *Principles of Public Speaking,* Ronald, 1958, chap. 7.

Soper, Paul L., *Basic Public Speaking,* 2nd ed., Oxford University Press, 1956, chap. 13.

White, Eugene E., *Practical Speech Fundamentals,* Macmillan, 1960, chap. 4.

Delivery

爲 12 爲
The Dynamics of Delivery

Delivery, the means of bringing the minds of speaker and listener together, is the final step of the speech act. All the previous thinking and planning of the speaker are brought to fulfillment by auditory and visual codes for conveying meaning. Thus the purpose of delivery is to carry out the function of the other five dimensions of speech in one single act of integration.

FUNCTIONS OF DELIVERY

Delivery helps to bring the speaker's image into close perspective. The audience gets its most intimate and close view of the speaker during the actual progress of the speech. The many attributes of the speaker's personality—his character, his attitudes, his knowledge, his sense of values, and his ideas—are reflected by voice and action. The whole dimension of the speaker becomes operative for better or for worse in this act of the speech communication process.

Delivery helps speaker and audience to function as a team. The speaker-audience relationship is best when they react to each other in the spirit of cooperation. Have you ever noticed how tired you feel after watching your favorite football team in an exciting game? This is because you were not only pulling for your team with mind and spirit but also shoving and pushing unconsciously to help get the ball across the goal line. This response of identification is called *empathy*. When listeners tend to react in empathy with the speaker's language expression, his vocal inflection, and his bodily action, we have a manifestation of team support. Listeners and speaker should function as a team, each striving for the other's success. Harnessing empathy is a matter of degree, but an empathic response should always be the goal.

Speaker and audience are not separate entities but an integral part of a common core in a given social experience. Delivery is the essential medium by which the speaker not only responds to the group, but directs and controls it and maintains vital contact with it. Delivery gives the speaker his only chance to join and hold together the giver and the receiver of the spoken word.

Delivery helps give meaning to the speaker's raw product of thought and feeling. Delivery has a vital bearing on the way speech content is communicated. Although what the speaker says is certainly the dynamic center of the entire speaking process, in most instances an idea poorly delivered—no matter how worthy it may be—loses much of its impact upon an audience. An important function of delivery is therefore to preserve or enhance during communication, the full value of content. Good delivery cannot make a good speech, but poor delivery can ruin what would otherwise be a good one. Make sure that by means of delivery you realize fully the benefits of the dimensions of thought and content.

Delivery helps make the organized thought picture clear and compelling. The over-all structure of your speech can be brought into sharper focus by vocal emphasis and bodily action. The architectural aspects of your speech remain static on paper, but by skillful delivery its beauty, simplicity, and strength can be effectively revealed to an audience.

Delivery helps color and shade the meanings symbolized by language. Delivery is specially suited to add new meaning and emotion to words and phrases. Great actors have been known to practice hours on a single phrase to produce a desired dramatic response. The whole scale of emotion may be sounded by tone quality, vocal emphasis, and gesture. Here the speaker has his greatest leverage for governing the meaning of words he utters. No matter how beautiful or powerful the language, it is the speaker's delivery which finally will electrify the audience or lull it to sleep.

SPECIAL CHARACTERISTICS OF DELIVERY

Delivery in speech is both shared and retained. When the merchant delivers a product to his customer there is a transfer of goods from one hand to another. This is not so with the speaker. The speaker who delivers an idea does not give it up; he still retains it. He may deliver the same ideas dozens of times to different audiences and never surrender any portion of his product. In fact, the idea he delivers then becomes more firmly his own—for him its value will increase by the experience of sharing it with others.

The importance of delivery varies with the speaker's purpose. When your purpose is to stimulate, entertain, or actuate, delivery becomes especially important. An appeal directed more to the heart of the listener than to his intellect must be effectively presented. This does not mean that delivery is unimportant in speeches to inform or convince; it means that when emotions and motivation are the chief concern, delivery assumes a more significant role.

Delivery provides the best means by which all the speech processes can be rewardingly rehearsed. The other five dimensions of speech taken separately do not lend themselves well to effective rehearsal. You can, to some degree, make trial runs in organizing and outlining your ideas or in reshaping your thought; you can perhaps make numerous trial runs in the use of words. But there can be no complete "dress rehearsal" without delivery. In such practice, you test not only the skills of delivery itself but also rehearse your organization, your central idea, your language, your logical and emotional supports, and even the manner of utilizing the attributes of your character and personality.

MODES OF DELIVERY

Impromptu

When we speak on the spur of the moment without having a chance to prepare for the speech, we are speaking *impromptu*. We are seldom asked to speak impromptu about something totally unfamiliar or uninteresting to us, but we may well be called upon without warning to say something about a particular field of interest or a special experience. We must be ready to meet such a challenge.

In most impromptu situations, the audience will respond sympathetically. The listener, sensing your predicament, will, as a matter of sportsmanship, rally in your behalf. Since your listeners will not expect a polished speech, they will be all the more delighted should you happen to do a good job. Impromptu speeches can be exceedingly dull or very exciting. They are dull when the speaker flounders about, hemming and hawing as he struggles to utter a few vague disconnected phrases and sentences. They are exciting if the speaker has the good fortune to hit upon a rich idea or belief of long standing, or if he has a sudden burst of insight. A number of helpful approaches for facing impromptu situations are discussed on page 353 of Part Three.

Extemporaneous Speaking

Extemporaneous delivery is often confused with impromptu, although the terms are far from synonymous. The extemporaneous speech is prepared; it is often the product of careful thought analysis and assiduous planning and assimilation of materials. It is often preceded by detailed outlining; portions of it may even be written out. It should be, and usually is, rehearsed from outline, although only the outline of ideas should be memorized. With such a backlog the speaker thinks his thoughts as he expresses them in a spontaneous, lively, and fresh manner. Words, phrases, and sentence patterns are formulated largely on the spot as the speech is delivered.

Extemporaneous speech is the most common and the most useful method of speaking. We may read our speeches occasionally from manuscript, but we have endless opportunities to speak extemporaneously. This method offers definite advantages over other forms of speaking. It utilizes the full benefits of careful and thorough preparation, yet permits the speaker wide latitude in adapting to the audience and the occasion. He is free to refer to speakers preceding and following him or to persons in the audience; he can refer to incidents and happenings which grow out of the occasion and can relate them to his subject and his purpose. It is this freedom to capitalize on local color and sudden turns of events for heightening interest or reinforcing a point which makes extempore speech desirable. Listeners usually prefer it over other types of delivery; it is most likely to be refreshing, spontaneous, natural, and realistic.

Classroom lectures, speeches at civic clubs, sermons, courtroom trials, and most professional addresses are usually extemporaneous. Nearly all the speeches in your speech class are of this type. Extemporaneous speaking is not always characterized by the most polished style of delivery, yet the wise student of speech will learn to speak extemporaneously before he speaks from manuscript—certainly before he ever memorizes an address. That is why this course is devoted almost wholly to the theories and principles in the planning and delivery of extemporaneous speeches. As Quintilian declared, "The richest fruit of all our study, and the most ample recompense for the extent of our labor is *the faculty of speaking extempore.*"

Manuscript Speaking

Manuscript speaking is becoming more and more common, partly because of the influence of radio, television, and improved public address amplifiers, and partly because busy industrial executives and government officials must guard themselves against inaccuracies in statement and avoid the possibility of being misquoted. Moreover, men in responsible positions with limited public speaking experience and training view the manuscript speech as something they can handle with greatest ease and self-assurance.

A common weakness of manuscript speaking is poor delivery, which may be due, in part, to faulty language style. The language of the speech to be read should resemble as nearly as possible that of extemporaneous speech. Too often, however, it is prepared as an essay to be read aloud. Churchill always insisted on reading every sentence aloud until he was satisfied that it sounded as eloquent as possible. The written speech should really be an extemporaneous speech that has lodged itself on paper. Its words, phrases, and sentences should spring forth with conversational freshness suited to the thought, the occasion, and the speaker.

Speech delivery from the manuscript calls for special skills and techniques. A principal cause for poor manuscript reading lies in the speaker's failure adequately to utilize and master the essential principles of effective oral reading.

Here are some suggestions for improving your ability to deliver a speech from manuscript:

1. *Think and relive the thought as you speak.* Re-experience as fully as possible the true meaning of what you say at the moment of utterance.

Live anew the thoughts and feelings, sensing their vitality, reality, and importance. Concentrate on your ideas rather than the words.

2. *Speak with a sense of communication*—a sense of sharing your thoughts, your feelings and attitudes with your audience. "Talk it over" with your listeners; look directly at them so you may sense their reaction. *Practice until your eyes rest upon the audience at least twice as much of the time as upon your manuscript.*

3. *Practice your speech aloud at least six or eight times.* Thought progression lies in your ability to keep thinking ahead of your tongue. Practice until you can speak from memory a sentence or more ahead of the spot where your eyes fall at any moment. Mark on your manuscript thought units composed of groups of words, each representing one eyeful of meaning. These will serve as guideposts which will help you to speak with a certain rhythm and with effective pauses, yet all the while keeping your thoughts marching along with easy fluency.

4. *Keep the manuscript as inconspicuous as possible.* The manuscript should never become a barrier between you and the listener. Be sure it is neat and easily legible. Use a lectern or reading stand where papers can lie flat and your eyes can easily focus on the words without stooping or lowering the head. Glance down *with your eyes* to pick up the meaning—don't keep nodding your head up and down. Sheets of paper should not be flipped over but slipped aside or under the manuscript.

5. *Develop sound attitudes toward manuscript speaking.* Use of a manuscript is not the lazy way out or an easy substitute for the extemporaneous speech. Work hard to overcome poor delivery. Don't think that once the speech is written your job is finished. The key to effective manuscript delivery lies in industrious and diligent rehearsal.

The Memorized Speech

The practice of memorizing *all* speeches word for word should be strongly discouraged. Beginning speech students may feel that with a memorized speech they are "safe," but it often gives only a false sense of security. The memorized speech has its limitations and hazards. It often *sounds* memorized—stilted and artificial. The speaker with a memorized speech may tend to sound like a schoolboy reciting his piece, declaiming with his mind on the words, not the ideas. If he forgets, as he often may, he can be in real trouble. Faulty memory breaks the continuity of thought and leaves the speaker floundering. As he struggles to get back on the track but is unable to do so, he is seized with fright and even panic. The resulting embarrassment is not only his own but is shared by the audience.

Although memorized delivery has its hazards and pitfalls, this does not mean it should be ruled out in all instances, for it can on some occasions and for some speakers be the most effective mode of delivery. Memory helps to assure fluency and to improve the speech's stylistic quality. Many great speakers memorized their speeches. They trained themselves to be consummate actors and spent endless labor and effort in attaining artistic perfection. Most students in speech classes cannot afford the time, nor do they have the dramatic ability to refine their original speeches to such perfection—nor would this ability generally be very useful to them. Perhaps for one or even two assignments the memorized technique can be employed as a training experience. Moreover, there are frequent instances when memorization of certain parts or passages of an extemporaneous speech may be wise. For instance, it may be helpful to memorize the opening or closing sentences of your speech, or a dramatic incident, a literary quotation, a piece of description, or a few lines of poetry. These memorized portions must, however, be carefully blended with the thought and mood you wish to convey and the general extempore style of delivery used.

STANDARDS OF EFFECTIVE DELIVERY

Effective delivery communicates meaning without apparent artifice. Delivery is best when the speaker takes the listeners on a thought journey while they remain unaware of his method of conveyance. Delivery is best when listeners forget who is talking or what he is trying to do, yet go strolling with him mentally.

The listeners may fail to join the speaker on his thought journey for many and varied reasons. They may not like the way he stands or the way he paces back and forth, his fidgety, meaningless gestures, the way he fumbles with his notes, jingles the coins in his pocket, or pronounces some of the words. They may be conscious of his peculiar vocal inflections, his artificial smile, the way he screws up his face, and so on. Anything the speaker does which seems strikingly different or irregular and appears out of keeping with what the listeners are accustomed to may call attention to itself, thus causing them to become conscious of the speaker and his manner. In a sense, of course, every speaker's delivery is unique, and this uniqueness should be capitalized upon. The point is that when differences are so striking that the listener's mind is drawn more toward them than toward the meaning the speaker wishes to communicate, the speaker fails to meet the first purpose of delivery.

Effective delivery maintains a spirit of communication. Modern speech must be direct and communicative; the days of the elocutionary style of delivery are long gone. In that period, gestures, voice, and vocal inflection were often studiously rehearsed with the view of adding grace and beauty to expression. The intent was to impress or perhaps cast a kind of hynotic spell upon the audience. Audiences may have been impressed at the moment, but individual listeners were often at a loss later to tell much about what the speaker actually said. This style of delivery placed too much emphasis upon outward display and exhibition. Today the central focus is upon a lively sense of communication. The extemporaneous manner dominates the mood and the tone of delivery. The speaker thinks and relives his thoughts and feelings as he speaks in a natural, spontaneous, and animated enlarged conversational style. He talks *with* his listeners, not *at* them; he shares his ideas with them instead of projecting ideas toward them.

Effective delivery makes ideas sound important. What can be more depressing than an indifferent, I-don't-care, ultra-casual speech delivery? No matter how small the audience or how ordinary the subject, never allow your manner of speech to sink to the level of the commonplace. Every word and phrase should always be worthy of the listener's respect and attention. The first rule of salesmanship is to consider every sale an important one, whether it involves a ten cent lead pencil or a twenty-five thousand dollar house. One of the secrets of Theodore Roosevelt's speech delivery was his determination to make every word and syllable sound important to his listeners. He gave the impression that he cared about every thought he uttered.

Effective delivery is appropriate to the thought and the occasion. Certainly the speaker's manner of delivery must be in harmony with his ideas. Insignificant thoughts should not be presented in an eloquent manner, nor are lofty ideas to be treated matter-of-factly. Voice and bodily activity should always fit the thought; for, says Cicero, "every emotion has from nature its own peculiar look, tone, and gesture." However, when treating extremely emotional subjects, it is better somewhat to underplay emotion in delivery; otherwise the performance may become too painful for the listener. At least part of the speaker's feeling should be "pent up" emotion: he should communicate strong feeling but demonstrate proper restraint.

PROJECTS AND EXERCISES

For speaking projects see Part Three.

1. Attend a campus speech and determine if the speaker: (1) communicates meaning without apparent artifice, (2) maintains a spirit of communication throughout his speech, (3) makes ideas sound important, (4) uses delivery appropriate to the thought and the occasion.
2. Make a list of all the advantages and disadvantages you can think of for these modes of delivery: (1) extemporaneous, (2) memorized, (3) manuscript.

TOPICS FOR DISCUSSION

1. What is meant by a "conversational mode" of speaking?
2. How can poor delivery be an impediment to the speaker's ideas?
3. What advantages and disadvantages can you see for extemporaneous speaking?
4. When would memorization be a good mode of speech?
5. What are the biggest problems of manuscript speaking?

ADDITIONAL READINGS

Gilman, Wilbur E., Aly, Bower, and Reid, Loren D., *The Fundamentals of Speaking,* Macmillan, 1951, chap. 7.

Oliver, Robert T., and Cortright, Rupert L., *New Training for Effective Speech,* rev. ed., Dryden, 1951, pp. 107–119.

Oliver, Robert T., Dickey, Dallas C., and Zelko, Harold P., *Communicative Speech,* rev. ed., Dryden, 1955, pp. 38–51.

Sarett, Lew, Foster, William Trufant, and Sarett, Alma Johnson, *Basic Principles of Speech,* 3rd ed., Houghton Mifflin, 1958, chap. 2.

Smith, Raymond G., *Principles of Public Speaking,* Ronald, 1958, chap. 15.

White, Eugene E., *Practical Speech Fundamentals,* Macmillan, 1960, chaps. 16 and 17.

Winans, James Albert, *Public Speaking,* rev. ed., Century, 1917, chap. 2.

Woolbert, Charles Henry, and Smith, Joseph, *Fundamentals of Speech,* Harper, 1934, chap. 5.

❧ 13 ❧
Bodily Communication

BODILY ACTION—CODE FOR COMMUNICATION

Bodily action includes any possible movements of the body—such as walking about the platform, posture, shrugging the shoulders, head movements, hand gestures, facial expressions, and eye glances. Some bodily actions are meaningless and random, serving no purpose other than to ease the tensions of the speaker. When such nervous, fidgety movements are pronounced and continuous, they distract attention from the meaning, are annoying to the listener, and are a general interference in the communication process.

Bodily action is an important part of the natural code for communicating thought. Longfellow realized this when he wrote, "He speaketh not and yet there lies a conversation in his eyes." The fact is that we do talk with our bodies. It was not a joke when the Frenchman said, "Let go of my hands, I want to talk." Have you ever observed children at play, particularly when adults are not supposed to be present? Have you noticed how naturally and expressively they use their hands, feet, legs, face, eyes, head, and entire bodies as they chatter and carry on their world of make-believe? Infants learn early in life to express their wants by all kinds of bodily actions. Primitive people develop intricate systems of signs to supplement their vocalization, or even as a substitute for language.

287

The language of action is undoubtedly far older than the language of words. Even in relatively modern times, Columbus and other explorers must have placed great reliance upon pantomime and signs of all sorts in their efforts to communicate with the native inhabitants of lands they discovered.

A speaker is seen as well as heard, except when talking over the telephone or radio, and even then his vocal expressiveness is influenced by the way he sits or stands, and by the bodily actions which release his motor tensions. A speaker facing an audience cannot escape action as part of the communication code. Every speaker must use both words and action—he cannot use words alone. Emphatic motor responses are natural even when talking to oneself. It is natural for a person to gesticulate, even violently at times, while talking over the telephone—amusing as this may be to others observing him.

There are many reasons why we should make effective use of bodily expression in speech delivery. Some of these reasons have a direct bearing upon the clarification, emphasis, and reinforcement of thought; others contribute more indirectly to effective speech communication—help to give ease and comfort to both speaker and audience, increase speaker confidence, activate his mind, increase audience interest and attention, and establish a closer relationship between speaker and audience.

USE BODILY ACTION FOR MORE EFFECTIVE COMMUNICATION

At least seven reasons can be cited for using bodily action to make your speech communication more effective:

1. *It helps break up stiff posture and awkward appearance.* When the speaker is tense, he looks awkward—easy bodily movements and action will counteract the stiff, awkward appearance.
2. *It helps release warmth and humanness of the speaker.* Lifeless, inactive speakers appear cold and aloof—physical animation helps bring the inner man out of his shell, helps to radiate and reveal essential qualities of the real personality.
3. *It helps activate the mind of the speaker.* We think with our bodies as well as with our brains. Freeing the body helps free the mind—processes of thought and feeling are energized through muscular activity.
4. *It helps control speech fright and develops poise.* Action breaks up physical tensions of the speaker—helps him feel more comfortable and at ease.

5. *It helps create and hold listener attention.* Action is a most common and effective device to get attention. Attention is the door to the mind, and what holds attention tends to lead to action. Action helps to keep audience awake.

6. *It helps strengthen the tie between speaker and listener.* Action brings the law of empathy into effect. Listeners tend to participate in what the speaker is doing; they tend to push themselves into what they perceive; they unconsciously work with the speaker. Action helps this cooperation more than voice.

7. *It helps give life and tone to the speech act.* Action gives the whole speech a lift. It helps to add tone and spirit to the whole occasion. The speaker is not a statue—he is a live human being. He should act like one.

THE RELATION OF GESTURES AND BODILY EXPRESSIONS TO MEANING

Gestures punctuate thought and emphasize meaning. The writer can punctuate his thoughts and give emphasis to them; so can the speaker. One effective method for the speaker is the *emphatic gesture.* The grade school teacher may snap her fingers to emphasize a point or reinforce room discipline. Some speakers use the index finger or the clenched fist, the shake of the head, or the stamp of a foot to stress a point. The emphatic gesture is usually sharp and sudden; it follows no set pattern.

Gestures help make pictures clear. The picture or *descriptive gesture* may be any kind of bodily response which indicates distance, space relationship, shape, size, or direction. If you try to tell someone how to put on a glove and you have no glove, you will have to describe or suggest the action by using your fingers and hands. Suppose you are telling someone about your first trip to a big city; as you describe the tall skyscrapers, you may suggest great height by throwing your head sharply back and looking nearly straight up. Here hand, body, head, and eyes can help create the picture. Picture gestures are used especially in pantomime, in the parlor game called "charades," and when telling about "the fish that got away." The speaker can make narrative and descriptive parts of his speech exciting and vivid by the skillful use of gestures of this type.

Gestures reflect personal reactions and attitudes. We react naturally with facial expressions and bodily movements to things we like or dislike. Suppose you bite into an apple or plum and find it very sour—you will probably make a sour-looking face. Or suppose someone offers your little sister a ripe, sweet, juicy peach; if she is fond of peaches her eyes will widen, her face light up, and she may hop up and down with glee. If a cat were to jump suddenly into the lap of a woman who hates cats, you would probably see a swift gesture of rejection. Speakers use gestures to reflect their attitudes and feelings of approval and disapproval of things which annoy and disgust them and of things which give them pleasure and delight.

Gestures help dramatize the thought. The *arrestive gesture* gives the signal that the speaker is about to say something he especially wants his listeners to hear. Its function is similar to that of the chairman of a meeting rapping for order or a master of ceremonies clapping his hands in a group to get attention before making an announcement. The speaker's dramatic gesture will probably be more subtle. He may shrug his shoulders, raise his hands, move forward a step or two, or strike a certain pose to arrest the attention of the audience preparatory to the point he wants to convey or to the mood he wishes to create. These dramatic gestures give the thought an edge of excitement and importance.

Gestures identify and discriminate ideas. Gestures of this type often blend with those made for clarity or emphasis. They help to point out something specific, to indicate a comparison, to enumerate and classify ideas, and to give shades to meanings in general. The speaker may use his fingers to count off a number of points, as, for example, "in the first place," "the second place," and so on. He may use hands, arms, and body to indicate contrasts or division of thought with such phrases as "on the one hand this may be true, but on the other the fact may be that . . . ," or "may I point out this difference, however," or "now get this."

MAKE YOUR GESTURES EFFECTIVE

Gestures should seem natural and spontaneous. Studied, mechanical gestures are artificial, unreal, and annoying to the listener. People gesticulate easily, naturally, and spontaneously in their everyday interpersonal relations. We are accustomed to this genuine bodily expression. This is probably why the studied, mechanical gesture comes as a kind of distasteful shock to the audience.

Freedom and spontaneity of bodily expressions spring basically from good mental attitudes. Inhibited bodily responses are often conditioned by tensions brought on by feelings of speech fright and apprehension. Lack of experience in speaking and feelings of inadequacy aggravate the problem. If this applies to you, it does not mean you should wait until you feel comfortable and self-confident before you try to use gestures in a speech. On the contrary, you should be encouraged to use more bodily action than usual, especially such action as is used for demonstration and description. Don't worry about a little awkwardness—awkwardness and mechanical stiffness are not the same. One of the best ways of developing spontaneity is to prepare your speech carefully, while cultivating the desire to speak. As you gain in experience and strengthen your will to talk, you will improve in spontaneity of bodily expression.

Gestures should be suitable to the meaning. Hamlet advises us, "Suit the word to the action and the action to the word." Action must be in harmony with the meaning which the words symbolize. Occasionally we see a speaker who hops about, swinging his arms wildly like a jumping jack—obviously overdoing it. He is, again as Hamlet put it, "tearing a passion to tatters." More often we see the other extreme, the speaker who scarcely moves a muscle to color or reinforce the thought. A "feeling" for what action to use, how much, and when to use it is something which is developed only by experience, by observation, and by good taste. A speaker who relates an experience such as walking up three flights of spiral steps only to be met on the third flight by scores of cardboard boxes of various sizes bouncing and tumbling down toward him, without making a single gesture or changing his eye glances, fails to suit action to meaning. By the same token, a speaker who shouts and beats his fist into his hand while discussing such a trivial topic as what kind of chewing gum is best, similarly fails to suit the action to the thought.

Gestures should be suitable to the speaker, purpose, and occasion. Some people tend to be motor types, others sensory types. Theodore Roosevelt was clearly the former, Woodrow Wilson the latter. Naturally, a motor type should use more bodily action than a sensory type. It is more becoming to him. In general, men should use more action than women, especially gestures of the broad, sweeping type, and young speakers should use more than mature.

The amount and type of bodily action should suit the speaker's purpose, audience, and occasion. Obviously the kind of action a speaker might use for a pep talk at a football rally in the college field house on Friday night before the big game would not resemble what the rector would use in church on Sunday. A speaker telling stories to grade school children will probably exaggerate the action; the college dean, making a report on some academic topic before his faculty, will minimize it. The size of the room and the size of the audience will also govern the speaker's action in kind and degree. A speaker gesturing vehemently in a small office room before an audience of six or eight people would probably seem ridiculous. On the other hand, a speaker in a large auditorium before several thousand people needs to use broad, sweeping gestures and bodily movements.

Gestures should be properly timed. The key to effective action lies in its timing. Like the drum beat in the orchestra, proper timing gives emphasis without making the listener aware of it. The climax of the emphatic gesture especially should synchronize with the vocal punch given a word or phrase. The peak or climax of the gesture puts fire and force into the thought. In this sense a gesture resembles the stroke of the tennis player. The moment and point of the racket's impact on the ball is all-important; it is everything. The same is true of the impact of the emphatic gesture at a climactic moment in the speech.

Gestures should show balance and variety. The effective speaker will use variety in his bodily action. He will move about on the platform, gesture with either or both hands, mix up gestures of the clenched fist, open palm, and index finger, and vary his head movements, facial expressions, and eye glances. Repetition of the same type of gesture again and again becomes monotonous. Distracting attention by its very monotony, it eventually tempts members of the audience to mimic the speaker as he continues his habitual single gesture.

Gestures should be definite and complete. Definiteness of action helps to make thought more specific. Effective gestures will point, separate, stress, clarify, or emphasize some particular idea or feeling. They should be so sharp and clean-cut that there can be no doubt in the listener's mind as to the meaning of the ideas presented or the speaker's attitude toward them. Halfhearted, uncertain, droopy, incomplete gestures are not only damaging to the speaker's prestige, but their utter lack of force will spoil the total effect of his ideas by suggesting timidity. Characteristic features of the definite and complete gesture are: (1) vigor, (2) good timing, and (3) proper stroke. The timing of the weak gesture is offbeat, and the final punch in the stroke, if there is one, does not synchronize with the key word or phrase. The stroke of the gesture lacks snap or punch, for the movement is not carried through to a clean-cut finish.

Gestures should be made with the whole body. We have stressed many times that it should be the whole man who talks. This applies with special point to bodily action and gesture. The contender in the 100-yard dash runs with his arms, back, and head as well as with his legs. He uses the whole body, and so do the baseball pitcher, the tennis player, the golfer. The speaker similarly talks and gestures in one operation; only a puppet gestures in pieces. The index finger gesture, or any movement you make, is best when coordinated with your entire body, including even your toes. Gestures should be unified with your total physical self.

POSTURE AND PLATFORM APPEARANCE

Your platform bearing is an important and inescapable part of your speech delivery. Before you utter a word, the audience already is sizing you up. Right or wrong, it forms opinions about you by the way you look, the way you walk to the platform, the way you are dressed, and the way you stand. Unconsciously, listeners score points for or against the speaker on the basis of his appearance and posture.

Posture is a subtle factor; yet it plays an important role in creating the initial image of the speaker—an image which tends to linger in the minds of the listeners. The speaker's physical bearing, which includes the way he stands and moves about on the platform, not only affects the attitudes of the listener toward him but influences his attitudes toward himself, his purpose, and his ideas. Every speaker communicates best when his posture and mental faculties are fully cooperative. The speaker who stands or moves about with arms folded or hands locked behind his back for long periods of time is physically holding back part of his personality. The speaker who habitually stands either rigid and tense or in a deep slouch does not talk with his whole body; thus his mind cannot function with complete freedom. Even the quality and vigor of his voice will be adversely affected by a sagging, drooping posture.

Characteristics of Good Posture

Both conscious and voluntary bodily action are necessary to develop good habits of posture. First, you must think about your carriage; you have to put your mind on it. Most of us straighten up and spruce up when we go out to dinner, go to church, when company comes, or when we pay a social call. We pay attention, not only to our conversation, but to the way we walk about, and the way we stand and sit. Why not do the same before an audience, when we have a group of listeners as our guests?

Unfortunately, the very word *posture* suggests some kind of an uncomfortable pose. Mention the word and the average person thinks he has to snap to attention and stand like a ramrod with chest out and chin in. This may be all right for a West Point cadet, but it is not good for walking, dancing, eating a meal, or playing a game. Janet Lane, in her book, *Your Carriage, Madam!*, says: "Really good posture, everyday, useful posture, means being lined up for grace and action, your body carried in perfect balance, your bones lying smoothly in place, and all your muscles working on the right tracks. It means Katharine Cornell leaning back in a chair, or Greer Garson floating down a stairway. . . . It's a diver in the air, an aquaplaner keeping his footing, a tennis player running to the net for a kill, or an old lady who knows how to sit at ease when her work is done—look at Whistler's portrait of his mother."[1]

Plato, commenting about the role of posture, says, "The beautiful motion is that which produces the desired result with the least effort." Whether you are an athlete trying to improve your form, a concert artist trying to develop poise, or a speaker concerned about communicating ideas with an audience, the key function of posture is to help you look your best and do your best with the greatest ease.

Usually the speaker makes his speech standing. This means standing up erect and tall—not slouching over a table or leaning on the back of a chair or the lectern. It does not mean to stand rigid and immobile, although the upright position must be kept in mind. Some speech teachers think it helpful to say, "Pull yourself up to your full height and stand tall, think tall, walk tall, talk tall, and remain tall throughout your speech." This "attitude of tallness" guards against a droopy, slouchy appearance; but of course we ought not to overstrain muscles just to create the illusion of tallness.

[1] Janet Lane, *Your Carriage, Madam!*, 2nd ed., John Wiley, 1947, pp. 6–7.

You should be able to feel the main weight of your body as it falls naturally and easily through the center of your ankle bones. This position should give you the feeling of standing firmly, comfortably, and in good balance. Your knees should not be stiff, with legs perfectly straight, but should be slightly flexed, as your elbows are when the arms swing naturally at your side. Neither throw out your chest nor let it cave in, but keep the center of your chest lifted to suggest alertness and aliveness.

Posture approaches its best level of effectiveness when it has the following characteristics:

1. *Alertness.* We have all seen the basketball player move about on the floor, poised and ready for action, relaxed yet mentally on his toes, ready to spring into action with lightning speed. He is awake and ready for whatever may happen. The speaker should develop a similar attribute in his posture.

2. *Poise and balance.* The speaker's apparent ease helps put the listeners at ease and gives them a comfortable feeling. Poise and balance are attributes which give grace to the speaking performance.

3. *Purposefulness.* The speaker who is businesslike and who creates the impression of having a definite purpose will be respected by the audience. He makes his listeners feel that he will not fritter away their time or give way to a lot of nonsense and foolishness. He has the traits of a leader.

4. *Friendly dignity.* The ideas of friendliness and dignity are here combined. Not only should the speaker reflect warmth and cordiality, but he should register a dignity which enlists the respect of the audience.

Awkward Posture

Underlying the principles of good posture are the law of gravity and the physical phenomenon of muscular fatigue. Muscles, sinews, bones, and sense of balance must cope with the force of gravity. Keeping in mind the essential characteristics of good posture, the speaker must first of all distribute the weight of his body on the balls and heels of his feet for general ease and comfort.

Awkwardness of posture is usually a matter of degree. Some speakers have better muscular co-ordination than others, and some have an advantage in figure and general bodily build. Men are usually more guilty of awkward posture than women. Yet because we expect better posture from women than we do from men, when they fail to demonstrate it an audience is slow to forgive them.

There are four common types of awkward posture, all of which should be avoided. The first type may be identified as the *tired farm horse*. Here one hip is thrown out of line from one side to the other, and the speaker shifts his full weight at regular intervals from one foot to the other—much in the manner of a tired farm horse standing drowsily in the hot summer sun. This gives him a slouchy, droopy, unbecoming appearance, one that is much more common among men than among women.

The second awkward type might be called the *wooden soldier*. In this posture the heels are clicked together, toes are parallel and straight forward, knees stiff, chest thrown out, and the whole body tense like a rookie soldier at attention. The speaker with this type of posture appears rigid, formal, and aloof. This position is quite likely to cause him discomfort, and as he seeks relief from the tension he often starts to teeter up and down on his toes.

The third awkward posture reminds us of a tripod with one leg missing; it is often called the *Colossus of Rhodes*. Here the feet are planted wide apart and the chin is thrust forward; the arms may be folded across the chest or the hands locked behind the speaker's back for long periods of time. This stance is not only undignified and unbecoming to a speaker but it also is so uncomfortable that soon he may seek to relieve his overstrained muscles by swaying back and forth from one side to the other in a kind of rocking chair motion.

The fourth awkward posture is that of the *podium leaner,* occurring only when the speaker has something on which to lean. Here the speaker who has an aversion to standing erect seeks something on which to rest part of his weight. He may place the palms of his hands flat on a table, a lectern, the back of a chair, or anything he can find, and lean on them. If the lectern is high enough, he may rest one elbow on it and lean on that. This posture suggests laziness and lack of poise. It is utterly lacking in dignity.

EXPRESSIVE AGENTS

Hands

Your hands represent one of the most expressive aspects of gesture and bodily action, superbly convenient and useful for description and emphasis. Imagine, if you can, how handicapped you would be if you tried to speak with hands and arms tied or paralyzed. Yet although your hands are a most expressive medium, they are also a source of worry and concern, particularly for beginning speakers. The speaker bothered by self-consciousness seems to have his tensions come to a focal point in his hands. As a result he uses meaningless gestures and fidgets about nervously, locks his hands behind his back, rubs his chin, rubs his hands together as though giving them a dry wash, and fumbles with his notes. Women usually control their hands better than men, but they twirl their beads and adjust their hair. "I don't know what to do with my hands," is commonly heard from beginning speech students, and teachers commonly reply, "Forget them." But this advice hardly gets at the root of the problem. The key is not in forgetting your hands but in forgetting yourself by concentrating on what you are saying and sensing your responsibility to communicate with your audience. If you care enough about your subject and about getting it across to your listeners, your hands will take care of themselves—you will use them to help express your ideas.

Since it is in our nature to doodle or handle things, it is often helpful to use the blackboard, charts, objects, notes, books, or other items which have some connection with the subject. The use of visual aids or demonstration devices in which hands are necessary for developing or making the thought clear is sound practice, provided that the visual aids used are appropriate for your purpose and your subject.

Head

A certain degree of action and specific gesturing is naturally associated with the head. Head gestures are usually not so marked or distinctive as those of the hands and arms, but, be it ever so slight, head action should supplement and reinforce other gestures. Nodding the head, for instance, for approval and shaking it for disapproval is natural and effective and can be co-ordinated with other gestures which convey this meaning. However, meaningless head gestures should be avoided. Some speakers have an annoying habit of bobbing the head monotonously every time they want to stress a word or an idea.

Face and Eyes

Facial expressions are important in the communication process, for they reflect not only the speaker's thoughts, emotions, and attitudes but many other attributes of his character and personality. The collective mind of the audience may say of the speaker, "He has an honest face," "—a friendly disposition," "—an intelligent look," "he is an old sour puss," and so on. The poker face, which is almost expressionless, and the face of the speaker who exaggerates his expressions and "hams" the speech act are extremes which should be avoided; the importance of doing so is convincingly demonstrated in moving pictures and television.

The eyes are the focal point of expression in the face, the windows through which we discern the person inside. Imagine how difficult it would be for a speaker wearing dark glasses to make contact with his listeners. It is with the eye that the speaker pierces the minds of his listeners. *Therefore the speaker should look directly and constantly at his audience.* The downcast glance at the floor, the vague gaze over and above the audience and at the ceiling, and the mechanical sweeping of the eyes from one side of the audience to the other like a water sprinkler are habits which distract and annoy the listener. Avoid such eye behavior. Instead, talk directly to the members of your audience. Meet the eyes of as many individuals as the situation permits. Some speakers find it helpful to pick out the friendly, sympathetic faces in the audience and talk primarily to them. Others find the indifferent, disinterested listeners a special challenge and make a point of trying to wake them up and win them over.

Some of history's greatest speakers have been known for their unusual eye appeal. For example, Lord Chatham is said to have influenced many with his strong expressive eyes; in debate he sometimes was able to stare down an opponent. Most effective speakers reveal a strong personality through expressive eye contact.

PROJECTS AND EXERCISES

For speaking projects see Part Three.

1. Attend a campus speech and make a list of the speaker's most effective bodily actions. Make another list of any distracting mannerisms he may have.
2. Make a list of ten topics particularly suited for a demonstration speech and write a brief statement explaining why you think each choice is a good one. Read the assignment, Part Three, page 351, before you start this project.
3. Have a contest in which four or five members of the class get on the rostrum and all repeat the alphabet for one minute with gestures and action. Let the class vote on whose visual communication ranked first.

TOPICS FOR DISCUSSION

1. Describe the most common defects of gestures.
2. How can bodily action make the speaker's meaning more expressive?
3. Why is good eye contact important?
4. What is meant by the speaker's movements and what are their value?
5. Can gestures be learned or does one have to wait for them to come naturally?
6. A speaker's mannerisms may be a help or a hindrance to effective communication. Explain the conditions under which they are helpful and harmful.
7. Which is more objectionable—too little or too much bodily action? Why?
8. Discuss the theory underlying the expression: "Free the body, free the mind."

ADDITIONAL READINGS

Brigance, William Norwood, *Speech, Its Techniques and Disciplines in a Free Society,* 2nd ed., Appleton-Century-Crofts, 1961, chap. 16.

Bryant, Donald, and Wallace, Karl, *Fundamentals of Public Speaking,* rev. ed., Appleton-Century-Crofts, 1953, pp. 244–248.

Gray, Giles W., and Braden, Waldo, *Public Speaking,* Harper, 1951, chap. 22.

Lane, Janet, *Your Carriage, Madam!,* 2nd ed., Wiley, 1947.

Oliver, Robert T., and Cortright, Rupert L., *New Training for Effective Speech,* rev. ed., Dryden, 1951, chap. 12.

McBurney, James H., and Wrage, Ernest J., *Guide to Good Speech,* Prentice-Hall, 1955, chap. 10.

Monroe, Alan H., *Principles and Types of Speech,* 4th ed., Scott, Foresman, 1955, chap. 3.

Sarett, Lew, Foster, William Trufant, and Sarett, Alma Johnson, *Basic Principles of Speech,* 3rd ed., Houghton Mifflin, 1958, chap. 10.

White, Eugene E., and Henderlider, Clair, *Practical Public Speaking,* Macmillan, 1954, chap. 10.

Woolbert, Charles Henry, and Smith, Joseph F., *Fundamentals of Speech,* 3rd ed., Harper, 1934, chaps, 6 and 7.

❧ 14 ❧
Vocal Communication

Speeches are essentially designed to be heard. Although we may read and study them later, the voice is the chief medium by which speeches are delivered. Bodily action and gesture reinforce and amplify the meaning conveyed by vocal expression; the voice, however, can transmit thought and emotion by itself—as demonstrated by radio, telephone, and voice recordings. Even before the advent of these modern inventions, communicative speech was conceived of as being carried on by voice only. In Exodus, for example, chapter after chapter begins with "and the Lord spoke to Moses," yet Moses never sees the face of the Lord. The sound of a voice culminated in the conversion of the apostle Paul to Christianity; the ancient Greeks sought guidance from oracular voices which issued from caves; and the story of Joan of Arc is the story of voices she heard. Although these instances have the aura of the supernatural, they suggest that in human experience the voice has a firm and personal hold as a communication agent.

THE VOICE—ITS THREE MAJOR ROLES

In all forms of oral communication—conversation, reading aloud, acting, public speaking—the voice plays one or more of three major roles.

Role One: An Aid to Meaning

The voice provides the speaker with remarkable leverage for making his ideas more effective. Its potential is limitless for emphasizing, coloring, and shading speech substance. The speaker can avail himself of all the vocal mechanics: inflection, vocal force, speed of utterance, pauses, patterns of rhythm, variation in pitch, in duration of tone, and in articulation and pronunciation. With the aid of these devices he can express thought, imagery of all kinds, emotions, subtle feelings, attitudes, and his whole personality.

A speaker can create many shades of meaning and emotion by the way he expresses a single word. For instance, the word *yes* may be voiced to convey doubt, surprise, anger, disappointment, uncertainty, certainty, and so on. The central thought of a sentence may turn on the manner of emphasis of a particular word. For instance, five different meanings of the following sentence are suggested by shifting emphasis to a different word:

I hope you will go. (I personally feel that way about it.)
I *hope* you will go. (I am encouraged to believe.)
I hope *you* will go. (No one else is concerned here.)
I hope you *will* go. (Let there be no doubt about this action.)
I hope you will *go*. (No question of staying or writing or other action.)

Sometimes the tone of the voice can be so strong and convincing that it contradicts the meaning of words to which the listener is accustomed. Have you ever heard someone say, "Good morning, I am glad to see you," when it sounded more like, "You scoundrel, I'm sorry we met"? Vocal tone may carry meaning opposite to what the words say. This often happens in sales work and interpersonal relations when the tone in the salesman's or customer's voice betrays the meaning of the words and causes communication failure.

Role Two: Creates the Speaker's Image

Much has been said and written about the voice as a medium for expressing the personality of the speaker. Since this point has already been discussed in Chapter 2, only brief mention of it needs to be made here.

When you listen to a person over the telephone, the radio, or on a voice recorder, your only basis for judging his delivery is his voice and how he uses it. The American Telephone Company, realizing the importance of voice as a factor in human relations, trains its switch-board operators to develop "a voice with a smile." Over the radio or telephone your voice is *you*. The listener who cannot see you wants to sense the sparkle, the warmth, the cheerfulness, and sincerity in your voice. A dead, dull, bored tone of voice does not give the listener a very attractive image. Such traits as conceit, arrogance, bitterness, and petulance, when reflected in the voice, can be a serious barrier to communication.

The personal popularity of many radio commentators, speakers, and actors is in large measure determined by a magnetic, colorful, and well-modulated voice which reflects pleasing, interesting, and desir-able traits of personality and character. These basic attributes of suc-cessful vocal expression are inescapable, no matter how subtle they may be when the speaker meets his audience face to face.

The image of the speaker as created by the voice remains a mysteri-ous phenomenon. Socrates was said to have been perhaps the home-liest man in all Greece, an ugly man living among people who prized physical beauty. One of his students said he looked like a satyr; but it was also said of him, that when he spoke the words seemed divine, and that when anyone else said the same words, they were flat and dull.

Role Three: Provides a Psychological Agent

Dr. John Watson, an eminent psychologist, tells us that we start out in this world with only two basic fears—the fear of falling (sensing the loss of bodily support) and the fear of loud noises. This second source of fear reaction, primitive in our nature, reaches us through our ears. Thus we never seem to fail to be startled by a clap of thunder.

Sounds may cause emotional reactions of various degrees of in-tensity. People who have heard the cry of a fox or a mountain lion or the scream of a horse when a barn was burning are often unable to erase such an experience from their memories. Music, probably the most purely emotional of all the arts, is usually regarded as a source of pleasant experience; its power to soothe and to stimulate is almost as old as man. The Biblical David, for instance, acted as a musical therapist, relieving the melancholia of King Saul by playing his harp.

The voice is the speaker's primary tool for emotionalizing or dramatizing his ideas and giving sparkle and color to his delivery. As a psychological tool the voice is particularly important in sermons, speeches of inspiration, commemoration, and those to activate the audience. Since people tend to base their actions more upon emotion than reason, the role of the voice in delivery is particularly significant.

BASIC STANDARDS FOR VOCAL DELIVERY

The prime function of the voice in delivery is to help the speaker communicate effectively. This central function depends upon the speaker's ability to meet three required standards: the speaker must be *heard*, he must be *understood*, and he must be *pleasing*. These three standards, while representing distinctive objectives, tend to complement each other in some degree. The speaker who is easily heard helps himself also to be understood, and vice versa. The speaker with a well-modulated, pleasing, and melodious voice will also find that this helps him to be heard and understood.

The speaker must be heard. A speech teacher once remarked to a student, "If you can't be heard, you might as well stay home." Obviously, there is merit in this comment, for there can be no communication if the audience cannot hear the speaker, and without undue strain or effort. If the listener must squirm about, turn his head, or cup his hand behind his ear, then the speaker fails to reach him. Nothing is more distressing to the listener than to have to work hard to catch a few words and phrases which now and then come in a thin, weak murmur from the platform. To be heard requires adequate and sustained vocal loudness, vocal energy, and proper tone placement.

The speaker must be understood. To be understood requires clear and distinct utterance of all words and syllables in a scheme of articulation and pronunciation representing standards to which the audience is accustomed. Diction should be precise, accurate, and clean-cut. Words should fall from the speaker's lips like newly minted coins—bright, clear, and distinct. Language should be instantly intelligible without the listener's being conscious of it as language. The speaker must not mutilate his words by omitting or adding sounds or syllables. Careless, slipshod, indistinct mumbling not only annoys and disturbs the listener but gives the impression that the speaker is fuzzy and careless about his thinking. Being understood, like being heard, is crucial. The speaker who cannot be understood is merely using up the listener's time.

The speaker must be pleasing. Just to be heard and understood is not enough. The speaker must go beyond the mere mechanics of projecting his voice to be heard and articulating words and syllables to be understood. Since it is important that his vocalization not be dull or unpleasant, he must learn to modulate his tones and control the intricacies of inflection, tempo, volume, and rhythm to make listening easy and enjoyable.

Obviously, his vocal expression will be more pleasant and enjoyable if he can keep his ideas moving along fluently and at a comfortable pace. A jerky, hesitant delivery, cluttered up with random meaningless "uhs" and "ers," can be unpleasant and annoying. But this is not to say that he must be glib or race toward his goal. The point is that there should be thought progression without creating the impression either of glib superficiality or of tense, laborious effort.

A besetting sin of many speakers is vocal monotony. Speech which lacks variety of pitch, rate, force, or melody is monotonous. Nothing is as boring as a one-note, one-rate, one-force, or one-tune speaker; listeners like vocal variety and color. A voice that is rigid, stiff, and unresponsive to changes of mood and meaning is distressing to the ears of any audience; a flexible voice is restful and pleasing. Make listening easy and enjoyable and you will make communication more effective.

√ THE VOICE MECHANISM AND HOW IT WORKS

No separate bodily apparatus can be singled out and exclusively identified as the speech mechanism. Speech uses organs and parts of the body that serve other and more basic biological needs, and in that sense it is an "overlaid" function. This concept of the dual functions of parts of the body to serve both biological and communication needs is well stated by Virgil Anderson in his book, *Training the Speaking Voice:*

Strictly speaking, there are no speech organs as such in the human animal. The larynx, for example, of first importance in speech, was originally developed as a valve to prevent foreign matter from entering the trachea. The lungs, which furnish the motive power for voice production, have as their primary purpose the ventilation of the blood by supplying it with oxygen and carrying off waste products arising from the process of metabolism. The primary functions of the mouth are concerned with the intake and mastication of food. Speech, therefore, is an activity "invented" and developed by man for the purpose of better adjusting himself to his social and physical environments. It is no more a natural activity for him than is dancing or singing, probably not as much. The principal difference is that speech has come to have a much deeper social significance and psychological involvement.[1]

In other words, we have within the framework of the human body a complex of organs designed to serve biological functions, but which also co-ordinate as a mechanism to produce speech. This mechanism for producing sound has much in common with most musical instruments, in that there are in all of them three main phases of tone production: (1) the energy or motor phase, (2) the vibration phase, and (3) the amplifying or resonating phase. The human instrument, however, goes one step further; it modifies or refines the tones produced to give us articulate speech. These four phases are often called *breathing, phonation, resonation,* and *articulation.*

Breathing

The production of tone in both human speech and musical instruments requires a source of energy. For the violin it is the bow drawn by the player over the strings; for the saxophone, clarinet, and reed instruments, the energy is supplied by the breath of the player; in the pipe organ the bellows are filled by an electric motor or a hand wind pump. In the voice, energy is provided by the breath, controlled by the diaphragm and the intercostal muscles. The mechanism for breathing which supplies this motor consists of the lungs, the bronchial tubes, the trachea, the ribs and other bones, cartilages, and tissues, along with the intercostal muscles, which contract and expand the air space occupied by the lungs.

Apparently there is little correlation between the capacity of the lungs and the actual support of tone. Tone support depends upon breath control and the extent to which breath is kept either deep or shallow. Deep breathing is activated by the abdominal muscles, shallow breathing by the upper chest muscles. If you lie in bed with a high fever, you will probably breathe very rapidly, but your breathing will be shallow and mostly from the chest, very little from the diaphragm. Opera singers, experienced public speakers, and actors learn to breathe deeply and keep the muscles about the midsection

---

[1] Virgil A. Anderson, *Training the Speaking Voice,* 2nd ed., Oxford University Press, 1961, p. 5.

firm and hard in order to produce strong and steady tones. However, this does not mean, except in cases where a singer holds a long note, that they consciously try to get more breath to speak more loudly. Gray and Wise point out that "not everyone requires more breath to speak loudly than to speak in a normal voice." They go on to say: "In fact, in a study of this subject, almost one-third of the 140 people studied used even less breath in speaking loudly than in speaking normally. Increase in loudness in such cases seems to be achieved by adjustments in resonance, resulting in a greater audibility of a tone without corresponding increase in volume of breath used."[2]

Phonation

Resin on a bow helps to vibrate violin strings. The reeds of the saxophone and clarinet are made to vibrate by the breath of the player, and the reeds of the pipe organ vibrate when a column of air passes over them from the bellows of the organ. In the human instrument, the vibrations take place in the larynx, which houses the vocal cords. The vocal cords or bands are membranes similar to lips and are controlled by some of the most sensitive and rapidly moving muscles of the entire body. Within the larynx the vocal cords are lengthened or contracted by the action of various cartilages and muscles. These initiate the original, raw speech tone. When the doctor looks down your throat and asks you to say "ah," your throat is in a strained position and your tone will not be very rich in quality, yet this tone is part of the basic texture of your voice. In normal speech the tone is refined and made more pleasant in quality by proper relaxation of the throat muscles, proper control of the vibrating mechanism, and proper placement of these tones in relation to the resonating chambers. When you yell yourself hoarse at a football game you put undue stress upon the muscles which control the vocal cords. This overstrain may even cause the formation of nodes on your vocal cords which give your voice a husky, raspy tone quality. Children who grow up in the slums in the midst of constant noise and tension, and who must frequently yell as a matter of survival, often have coarse, husky voices. In order to have round, full, clear tones, you must develop habits of speaking with relaxed throat muscles.

[2] Giles Wilkeson Gray and Claude Merton Wise, *The Bases of Speech*, 3rd ed., Harper & Brothers, 1959, p. 140.

Resonation

Raw tone is enlarged by various means. Sounding boards or resonating cavities are an important part of this phase of vocalization,
which is commonly called tone projection. The violin has a sounding
box; the clarinet and saxophone have tubes as sounding chambers;
the organ has pipes. These resonating chambers correspond to the
resonating cavities and sounding boards of the human body: the
trachea, the nasal cavities, cheek bones, palate, teeth, bony structure
of the head, sternum, ribs, and even the backbone. Not all the bony
parts serve as direct sounding boards—some merely help to conduct
the resonating tone; for instance, you have certainly noticed how a
bad head cold affects the quality of your voice. But all of these
resonating parts determine largely the richness and mellowness of
your voice.

Resonance, the key to the carrying power of your voice, can be of
three types. You can reproduce *cavity* resonance by blowing across
the mouth of empty bottles of different sizes, or by making a clacking
sound with your tongue while changing the size of the mouth cavity
by means of lips and cheeks. Cavities in the head and chest affect
the resonance of the voice; we speak of a voice having nasal, head, or
chest resonance. The second type of resonance is produced by *forced*
vibration. If you hold in your hand a tuning fork with its prongs
vibrating, the tone sounds relatively weak; but touch its base on the
top of a table and the whole surface seems to pulsate; the sound becomes much louder. In like manner, the bony structures of the body
help to intensify the sound of your voice. The piano, which is well
equipped for this kind of resonance, is also a good comparison.

The third type of resonance is that of *sympathetic vibration*. A
person with a strong voice singing by a piano when the soft pedal is
depressed may start certain strings vibrating which correspond to his
singing pitch. This type of resonance, however, is probably not
operative in the speaking voice.

Articulation

The fourth phase in the production of human speech, as stated
above, goes beyond energy, phonation, and resonance of tone. It
concerns the process of articulation and pronunciation and is often
called the *modification* or *refinement* phase. The principal organs

which make articulation possible are the tongue, lips, teeth, jaws, and palate. Chiefly by means of these organs sounds are modified into words and syllables. These parts of the speech mechanism also affect the quality, pitch and carrying power of the voice, but their most important function is to implement the mechanics of articulation and pronunciation.

THE VARIABLE ELEMENTS OF THE VOICE

Now that we have seen how the voice is produced and the tone modified into articulate speech, we are ready to consider the attributes of vocal sound and how variety may be attained from each. The characteristics or elements of the voice are pitch, force, quality, and time.

Pitch

Pitch is determined by the frequency of sound vibrations per second. The ear identifies a sound vibrating at a frequency of 256 cycles per second as middle C. Twice that number, or 512 cycles per second, is the C an octave higher. Pitch plays a most important role in the mechanistic aspects of making music enjoyable. Similarly it is the basic element in the voice by which a speaker can convey meaning and obtain variety and color.

KEY. Most of us normally speak with a certain average pitch level in a range of one to two octaves, the normal level varying from person to person. It is best for a speaker to stay within range of his normal pitch, but if his voice tends to be high he can favor the lower half of it. When angry or excited, it is especially important to control vocal pitch in order to avoid the impression of tension or strain.

STEPS AND INFLECTION. A *step* is an abrupt change of pitch, whereas an *inflection* or slide or glide is a gradual change of pitch level. Using them may be compared to going up or down from level to level by either an escalator or stairs. If you say "look up," the word *up* will probably be a step higher in pitch than the word *look*. An inflection or slide is, in contrast, an uninterrupted glide of the voice upward or downward on the scale. Try saying, "Oh, I don't know," in a credulous—and continuous—tone of voice which exag-

gerates the inflection. The pitch curve would probably resemble ⁓ .
All the sounds of syllables in this four-word expression are made
in a sweeping, continuous glide downward, around, and then upward—a curve which could be imitated by a sliding trombone. If
the words were expressed in separate steps, it would seem mechanical
and unnatural.

MELODY PATTERNS. Speech melody is the result of variations in
speaking rate, tone duration, force, and pitch, interwoven with
rhythm and cadence. In most instances, variations in pitch are, as in
music, a dominant factor in formulating melody patterns. As the
words and phrases are spoken, shades of meaning are expressed in a
continuous pattern of inflections and steps. If pitch changes, however, fall into fixed patterns, they can take on a singsong effect and,
when carried to extreme, become deadly monotonous.

Melody pattern can be a distinctive characteristic of human
speech. A particular melody is often associated with people of various professions: the minister, the politician, the prosecuting attorney,
the circus barker. National characteristics are reflected in the characteristic melody patterns of the Irish, the Swedes, the French, the
Chinese, and so on. Even children of the same family often develop
a peculiar speech melody by which others can recognize them. Actors,
when creating a character for a stage performance, are often as careful about developing a particular melody pattern as they are about
mastering a dialect required in their characterization.

Force

The term *force* may have many meanings when used in connection
with making a speech. When we say, "the speaker was forceful," or
"that was a forceful speech," we are probably referring to more than
one kind of force. Force may come from the nature and quality of a
thought—how it is developed with factual and logical supports; it
may come from words, sentences, or general rhetorical style; it may
come from the speaker's ethos and character; it may come from the
speaker's energetic delivery; or it may be a combination of two or more
of these factors. Our concern here is with vocal force and energy, its
mechanical aspects and its relation to communication and meaning.

Force is intensity or loudness of sound, essentially determined by
the amount of energy exerted by the stream of air over the vocal

cords. The intensity of the sound is affected by the amplitude of the object in vibration, as can be illustrated by plucking a string on a guitar. Pluck it lightly and the steel wire vibrates only slightly; the sound is weak. Pluck it violently and the string vibration is much wider, the amplitude greater, and the sound much louder. The same principle applies to the vocal cords: a stream of air passing over them expands their amplitude and increases the loudness of the voice. This loudness may be reinforced by resonance and accompanying overtones.

Vocal force is usually classified into three types: effusive, expulsive, and explosive. The effusive tone is drawn out as in a mother's cooing over her baby or as your probable tone in saying, "Oh, what a beautiful morning." The expulsive tone is most commonly heard in normal conversation; if you say to a friend, "Did you see Jim last night?" you will probably use this type of force. Explosive force is characterized by sudden sharp sounds such as those heard on military drill fields and on football fields when players count in cadence and bark their signals.

We have already said that the speaker must speak loudly enough to be easily heard. A firm, strong, vibrant voice usually indicates positive attitudes in the speaker and is often the hallmark of leadership, whereas a thin, weak, puny voice seldom inspires the listener in thought or action. Loudness in itself is not, however, a virtue and, when overdone, can become both tiring and obnoxious. Monotony in vocal force can be almost as distressing to a listener as monotony in pitch.

Vocal energy should be varied in the interest of pleasant listening. It should serve as a tool for emphasizing meaning and placing proper stress on syllables in the pronunciation of words. There are times when an explosive shout may be the best way to achieve impressive emphasis. On the other hand, a mere whisper appropriately applied may be equally or even more effective. It is not the degree of loudness but its variation that is important. Silence at the right moment may be the most impressive of all.

The way we use force in articulating words, phrases, and syllables is called *stress*. Stress is not a matter of vocal energy alone; it is reinforced by changes in rate and pitch and, to some degree, in quality. We give more stress to certain syllables than to others in pronouncing individual words and more to certain words than to others to convey a specific thought in a sentence. If you say, "I lost my pencil," and stress the word *pencil,* the image of a pencil stands out. Sometimes we give equal stress to words in a phrase or whole sentence. Suppose you and a friend are sitting quietly in your room studying and you hear an odd noise outside your window. You might turn to your friend and say, *"Did you hear that?"* All words are equally stressed. In this way you lift the entire thought into focus by stressing the sentence as a single thought unit.

Quality

There are many ways of defining the term *vocal quality.* In one sense, quality is a matter of the feelings of pleasantness or unpleasantness toward a sound. In another sense, quality is the peculiar character of one voice compared to another. We learn to identify and recognize people by the quality of their voices, no two of which are ever completely identical. This individualistic tone and texture of a voice is more quickly detected by the blind, who train themselves to recognize people primarily by their voices.

Quality is also explained on the basis of the *timbre* or *tone color* of the voice. In this sense, quality is that characteristic of sound which makes it different from a similar sound with the same degree of force, pitch, and duration. Tuning forks of the same pitch have identical sounds. They do not produce distinctive tone quality, since each prong of a fork is identically constructed to vibrate as a complete unit to produce a pure tone. Two violins, however, made by the same manufacturer, apparently of identical materials, and subject to identical processes in workmanship yet have distinctive tone quality. In each violin, sound waves are formed as complete units but are blended with segmental vibrations of higher frequencies to give overtones which produce its timbre or tone quality. The overtones are not heard as separate pitches but blend with the fundamental sound producing the quality of tone. It is the overtones which help create the peculiar quality of human voices.

Many adjectives are used to describe the attributes of quality in voices. We speak of a voice as clear, husky, harsh, nasal, guttural, falsetto, orotund, hard, soft, masculine, feminine, youthful, old, metallic, shrill, warm, weak, and so on. Although the voice quality of an adult person is largely conditioned by the fixed physical structure of the body, it may be modified and improved by the speaker's emotions, mental concentration, and by his use of specific voice exercises designed for tone support, controlled breathing, and throat relaxation.

Time

Every tone must have a beginning and an end. *Rate* refers to the speed at which words and syllables are uttered. A very slow speaker may speak only 90 words a minute, whereas a rapid speaker may exceed 200 words a minute. The average rate is from 120 to 150 words a minute. Rate should naturally vary according to the size of the audience, the nature of the thought and emotion conveyed, and the natural gait of the speaker. You should slow down the tempo for large audiences and for those parts of the speech which involve moods and thoughts of grandeur, reverence, and the like. You would not speak the lines of the Twenty-third Psalm in the same tempo as the sportscaster during intense moments of a basketball game.

Duration is a special factor in the speaker's rate which involves the prolongation or brevity of his vowel sounds. If someone speaks with a drawl, he is probably doing more than just speaking slowly; he is prolonging vowel sounds. In order to project clearly and accurately in a large auditorium, or outdoor speaking situation, a speaker usually increases the duration of sounds—the circus barker and the public address announcer at football games are good examples.

Some student speakers tend to speak far too rapidly for easy comprehension; their excessive speed of speech interferes with the accurate and precise activity of the articulatory organs. Others speak at a rate which is painfully slow. Your teacher and classmates can give valuable guidance on what would approximate a desirable rate for you. Unless your regular speaking pace is extremely slow or extremely rapid, it is usually best to seek out your most natural speaking gait and try to approximate it.

CHARACTERISTICS OF THE EFFECTIVE SPEAKING VOICE

Earlier in the chapter we pointed out that on a functional basis a speaker must be heard, be understood, and be pleasing. Let us now consider those qualifications in the speaking voice which more specifically meet the requirements of the listener. Analyze your vocal needs carefully. If you are deficient in any category, studiously practice the appropriate exercises of this section.

Adequate Force and Energy

We have already discussed why vocal force is important. A more important matter is how to develop it. The key to vocal energy is breath control and the proper use of the abdominal muscles, but never think that the working of the voice mechanism depends solely upon any one area of the body. Your motor may provide the driving force of your automobile, but it will not transport you if the steering gear is broken. Vocal force is similarly also influenced by the attitude of the speaker and is greatly aided by relaxed throat muscles, a properly opened mouth, and resonation. The voice functions best when all phases of the mechanism are co-ordinated to attain a specific purpose.

You should be able to develop an appreciation of breathing and breath control by watching a healthy sleeping baby. When he sleeps, when he wakes up, as he gurgles or laughs, or when he cries angrily, you will see the natural and perfect functioning of the diaphragm and abdominal muscles. The big voice from the little person gets its force, not from the lungs, but from the intercostal muscles that control the diaphragm. Have you ever laughed until your sides ached? If you have, your diaphragm and the abdominal muscles were overworked and the following day may have even felt sore.

EXERCISES

1. Count to 40 with firm, full tones, vocalizing only the odd numbers and substituting three sharp and vigorous hisses for the even numbers. Breathe as often as is comfortable. Normally, you should take a breath at 4, 8, 12, 16, and so on.
2. Observe your own breathing and the way your diaphragm works. On your bed without pillow or on the floor, lie flat on your back. Balance a heavy book on your waistline. Try bouncing the book up and down only by the stroke of your diaphragm as you hiss sharply and explosively. Also, watch the action of the book as you cough several times or as you give sharp military commands such as, "Company halt!" "Forward march!" "Number one fire!" "Number two fire!" and so on.
3. Be sure you use properly the diaphragm and the muscles around your lower ribs in supporting the tone. Pack the tone against your belt and let it float out fully and freely on the breath. As you hold this attitude, try a train-calling exercise. Imagine you are in a large railroad station where no loud-speaking device is available and you are calling trains.

Here is an example: "All aboard for Chicago, Toledo, and Buffalo! Train on Track 7 now ready! All aboard!" Use a round, full, effusive voice.

Purity of Tone

The voice should sound clear as a bell, free from harshness, huskiness, breathiness, or other distracting components of noise. Purity of tone depends primarily upon the combination of relaxed, open-throat phonation and adequate resonance—this is the basis for a clear musical quality. Singing the vowels is a standard exercise for developing purity of tone; it is believed that by holding the vowel sounds one can develop a fuller, richer tone and can thus improve the quality of the voice. In speech we try to carry over tone qualities of the sung vowel to the spoken vowel as we utter words. Developing a good singing voice usually helps to improve the speaking voice.

RELAXATION EXERCISES

1. The yawning position is a good starting point for relaxation of the throat. Open the mouth wide and yawn heartily several times. Try to carry over the open, relaxed tone of the yawn as you vocalize in normal pitch the sounds "wah-wah-wah-wah-wah, woe-woe-woe-woe-woe, woo-woo-woo-woo-woo," in an effusive chant.
2. If yawning is difficult, try to relax tensions in your neck, throat, tongue, lips, and face. Stand with your body relaxed and breathe normally. Roll your head around slowly a few times, allowing it to drop as limply as possible, as if you were imitating a Raggedy Ann doll.
3. Lie down on your bed or cot without a pillow, or on the floor. Yawn a few times and say, "unh huh, huh unh," (meaning yes and no) with your lips closed. Swoop the tone widely upward for yes and widely downward for no. Do the same for the vowels, a, e, i, o, u. Also try shifting quickly from the nasal tone ng to the open throat tone "ah," "oh," and "ooh."

Resonance provides the means by which vocal tone attains its carrying power; it does not add to the original sound but amplifies and enriches it. The three principal resonators are the pharynx, the mouth, and the nasal areas.

The mouth is the most important single resonator of the voice because its size and shape can be instantly changed by tongue, lower jaw, cheeks, and lips, and this modification produces the various

vowel sounds. We seem to be particularly conscious of nasal resonance, probably because we associate it with nasality. *Nasality* results from the lack of proper resonance and produces an unpleasant,
narrow, tinny and twangy sound, whereas *nasal resonance,* which
should be blended in judicious balance with throat and mouth resonance, helps to give a ringing sound to the voice. The consonants
m, n, and *ng* employ nasal resonance. An exaggerated nasality combined with nasal resonance often characterizes the voices of circus barkers, street vendors, and newsboys. They are usually noisy,
penetrating, and unpleasant but have great carrying power. Often
what we identify as nasality is actually denasality, meaning that the
speaker fails to achieve proper resonance on the nasal sounds. When
we have colds we frequently develop a denasal quality, even to the
point of being unable to produce the nasal sounds *m, n,* and *ng,*
which, denasalized, become *b, d,* and *g.*

RESONATING EXERCISES

1. Hum loudly with your lips closed. Notice the tingling sensation in the
   front of your face, on the tip of your tongue touching your teeth, and
   on your lips.
2. Repeat the vowels, *a, e, i, o, u,* in a chanting manner and imagine you
   are sending your tones through the keyhole of a door some 20 feet
   away.
3. Repeat in an even chanting manner, first rapidly, then slowly, words
   which have nasal consonants—*m, n, ng.* For instance, *one-one-one, me-
   me-me, ringing-ringing-ringing, nine-nine-nine, time-time-time,* and so
   forth.
4. Read aloud a line or two from literary prose or from a speech, and
   sandwich between the lines the *me-me-me* exercise. For instance, "Four
   score and seven years ago—*me-me-me-me-me*—our fathers brought
   forth upon this continent—*me-me-me*— . . ."

Clear and Distinct Diction

Precision of articulation and accurate pronunciation are basic in
the process of attaining clear, distinct utterance; here lies the key to
being understood. Many approaches may be made to developing clear
and distinct diction. The organs most vital and essential to clear diction are lips, tongue, jaw, teeth, and velum, all of which are employed in varying degrees when we speak distinctly. The special

exercises which follow give individual attention to (1) the tongue, (2) the lips, and (3) the jaw.

TONGUE EXERCISES

1. With the mouth relaxed, put your tongue out as far as it will go, then draw it back again. Do this 10 times. Now repeat slowly, *lāy, lēē, līe, lōw, lōō,* increasing your tempo until you are going as rapidly as possible. Try repeating successive sounds like "tah, nah, lah."
2. Fight both lazy lips and tongue by repeating the alphabet rapidly with teeth tightly clenched; exaggerate the action of lips and tongue, and, thus handicapped, speak as distinctly as possible.
3. Repeat rapidly the following sounds: *nā-nē-nī-nō-nū; dā-dē-dī-dō-du.* Use the same sequences beginning with the letters *t, b,* and *s.*
4. Count to 100 in units of 10. Count the first 10 with teeth clenched; from 10 to 20 open the mouth a little wider than you normally do and let the tones fly out. From 20 to 30 clench teeth again, switch back to open mouth from 30 to 40, and so on.
5. Examine carefully the plosive consonant *t.* It should be made without waste of breath; the slight sound it produces without air build-up resembles the sound when a cork is pulled suddenly from an empty bottle. Practice making the t sound rhythmically, using three light stresses, then a heavy stress.

t′	t′	t′	t″
tt′	tt′	tt′	tt″
ttt′	ttt′	ttt′	ttt″
tttt′	tttt′	tttt′	tttt″

LIP EXERCISES

1. For flexing and stretching the lips, speak clearly and in an exaggerated manner the letters *Q-X* at the rate of about thirty times per minute. Stretch your lips to the extreme limit each time. Notice how tired your lips become in less than thirty seconds.
2. Practice the words *who, me* fifteen or twenty times, stretching your lips until they feel tired.

JAW EXERCISES

1. Drop the jaw lazily and allow the mouth to fall open as if you were impersonating an idiot.
2. Speak in a regular marching cadence, using the word *hup, hup, hup.*
3. Pronounce the words *pouch, ouch, couch* by opening the mouth widely, repeating each word several times.

4. Practice speaking at a brisk cadence the word combinations *ring wasp—ring wasp—ring wasp* . . .

SPECIAL EXERCISES FOR DISTINCTNESS
(*Tongue, Lips, and Jaw Combined*)

1. Practice reading the following as distinctly as possible:

The perfectly purple bird unfurled his curled wings and whirled over the world.

Some folks say I lisp when I say "soup," "soft soap," or something similar; I perceive it myself.

Bill had a billboard. Bill also had a board bill. The board bill bored Bill so that Bill sold the billboard to pay the board bill. So after Bill sold his billboard to pay his board bill, the board bill no longer bored Bill.

Judge not that ye be not judged, for with what judgment ye judge ye shall be judged.

Pearl's purple parrot said, "Pucker your pretty lips and say 'prunes and prisms.' "

Leaping up the steep, slippery slopes of Pike's Peak is the pleasant pastime of mountain sheep.

Strolling leisurely along the cool lanes beside the lake, Paul flipped pebbles to ripple the water.

The noise of the zephyr as it whizzes past the zoo bothers the zebras grazing lazily nearby.

Mirage and camouflage usually are visual illusions which present confusion upon occasion.

Amidst the mists and coldest frosts,
With stoutest wrists and sternest boasts,
He thrusts his fists against the posts
And still insists he sees the ghosts.

2. The following exercise is more difficult than it sounds. Say these words accurately and distinctly, beginning slowly and accelerating your speed to over 200 words per minute: yellow leather, red leather—yellow leather, red leather—yellow leather, red leather . . .

3. An excellent exercise, because it offers so many difficulties to clear enunciation and right diction, is the following passage from Shakespeare's *Hamlet*. David Belasco once said that these five lines were the most difficult lines in English literature to enunciate. Practice them until you can read them as smoothly and easily as you can reel off your home address.

Thoughts black, hands apt, drugs fit, and time agreeing:
Confederate season, else no creature seeing;
Thou mixture rank, of midnight weeds collected,
With Hecate's ban thrice blasted, thrice inflected
On wholesome life usurp immediately.

4. Practice consonants rhythmically. Use three light stresses, then one heavy, as:

p′	p′	p′	p″
PP′	PP′	PP′	PP″
PPP′	PPP′	PPP′	PPP″
PPPP′	PPPP′	PPPP′	PPPP″

Do the same with: *b, t,* and *d, k* and *g, f* and *v, s* and *z, sh* and *zh, m, n, ng, l, r, th,* and *th, sh, w, h, hy, ch-tsh* or *k, j-dzh, x-ks,* or *gz, y.* Practice the following words, paying special attention to the consonants.

pipe, bat, back, fife, hiss, push, maim, lull, very, breath, babe, bad, bag, valve, buzz, azure, nun, ran, breathe, song, war, when, hat, church, judge, lax, yet, cock, wee, human, chorus, example

5. Practice the following many-syllabled words, paying special attention to precision of diction:

innumerable	incendiarism	unanimously
congratulatory	temporarily	necessarily
chronological	heterogeneous	inexplicable
absolutely	unanimity	extraordinarily

Flexibility and Vocal Variety

This requirement grows out of the listener's strong aversion to dull, monotonous speech on the one hand and the satisfactory rewards of a pleasing vocal delivery on the other. Everything else being equal, the speaker whose voice is dull and annoying will probably be more severely penalized by the listener than the one who cannot be heard or understood. In other words, most listeners are slower to forgive lack of vocal variety than lack of vocal energy or vocal distinctness.

Lack of vocal variety may result from monotony of force, pitch, tone duration, or quality, or from use of a set pattern of speech melody. The problem of monotony may be aggravated by poor mental attitudes, inadequate powers of concentration, feelings of inhibition, limitations in muscular coordination, and a generally unresponsive

voice mechanism. Not everyone has the needed muscular coordination or the physical aptitude to be a graceful dancer or an expert
golfer, nor is everyone endowed with a perfect vehicle for vocal expression; however, most people, with proper training and practice,
can develop adequate vocal flexibility and variety.

Physical potential often remains undiscovered or fails to be fully
utilized if the speaker is inhibited. We only have to watch children at
play to understand this point; a child usually cries "Ouch!" or "Give
me that!" with utter abandon, thereby demonstrating what natural
uninhibited vocal expression can be. The speaker must first banish
his repressions and work at reducing inner tensions which thwart the
natural functioning of his voice mechanism. One of the best ways he
can do so is to focus his mind on the meaning of what he is saying
and respond as a total person to the central purpose. In simpler terms,
the speaker must begin within himself. Then he may take steps
toward developing vocal variety by practicing exercises to enable him
deliberately to control rate, force, pitch, duration of tone, and vocal
quality. Such exercises are more or less mechanical in character but
helpful in developing types of variety, just as finger exercises are
helpful for mastering techniques of piano playing.

Exercises for Vocal Variety

1. Read the following sentences from five to ten different ways, each time
   changing the melody pattern composed of rate, pitch, and force. Be
   sure always to maintain the full sense contained in the language,
   making it as interesting and meaningful as possible.
   a. An old clock, that stood in the family kitchen for fifty years or more
      without giving its owner any cause for complaint, early one Sunday
      morning, before any of the family were stirring, suddenly stopped.
   b. I walked across the street and whom do you think I saw? I saw my
      old friend Charlie, all dressed up, wearing a top hat, carrying a cane,
      and smoking a big, black cigar.
   c. We started for the woods early one Sunday morning, when all of a
      sudden something black appeared near the path. Alice grabbed my
      arm excitedly and started to scream. She thought it was a bear, but
      it was only a big black stump.
   d. Oh, I don't know. I have heard people say that before, but I am sure
      it will be a long, long time before we live in a world of permanent
      peace.
2. Take the simple sentence "You need me." It has only three words, but

it can be expressed to suggest a dozen different meanings. Try to get as many shades of meaning from it as possible.

Repeat the following sentence five times, each time changing the thought by emphasizing a different word. Exaggerate your inflections as much as you can.

Yes, he is a guilty man.
Yes, *he* is a guilty man.
Yes, he *is* a guilty man.
Yes, he is a *guilty* man.
Yes, he is a guilty *man.*

3. Practice the following expressions, and exaggerate the inflections even to the point of absurdity.
   a. Oh, I don't know.
   b. Oh, yeah, that's what you think.
   c. Why, of course I'm going to the ball game.
4. Practice the following sentence with special emphasis on gaining variety in the duration of the vowel sounds:
   "Oh, I'm weary and lonely and I long to go home."
   First say it in a staccato manner, smothering the vowel sounds. Now say it allowing the vowels all possible freedom and fullness of expression. Notice the effusive tone in the words "weary," "lonely," and "long." Notice how much more pleasing to the ear is the second manner of expression.
5. Practice the three sounds ä, ō, and ōō separately. First try to get a smooth, even, drawn out tone, then practice each sound with a swell or crescendo, giving a light touch at the beginning and end of the tone and maximum volume in the middle, thus ä, ō, ōō.
6. Also try to get as much inflection and variety of pitch as you can by saying the following words and phrases: Oh, yeah, that's what you think; Oh, I don't know; Why, of course, I am going to the fair; Well; Yes; Oh.
7. Read the laundry list or a description of a course in your college catalogue and make it sound very dramatic and exciting. Exaggerate the variety of rate, pitch, force, and quality. Do the same with the alphabet.
8. Read aloud poetic selections which are written in a reverent or sublime mood, such as Kipling's "Recessional" or the Biblical Psalms. Work for rich, round, full tones.

Easy Fluency

Fluency in speech makes listening easy and enjoyable. The speaker should develop the ability to advance his ideas smoothly, like a person walking with an easy rhythm and a positive and confident stride. The hesitant, jerky speaker who clutters his speech with an assortment of grunts, pauses, and "er-r-rs" can be very tiresome. Pauses applied properly are effective for emphasis, but pauses which reflect the sputtering mind, or the mind that has stopped dead, break the progress of thought.

The goal of fluency is largely reached through two factors, language and thought. The hesitant speaker may search—and search too hard at times—for the correct word; this groping for the right word often interferes with the oral momentum of his meaning. Both knowing what one wants to say and having facility in the use of language are prerequisites to fluency. However, many speakers still find it difficult to attain fluency, no matter how familiar they are with the subject or how well they have language in hand. In such instances, the key to the problem often lies in thought rhythm and thought grouping. Beyond the grammatical punctuation of a passage of spoken prose is the subtle oral punctuation a speaker uses to express the thought in word groups which seem most natural. This phenomenon may be observed by listening to responsive readings in church or to the Lord's Prayer spoken in unison.

Effective vocal phrasing requires not only insight into the meaning within a specific phrase but a sense of timing and an awareness of how the minor thought phrases are related to the larger thought units of a paragraph or a major portion of the speech. Read the following sentence aloud and observe its simple phrasing: "He rose from his chair/walked to the window/looked across the street/ turned/put on his hat and coat/and departed." The following sentence is a little more difficult: "The beginning student of public speaking/will find that advice on how to make a speech/is plentiful/ and sometimes inconsistent/but he can be reasonably sure/that all reliable advisers/will urge him to listen to good speaking/to read many speeches carefully/and to practice making speeches/as often as possible." Grammatical punctuation is often helpful in making the meaning clear, but it is usually totally inadequate as a guide for vocal thought phrasing.

Exercises for Fluency

1. Read aloud five or ten minutes every day some well-written passage of prose or verse. Imagine you are reading to a radio audience and that

stumbling on words or phrases or any sharp breaks in your fluency will be criticized by your listeners. Don't expect to be flawless in attaining rhythm and fluency at first. Keep on practicing until you sense you are making real progress. At first read over your selections to yourself in an undertone to get the sense. Later, try sight reading (reading aloud from printed matter you have not seen before).

2. Two or three times a day for a period of three or four weeks practice making an impromptu speech about some familiar object. Look out of your bedroom window every morning and select the first object you see, call it by name, and talk about it for two minutes. Describe it, comment upon its size, shape, color, weight, uses, and so forth. Tell what you like and don't like about it and comment upon any experience you have had with it. Stay on the topic if you can, but don't worry if you wander off the subject. The point is to keep the talk flowing for two minutes.

Element of Human Warmth

Much has already been said about how the voice reveals the individuality and personality of the speaker. Much of the charm in the voice lies in its naturalness and its humanness, as reflected in quality, method of emphasis, peculiarities of rate, force, pitch, and melody. This charm is markedly influenced also by the speaker's style of language and general manner of delivery; yet its power is determined in large measure by intangibles. There is no doubt that listeners tend to be repelled by the voice which lacks human warmth and are drawn toward the speaker who clearly manifests it. To achieve it, the speaker should first of all dare to be himself and not pretend to be someone else. He should strive to avoid all artifices, such as theatricality, sanctimony, over-formality, ornateness, or too precise diction. He should try to be direct, genuine, natural, and unafraid of being human.

EXERCISES

1. Practice reading aloud short prose or poetic passages which express strong sentiments and have an inspirational meaning for you.
2. Make an inventory in sentence form covering the main points on the subject, "Things for Which I Am Grateful." Practice reading these aloud with a round, firm voice, and make a special effort toward sincerity.
3. Write a short essay, from 200 to 500 words, lauding some person who has greatly influenced your life. Read this aloud to yourself several

times and surrender inwardly to your true feelings and sentiments. Don't be afraid to overdo this in the privacy of your room.

ARTICULATION AND PRONUNCIATION

Articulation concerns utterance of speech sounds, either good or bad. When someone says, "What did you say? I didn't hear you," he often means he did not understand you: you were not sufficiently distinct. Speech is a flow of a variety of sounds, a moving process. Adjustments in vocal utterance must be made quickly and on the run, for a speaker may utter more than 300 variable syllables in a minute. Yet these syllables are formed of still other sounds, the vowels and consonants which are supplied by phonation and resonance. Articulation is the process of forming, joining, modifying, and separating these sounds into syllables, words, and phrases. The organs which modify and refine these sounds in articulate speech consist of lips, teeth, jaws, tongue, palate, velum or soft palate, and the vocal folds themselves.

Articulation is usually best when there is a proper balance between tone quality and distinct utterance of the consonants. In general, the vowels give tonal richness to speech, whereas the consonants give it clarity and distinctness. The goal is to speak with full, open vowel sounds and definite, precise consonant sounds.

Good voice and diction require diligent and careful use of the mechanics of articulation. Much indistinctness is the result of carelessness; we remain indistinct out of indifference. The first requirement for improvement in articulation is to begin to think about it.

Pronunciation involves sounds and accents given to words and syllables according to the standards prescribed by common usage. Articulation concerns distinct utterance, whereas pronunciation concerns acceptability of utterance. In one sense, pronunciation is to speaking what spelling is to writing; however, spelling is more widely standardized, not subject to regional differences, and does not fluctuate or change from time to time as much as pronunciation. But if some pronunciations customary in Boston are quite uncommon in Atlanta or Seattle, that does not mean a speaker should vary his pronunciation to conform with the practices of every region where he happens to speak. Instead, *it is best to follow as nearly as possible the usage of the educated people of your home community*. You should in general, strive to use pronunciation which will attract the least attention to itself.

IMPROVE YOUR PRONUNCIATION HABITS

Combine the functions of articulation with pronunciation. Articulation and pronunciation together produce the flow of spoken discourse. In pronunciation, sounds are produced, shaped, and modified into meaningful symbols; articulation concerns the distinctness and precision of utterance. Pronunciation brings out the meaning in words, whereas articulation produces, refines, and controls the sounds or noises and fits them into connected speech. The speech sounds themselves may be classified roughly as vowels or consonants. Vowels, according to Virgil Anderson, "are defined as sonorous speech sounds produced by relatively open and unobstructed throat and mouth passageways. . . . Consonants, as a class, are made up of less sonority and more noise elements than vowels—the result of a greater degree of obstruction imposed upon the outgoing tone, or, as in the case of the voiceless consonants, upon merely the unvocalized breath."[3] The vowels thus give carrying power to the voice; the consonants give it clarity and distinctness. Separately and together, articulation and pronunciation depend upon these vowel and consonant attributes and their control.

Develop a critical ear. Develop the habit of observing the pronunciation of others as well as your own to detect differences in the pronunciation of common words, especially where a slight variation distinguishes the acceptable from the unacceptable. For example, train your ear to detect the difference between the word *catch* when it rhymes with *patch* and its careless pronunciation which rhymes with *fetch*. Learn to hear the sounds you give to the vowels and observe the way you articulate such consonants as *b, d, t, l, wh, th,* and *r*.

Develop the dictionary habit. First become familiar with the key to the diacritical markings your dictionary uses. Since keys to the diacritical marks are not identical in all dictionaries, we recommend those used by the latest edition of *Webster's New World Dictionary of the American Language, the American College Dictionary,* or *Webster's Collegiate Dictionary* (Merriam-Webster). Learn how to use the marks as you do words in sight reading. Use the dictionary

[3] Anderson, *op. cit.,* p. 260.

regularly to reinforce your knowledge of preferred pronunciations. Remember that the role of the dictionary is limited. Since there is no single standard of pronunciation to which we can turn for absolute authority, the dictionary, as a general rule, simply offers the best single source for guidance. Dictionaries are not infallible and in many instances disagree among themselves; *correct pronunciation,* therefore, is an elastic term. Pronunciation is most nearly correct if it is used by large numbers of educated people. Dictionaries seek to *observe* and *record* the language usage of this group rather than to dictate what forms are correct. In its Preface *Webster's New World Dictionary of the American Language* states: "With pronunciation, as with all other aspects of lexicography, it cannot be repeated too often that dictionaries are not the lawmakers—they are merely the law-recorders. A pronunciation is not correct, or standard, because it is given in a dictionary; rather, it should be found in a dictionary because good usage has already made it standard."[4]

Study and practice the words in the following lists. When we mispronounce words, we commit one or more errors which may be classified into the following categories: (1) incorrect sounds—vowels or consonants—due to substitution, (2) incorrect accent, (3) adding a sound, (4) omitting a sound, (5) incorrect sound sequence.

On the following pages are found many examples of these mispronunciations. Become familiar with the types of errors identified with each pronunciation failure. Review first the examples given in each category; then try to pronounce the remaining list. Be sure to check your pronunciation with a standard dictionary.

INCORRECT SOUNDS DUE TO SUBSTITUTION

Examples of wrong vowel sound:

Word	Sounds Like	Not Like
again	pen	pin
aye (meaning "yes")	buy	bay
bade	mad	made
because	pause	buzz
been	pin	pen
bury	berry	furry
catch	latch	fetch

---
[4] *Webster's New World Dictionary of the American Language,* College ed., World, 1958, p. x.

Word	Sounds Like	Not Like
deaf	Jeff	reef
egg	beg	vague
err	fur	fair
fete	fate	feet
get	pet	sit
mien	mean	main
thresh	mesh	mash
wash	squash or bosh	worsh

How do you pronounce these?

apropos	figure	naïveté
Arab	forte	nape
because	fungi	pathos
blatant	gaseous	plait
bona fide	genuine	provoke
breeches	heinous	senile
chic	Italian	solace
clientele	italics	sycophant
deign	livelong	wrestle
de luxe	long-lived	worship
draught	mauve	zealot
era	naïve	zoology

Examples of wrong consonant sound:

Word	Acceptable Pronunciation	Unacceptable Pronunciation
chasm	kaz'm	chaz'm
corps	kor	korps
draught	draft	drawt
gesture	jes'cher	ges'cher (*hard g*)
orgy	or'ji	or'gi (*hard g*)
quay	key	kay or kway
schism	siz'm	skiz'm

How do you pronounce these?

accessory	exit	longevity
blackguard	façade	magi
chiropodist	gesticulate	nauseous
diphtheria	gimlet	pantomime
dishevel	height	posthumous
drought	hypnotize	xylophone

INCORRECT ACCENT

Word	Correct Accent	Wrong Accent
aggrandizement	ag-GRAN-dize-ment	ag-gran-DIZE-ment
cement	ce-MENT	CE-ment
clandestine	clan-DES-tine	CLAN-des-tine
combatant	COM-ba-tant	com-BAT-ant
demonstrative	de-MON-stra-tive	dem-on-STRA-tive
formidable	FOR-mid-a-ble	for-MID-a-ble
garage	ga-RAGE	GAR-age
genuine	GEN-u-win	gen-u-WINE
gondola	GON-do-la	gon-DOL-a
grimace	gri-MACE	GRIM-ace
irrefutable	ir-REF-u-ta-ble	ir-re-FUT-a-ble
irreparable	ir-REP-a-ra-ble	ir-re-PAR-a-ble

How do you pronounce these?

despicable	infamous	positively
dirigible	influence	preferable
ignominy	insurance	respite
impious	irrevocable	spontaneity
impotent	mischievous	theater
incongruous	orchestra	vehement

ADDING A SOUND

Word	Pronounced	Not
athlete	ath'lete	ath'a-lete
elm	elm	el'lum
grievous	grie'vous	grie'vi-ous
preventive	pre'vent'ive	pre-vent'a-tive
toward	tord	to'ward

How do you pronounce these?

alms	bomb	mischievous
almond	film	poignant
balm	height	salmon

OMITTING A SOUND

Word	Pronounced	Not
arctic	ark'tic	ar'tic
library	li'brary	li'ber-ry
sophomore	sof'o-more	sof'more

How do you pronounce these?

geography	golf	statistics
government	medieval	February

INCORRECT SOUND SEQUENCE

Word	Right	Wrong
cavalry	cav'al-ry	cal'va-ry
children	chil'dren	chil'dern
hundred	hun'dred	hun'derd
larynx	lar'ynx	lar'nyx
modern	mod'ern	mod'ren
perspire	per-spire'	pre-spire'
perspiration	per-spir-a'tion	pres-pir-a'tion
predicament	pre-dic'a-ment	per-dic'a-ment
presume	pre-sume'	per-sume'
relevant	rele'e-vant	rev'e'lant

IMPROVE YOUR VOICE THROUGH ORAL READING

One of the best and easiest ways to vocal development is through oral reading. Through reading we can polish our voice habits without the routine of pure exercise. While we are improving our voices we are also acquiring skill in reading aloud, which is useful in social gatherings, in church and in school. Parents, moreover, find that reading aloud delights their children.

Oral reading has advantages for vocal development as compared with extemporaneous speech. In oral reading, first, we read the thoughts of others and therefore need not worry about thinking our own thoughts. Thus the beginning student frequently experiences less stage fright when he is reading than he does when he is making a speech. Since he need not worry about forgetting, he can utilize this freedom from tension in concentrating upon vocal expression. Second, we can reread passages many times in oral reading. It is simple for the teacher to stop the reader and ask him to read a passage again with a different vocal inflection and perhaps a faster or slower rate. Such practice is as useful for maximum vocal development as it is for acquiring adequate reading skills.

On the other hand, in one way it may be more difficult to read from the printed page than to make a speech. In a speech we think our own thoughts as we present them, and this leads to naturalness of expression. In reading we must recreate the thoughts of others, and this often leads to artificial vocal patterns. Many people speak extemporaneously with ease and skill but when they read suddenly proceed at a very rapid, artificial rate with only slight vocal inflection and virtually no feeling or emotion. The reading of highly cultivated people is generally inferior to their conversation in expressiveness, liveliness, and genuineness.

We must read orally the way we speak, thinking the thought as we present it. A good reader will use all his effort to recreate the author's thought as he reads. Effective oral reading first of all requires, then, that we thoroughly understand the material we are going to read. To achieve proper understanding, careful study and analysis are necessary.

Logical Elements

Most writing has both a logical and an emotional meaning, and you need to understand both before you can adequately interpret your selection. Begin by determining the logical meaning. Follow these steps:

1. Read the selection completely through, silently and rapidly.

2. After this initial reading, try to recall the main ideas and determine the key thought of the selection, often called the theme. Theme has been defined as "the total comment made by the writer. It may or may not be a positive belief, but it is indicative of a set of values and a view of life."[5] Sometimes the author's theme emerges very plainly; occasionally, however, the interpreter has to search for it.

Grimes and Mattingly point to a set of clues which lead to the discovery of theme. First, the title may reveal it. Look for ways that the title connects with the work itself. Does it merely identify the subject? Is it an ironical statement of the theme? Or does it clearly point to the theme? Second, study the author's life and any statements made by him or about him. His education, position in life, environment and cultural and personal influences affect his point of view and his choice of theme. Third, key lines are clues to meanings:

When an author interrupts the action of a story to make comments applicable to all men, not just to the John or Jane of the story, when he moves

[5] Wilma H. Grimes and Alethea Smith Mattingly, *Interpretation*, Wadsworth, 1961, p. 38.

from the particular to the general, he is giving us a signal . . . In Sophocles' *Antigone,* at the close of the play, the leader of the chorus speaks these key lines: "There is no happiness where there is no wisdom;/ No wisdom but in submission to the gods./Big words are always punished,/ And proud men in old age learn to be wise." Here, a general statement points to theme and helps us to know what, within the play, to emphasize, what to subordinate.[6]

Sometimes a key line introduces the work, and the rest of the composition is essentially a development of this idea. Key lines are often repeated in the poem, thereby setting up a rhythm and an echo of the author's theme.

3. What is the author's over-all attitude, and does it change during the selection? A writer may be joking, sarcastic, ironical, or in dead earnest; he may be asking a question when he intends an assertion; he may understate or overstate his meaning for a desired effect. Therefore, we must do more than discover the literal meaning of a composition; we must also find out how the author means the writing to be taken. The author's attitude, furthermore, sometimes changes during the selection. If so, the reader should know this and reflect it in his interpretation.

4. Read the entire selection again, and this time analyze every word, word grouping, and sentence. Keep a dictionary handy and look up the meaning and pronunciation of all words of which you are not completely sure. If you think you know the meaning of a word but find that the author's use of it does not fully make sense, look it up; for the dictionary may give more than one meaning or several shades of meaning that will clarify the author's usage.

After you have analyzed individual words, try to determine how they relate to other words. The meaning of a sentence becomes clear only when we know which words are subordinate to other words and which should be emphasized—as was mentioned earlier under "The Voice Should Have Easy Fluency." Words in isolation do not give the real meaning of the author. Only as words are used together do they become meaningful. Word groupings are the units of thought. In fact, the last three sentences can be used to illustrate the concept of word groupings in sentences:

6 *Ibid.,* p. 40.

Words in isolation/ do not give the real meaning/ of the author./ Only as words are used together/ do they become meaningful./ Word groupings/ are the units of thought.

If the reader does not place the right words in a group, meaning can easily be distorted. Note the two different word groupings of this sentence:

Two players/ found themselves sliding into the same base.
Two players found themselves/ sliding into the same base.

In the first case the meaning is accurate; namely, two players, because of poor base-running, slid into the same base. In the second case, however, it is implied that the players made some mysterious discovery about themselves while sliding into the same base—obviously not the meaning intended by the author. Another good example is Christ's words spoken to the dying thief on the cross:

Verily I say unto thee/ today thou shalt be with me/ in paradise.
Verily I say unto thee today/ thou shalt be with me/ in paradise.

In the first grouping of this sentence, a time is given: the thief: he is to be with Christ in paradise that very day. In the second interpretation, *today* refers merely to when the statement is made.

Next, decide which words should be emphasized. Emphasis consists of making one word or group of words more pronounced than others in a sentence; thus the reader centers attention on words that reveal the author's meaning. Certainly, varying emphasis in a sentence produces varying meanings. "Yes, I WILL do that" has a different meaning from "Yes, I will do THAT." A portion of Lincoln's "Gettysburg Address" serves well for illustrating stress or emphasis:

Four score and seven years ago our fathers brought forth upon this continent, a NEW NATION, conceived in LIBERTY, and dedicated to the proposition that ALL men are created EQUAL.

Now we are engaged in a great CIVIL WAR, testing whether that nation or ANY nation so conceived and so dedicated, can LONG endure. We are met on a great BATTLE-FIELD of that war. We have come to DEDICATE a portion of that field, as a final resting place for those who here GAVE their LIVES that that nation might LIVE. It is altogether FITTING and PROPER that we should do this.

In sum, note carefully the word groupings of the selection you plan to read, find the thought center in each group, and note which words should receive emphasis within the sentence. Adequate logical interpretation in oral reading is the result of careful study and analysis.

Emotional Elements

Good literature is rich in emotional tone, which the good reader seeks to capture in his oral reading. It is as important to understand the emotional meaning of your selection as it is to understand its logical meaning. An analysis of emotional aspects is thus the second major step in preparation for reading.

First determine the underlying *mood* of the selection, by which is meant the total effect of an author's words and images: despair, nostalgia, fear, or a long list of other feelings. Read the selection carefully in order accurately to determine mood; often the theme will clearly imply the proper mood. It should be your aim to recreate as nearly as possible the author's mood and impressions.

Imagery is an important source of emotion and vivid expression. A number of different types of images can be built, but by far the most common are those of sight, sound, and smell. The following passage from Barrington's "The Unveiled Woman" contains unusually strong visual and olfactory images:

> Sitting in the pavilion, looking down into the moon-mirroring water, was a woman in the ancient dress of Persia, golden and jeweled. She flung up her head magnificently, and looked at them, the moon full in her eyes. The garden was peopled now, not only with roses, but with large white blossoms sending out fierce hot shafts of perfume. They struck Beatrice Veronica like something tangible and half dazed her as she stared at the startling beauty of the unveiled woman, revealed like a flaming jewel in the black and white glory of the night.[7]

Analyze your selection carefully for images and in your reading try to make them as vivid and expressive as possible. An occasional well-placed pause after especially graphic passages usually helps to create the intended image.

Figures of speech, which are basically imagistic, are another special source of emotion in writing. Since figurative speech has been discussed in some detail in Chapter 11, pages 268–269, suffice it to say

[7] *The Atlantic Monthly*, February, 1925, p. 223.

that a good reader must first of all understand the figures in his selection and then try to make them meaningful and expressive for the listeners.

Special Problems in Reading Poetry

Thus far our discussion of oral reading has had application to both prose and poetry. Poetry, however, has three special reading problems: (1) it is highly imaginative, (2) it is rhythmic and often metrical, (3) it frequently is in rhyme.

Imagination and its accompanying state of emotional intensity are important aspects of poetry. Edgar Allan Poe said that a poem should elevate the soul. To do so the poet generates emotion and imagination through imagery and various stylistic effects, such as alliteration and onomatopoeia. It is especially important in reading poetry that these elements be handled skillfully.

Rhythm and rhyme tend to be problems for the inexperienced reader. He tends to handle rhythm in a singsong, monotonous manner, emphasizing meter instead of meaning; rhyme he usually accentuates whether his interpretation makes sense or not. Certainly the reader should capitalize upon rhyme and rhythm to achieve the true beauty of a poem—poetry is not prose and should not be interpreted in a prosy rationality. A skillful reader will use meter and rhyme to advantage, not only to create a pleasant effect but especially to interpret meaning.

Monotony often is the result of improper phrasing and pausing. In reading verse, the beginning reader will often pause at the end of every line, regardless of whether the thought passage stops there or not. Punctuation sometimes serves as a guide here: if there is no punctuation at the end of a line, it is likely that a pause at that point would be out of place. A careful study of thought or word groupings will help the reader to determine proper phrasing and pausing. A poem should be read just so rhythmically that the rhythm does not call attention to itself but increases the meaning of the author's words. Thus the reader will find a happy medium between singsong and prose.

Oral Rehearsal

After you have made a proper analysis of your selection, rehearse your presentation often; an assignment to read from the printed page instead of making an extemporaneous speech does not mean that rehearsal is unimportant. Good reading is usually the result of diligent rehearsal.

First, plan your introduction to the reading so that you will not have to rely upon notes during its presentation; the introduction should be extemorized as though it were in a speech. Second, practice reading thought groups until you can read them easily and fluently. Place adequate stress upon the words to be emphasized in order to convey the right meaning. Third, practice varying your pitch, rate, and force in an expressive and interesting manner to make the author's meaning come to life. Most readers read too fast; therefore, pay special attention to the pacing of your reading. Fourth, practice with bodily action. Facial expression is extremely important in reading, and an occasional purposeful gesture will enhance and strengthen your presentation.

Delivery

The reader is not acting nor making a speech; he is trying to communicate the printed page, prose or poetry, to a group of listeners. It is important that at all times he observe good speech communication habits. This means, first of all, that he maintain a high degree of personal directness with his audience. A good reader does not keep his eyes glued to the pages of his manuscript; rather, he maintains eye contact with his listeners at least 50 percent of the time. The skillful interpreter also reads with feeling. The inexperienced student, who is often afraid to read with feeling for fear of overdoing it, as a result reads in a lifeless and unimaginative manner. The reader has the task of making the printed page come to life for the audience; no monotonous, inflexible, hurried style of delivery will do this.

Use a lectern for your reading only if it is high enough for you. If you are tall and the lectern is too low for you, hold your book or manuscript in your hands. Hold it high enough so you can read comfortably. Do not hold it tightly against your chest, for this impedes eye contact with your audience. If you use a lectern you may find it practical to stand back from it a step or two so that you need not look down your chest at the manuscript and can maintain maximum eye contact with your audience.

The voice is of primary importance in oral reading. Since reading requires the skillful use of all vocal qualities, as you improve your oral reading you will undoubtedly experience considerable vocal development and improvement.

SUMMARY

The problem of improving voice habits is infinitely complex. Two basic approaches are essential, one motivational and one mechanical, but the two must work together harmoniously. To develop a desirably constructive attitude, start by being concerned about the listener, his likes and his needs. A little role-playing is in order: trade places with the listener. For instance, if you cannot be heard and your teacher or classmates suggest that you speak louder, make the suggestion less mechanical and more motivational. Ask yourself instead, "Are you sure those in the back row can hear you easily and without effort?" and thus think about the listeners' needs and your responsibility toward them. The emphasis should be upon true communication, not upon mere loudness.

Most speakers are endowed with an adequate vocal mechanism but do not make full use of this equipment because they lack the necessary attitudes. Many poor or mediocre vocal performances in interpersonal relations and in speaking before groups spring from poor mental attitudes. We do not give enough thought to our voice; we take it too much for granted. If we could develop the habit of being one-tenth as concerned about how we sound in our daily personal relationships as we are about how we look, our voice and speech would be more pleasing to others and our oral expression much more effective. Yet we seem to care a lot about how we look but not about how we sound. These habits of thought, unfortunately, are carried over into the speech class. We therefore need to start by reconstructing our attitudes—developing a sense of awareness about our vocal appearance and deepening our sense of listeners' needs both in and out of the classroom.

An organic voice deficiency or a functional weakness which may be more or less independent of our attitudes can often be rewardingly approached by mechanical means. Better voice habits can almost always be developed by a sustained program of voice exercises; however, anyone with a clearly unusual voice defect or weakness should consult a specialist in speech therapy. The exercises outlined in this chapter are designed for those with normal voice mechanisms who need special self-training to improve their abilities in voice and articulation.

PROJECTS AND EXERCISES

For speaking projects see Part Three.

1. The words below are grouped in three divisions—A, B, and C—and in four separate columns. Words in each column sound very much alike. Practice articulating them distinctly with your back to the class or with your voice coming from behind a screen or from another room. Test the intelligibility of your speaking by reading four or five words from each column of one division while your classmates check the words they think you pronounce. Pronounce each word only once, and pause a few seconds after each group.

A

burn	care	tour	manner
earn	rare	poor	stammer
yearn	tare	pure	hammer
learn	blare	lure	banner
firm	hair	cure	fanner
term	mare	your	glamor
turn	ware	sure	clamor

B

hold	attacked	subsist	maintain
told	retract	desist	restrain
bold	exact	resist	obtain
ode	enact	enlist	abstain
scold	intact	insist	retain
rowed	impact	persist	regain
mowed	extract	mist	attain

C

mutter	stumble	bother	settle
subtle	rumple	bottle	medley
muddle	stubble	mottle	rental
puddle	fumble	waddle	medal
muzzle	bubble	throttle	metal
rudder	jumble	grotto	mental
puzzle	rumble	model	dental

2. Make a list of twenty common words which you have recently heard mispronounced, indicating both wrong and correct pronunciations.

3. The following words, as paired, are often confused because they have similar sounds but different meanings. Practice articulating these words with precision.

abominable	abdominal	exult	exalt
adapt	adopt	garnered	garnished
accept	except	hanged	hung
ascent	accent	immorality	immortality
assess	excess	incidents	instances
calvary	cavalry	morning	mourning
consolation	consultation	pitchers	pictures
congenital	congenial	respectively	respectfully
deposed	disposed	sense	cents
disillusion	dissolution	sex	sects
drug	drag	statue	statute
effect	affect	suburb	superb
exit	exist	wandered	wondered

4. Practice articulating accurately the following words, which have difficult sound combinations.

amphibious	statistics	despicable
catastrophe	inevitably	abominably
heterodox	articulatory	fortuitously
homogeneous	indisputably	justificatory
hyperacidity	sublunary	accessorily
hypodermic	confiscatory	congratulatory
perimeter	inexplicable	incontrovertible
synthesis	extraordinarily	disingenuousness
ambivalent	indissolubly	fratricidal
antecedent	authoritatively	elliptically
circumnavigate	apocalyptically	supererogatory
dehumanize	innumerably	indefensibly
multicolored	annihilation	lamentably
nonentity	lugubrious	intransigent
subterranean	deplorably	simultaneity
deleterious	interpolate	exhortatory
repugnant	indefatigable	substantively
heterogeneous	angularly	disinterestedly

VOICE ANALYSIS CHART

(Positive Factors)

This chart may be used to rate yourself or other members of the class. First try to rate yourself on each item in the privacy of your room; then collect unsigned rating charts on *your* voice from other members of the class. Compare results. Check score in the proper square in the columns on the right hand side of the chart according to the scale: excellent = 4, good = 3, fair = 2, poor = 1.

	Excellent 4	Good 3	Fair 2	Poor 1
1. Adequate vocal energy				
2. Fluency in vocal utterance				
3. Clear, distinct, and precise articulation				
4. Vocal flexibility and pleasing variety				
5. Voice vibrant with human warmth				
6. Purity of vocal tone				
7. Use of desirable level of pitch				
8. Use of desirable speaking rate				
9. Speech that is natural and unaffected				
10. General use of accepted pronunciation				
11. The practice of completing sentences in a speech with adequate vocal force				
12. Giving emphasis to the thought rather than words				
13. Habit of making what is said sound important				

VOICE ANALYSIS CHART

(Negative Factors)

This chart lists faults and weaknesses of voice in speech. Indicate in the proper square in the columns on the right the degree, if any, of the faults which apply to the person rated. Low score is best. Application of negative factors is made on the following scale: Definitely = 4, moderately = 3, slightly = 2, none = 1. Rate yourself first and compare your score with ratings given you by members of the class.

	Definitely 4	Moderately 3	Slightly 2	None 1
1. Difficulty in being heard				
2. Articulation sounds mumbled, fuzzy, indistinct				
3. Monotony of pitch				
4. Monotony of force				
5. Monotony of rate				
6. Monotony of melody				
7. Lacking in fluency—speech jerky and hesitant				
8. Speech cluttered with "uhs" and "ers"				
9. Voice unpleasantly high and shrill				
10. Tone of voice tends to be flat and dull				
11. Too much nasality				
12. Speech seems artificial and affected				
13. Tone tends to fade out too much at end of sentences				
14. Failure to make what is said sound important				
15. Careless habits of pronunciation				
16. Tendency to choke off open vowel sounds				

TOPICS FOR DISCUSSION

1. Discuss the voice and diction of national news commentators, political officers, and entertainers heard over the radio and television. Comment

upon their vocal qualities, regional dialect, pronunciation, voice personality, melody patterns, and distinct articulation.

2. Many of our speech habits are formed by imitation. Discuss the influence of family conversations and the voice habits of grade school teachers as they have affected the individual members of a speech class.

3. Explain why others can often tell our state of health by the quality of our voices.

4. The voice is very sensitive in registering our inner moods and feelings. Discuss the problem of controlling your voice when you are excited and emotionally stirred up.

5. What are some of the peculiarities of pronunciation and dialect associated with Boston, Texas, Arkansas, Brooklyn, upper New York, Maine, Kansas, and other parts of the country?

6. Discuss some of the objectionable characteristics of voice and speech of people in everyday life. For instance, what about baby talk, the whiney voice, the gushy tone, the boisterous voice, the confidential tone, the nasal twang, the husky voice, the feminine tone, and the masculine voice? What other annoying types of voices can you think of?

EXERCISES FOR READING

1. For strong, full, vibrant tone of voice:

> Roll on, thou deep and dark blue Ocean—roll!
> Ten thousand fleets sweep over thee in vain,
> Man marks the earth with ruin—his control
> Stops with the shore;—upon the watery plain
> The wrecks are all thy deed, nor doth remain
> A shadow of man's ravage, save his own,
> When for a moment, like a drop of rain,
> He sinks into thy depths with bubbling groan,
> Without a grave, unknelled, uncoffined, and unknown.
>   —LORD BYRON

2. For rhythm, rhyme, and melodic beauty:

> I must go down to the seas again, to the lonely sea and the sky,
>   And all I ask is a tall ship and a star to steer her by;
> And the wheel's kick and the wind's song and the white sail's
>   shaking,
>   And a gray mist on the sea's face, and a gray dawn breaking.
>
> I must go down to the seas again, for the call of the running tide
>   Is a wild call and a clear call that may not be denied;
> And all I ask is a windy day with the white clouds flying,
>   And the flung spray and the blown spume, and the seagulls
>   crying.

I must go down to the seas again, to the vagrant gipsy life, .
   To the gull's way and the whale's way where the wind's like a
   whetted knife;
'And all I ask is a merry yarn from a laughing fellow-rover,
   And quiet sleep and a sweet dream when the long trick's over.
                                        —JOHN MASEFIELD

        I wandered lonely as a cloud
          That floats on high o'er vales and hills.
        When all at once I saw a crowd,—
          A host of golden daffodils
        Beside the lake, beneath the trees,
        Fluttering and dancing in the breeze.

        Continuous as the stars that shine
          And twinkle on the Milky Way,
        They stretched in never-ending line
          Along the margin of a bay;
        Ten thousand saw I, at a glance,
        Tossing their heads in sprightly dance.

        The waves beside them danced, but they
          Outdid the sparkling waves in glee;
        A poet could not but be gay
          In such a jocund company;
        I gazed—and gazed—but little thought
        What wealth the show to me had brought.

        For oft, when on my couch I lie,
          In vacant or in pensive mood,
        They flash upon that inward eye
          Which is the bliss of solitude;
        And then my heart with pleasure fills,
        And dances with the daffodils.
                                —WILLIAM WORDSWORTH

3. For clear and precise articulation:

        There was a rustling that seemed like a bustling
        Of merry crowds justling at pitching and hustling;
        Small feet were pattering, wooden shoes clattering,
        Little hands clapping and little tongues chattering,
        And, like fowls in a farm-yard when barley is scattering,
        Out came the children running.
                                    —ROBERT BROWNING

        The sun is set; the swallows are asleep;
        The bats are flitting fast in the gray air;
        The slow soft toads out of damp corners creep;

And evening's breath, wandering here and there
Over the quivering surface of the stream,
Wakes not one ripple from its silent dream.
                              —PERCY BYSSHE SHELLEY

4. For gaiety and light-hearted mood:

> Eight fingers,
>   Ten toes,
> Two eyes,
>   And one nose.
> Baby said
>   When she smelt the rose,
> "Oh! what a pity
>   I've only one nose!"
>
> Ten teeth
>   In even rows
> Three dimples,
>   And one nose.
> Baby said
>   When she smelt the snuff,
> "Deary me!
>   One nose is enough."
>   —LAURA E. RICHARDS

5. For solemn and reflective mood:

> The day is cold, and dark, and dreary;
> It rains, and the wind is never weary;
> The vine still clings to the mouldering wall,
> But at every gust the dead leaves fall,
>   And the day is dark and dreary.
>
> My life is cold, and dark, and dreary;
> It rains, and the wind is never weary;
> My thoughts still cling to the mouldering Past,
> But the hopes of youth fall thick in the blast,
>   And the days are dark and dreary.
>
> Be still, sad heart! and cease repining;
> Behind the clouds is the sun still shining;
> Thy fate is the common fate of all,
> Into each life some rain must fall,
>   Some days must be dark and dreary.
>   —HENRY WADSWORTH LONGFELLOW

6. For sublime and serene mood:

> It was many and many a year ago,
>   In a kingdom by the sea,
> That a maiden lived, whom you may know
>   By the name of Annabel Lee;
> And this maiden, she lived with no other thought
>   Than to love, and be loved by me.
>
> I was a child and she was a child,
>   In this kingdom by the sea;
> But we loved with a love that was more than love,
>   I and my Annabel Lee,
> With a love that the winged seraphs of heaven
>   Coveted her and me.
>
> And this was the reason that long ago,
>   In this kingdom by the sea,
> A wind blew out of a cloud, chilling
>   My beautiful Annabel Lee;
> So that her high born kinsmen came,
>   And bore her away from me,
> To shut her up in a sepulcher,
>   In this kingdom by the sea.
>
> The angels, not so happy in heaven,
>   Went envying her and me.
> Yes! that was the reason (as all men know)
>   In this kingdom by the sea;
> That the wind came out of the cloud by night,
>   Chilling and killing my Annabel Lee.
>
> But our love it was stronger by far than the love
>   Of those who were older than we,
>   Of many far wiser than we;
> And neither the angels in heaven above,
>   Nor the demons down under the sea,
> Can ever dissever my soul from the soul
>   Of the beautiful Annabel Lee.
>
> For the moon never beams without bringing me dreams
>   Of the beautiful Annabel Lee,
> And the stars never rise but I feel the bright eyes
>   Of the beautiful Annabel Lee.
> And so, all the night-tide I lie down by the side

Of my darling, my darling, my life, and my bride,
   In her sepulcher there by the sea,
   In her tomb by the sounding sea.

—EDGAR ALLAN POE

7. For grand and reverential mood:

Seated one day at the organ,
   I was weary and ill at ease,
And my fingers wandered idly
   Over the noisy keys.

I do not know what I was playing,
   Or what I was dreaming then;
But I struck one cord of music,
   Like the sound of a great Amen.

It flooded the crimson twilight,
   Like the close of an Angel's Psalm,
And it lay on my fevered spirit
   With a touch of infinite calm.

It quieted pain and sorrow,
   Like love overcoming strife;
It seemed the harmonious echo
   From our discordant life.

It linked all perplexéd meanings
   Into one perfect peace,
And trembled away into silence
   As if it were loth to cease.

I have sought, but I seek it vainly,
   That one lost chord divine,
That came from the soul of the Organ,
   And entered into mine.

It may be that Death's bright angel
   Will speak in that chord again;
It may be that only in Heaven
   I shall hear that grand Amen.

—ADELAIDE A. PROCTOR

8. For a feeling of quiet solitude:

The curfew tolls the knell of parting day,
   The lowing herd wind slowly o'er the lea,
The plowman homeward plods his weary way,
   And leaves the world to darkness and to me.

Now fades the glimmering landscape on the sight,
And all the air a solemn stillness holds,
Save where the beetle wheels his droning flight,
And drowsy tinklings lull the distant folds;

Save that from yonder ivy-mantled tower
The moping owl does to the moon complain
Of such, as wandering near her secret bower,
Molest her ancient solitary reign.

Beneath those rugged elms, that yew tree's shade,
Where heaves the turf in many a moldering heap,
Each in his narrow cell forever laid,
The rude forefathers of the hamlet sleep.

—THOMAS GRAY

9. For strong feeling:

When, O Catiline, do you mean to cease abusing our patience? How long is that madness of yours still to mock us? When is there to be an end of that unbridled audacity of yours, swaggering about as it does now? Do not the nightly guards placed on the Palatine Hill—do not the watches posted throughout the city—does not the alarm of the people, and the union of all good men—does not the precaution taken of assembling the Senate in this most defensible place—do not the looks and countenances of this venerable body here present have any effect upon you? Do you not feel that your plans are detected? Do you not see that your conspiracy is already arrested and rendered powerless by the knowledge which everyone here possesses of it? What is there that you did last night, what the night before—where is it that you were—who was there that you summoned to meet you—what design was there which was adopted by you, with which you think that any one of us is unacquainted?

Shame on the age and on its principles! The Senate is aware of these things; the consul see them; and yet this man lives. Lives! aye, he comes even into the Senate. He takes a part in the public deliberations; he is watching and marking down and checking off for slaughter every individual among us. And we, gallant men that we are, think that we are doing our duty to the Republic if we keep out of the way of his frenzied attacks.

You ought, O Catiline, long ago to have been led to execution by command of the consul. That destruction which you have been long plotting against us ought to have already fallen on your own head.

—CICERO

ADDITIONAL READINGS

Andersch, Elizabeth G., and Staats, Lorin C., *Speech for Everyday Use,* rev. ed., Rinehart, 1960, chap. 6.

Anderson, Virgil A., *Training the Speaking Voice,* 2nd ed., Oxford University Press, 1961.

Brigance, William Norwood, *Speech, Its Techniques and Disciplines in a Free Society,* Appleton-Century-Crofts, 1952, chaps. 13, 15, 17, and 18.

Brown, Charles T., *Introduction to Speech,* Houghton Mifflin, 1955, Part 4.

Dickens, Milton, *Speech, Dynamic Communication,* Harcourt, Brace, 1954, chaps. 8 and 9.

Fairbanks, Grant, *Voice and Articulation Drill Book,* rev. ed., Harper, 1960.

Karr, Harrison M., *Developing Your Speaking Voice,* Harper, 1953.

Oliver, Robert T., Dickey, Dallas C., and Zelko, Harold P., rev. ed., *Communicative Speech,* Dryden, 1955, chap. 3.

Gray, Giles Wilkeson, and Wise, Claude Merton, *The Bases of Speech,* 3rd ed., Harper, 1959, chaps. 2 and 3.

Lewis, Norman, *Word Power Made Easy,* Doubleday, 1953.

McBurney, James H., and Wrage, Ernest J., *Guide to Good Speech,* 2nd ed., Prentice-Hall, 1960, chap. 13.

Reid, Loren, *First Principles of Public Speaking,* Artcraft, 1960, chap. 13.

Sarett, Lew, Foster, William Trufant, and Sarett, Alma Johnson, *Basic Principles of Speech,* 3rd ed., Houghton Mifflin, 1958, chap. 9.

Soper, Paul L., *Basic Public Speaking,* 2nd ed., Oxford University Press, 1956, chaps. 8 and 9.

White, Eugene E., *Practical Speech Fundamentals,* Macmillan, 1960, chaps. 4, 6, and 7.

White, Eugene E., and Henderlider, Clair R., *Practical Public Speaking, A Guide to Effective Communication,* Macmillan, 1954, chap. 11.

PART THREE

A Program of
Speaking Experiences

It has been said that the three rules for the public speaker are: (1) practice, (2) practice, (3) practice. However, as educators we know that aimless practice by itself may only serve to fix more firmly wrong habit patterns. Unguided practice only makes permanent, not perfect. Growth and development of speaking ability can best be achieved through an intensive study of theory and the right kind of practice under the able guidance and direction of a teacher. Here lies the ultimate challenge to this book and the speech course in general.

The speaking assignments in this part of the book have been designed to give the student an acquaintance with the many facets of the speech act. *What* to do, rather than *how* to do it spelled out in great detail, has been stressed in the presentation of the speech projects. Thus the student, exercising and developing his creative talents and powers of speech in his own way, is challenged to draw upon his individual resources and abilities. This method in the long run will contribute most to his total growth as a person.

GUIDED SPEECH PRACTICE

Speaking experiences under the guidance and direction of an instructor form the backbone of this course; invaluable learning takes place as you practice making speeches before the class. These assignments, involving acts of oral communication, are arranged in three major divisions. Group One contains short speeches in which the content is drawn largely from personal background experiences and evaluative thought. Group Two contains longer speeches, of five to ten minutes, which more fully challenge the student's ability to develop creative speech based upon research, thought analysis, careful organization, assimilation of materials, and general grasp of the subject. Group Three consists of miscellaneous projects offering experiences valuable to oral communication which may fit in at certain intervals in the course and generally enrich the total program.

Each speaking assignment has its essential characteristics and its individual requirements. Each speech must be tailored to fit a specific need. However, there are some common rules which should be considered for all speeches requiring advance preparation.

1. Rehearse your speech carefully and often enough to make certain your materials are manageable within the allotted time.
2. Observe the time limit.
3. Keep firmly in mind the central or major focus as designated in the description of the assignment.

GROUP ONE

These assignments are designed to supplement the more solid projects, listed in Group Two, which require study and preparation in depth. It is assumed that several speaking experiences of two or three minutes each early in the course, together with one or two similar or impromptu experiences interspersed later, are more helpful toward total growth and development of speaking ability than is a single speech of eight or ten minutes. This does not mean, however, that these assignments should be viewed lightly. Except for the impromptu speeches, they should be carefully and thoroughly worked out in advance to reflect thought which has been effectively designed and carefully digested and rehearsed. These are not mere finger exercises preparatory to the main performances. They are, moreover,

349

effective in building a congenial class spirit, in developing freedom and spontaneity of oral expression, and in increasing personal confidence.

It is therefore important that you approach these ventures with a cooperative and spirited attitude during the opening days. Don't worry about the speech mechanics. Launch out freely and lose yourself in the ideas and your development of them. Stand up and speak out in a full, firm voice from the very beginning, making sure everyone in the room can easily hear and understand you, and keep your mind on what you are talking about. Feel free to make occasional extemporaneous references to points made by others, relating them to what you have to say.

Do not expect much detailed criticism from your instructor during these early short speeches, but evaluate and criticize your own efforts and share comments with the other students between class sessions. In thus trying to orient yourself to the class you will contribute to its total success and its positive tone and mood.

INTRODUCTION OF A CLASSMATE (TWO MINUTES). The class will be divided into pairs preparatory to the following class session, when each member of the pair will make a friendly, informal biographical sketch about his partner. Part of the class period or a get-together between classes may be arranged for interviewing each other. This speech should be packed with information: name, nickname, home town, family, major course interest in college, hobbies, professional aims, unusual interests, achievements, honors, and so forth. This should not be a mere recitation of facts about each other but a pleasantly composed oral account of an important member of the group.

VALUE JUDGMENT SPEECHES (TWO MINUTES). The five separate speaking assignments included here should stimulate you to voice your opinions from your own point of view. These speeches should be carefully thought out in advance, but use notes if you wish. Also, we suggest that you discuss the subjects outside the class with other students, friends, or members of the family. The class should be divided into two groups, each dealing with a separate subject so that on a given day two areas of subject matter may be covered in a single class period. You may want to make a quick poll of the half of the class not speaking on your subject to get their ranking of the topics you discussed and to compare their totals with your own.

1. *Six factors of life.* Rank the following six factors in order of their importance, and give your reasons for so doing: (1) friends, (2) education, (3) family, (4) money, (5) religion, (6) health. Which do you rank first, second, and so on, and explain your evaluation.
2. *Six professions in civilization.* Use the same approach to the following six professions and occupations, evaluating them as to which has contributed most to civilization: that of (1) the preacher, (2) the farmer, (3) the scientist, (4) the artisan, (5) the politician, (6) the teacher.
3. *Give up six modern conveniences.* Imagine there are six modern conveniences which your parents must give up, one at a time, beginning a year from now. They are: (1) the telephone, (2) the radio and television, (3) the automobile, (4) the refrigerator, (5) the bathroom, (6) the washing machine. The decision of what to give up first, second, and so on is up to you. Explain your reasons for your choices and the order of their elimination.
4. *The lighthouse speech.* Suppose you and a companion of your own sex are to live two years in a lighthouse, isolated from the world. You can take three books other than the Bible and can have sent to you for the duration of your stay three subscriptions to magazines or newspapers. What books and publications would you choose? Support your selections.
5. *Life and death on the desert.* Suppose ten people are stranded in a desert and a helicopter can save only five; the other five must be left to perish. They are: (1) an Army captain, (2) Miss America, (3) a 12-year old boy, (4) a wealthy society woman, (5) a noted scientist, (6) a preacher or priest, (7) your high school principal, (8) a college football hero, (9) a bricklayer, (10) yourself. Whom would you save and why?

SPEECH FROM BACKGROUND MATERIALS (TWO MINUTES). This speech is based upon personal experience. Talk without notes and aim for a strong sense of communication. Choose one of the following topics: (1) my home town, (2) an interesting character, (3) what I hope to be when I am 50, (4) my first impression of our college.

SPEECH OF DEMONSTRATION (FOUR MINUTES). The speech of demonstration is an informative speech of the instructive type featuring visual supports, such as objects, other persons, blackboards, charts, descriptive gestures, bodily action, or visual aids of any kind. The listener should get the meaning by what he sees as well as by what he hears; therefore, it is important that you use an extra amount of gesture and bodily activity to clarify, amplify, and reinforce all phases of your demonstration. The following suggestions may help in the selection of your topic, its preparation, and presentation.

Suggestions

1. Select a topic which lends itself to broad bodily movements, in which all the details may be easily seen by the entire class. How to sew a button on a shirt is not a suitable topic; how to throw a football would be much better.
2. Work out a suitable introduction in which you justify your choice of topic and prepare the audience for a clear understanding of your demonstration.
3. Keep on talking at all times while you demonstrate. Talk and demonstration must be blended together. Guard against long pauses or moments of silence during the various phases of your demonstration.
4. When presenting your speech, maintain sufficient eye contact with your audience. There is always the danger of keeping your eyes too much on the visual aids or whatever you are demonstrating, thus neglecting adequate eye communication with your listeners.

Main focus:

1. Clarity
2. Plenty of bodily action
3. Specificity and details (this is usually the key to effective demonstration)

Typical subjects:

How to rescue a drowning person
Playing center on a football team
Basic football formation (use blackboard)
Seven ways of wearing a scarf (for women)
How to pack a suitcase
Principles of giving first aid
How airplanes fly
How to read a weather map
The science of meat carving
How to arrange flowers
Some key plays in baseball (blackboard)
Principles of modeling clothes (women)
The art of walking
Posture and carriage

How to play an instrument
Archery
How to control a fire
Tricks in tying knots
How to read a blueprint

IMPROMPTU SPEECHES. In a sense, there is no such thing as an impromptu speech, since all experience gives background preparation for speaking. When we speak in the manner we call "impromptu," we mean simply that there is no preliminary preparation on a specific subject for a particular occasion.

We all have much wider experience speaking impromptu in everyday relationships than we have making a prepared speech before a group. Discussions, conferences, social visits, class recitations are actually short, fluid impromptu speeches. Yet, although we may be called upon to speak impromptu 100 times a day, when we are called upon to do so before a speech class it comes as a kind of shock. But this is a type of speaking we should not neglect, since at times it can bring out the best in a speaker. In the light of the academic demands in a course of this kind, however, only passing attention can be paid to impromptu speaking.

The speaker must seek to make his own opportunities by means of dipping into his background of experiences and information; in other words, his problem is how to make the past work for him. There are many ways for thus improving one's ability to speak impromptu.

Suggestions:

1. Ask yourself the questions who, what, where, when, why, how. Usually at least one or two of these self-starters will dislodge some materials from your mind.
2. Consider the time factor—the past, the present, and the future. Not that you necessarily should fully explore the yesterdays, todays, and tomorrows, but it may be helpful to compare facts and events of one time period with those of another. Review pages 217–222 of Chapter 9, "Designing the Speech," for handy, stock organizational patterns.
3. Practice privately making impromptu speeches based upon the pattern described in the first exercise below, *Tapping your subconscious mind.*
4. Widen your experience in making extempore prepared speeches before groups, employing style which features spontaneity, fluidity, and conversational directness. This background should improve your ability to speak impromptu.

The following impromptu speaking exercises are easy to master. In each one there is a path which leads to background experiences from which you can draw. Make no plans as to what you might say before you get your topic. Then the instant you hear it announced throw yourself headlong into the opening statements without worrying too much about how you are going to make out. The point is to get going, and you will be surprised how you can collect your wits as you go along. When your ideas stop coming, don't try to hang on too long; simply end your talk. These speeches should at most be one minute to two minutes in length. Listen to your colleagues and play a mental game with yourself as to how you would have handled the subject had it been given to you.

1. *Tapping your subconscious mind.*   Topics are usually not announced until you stand before the class. Use the following formula if you need help; otherwise, pay no attention to it. First, speak from association; what is the first thing of which the topic reminds you? Second, talk about its size, shape, uses, kinds, and so forth. Describe it in detail. Third, weave in a personal experience connected with the subject. (This is also an excellent "daily dozen" type of practice exercise for speech improvement.) Provide yourself with a grab bag of thirty or forty topics from which you can draw two or three times a day for a period of two or three weeks, and practice privately as you walk or ride to and from school.

Here is a list of thirty topics successfully used by thousands of students: bicycle, hammer, snakes, pencil, chickens, cats, dogs, apples, watermelons, peanuts, popcorn, spiders, grasshoppers, jack rabbits, buttons, shoes, neckties, horses, watches, flies, hats, bananas, ice cream, brooms, trees, matches, string, telephone, baseball, dolls, birds.

2. *Narrative or descriptive speeches.*   Focus on specificity and details. Typical subjects:

The kitchen in your home
How you spent the first two hours of this day
How you are going to spend the two hours following this class
A description of a high school teacher
The difference between a cat and a dog
The inside of your church
How a blind man could get from this room to the library

3. *My first.*   This speech is about your first experience of some act or thing. Draw from the instructor's desk a card with three topics.

Read them aloud, and some designated member of the class or the class itself will pick the one you must use. Your card will have such typical subjects as:

The first time I drove an automobile
My first plane ride
My first big trip
My first day at school
The first pet I had
The first day in grade school
My first public appearance
My first speech
My first formal party
The first time I saw a snake
The first time I saw a big fire

4. *Evaluative type of impromptu speech.* Take a clear stand, and support your personal opinion, with facts and logic if possible. Three topics may be on a card, from which you choose one.

Typical subjects:

Women drivers
Steady dating in high school
Should 18-year-old citizens vote?
Cheating in examinations
Should fraternities be abolished?
Should speech be a required course in college?
Should rules for closing hours be changed?
Are college students snobs?
Is there too much emphasis upon athletics in college?
What I expect from a person I would marry
Should college entrance requirements be raised?
My words of advice to a high school senior
Careless drivers

THE HECKLING SPEECH. This speech teaches prompt audience adaptation and helps the beginning speaker to forget about himself and concentrate on what he is saying. Inexperienced speakers usually approach this assignment with some dread. But afterwards they frequently have far less fear of speaking in public, because they have learned to concentrate on their message and in the process have developed considerable bodily activity.

One of two approaches may be used to this assignment:

1. The audience may be allowed to heckle during the speech. Whenever the speaker makes a controversial point without adequate support, a member of the audience may interrupt him and question him on it. If this method is used, someone should act as chairman of the meeting in order to avoid sheer confusion. The speaker should have the opportunity to finish his speech; whenever the chairman feels hecklers are preventing adequate progress of the speech, he should prohibit further interruption.

2. Another approach to this assignment consists of a three to four-minute speech without interruption, after which three minutes are allowed for questions from the floor. If questions are not forthcoming from the audience, the instructor should be prepared to ask questions.

The speech itself should be on a highly controversial subject, in which research, documentation, and developing a polished piece are less important than bringing to focus a vital central issue about which you can strongly express your feelings and beliefs. This project is designed primarily to give you training in thinking on your feet.

Suggestions for answering questions:
1. Restate the question.
2. State your reply directly to the point.
3. Try to relate your answer to your speech.

This basic organizational pattern for answering questions serves well whether you present additional information or an argument in refutation of an objection. If someone asks a question you are unprepared to answer, do not try to bluff your way through but instead freely admit ignorance. If you know where the answer can be found, direct the questioner to this source.

Typical subjects:
Girls' dormitories should abolish closing hours for girls.
Athletic scholarships should be abolished.
Fraternities should be abolished.
National prohibition should be re-established.
All state universities should establish compulsory R.O.T.C. units.
A program of U.S. universal military training should be established.
Licenses of drunken drivers should be suspended for two years.
Women's modern emancipation has degraded womanhood.
College admission requirements should be stiffened.
Standard grading systems in college should be replaced with a "Satisfactory-Unsatisfactory" system.

Every college student should be required to take a minimum of twenty
credit hours of a foreign language.

GROUP TWO

This speech course is essentially anchored to the assignments described in this section. Here the important theories and principles of
the six dimensions come to fruition in the development and delivery
of various types of speeches. Obviously, all these speeches must be
carefully structured and outlined in advance. Review Chapter 5 for
sources of materials for making your speeches.

The Speech to Inform *(4 —6 min.)*

The speech of information is one of the most widely used types of
speeches which we make or hear in life. Furthermore, almost any
kind of speech, no matter what its central aim, is likely to contain
some informative matter. The objective of the speech to inform is
to secure understanding of uncolored factual materials. The information should have some academic worth—that is, it should have enough
value to the listener that he can weave it into his construct of general
knowledge. A speech about a fishing trip to Minnesota probably
would be of little value to the listener unless it helps him, for instance,
to understand the North Woods or gives insight about the nature of
fish and man. Anything which will help the listener understand himself, his environment, and his heritage will have value for him.

Students often confuse the speech to inform with the speech of
advocacy or conviction. This confusion often arises from the slanting
or coloring of facts or incidents. The speaker making the speech to
inform should be an objective reporter—he should seek to reveal the
truth carefully, accurately, and without editorializing or trying to influence listener opinion on controversial points. The informative
speaker must be neutral and unbiased. His business is to give insight
and information in a nonpartisan manner, letting the listener draw his
own inferences and conclusions.

Having selected your topic, read for background materials and prepare and finally present your speech with the following suggestions
in mind:

1. Make your speech rich in substance. The class should learn something
   from it. Three-fourths of what you say should offer new materials for
   most of your listeners.

2. Make information worthwhile. If the listener can say "so what?" and find satisfaction in answering his question, your information has probably met the test.
3. Make it interesting for the listener. Listener interest is a key link in the chain of communication. Interest may be inherent in the subject matter itself or can be created through imaginative treatment by means of language and delivery.
4. Make it clear. Listener understanding depends upon clarity.
5. Make delivery lively and enthusiastic. Since informative speeches free from prejudice or bias do not naturally fire the speaker's thought, he needs to compensate for this deficiency and provide self-generated enthusiasm.

INFORMATIVE SPEECH 1: REPORT BASED ON READING RESEARCH. Preparation for this speech requires specific reading research. Length of the speech is determined by the instructor. Suggested topics are arranged in three groups, representing relative levels of challenge or degree of difficulty in the mastery or assimilation of the central subject matter. Level One represents simple concrete objects, products, and specimens of animals and plants or of human achievements. Level Two represents religions, laws, organizations, agencies of government, philosophies, processes of production, and theoretical concepts. Level Three represents a challenge of inquiry about some alleged fact, condition, or theory where there exists an uncommon amount of confusion and conflicting beliefs; your purpose is to clarify and establish concepts more valid than the prevailing ones.

LEVEL ONE

diamonds	oil	squids	mosquitos
volcanoes	coal	lemons	potatoes
coffee or tea	fire	oysters	the Suez Canal
salt	windmills	apples	weeds
glass	eggs	the Bible	rubber
tobacco	matches	tornadoes	snakes
camels	rice	the Chinese	sugar
cats	wool	Wall	soy beans
wine	cathedrals	belts	dynamite
plastics	pigeons	bats	bells
smoking pipes	the circus	boxcars	bicycles
the violin	poisonous insects	leather	soap
the Nautilus	nails	cotton	cement
lightning	whales	peanuts	watches

LEVEL ONE (*Cont.*)

ink	paper	spiders	weather
bees	telephones	buttons	U.S. highways
elephants	olives	horses	geysers
milk	wood	Persian rugs	watermelons

LEVEL TWO

Religion

agnosticism	Hinduism
atheism	Judaism
paganism	Buddhism
Calvinism	Christian Science
Mohammedanism	Roman Catholicism
Shintoism	Orthodox Church

Government Agencies and Services

Social Security	U.S. Bureau of Revenue
Security Exchange Commission	Federal Prisons
Commodity Credit Corporation	Federal Bureau of Labor
Federal Communication Commission	Federal Board of Aeronautics
Federal Trade Commission	Atomic Energy Commission
U.S. Bureau of Printing	Federal Bureau of Investigation
Federal Reserve System	The Merchant Marine

Politics, Government, Economics

Fascism	Inflation
Communism	The Gold Standard
British Labor Party	The Sterling Bloc
Constitutional Monarchy	The International Bank
Imperialism	The Stock Exchange
Martial law	Co-op movement
Free enterprise	City Management
Capitalism	U.S. federal budget

Science, Invention, Industry

The sponge industry	Building a superhighway
Pearl culture	Hybrid corn
Motivational research	Vitamin pills
Peaceful use of atomic energy	Atomic submarines
Deep-sea diving	Skin-grafting
Jet airplanes	Controlling air traffic
The cork industry	Dealing with atomic waste
Modern methods of mining coal	

How It Works

Weather forecasting
Collecting income taxes
St. Lawrence waterways
How soccer is played
Mayor-council city government
Drilling offshore oil wells
Chinese counting system

Raising and curing tobacco
The art of emceeing
Reading a financial report
Brainwashing
Gresham's Law
Jet engines
The mobile

LEVEL THREE

What should we believe about the following?

Flying saucers
Leprosy—its treatment and cures
The status of our oil reserves
Treatment and cure of cancer
Why Johnny can't read
Trucks a threat to our railroads
Child prodigies
Extra-sensory perception
Mental telepathy

Smoking as a cause of lung cancer
Dangers of atomic fall-out
Racketeering among labor unions
England's public health program
Women drivers
The Abominable Snowman
Alcoholism
Sea serpents
Witchcraft

INFORMATIVE SPEECH 2: ORAL FEATURE REPORT. Content of this speech is based mostly on research other than from reading or background experience, although these may provide supplementary supports. Often in life we are called upon to make a report about a trip, a convention, a piece of research, or some project or event we have observed or investigated. Our Sunday newspapers frequently run feature articles containing materials that are newsworthy and of immediate public interest about some person, event, organization, or civic project. This speech in a sense resembles that type of journalism; only it is for the class-audience instead of a reading public. The materials for this speech should be obtained mainly by personal interviews, observation, and investigation. Use the reporter's tools of inquiry, *who, when, why, where,* and *how.*

This speech is of the informative type, and most of what you say should reflect worthwhile knowledge which the listeners did not have before. Trivial substance based upon such topics as habits of my roommate, how Jim was the life of the party, or table manners at our house are not acceptable.

Main focus:

1. Richness of subject matter
2. Adequate interest level for the class
3. Enthusiastic, lively presentation

Typical subjects:

Our county jail
Our fire chief and his problems
The city police court
A typical day in the Dean's office
The workings of a produce market
The operation of a city paper route
Maintenance of the college buildings and grounds
The court house
The local airport
A report on a local supermarket, restaurant, store, bank, unemployment
   agency, animal shelter, manufacturing plant, or chamber of commerce
A report on some function, service, or organization connected with your
   college or university—the extension division, hospital, library, book-
   store, college press, system of honors and awards, and so forth

INFORMATIVE SPEECH 3: SYMPOSIUM ON CURRENT AFFAIRS. A symposium consists of a chairman or moderator and a group of experts
who give speeches on important phases of a topic. Since the panel
examines the topic from all its important sides, a symposium discussion is one of the best ways of intelligently exploring a topic and
conveying a large body of organized information to an audience.

For this assignment the class should be divided early in the semester
into groups of three to five members, and each group should be given
a topic area in current affairs. It is best that the entire class take up one
common general subject of current vital interest, such as International
Developments. Group I may be assigned African Affairs; Group II,
Asian Affairs; Group III, Latin American Affairs; and Group IV,
European Affairs. Again, if the general subject is current domestic
problems, Group I might be assigned Public Education; Group II,
Civil Rights; Group III, Labor-Management Relations; Group IV,
Agriculture; and Group V, Public Health and Welfare. Throughout
the semester, students should read about their topic area in newspapers
and periodicals. Approximately two weeks before the symposium
discussion is to take place, groups should meet informally to discuss
the topic area and break it down into specific topics to be assigned to

group members. At the end of the meeting each student should know exactly what his speech in the symposium is to cover and how much time he will have for it.

There are two common methods of covering the topic area. One is strictly informative; for example, African Affairs may be handled thus: Speaker 1 discusses African religious problems; Speaker 2, economic problems; Speaker 3, social problems; and Speaker 4, political problems. The second method can be illustrated by the topic of federal aid to parochial schools: Speaker 1 presents an historical review of federal aid to education; Speaker 2 discusses current bills in Congress; Speaker 3 presents the most important arguments in favor of federal aid to parochial schools; and Speaker 4 presents the leading arguments against federal aid to parochial schools.

One member of each committee should serve as chairman for the group. The chairman introduces the topic for discussion, comments briefly on its importance, defines it, introduces the speakers, and invites the audience to participate if this is part of the symposium plan. Between each speaker he makes a transition into the next speech, possibly by crystallizing the preceding speech in two or three sentences and then showing how it logically leads into the next topic for discussion. After the speakers have concluded, the chairman should give a brief summary of the entire discussion and open the meeting to questions from the audience. During the forum period he must maintain complete control of the meeting and keep it moving from one question to the next. He should watch the minutes carefully and be sure to terminate the discussion at the specified time.

Sometimes the chairman himself is a participant in the symposium and presents the first speech. In this case his speech should usually consist of a definition of the topic and a presentation of background information.

Main focus:

1. Panel should give thorough coverage on an important current affair.
2. Each speech should be filled with up-to-date information.

INFORMATIVE SPEECH 4: SYMPOSIUM DISCUSSION OF THE SIX DIMENSIONS OF SPEECH. The beginning course in speech combines a body of theory and principles with practice in the application of speaking skills. Since speech improvement depends as much upon practice as upon theory, much valuable student speaking time is often lost by an excessive number of class lectures or recitations based upon the text.

To help remedy this situation the instructor may elect to let the students study and discuss the theory of the course—with, of course, a proper amount of guidance.

The student-committee plan represents one approach to understanding the basic theories and principles embraced in the six fundamental areas of the speech-making process and is a substitute for either the lecture or the recitation system. It is a learning device designed to stimulate creative thinking and to develop a sense of personal responsibility in the student, rather than to emphasize mere acquisition of knowledge.

The mechanics are quite simple. A class of about twenty students is divided into six committees with three or four students on each committee. The project is introduced early in the course, and students work at it for a period of about five or six weeks—three or four weeks for planning, briefing, and preparation and two for final reports. The initial procedure is determined by the instructor. Most teachers stimulate thought by calling for a carefully prepared written inventory of speech factors which contribute significantly to effective speaking, and one of speech factors most annoying or objectionable in a speech or speaker. A class period then, devoted to thorough exploration and evaluation of the items presented, serves to determine common deminators and their relationships with the six fundamental problem areas of speech: the speaker, the audience, thought and content, organization, language, and delivery.

After the students understand the scope of all six dimensions, committees are organized—one group of students for each of the six topics. If possible, each student is allowed to join the committee of his choice. Each committee selects its own chairman. All students are then supplied with a selected bibliography (the Additional Readings at the end of each chapter in this book, for example).

One or more class periods are now devoted to committee workshop, with the instructor moving from committee to committee, giving counsel as needed. The committees are also encouraged to meet together outside of class to crystallize their assignments. After the committees are organized and individual responsibilities determined, the regular class speaking projects are resumed for two or three weeks before committee reports begin.

Each committee has a class period for presentation. On the day of presentation, the leader takes care of physical arrangements, such as seating. He collects an outline from each participant for the instructor's file (they are useful in preparing examinations on the subject matter). The symposium-forum method is used: the chairman gives a brief explanation of the problem area, sets the tone for the talks which follow, introduces the first speaker, and provides transitions from speaker to speaker. Each member gives at least one carefully prepared informative speech on a subtopic, but any member may give more than one talk if (in order to give maximum coverage of the subject) the organization pattern of the committee calls for it. The use of charts, diagrams, and other visual aids is to be encouraged.

After all have spoken, the chairman conducts the forum-period, inviting questions from the audience. At this time, the instructor may fill in important points and give such emphasis as he considers advisable. It is his job to reinforce and supplement the most important concepts. The final step is an examination on the theory covered during the discussions.

Main focus:

1. Adequacy of coverage of assigned topic
2. Interestingness of presentation
3. Clarity and specificity of materials presented
4. Breadth of knowledge on assigned topic

The Speech to Entertain

This speech need not be hilariously funny nor unusually clever; you are not competing with celebrated comedians and humorists. The important thing is to keep it in a light vein, to make the listening enjoyable. Give the audience a good time and leave it with a pleasant impression.

Suggestions:

1. Weave ample attention and interest factors into your speech.
2. Wit and humor, if used, should be related to your ideas. Dry, subtle humor is preferable to the broad, obvious type.
3. Put more emphasis on your own ideas and method of treating substance than upon "canned" jokes or specific research.
4. Choose a subject from which you yourself can get fun and enjoyment.

Main focus:

1. Interest level of speech
2. Ability to deliver speech in a light vein

Typical subjects:

Class reunions—are they fun?
How not to make an after-dinner speech
Pets I have known
How to win an award in the national Liars' Club
An interesting and exciting hobby
Some professors I have known
Customs of Eskimos and college coeds
Parlor tricks that don't work
Is Emily Post necessary?

The Speech to Persuade

PERSUASIVE SPEECH 1: TO SECURE RATIONAL BELIEF. The emphasis in this assignment is upon rational thinking. As background for it be sure to review pages 166–176 on "Evidence." Every idea in this speech should be either fully documented with reliable evidence or thoroughly convincing on the basis of logic. Convince the listener rationally that he should believe your proposition.

Suggestions:

1. Collect evidence from a variety of sources.
2. Vary the way you introduce your evidence.
3. Give the source of your evidence.
4. If you read from a source, make it talk for you; read to the audience, not the lectern. Just because you have evidence is no indication the listener will react favorably; you must communicate your evidence to him in the most effective manner.
5. Organize your speech as clearly as possible, thus making your logic clear and easy to follow.
6. Use internal summaries or brief reviews in the speech.
7. Approach the speech with an unemotional attitude.

Main focus:

1. Logical appeal
2. Documentation of controversial points
3. Clarity of thought relationships

Typical subjects:

Tuition for in-state college students should be abolished.
Mercy killings should be legalized.

The legal voting age should nationally be reduced to 18 years.
The United States should unilaterally discontinue testing of nuclear weapons.
Capital punishment should be nationally abolished.
R.O.T.C. programs should be abolished.
Labor unions are detrimental to our economy.
Political campaigning should be confined to one month before the election.
Integration should be postponed 25 years.
Gambling should be legalized nationally.
Sale of narcotics should be made legal.
Socialized medicine should be adopted.
The United Nations should have a permanent police force.
Major league baseball should curb its bonus spending.
Boxing should be abolished as a legal sport.
College football is contrary to sound educational principles and objectives.
The American trend toward socialism is to be deplored.
Red China should be admitted to the U.N.
Agricultural price supports are undesirable.
The Fifth Amendment is detrimental to effective democracy.

PERSUASIVE SPEECH 2: TO SOLVE A PROBLEM.   The problem-solution speech is one of the most common types of persuasive speeches. In it, you have a three-fold objective: (1) make people actively aware of an existing problem, (2) sell your listeners on your solution to the problem, (3) get the listeners to act upon your solution.

Begin your speech with an introduction which leads smoothly and logically into the development of the problem—this is often called the "need" step; second, outline a specific solution to the problem; third, show that it is practical by giving evidence that your proposal will do what you say it will; fourth, show that it is desirable—its results will be beneficial instead of harmful; fifth, ask for action from your listeners in the conclusion of your speech.

Suggestions:

1. Make the problem as vivid as possible. Show that it affects your individual listeners.
2. Outline your solution clearly.
3. Support your solution adequately.
4. Spend an adequate amount of time in discussing your solution. A frequent weakness of problem-solution speeches is that so much time is

spent on the problem that very little is left for the solution. Approximately one-third of your time should be allotted to development and support of your solution.

5. Tell the listeners exactly what you want them to do about your proposal.

Main focus:

1. Vividness and impellingness of problem
2. Clarity and definiteness of solution
3. Logical support of solution
4. Effective action appeal

Typical subjects:

The water pollution problem
The problem of abortion
The American Indian
Drunken drivers
Latin American relations
Divorce
Our farm surpluses
Our overcrowded universities
Scarcity of science teachers in high schools
Flood control in the Missouri Valley
Our missile development program
The care of our mentally ill
Education for birth control
Alcoholism
Comic books and comic strips
Vandalism
Our public highways
Recreation facilities in our large cities
Our overcrowded airports
Care of the aged
The high cost of dying

PERSUASIVE SPEECH 3: TO STIMULATE ATTITUDES. This speech, which is also known as the speech to impress, strikes at the common human weaknesses of indifference and apathy. People often blind themselves to undesirable happenings and conditions about them because it is the easiest course of action. This apathy is often the cause of crime and many other social ills. The speaker trying to cope with these problems must arouse people's attitudes, making them sharply aware of a problem or condition; he must stir up their feelings. No solution is offered in this speech; the speaker's purpose is to wake up the listener to a new and deeper appreciation of something about which he already has a basic belief.

Speeches to stimulate can be given for the simple purpose of stirring the emotions, for people are emotional beings and enjoy emotional experiences. Speeches of tribute are given for emotional and sentimental reasons; so are anniversary and dedicatory addresses, rally speeches, and a long list of others. Religious sermons are usually speeches to stimulate attitudes. Congregation members usually agree with the pastor in belief but often are apathetic in action and attitude.

Suggestions:

1. Base your speech on a definite emotional goal.
2. Make your ideas as sharp and vivid as possible. Illustrations usually are effective.
3. Strive for a certain sublimity in style. Some loftiness of language and thought is helpful in this speech.
4. Try to bring your speech to a climactic close.
5. Deliver your speech with feeling.

Main focus:

1. To inspire the listener.
2. Sincerity in delivery.

Typical subjects:

Values of Greek philosophy in present-day life
What is progress?
Keys to success
Happiness—who can find it?
Values in a nuclear world
Materialistic standards and human dignity
The value of liberal arts
Conformity in American society
Contemplation of beauty—an art or a gift
The meaning of "I put away childish things"
Cultivating the gift of gratitude
A rebirth of manners
The movement from farm to city
The deplorable condition of our jails
Heart disease
America's weight problem

Public indifference at the polls
Our neglected talents
The need for better critical thinking
The neglected pastime of reading

PERSUASIVE SPEECH 4: TO CHANGE HOSTILE ATTITUDES. This speech deals with subjects about which people feel very strongly. In a sense it is the opposite of the "speech to stimulate attitudes." The speaker's task is to conciliate people and get them to take a new (and, it is to be hoped, objective) look at the subject. In other words, this assignment is essentially an exercise in dealing with a hostile audience. The speaker has to create a feeling of good will for himself and for his subject. For a general background of essential concepts, review Chapter 2, "The Speaker's Image," and pages 176–184 in Chapter 7, "Developing an Idea," for this assignment.

Hostility may vary widely in degree from mild resentment to bitter and blinding emotionalism. Some of the areas where hostile feelings are most likely to be encountered are religion, race, and politics. Feelings and prejudices rooted in school, fraternity, class, and group rivalry may also prevail. Try to choose some topic which will meet with hostility from at least a fair portion of the class. Like the "Heckling Speech" of Group One, this speech requires careful audience adaptation.

Suggestions:

1. Begin with material that will help create good will for both speaker and speech.
2. Try to begin with points of agreement.
3. Use an indirect organizational approach.
4. Decide on a basic appeal for your speech. People are never so likely to change their attitudes as when there is an emotional or motivational reason for doing so.

Main focus:

1. Amelioration of hostile attitudes toward speaker and speech
2. Audience adaptation

Typical subjects:

Racial intermarriage
Contributions of the Democrats in Congress

Contributions of the Republicans in Congress
Books that should be burned
Federal aid for private schools
Parents should stand trial for their delinquent children
The Fifth Amendment should be repealed
Integration
The U.S. should abandon Quemoy and Matsu to the Chinese Communists
The Federal government should abolish all agricultural price supports
We should adopt national Sunday "Blue Laws"
Protestant churches should merge under single leadership
Unilateral disarmament
Compulsory federal health insurance

GROUP THREE—MISCELLANEOUS PROJECTS

SPEECH OF TRIBUTE.   Most of us will at some time be called upon to deliver a speech of tribute to a person or organization. Commemorative dinners, farewell banquets, dedications, and similar occasions as a rule call for verbal tribute. The best known speech of tribute is the eulogy; the death of almost every prominent person calls for a eulogy commemorating his life and his services. Upon the death of one of its members or of a high-ranking federal officer, Congress sets aside time for eulogistic services.

For this assignment you are to prepare a speech in which you pay tribute to some person, living or dead. You should have some specific reason for your choice of subject. It helps if you have some connection with the person, if he has affected your life in some way; he may be a relative, a close friend, or an historical or public figure you have always admired. If you choose to pay tribute to a friend or relative not generally known by the public, there should be something about this person's life that holds a message for the listener. Avoid choosing someone merely because you like him.

Suggestions:

1. Choose a subject to whom you have some emotional attachment.
2. Avoid making your speech a biographical sketch of your subject. From the cradle to the grave is too long a time to pack into a 5-minute speech.
3. Organize your speech around the person's leading characteristics—such as courage, imagination, and integrity. Or discuss his virtues first and his important accomplishments next. As a final point you may

want to show what effect his life had on those around him, or what his accomplishments did for mankind.

4. Bring in pertinent biographical data in the development of your main points. They are a type of supporting material.
5. You may want to end the speech by pointing out to the audience what can be learned from this person's life.
6. Present the speech with a fair amount of feeling. It should be more than a mere itemization of the person's life; it should create some sentiment.

Main focus:

1. Make a person's life and accomplishments come to life for the listeners in a vivid and interesting manner.
2. Carefully decide what are the important aspects of this person's career.
3. Present your speech with the proper feeling.

Typical subjects:

Horace Mann	Martin Luther King	George Gershwin
Jonas Salk	Clara Barton	Ira Gershwin
Susan B. Anthony	Ralph Bunche	Oscar Hammerstein
Jane Addams	Jim Thorpe	Ludwig von Beethoven
Frank Lloyd Wright	Billy Graham	Jack Benny
Thomas Edison	Boris Pasternak	Al Jolson
Satchel Paige	Florence Nightingale	Will Rogers
Lou Gehrig	Joe Louis	Robert E. Lee
Babe Ruth	Wilma Rudolph	Nathan Hale
Helen Keller	Jackie Robinson	Samuel Adams
Louis Pasteur	Cardinal Spellman	Winston Churchill
Margaret Fuller	Albert Schweitzer	Frances Wright
Eleanor Roosevelt	Jascha Heifetz	Babe Zaharias
Booker T. Washington	Henrik Ibsen	Sam Snead
Alexander Graham Bell	Mark Twain	Your father
Lucy Stone	Colin Kelly	A close friend
Wyatt Earp	Daniel Boone	A teacher
Buffalo Bill	The Wright Brothers	A pastor

ORAL READING OF PROSE. The aim of this assignment is to develop skill in the expression or interpretation of written language. You may choose your reading material from a variety of sources: a newspaper, a letter, a book of philosophical essays, or even the Boy Scout manual. All are practical choices; however, a story permits you to demonstrate your full capability in reading and vocal expression.

Therefore, unless otherwise instructed, select a short story (cut it down, if necessary), take an incident from a novel that is complete in itself, or take several portions from a novel, using narrative transitions between incidents. Whatever you choose, be sure that it fits the time limits of this assignment.

Prepare a brief introduction for your reading. Identify your reading selection and its author. Relate any important information about the author that will help to enlighten your listeners on your selection. Tell anything about the selection itself that is necessary for its comprehension and appreciation by the listeners. If you have taken a portion of a novel, you may need to tell what precedes the incident you are going to read; and if important material follows your incident you may want to summarize that after you have read your selection. Deliver your introduction to the reading extemporaneously, and be sure to observe good speech habits.

Main focus:

1. Demonstrate that you understand your reading selection logically and emotionally.
2. Create the proper mood and feeling about your reading.
3. Read with meaningful vocal and bodily expression. Make the composition live for the audience.

ORAL READING OF POETRY. You may select one long poem for this assignment or several short ones. In the latter case, the poems may be by the same or several authors but on one theme; you may, for example, read three poems on the theme of death. Any standard anthology will provide a wealth of suitable poems for this assignment. Select poetry which you personally like, for it will be easier to read with emphasis and feeling.

Introduce your poetry reading just as you did your prose reading: give the essential information about the author and the concepts necessary for the listeners properly to understand and appreciate your selection. Avoid the temptation to make your introduction too long. It should be no longer than the introduction to a speech of similar length.

Main focus:

1. Demonstrate that you understand your reading selection emotionally and logically.

2. Create the proper mood and feeling about your selection.
3. Demonstrate that you are capable of reading rhyme, rhythm, and meter effectively.
4. Capture the imaginative aspects of the poetry, especially the imagery.

SHORT OCCASIONAL SPEECHES. Many times we are called upon to deliver a short speech for some special occasion—to welcome someone, bid someone goodbye, present or accept an award, or introduce a public speaker. These short speeches should be close-knit and carefully prepared. The precepts for these speeches are few yet important, since an occasional speech should proceed with dispatch but not overlook any niceties. Below is a skeleton outline for a number of occasional speeches. Your instructor may want to designate which occasional speech you are to give, perhaps by breaking the class into pairs for the speeches of welcome and response, farewell and response, and presentation and response.

1. *Speech of welcome*

   a. Make a definite statement of welcome to the person or group.
   b. Indicate pleasure at having him (or them) with you.
   c. Tell the audience important facts about your visitors: Who are they? What are they known for? Why are they here?
   d. Tell your visitors anything of special interest concerning your group or city.
   e. Once more indicate pleasure at having your visitors with you and express hope that they will enjoy themselves.

2. *Response to welcome* (adapt your speech to the welcome)

   a. Thank the speaker welcoming you.
   b. Indicate pleasure and purpose for being here.
   c. Report anything of special interest concerning your group (if you are representing one).
   d. Once more indicate pleasure at being here.

3. *Speech of farewell*

   a. Indicate to whom you are bidding farewell.
   b. Express regret at his leaving.
   c. Praise him for his influence during his stay in your midst.
   d. Tell your audience where he is going and wish him success in his new undertaking.
   e. Bid him farewell.

4. *Response to farewell* (adapt your speech to the farewell)

    a. Express regret at having to leave.
    b. Point out how you enjoyed your associations here.
    c. Tell reason for leaving and what you expect the future to hold.
    d. Farewell.

5. *Speech of presentation*

    a. Name the award to be given.
    b. Name the donor or donors.
    c. Outline the history of the award.
    d. Cite the conditions for making the award.
    e. Cite virtues and accomplishments of the recipient.
    f. Present the award.

6. *Response to presentation* (adapt to presentation)

    a. Express gratitude.
    b. Express pleasure of owning the gift.
    c. Thanks.

7. *Speech of introduction of a speaker*

    a. Build up the prestige of the speaker.
      (1) Who is he?
      (2) What are his credentials?
      (3) What are his special abilities for speaking on his subject?
    b. Announce the speaker's subject.
    c. Indicate the importance of subject. (But don't steal his speech.)
    d. Introduce the speaker.

THE SALES SPEECH. In a sense, the world is one vast salesroom with everyone in it a salesman of sorts—selling himself, a service, a product, a belief, a way of life. When we seek to influence others to do something we want them to do, we are practicing salesmanship—persuasion.

There may be endless variations in the sales approach. In this sales speech neither try to undertake the impossible, nor just go through the motions of an academic oral exercise, but seek a definite action response, immediate or delayed.

In this speech, as in any sales situation, we must consider three key factors—the salesman (speaker), the product or proposal (thought and content), the customer (the audience). The initiative lies with the salesman or the speaker, who must make the oral maneuvers that will bring the product and the customer into realistic relationship. The standard pattern of procedure in the sales speech is usually as follows:

1. Secure and hold attention of the audience.
2. Stimulate the interests of the audience.
3. Create a desire for the idea or product.
4. Convince the mind and motivate the will.
5. Secure action. Make the proposal and close the sale.

Of course these steps should not stick out obviously as separate gimmicks but should be artfully blended into an unfolding continuum of facts, reasons, suggestions, and motivational appeals. The crux of the sales speech lies in steps 3 and 4—namely, creating a desire and clinching that desire with motivational appeals.

Suggestions:

1. Take some topic about which the class has a neutral attitude or mild sales resistance.
2. Try to arrange your materials in a compelling order, in which logic and wants accumulate toward a climax.
3. Design your speech for some kind of a verdict by your audience. Work out your close on a "take it or leave it" basis.
4. If possible, get some kind of audience participation or feedback.
5. It is more important that you "almost persuade" the listener on a difficult subject than to sell him something which he already wants.

Main Focus:

1. Positive suggestions throughout the speech
2. Building ethos for yourself and magnetic power for the object or idea you are selling

Typical subjects (delayed response):

Stop eating candy between meals
Control your weight
A vacation trip
A course in the university
A theatrical production
A visit to an art museum
Forming or joining an investment club
Forming or joining a reading club
An insurance policy—accident, life, health.
Why support some law, campaign, or movement?

Typical subjects (immediate response):

Give money to heart fund, polio fund, cancer fund, Community Chest, Salvation Army, the blind, CARE, and so forth

Buy a specific product or article—a kitchen gadget, a mechanical pencil, a book, a magazine subscription, an item of clothing, a house ornament, a decoration for the person, a puzzle, a picture, a wastebasket, a brand of cosmetics, a novelty item

Join some club or organization which requires a commitment, signature, or fee

Credo—a Declaration of Faith Concerning Speech Education

I believe that of all human functions the gift of speech is most miraculous. I believe that, if speech were to stop, all civilized living would suddenly vanish.

I believe that the ability to be articulate is essential to inner harmony, to emotional maturity, and to mental balance. If all people could be completely articulate at all times, there might be no more wars and no more jails, more stable homes and more happy people.

I believe that speech is essential to the growth of the human personality and that it provides a way for self-discovery and renewal. For many, it is a way of self-expression without brush or pen.

I believe that the act of speech is a total process, that when it reaches optimum effectiveness the whole man communicates. What one is, is always part of what one says.

I believe that there is no substitute for content in the speaking process. Material of intellectual worth provides the essence of eloquence. Speech skills have their importance, but they no more make the speech than clothes make the man. The center of gravity in all oral communications is thought and idea.

I believe that every student should develop a concern for truthful and responsible speech, exhibiting sense—not nonsense, sincerity—not cleverness. He should at all times condemn charlatanism and superficiality, and should never be a party to plagiarized or dishonest work.

I believe that speech has no absolutes, that a completely perfect speech has not yet been made. I believe that speech offers a lifetime challenge in which there is never a final summit of achievement beyond which one cannot climb.

I believe that the individuality of the speaker is a valuable asset in the speaking process, and that any person with normal intelligence, normal emotional balance, and normal speech mechanisms has at his command the resources enabling him to make certain speeches which can be equaled by no other person. Every student has the potential to speak superbly at some time.

E. C. B.

APPENDIX

Evaluation Charts

Evaluation charts or scoring cards of individual speeches are commonly used by instructors or class members or both. Although they have their limitations as teaching aids, they are at times useful for pointing out a speaker's strength and weakness; moreover, they help keep the major goals and basic principles in perspective. Sample charts are offered here with the view of showing variations in patterns, goals, and items emphasized. The first general chart features rating of separate items clustered about each of the Six Dimensions of Speech; the second identifies the specific needs of a speaker; the third concerns the informative speech; the fourth is designed for speeches of the persuasive type, with a ballot to indicate listeners' shifts of opinion; the fifth provides a final summary rating of individual achievement in certain categories of the speech process. Mimeographed copies may be made of each chart and used, by teacher or students, with the appropriate speechmaking project.

Speaker _____ Date _____

Topic _____

Ratings in scale range from 1 to 7. In each category, 1 represents the lowest level you would expect to find in a beginning speech class, while 7 indicates the very highest. Check only those items which seem to you pertinent to the speech you are evaluating.

Comments

	Check in proper square						
SPEAKER	1	2	3	4	5	6	7
Poise and confidence							
Warmth and friendliness							
Enthusiasm							
Positive attitudes							
Maintaining ethos during speech							
AUDIENCE ORIENTATION							
Awareness of audience needs and interests							
Adaptation to control audience							
Use of interest and attention methods							
THOUGHT AND CONTENT							
Choice of subject							
Richness of content							
Logical adequacy							
Concrete supporting matter							
Worthiness of ideas							
Preparation—grasp of subject							
ORGANIZATION							
Unified thought picture							
Tailored to fit time limit							
Thought sequence							
Introduction							
Conclusion							
LANGUAGE							
Clarity							
Concreteness and specificity							
Oral style							
Saying much with few words							
DELIVERY							
Easily heard							
Easily understood							
Pleasing vocal coloration—variety							
Extempore directness							
Fluency							
Eye contact							
Bodily animation and life							

GENERAL CHECK LIST

Speaker _____ Date _____

Topic _____

Check only items which fit the case; write comments in margin at left.

Comments

SPEAKER
____Be more purposeful and earnest
____Self-consciousness seemed to be in the way
____Get more positive spirit
____Need more warmth and friendliness
____Need more enthusiasm
____Focus more on what you say, less on how you
    say it

AUDIENCE ORIENTATION
____Need to speak on level of audience
____Low interest value
____Poor communicative attitude
____Unresponsive to audience
____Personal indifference to listeners
____Need interest and attention devices

THOUGHT AND CONTENT
____Poor choice of subject
____Inadequate development of main idea
____Not rich enough in substance
____Need more specificity to support points
____Inadequate preparation

ORGANIZATION
____Introduction inadequate
____Need partitioning of ideas
____Need more interest build-up
____Need smoother transitions
____Need to create unified thought picture
____Need tailoring to fit time limit
____Conclusion step inadequate

LANGUAGE
____Need more specific language
____Vague and unclear
____Too many trite expressions
____Style unsuitable to speech or occasion
____Too verbose
____Poor grammar

BODILY COMMUNICATION
____Posture too casual or stiff
____Need more bodily animation
____General appearance too negative
____Poor eye contact
____Need more gestures

VOCAL COMMUNICATION
____Get more vocal variety
____Work for more fluency
____Make what you say sound important
____Need more vocal energy
____Need more conversational directness
____Need to speak more distinctly

CHART FOR INFORMATIVE SPEECH

Speaker _____ Date _____

Topic _____

What seemed to you to be the speaker's level of attainment relative to the assignment? Check in the proper square under the percentage scale to indicate your judgment of the speaker's success. 0% = poorest you might hear in a speech class, 50% = average, 100% = the best.

	Percentage										
	0	10	20	30	40	50	60	70	80	90	100
1. Speech offers new knowledge or added light and information											
2. General worthiness and value of the content											
3. Richness of substance—a solid, meaty speech											
4. General interest value inherent in the content											
5. General interest value as created by method and manner											
6. Enthusiastic, spirited delivery											

CHARTS FOR SPEECH OF CONVICTION OR PERSUASION

Speaker _____ Date _____

Topic _____

(P = poor; S = satisfactory; G = good.)

Comments

SPEAKER	P	S	G
Ethos factors			
Self-control			
AUDIENCE ORIENTATION			
Interest and attention			
Sensitivity to feedback			
THOUGHT AND CONTENT			
Clarity			
Logical supports			
Psychological supports			
COMPOSITION			
Organization			
Language			
DELIVERY			
Bodily responsiveness			
Vocal factors			
Extempore directness			

ATTITUDE TOWARD SPEAKER'S SUBJECT

Indicate honestly on the following scale how you felt about the speaker's subject before and after the speech. 0 = extremely opposed, 5 = neutral, 10 = extremely favorable.

	1	2	3	4	5	6	7	8	9	10
Before										
After										

FINAL SUMMARY RATING OF THE CLASS AUDIENCE

Rate the three highest ranking speakers in order in each column. Use the 1, 2, 3, system—1 for first, 2 for second, and 3 for third; rank only the first three places. The final result may be determined by adding the total number of points of all class members. Give 3 points for each first, 2 points for each second, and 1 point for each third; all others in the column are not ranked and get no points. This chart shows how each student should rate his classmates.

	Name of Student Speaker	Most Improvement During Course	Best Listener	Best in Thought Content	Best Organized Talks	Most Effective use of Language	Most Effective Delivery	Most Originality and Invention	Most Friendly Speaker
1	Adams	3							1
2	Burns		1						
3	Bucknell			2					
4	Clark								
5	Carlson								
6	Dixon								
7	Frost				2				
8	Guild						3		
9	Hanson	2							
10	Jackson								
11	Jaeckel					1			

#	Name						
12	Kritner	1					
13	Lamb					2	
14	Lincoln		3				2
15	Meyer						
16	Moses	2			3		
17	Morse		1				
18	Ober						
19	Porter		3				3
20	Rush						
21	Rose	3		3			
22	Stevens	3		2			
23	Thomas	1			2		
24	Wilson		1				
25	Zink				1		

Provide duplicate copies for the entire class and use at or near the end of the semester. Summary totals will indicate specific strength or weakness of each student.

Students and Experts Evaluate
Speech Factors

A recent study at the University of Kansas provides interesting data on the attitudes of college students and nationally known speech educators towards those factors which influence effective speaking. This search grew out of the hypothesis that speech teachers are often unaware of the attitudes of beginning speech students toward basic problems of speechmaking. The study shows where beginning college speech students and nationally known speech experts come closest together and where they are farthest apart in their concepts of what makes speech effective. The results offer some indications of the character of speech education as seen from both sides of the learning process. 493 college students, beginning the semester, and 77 nationally known speech educators, polled by mail, filled out identical questionnaires. The students were in the beginning speech course required for graduation; 51 percent were freshmen, 29 percent sophomores, 14 percent juniors, and 6 percent seniors. The ratio of men to women was 2 to 1. The speech experts were chairmen of respected speech departments, authors of widely used speech texts, and regular contributors to educational speech journals.

The survey was arranged in two parts: (1) positive factors which contribute to general effectiveness in speechmaking, (2) traits in a speech or speaker which are most objectionable or annoying to the person doing the rating. For the sake of simplicity, inventories of both positive and negative factors were limited to twelve items each. The factors listed are in some instances not mutually exclusive; where a total process is involved some overlapping in meaning obviously must occur. Moreover, factors must vary in their importance from one speech occasion to another. The aim, however, is to identify concepts and attitudes which stand out as relatively important in most speaking situations. Any item ranked first received five points, second four points, third three points, fourth two points, fifth one point. All other items received zero (0).

SUMMARY TOTALS OF ATTITUDE SURVEY

Part I.   Positive Factors: Concepts Concerning Elements Which Contribute Toward Effective Speaking

	493 Beginning Speech Students, Before Taking Course		77 Nationally Known Speech Experts	
	Rank	Percent ranking factor first	Rank	Percent ranking factor first
Adequacy in logical thinking	8, tie	7.03	4	8.96
Careful and thorough preparation	2	13.53	2	16.59
Clear and definite purpose of speaker	3	10.77	3	10.43
Self-confidence	1	15.46	12	2.43
Effective use of attention and interest devices	11	3.53	10	3.82
Having worthwhile ideas	5	8.60	1	19.98
Use of effective language and style	6	7.49	9	4.87
A desire to share ideas with audience	10	6.28	6	7.73
A lively and enthusiastic delivery	8, tie	7.03	8	6.10
Sincerity	4	9.46	7	7.21
Effective structure and organization	7	7.36	5	8.25
Creativity in treatment of ideas	12	3.46	11	3.50

Part II.   Negative Factors: Objections and Annoyances in a Speech or Speaker or Both

Egotistical attitude	9	7.01	6	7.26
Speaking overtime	10	6.62	11	1.47
Poor organization of a speech	5	9.01	3	13.84
Lack of eye contact with the audience	11	5.29	8	3.20
Insincerity	6	8.53	4	13.41
Poor preparation	3	10.44	2	17.37
Fidgety, nervous mannerisms	4	9.30	9	1.91
Apologetic attitude	7	7.14	10	1.56
Lack of enthusiasm	8	7.10	5	7.78
Monotonous vocal expression	2	12.10	7	4.32
Poor platform posture	12	2.00	12	.52
Lack of speech substance ("nothing to say")	1	15.46	1	27.40

The results of the above survey give the basis for many observations and various conclusions, of which the following seem most pertinent:

A. *Factual results to be noted:*

1. The experts regard speech substance more highly than the college students. This wide difference of opinion is indicated among positive factors not only in the matter of "having worthwhile ideas" but in those items which concern the treatment of ideas, such as logical thinking and organization, and which are more important to the experts than to the students. It should also be noted, on the basis of Part II, that students are more sensitive to fidgety mannerisms and monotonous vocal expression than are the experts. All of this indicates how highly the experts regard *speech substance.*

2. The widest of all differences of opinion between the students and the experts is indicated in the matter of self-confidence. Among the positive factors, the college students rank it first, the experts last. The fact that feelings of apprehension and personal tension are naturally at their peak among the college students during the opening sessions of a required speech course may explain this wide difference. Other wide differences concern having worthwhile ideas on the positive side and monotonous vocal expression and fidgety mannerisms on the negative.

3. There is considerable agreement among the college students and the experts on the positive factors of careful preparation, clear and definite purpose, use of attention and interest devices, enthusiastic delivery, and creative treatment of ideas. Among the negative factors, students and experts come closest to agreement on speaking overtime, poor preparation, insincerity, poor posture, and lack of substance.

B. *Constructive interpretation and conclusion:*

1. Beginning speech students may well be encouraged by the fact that the speech experts rated self-confidence so low in the list of positive factors. These veteran observers and practitioners are really saying: "Take heart. Don't let natural nervousness make you think that you cannot or are not doing a good job. Even the best and most experienced speakers still feel butterflies when they approach a public performance—but their nervousness may never be known to the audience. Success does not depend upon self-confidence—but upon content, preparation, and dedication to purpose." Although we may all feel better when we are relaxed and secure, it does not necessarily follow that we will speak better under such conditions. You may have all the self-confidence in the world, but this alone is no guarantee

you will make a good speech. Having something worthwhile to say may contribute more to effective speech than an abundance of self-assurance.

2. Students and speech experts were in wide disagreement on those negative factors which concerned monotonous vocal expression and fidgety mannerisms. This may indicate that the experts are looking at the forest, the students at the trees. No speaker was ever good because of monotonous vocal expression or fidgety mannerisms, but a speaker still may be relatively successful in spite of these annoying traits. Again we point out that sound ideas and preparation are central. Although habits of voice and bodily movement may be important, they lose their significance when compared to quality of thought, careful planning, and organization.

3. Beginning students too often think of speech as being based upon mechanical skills rather than communication. The essence of a speech situation is the flow of ideas, information, and feelings from one who talks to those who listen. Emphasis upon this flow, this exchange, is what we call the *communication concept*. It is significant that the experts ranked the sharing of ideas much higher than did the students—for *sharing* is at the heart of the best communicative attitude. Solid substance, careful treatment of the substance, and a genuine desire to share the substance are basic to effective communication.

Index